Nineteenth-Century Europe

Nineteenth-Century Europe

The Revolution of Life

Leo A. Loubère

*State University of New York
at Buffalo*

PRENTICE HALL
Englewood Cliffs, New Jersey 07632

Loubere, Leo A.
Nineteenth-century Europe: the revolution of life/Leo A. Loubere
    p. cm.
  Includes bibliographical references (p.) and index.
  ISBN 0-13-221086-X
  1. Europe—History—1815–1871. 2. Europe—History—1871–1918.
I. Title
D359.L82 1994   93-4487
940—dc20   CIP

Acquisitions Editor: Stephen Dalphin
Editorial/production supervision,
    interior design, and electronic page makeup: Marianne Peters
Cover Designer: Ray Lundgren Graphics, Ltd.
Prepress Buyer: Kelly Behr
Manufacturing Buyer: Mary Ann Gloriande
Editorial Assistant: Caffie Risher

All maps, excluding Map 1-1, are reprinted from William H. McNeill, *A History of the Human Community: 1500 to the Present, Volume II*, 3e, ©1990, pp. 538, 558, 559, 508-9, 586, 588, and 599. Reprinted by permission of Prentice Hall, Englewood Cliffs, New Jersey.

© 1994 by Prentice-Hall, Inc.
A Simon & Schuster Company
Englewood Cliffs, New Jersey 07632

Printed in the United States of America
10 9 8 7 6 5 4 3 2 1

ISBN   0-13-221086-X

Prentice-Hall International (UK) Limited, *London*
Prentice-Hall of Australia Pty. Limited, *Sydney*
Prentice-Hall Canada Inc., *Toronto*
Prentice-Hall Hispanoamericana, S.A., *Mexico*
Prentice-Hall of India Private Limited, *New Delhi*
Prentice-Hall of Japan, Inc., *Tokyo*
Simon & Schuster Asia Pte. Ltd., *Singapore*
Editora Prentice-Hall do Brasil, Ltda., *Rio de Janeiro*

Contents

Preface

The goal of this book is to provide the reader with a general descriptive and analytical text for the period 1814–1914. I have chosen to begin with the collapse of Napoleon's Empire—a traumatic event because the reaction against revolutionary upheavals and war was to determine the course of history for future generations. Also, the war of 1914 was destructive enough to close an era.

My objectives when writing this book were: first, to reveal the major trends in the time covered; second, to explain that within the major trends there were regional differences that must be investigated to deepen our awareness that generalizations, essential as they are, must be modified in light of variations from the norms; and third, to elucidate the dynamic forces in human societies.

The condition of Europe in 1914 was considerably different from that in 1814. Clearly there were powerful forces that brought about this transformation. In this book I attempt to discover those vigorous factors in the continuous relations among the four main activities of human groups. People, when clustered in groups, form governments to preserve order and to carry out certain other functions. They also undertake productive work to feed, house, and clothe themselves, which in turn creates economies. At the same time they form societies, hierarchical structures with each strata distinguished by its conditions of life. Over time, people also produce a culture made up of ideals and creative accomplishments. None of these aspects of human life exists isolated from the others; in fact, they are always highly integrated, resulting in modifications in one aspect based on broader activity taking place within the group.

Undoubtedly the most difficult task of the general historian is to explain these relations: to reveal how, for example, governments affected the lives of people and how an economy influenced a government to act in a certain way, and whether the ideologies of people prompt them to accept or to revolt against the authorities. The dynamic of history has been a continuous process of interrelations producing change. The chicken or egg question is hardly applicable to historical analysis of cause and effect because there was no chicken and no egg, only continuous mutation over time. Most notable was not only the extent of change, but its rapidity. Because its rate was unprecedented I have chosen a subtitle that best describes what really happened.

Acknowledgments

I wish to thank the following historians for reading parts of my manuscript: Roy Sandstrom, Georg Iggers, Christopher Guthrie, James Valone, Paul Guinn, Helju Bennett, and James F. Hood of Lindenwood College. Their comments were insightful and saved me from several errors of fact and interpretation. Naturally, the errors that may have been overlooked are entirely my own.

Nineteenth-Century Europe

Introduction

Overview of the Century

The theme of this book is *modernization*. This term came into fashion during the 1950s and was offered as a valid theory to describe the processes by which old regimes of Europe transformed themselves into efficient, liberal, or parliamentary, productive, and generally progressive societies enjoying high living standards. The theory has recently been either entirely discarded or modified to account for its shortcomings. My intention is to use the term not as a universally valid theory but rather as a model capable of explaining the different paths followed by European states over a century of time.

In the West, the area whose history gave rise to the theory, the general tendencies were fairly unambiguous. Governments became increasingly liberal, that is, they both granted and safeguarded individual freedoms, such as those of assembly, speech, religion, and private property. Beginning with 1830 each generation managed to curtail the once absolute power of rulership and subjected crowned heads to the limits imposed by constitutional law and parliamentary bodies. These assemblies themselves, at first chosen by upper-class voters, gradually fell under the sway of larger and larger electorates as laws defining the suffrage broadened to the point of granting full voting rights to all adult men.

Demands for female suffrage eventually arose but were not successful before 1914 in any major state.

This process hardly affected the multitude of sovereignties in central Europe—at least not until the last decades of the nineteenth century, or the first of the twentieth. Before then the main political goal of liberals and the few democrats who made up the political left was less a broader electorate than national unification. To achieve modernity was less a matter of the vote than of the formation of a united state. The middle decades witnessed the creation of the Italian kingdom and of the German empire. Paradoxically, the former was a liberal constitutional monarchy with a highly limited franchise, the new Germany, a semiautocratic state with manhood suffrage. The emperors of Austria and Russia survived liberal revolutions, and finally accepted the formation of narrowly elected parliaments. However, they succeeded in retaining ultimate control in their hands as hereditary monarchs, thanks to support of their respective nobilities, military, and clergy.

The general trends in politics, then, were complex and various, hardly the kind that lend themselves to simple theory. And yet, it can be argued that there was a contrapuntal relation between political and economic evolution: Where capitalism flourished so did liberal parliamentary forms of rulership. Or was it vice versa: Capitalism flourished because of the favorable economic policies of increasingly liberal governments? These two forms of human activity grew together in the West, and reinforced each other throughout the period. But the rise of a powerful German economy after midcentury revealed that capitalists could make their loyalty and wealth available to authoritarian regimes that equally supported their claims to economic power and endorsed their leaning toward industrial cartelization and monopoly. Even the tsars of Russia favored economic growth, provided that foreign investors financed it, and it did not disrupt society, or their autocratic rule. As a result of massive foreign investment and entrepreneurship even predominantly rural Russia began to appear as an awakening giant of industry. But Russian society was far from assuming the characteristics that modernization theorists attribute to advancing societies.

In the West, industrial growth developed from the rise of a native entrepreneurial class, which, in turn, assumed greater political importance as it grew wealthy. By the 1830s the bourgeoisie was a force to be reckoned with; not only was it growing in wealth but also in size. It was the "locomotive" of progress—at least certain members were; others, such as many small shopkeepers, were by no means locomotives, but cabooses at best. Whether dynamic or not, this bourgeoisie was renovated by the increase of manufacturers, merchants, professionals, bureaucrats, clerks, and scholars. They drastically changed the structure of Western society over the course of the century, as well as the locus of population. Thanks to their expansion the urban population moved steadily ahead of the rural both in numbers and voters. Farming families witnessed the departure of their young for better-paying jobs in towns and cities. Family structure, human relations, the position of women and everyday life became transformed beyond recognition.

With the rise of cities the former importance of religious practice diminished. Rural Europe had always formed the backbone of the various Christian denominations; this condition did not lessen, but after the 1870s there were fewer farmers in the West, and even fewer of their children were receiving an education in church schools. Centralized states began to provide free, compulsory, and secular education; in doing so, they offered a new cult, that of the nation, and a new emotional fervor, patriotism.

Western societies were also modified by the rise of a large factory working class. As the industrial revolution spread, there was a steady concentration of production in large establishments located in or near cities. Where there were no cities, factories were capable of creating urbanized communities out of small towns, peopled largely by propertyless wage earners. This new proletariat increased in number for both sexes. In the early stage of industrial growth, their working and living conditions were abominable. After midcentury, however, the men, especially the skilled among them, set up trade unions, and these, combined with a general increase in wealth, steadily improved their lives. Once they won the vote, they could also bring pressure to bear on their elected representatives to give the government a new mission, that of social reform. Just as the modern economy grew from free trade and individualism, so did Western governments slip from domination by the landed wealthy classes to that of the middle classes, which traded social reform for votes. The social reform movement, unlike the political effort, did not exclude women, but it did not give them an active role in the process; there was no serious effort to equalize living or working conditions between sexes.

European culture did not remain in ivory-tower isolation. Rather it was influenced by the general trends described earlier and contributed to them. Most important was the democratization of education, chiefly at the primary school level, but both secondary and higher education became more accessible to sons and even a few daughters of the expanding middle class. The spread of literacy created a new industry: the mass press and a new profession, journalism. The discovery and spread of scientific knowledge led to new world outlooks as evidenced by the theory of evolution put forward by Charles Darwin. His ideas modified traditional concepts about man and nature, furthering the secularization of society. Equally important were the advances in medicine, as well as private and public hygiene. The demographic revolution during which Europe more than doubled its population was in large measure a result of the spread of new knowledge about cleanliness, the causes of death, and the preservation of infants from disease and neglect. Science thrived in wealthy societies. The industrial revolution, the major source of wealth, was not merely an introduction of machines into manufacturing. Its early phase from the 1760s until about the 1830s, it is true, was largely a product of mainly technical knowledge and elementary entrepreneurship. From the 1840s, however, further advances came increasingly as a result of the application of science of a very high order—new theoretical knowledge in physics, especially electricity, and chemistry. Management came to rely somewhat less on shop-floor learning and more on acquaintance with advanced economics, finance, and technology. Before midcentury religion had dominated the minds of most people; afterward science where it spread made religious beliefs seem too simplistic. Other manifestations of culture, such as literature, art, architecture, and philosophy also escaped the grip of the churches as urban life offered new freedoms and opportunities for mental speculation.

If all of the preceding tendencies were part of the modernizing process, they did not produce identical results throughout Europe. The Russian and Austrian empires, and the emerging Balkans states remained predominantly rural, inhabited largely by peasants, most of whom were not even free of serfdom until midcentury or just after. Like southern Europe, large cities were rare because there was no industrial revolution nor middle class capable of carrying out such a concentration of people. Rulers were autocratic and supported by a still-powerful aristocracy and subservient churches. The peasant population was illiterate, grossly superstitious, and, when living conditions became unbearable, capable of violent rioting. One finds few of the signs of modernization in the East or in the Mediterranean South until the 1890s.

In Germany before unification in 1871 economic progress was initiated under Prussian leadership, and the formation of the empire hastened the process. By the turn of the century, German manufacturers, merchants, and bankers were rivaling those of Britain and had surpassed those of France. And yet the German middle class was politically reticent if not to say backward. It did not become the ruling class; its chief political party, the National Liberal, was more national than liberal, supported the autocracy of the kaiser and the arrogance of the aristocracy that controlled the two levers of power, the bureaucracy and the army.

A transition of considerable note did occur regarding the centers of power. Before midcentury it was commonly assumed by the ruling countries— Britain, France, Prussia, Austria, and Russia—that they formed a concert and that power was spread among them through the maintenance of an equilibrium of military might, a balance of power. That Europe enjoyed a century undisturbed by major wars comparable with those of the revolutionary and Napoleonic periods owes much to the ability of these states to respect one another's boundaries. With the 1850s came changes in the balance, and the rise of nationalistic fervor. Russian ambitions in the Balkans, matched by those of Austria, created a source of friction that ended the concert between these two bulwarks of conservatism. The unification of Germany and Italy brought into existence, along with Austria, a central European power block that isolated France and left Russia frustrated. In a sense, Britain held the balance after France and Russia formed a loose "understanding" of mutual defense in the 1890s. The scramble for colonies at the end of the century contributed to ill feelings; however, because the diplomatic corps of the great states were uncannily skilled at settling colonial territorial and boundary disputes, the big five did not resort to war over their dependent lands. It was rather Balkan nationalism, and the intervention of Austria and Russia that ended the hundred year peace. The four years of belligerency that began in 1914 proved to be the beginning of a new age of brutality and hatred, and therefore the weakening of the values that had endowed the nineteenth century with humane aspirations.

Certainly the 1800s were not unblemished. If there were no major wars there were major revolutions that reached a pinnacle in the spring of 1848. The uprisings were bloody, their suppression even bloodier. There was class hatred; there was distrust among nationalities and rabid racism; there was social injustice, selfishness, a gulf between rich and poor. And yet, our century drew to its close during the *belle époque*, that is, a time of improved living conditions, of greater security of life, of healthier cities, of governments more responsive to social reforms, and, finally, a widespread belief in progress, a hope in a better life in this world. And the arts were freer to express that hope then they had ever been since the golden days of ancient Athens.

The Value of Reading History

Because we cannot go back in time to experience past events directly, we must learn about them indirectly through the reading of books. Their contents are a form of substitute reality shaped by writers. Among them, historians go about this seemingly magical evocation not by slight of hand; they really cannot pull the past out of a sleeve. Rather they use artifacts, chiefly written documents, that people now dead left wittingly or unwittingly to posterity. From these various kinds of documents historians gather details that they organize into a narrative telling the story of the past. The narrative is called "written history." Therefore the nonspecialist, to acquire a knowledge about earlier societies, must undertake a program of reading the descriptions and analyses turned out by specialists.

Such a program raises the question: What is the best way to read history books? I think that one should read them in roughly the same way that one goes about solving a jigsaw puzzle. To solve a puzzle one must set each piece in its allocated slot so as to end up with an image. When studying the past, and then trying to recover it in words, historians put pieces (which are called facts or details) where they fit best to produce a verbal depiction for the reader. This analogy, of course, has its limits. Solving a jigsaw puzzle culminates in a static picture; however, past societies were no more immutable than our own—they certainly did not stand still, even though the rate of change varied considerably.

Our historical knowledge of them, in consequence, will emerge as a constantly changing frame that reflects the impulse to evolve.

Although this consideration reduces the value of the preceding analogy it does not negate it. Reading history books remains quite similar to solving a puzzle. First the reader should peruse each chapter rapidly to discover the period and topic it treats, as well as to obtain a general view of unfolding events. This reading will offer an understanding of the conditions that prevailed at the beginning and at the end of the period. If conditions changed then it becomes desirable to find out the cause and nature of change. Here historical study brings to light the dynamic elements of society. At this point the reader will want to go over the chapter more attentively to dig out the details—the jigsaw pieces of this changing image, and put them back together again to reveal the stages of mutation from an early period to a later one. History becomes more interesting and enlightening when the reader abandons the usually passive role for a more active one. A kind of test of one's knowledge can then be carried out by closing the book and trying to call up the facts, putting each in its proper position in an outline.

Above all reading as an active practice requires the asking of questions. What, when, where, why, and who are the five key words an interested scholar will constantly keep in mind. Historians try to discover the past by asking questions about it. The quality and significance of their discoveries depend in large measure on the value of the questions they ask of their data, their facts. Asking the right kind of questions is as important as finding the most plausible answers to them. Interrogating ordered details is a creative act giving rise to generalization. Historical writing consisting only of a vast array of names, events, and dates is often tedious. But if both the historian and the reader use such details to arrive at general conclusions, then interest is aroused by this creative approach. Even professional historians may, and often do, agree on the validity of a set of facts, but derive widely different conclusions from them. Readers, when discussing facts, often do the same.

Does this mean that history as a discipline is not a science? If by science one means a process of gathering data, drawing preliminary conclusions from them, and verifying these conclusions by repeated experiments under identical conditions, then no, the methods of history are not scientific. Simply put, past events do not repeat themselves, and conditions are never identical. There was only one July 1830 revolution in France, and the historian, although able to recall that event verbally, cannot repeat it, nor any of the myriad events that occurred and ended decades or centuries ago. In this sense past occurrences are unique, and historians deal with the unique. This undeniable factor puts their discipline in the realm of the humanities. Nonetheless history is also a social science and can use comparative methods to derive general interpretations as valid as many of those that emerge from the medical sciences. Although it is true that there was just one July revolution, there were many other revolutions and by comparing them, invoking for each the five key words indicated already, the imaginative researcher can validly offer some conclusions about their causes, nature, and result. To go further, by discovering similarities and differences about war, forms of governance, urban and rural life, death rates, the roles of women, the nature of family life, and so on, the reader, too, can find worthwhile general information about human nature, about causes of success or failure, the interplay between societies and environments, to mention only a few possibilities. From this exercise the reader may learn some particular lessons concerning one's conduct in present circumstances. Lessons, however, can be deceptive. As we shall later discover, François Guizot, a brilliant historian of the 1820s, sought to apply "lessons" about the historic rise of the upper middle class. Unfortunately for him, his conclusions were erroneous and brought him, not wisdom, but the arrogant pride that undermined the government he served. More important than lessons, which have been inaccurate at times, we can by careful and questioning study of the past, add to the wisdom that directs our thought and action. That should be the ultimate goal of the discipline.

1

The Geographic Perspective

Europe's Physical Geography

The continent of Europe, when observed on a global map, does not look greatly impressive. Its space comprises 1.4 million square miles, only 7.2 percent of the Earth's total land surface. In size it is just slightly larger than Australia and stands as the second smallest of continents. How then were Europeans able after 1800 to dominate and control for several generations more than half the world's land mass, and far more than half of its population? This is a question that we must answer during our course of study, and because we are considering the issue of space and man's conquest of it, we can begin by first investigating the geographical cradle of the Western powers. At the outset I want to make clear that the notion of geographical determinism has no appeal to me. Conversely, there is no doubt in my mind that the distribution of natural features such as topography, water courses and water masses, climate, arable land, and natural resources are all distinctly influential in how human societies arise, grow, and acquire the abilities by which we characterize them.

The Europe we are studying was bounded on the north by the Barents and North seas, on the west by the Atlantic Ocean, on the South by the

Mediterranean and Black seas and the Caucasus Mountains, and on the east by the Ural Mountains that separated European from Asiatic Russia.

Within these bounds Europeans were remarkably fortunate in their climate. Only a small number lived under temperatures too cold in the north or too hot in the south to discourage active, productive life. The average mean temperatures of the numerous divisions of the Continent made it possible for people to grow various kinds of food and raw materials under conditions that were acceptable without becoming life threatening or enervating. The land was more generous than on other, larger continents, offering inhabitants a generous 30 percent of arable land.

Much of the arable land lay in the North European Plain, stretching from the Pyrenees Mountains across northern spaces eastward to the Urals. Here was the bread basket of the Continent, where rich soils provided grains, especially wheat. In the west the band of flat or gently rolling land was rather narrow, two hundred miles at its widest, then it broadened to two thousand miles in Russia. There were also climatic differences. Southeastern England, northern France and the Low Countries, and northern Germany enjoyed a maritime effect that tempered the cold of winter and the dry heat of summer, creating a condition most favorable to agriculture. But much of northeastern Germany and Russia were more subject to arctic blasts and consequently suffered from colder winters and cooler summers with rain too highly concentrated in the warmer months. Agriculture was therefore somewhat more uncertain and less productive than in the west, if only because it was more extensive (used up more land) than intensive (higher yields within a given acreage).

Another region of rolling and flat land lay in southern Russia. The Steppes was a broad belt that extended from the Black Sea eastward into Asia, and in the distant past it had been the main route taken readily by invaders from central and eastern Asia. The founders of the early Russian state had tried to settle there but were constantly driven out by earlier inhabitants and finally penetrated the forest belt to its north. Not until the seventeenth century did the tsars wrench this land from the Cossacks, runaway peasants who had fled south to escape serfdom. Full control and exploitation came there mainly in the next hundred years after a massive peasant uprising was put down with the brutality customarily reserved for the lower classes in revolt.

Between these two plains topography was far more diverse. High mountain ranges hindered in places the free flow of peoples and goods. Some elevations became the natural boundaries between emerging states: the Pyrenees separated France from Spain; the Alps divided French-, Italian-, German-, and Slavic-speaking peoples; the Jura and Vosges divided French and Germans; the Carpathians formed a barrier among Germans, Bohemians, Poles, and Hungarians; the Caucasus and the Urals delimited Europe from Asia.

But these same high elevations furnished many essential elements of life. Most of the major water courses arose on their slopes, flowed swiftly downward

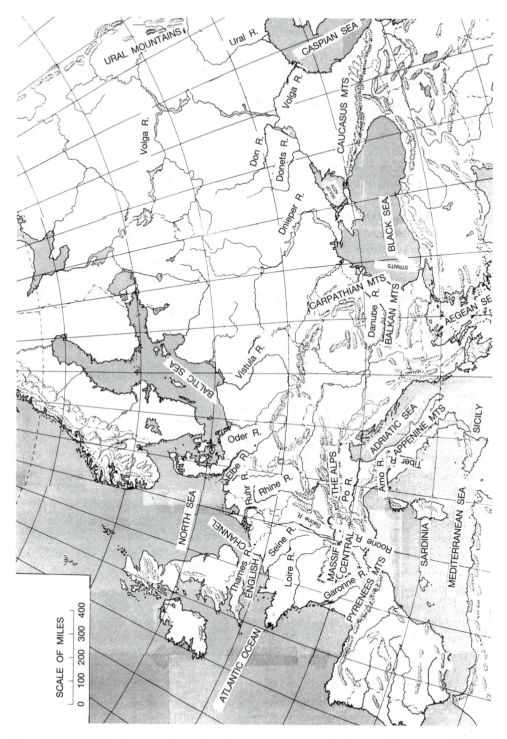

Map 1–1 Physical Geography of Europe

as turbulent mountain streams, then as they grew wider their waters calmed and they became majestic rivers offering the easiest means of transport before the advent of railroads. The Alps, the greatest range in Europe, was the source of the most impressive rivers: Rhine, Rhône, Danube, and Po. The Pyrenees fed the Garonne in France and the Ebro in Spain. The Apennines gave rise to the Arno and the Tiber from which Florence and Rome drew their water. Mountain streams were also the main source of irrigation systems that were indispensable in the more arid regions of the south. The lower slopes of most mountains became part of the cultivated surface available to European farmers. They were terraced by means of human and animal labor carried on for generations in the past, either because the local population exceeded the capacities of the fertile valleys, or because it was necessary to seek elevated sites as protection against barbarian invaders. Agriculture on terraced slopes was extremely arduous and not highly rewarding, with the result that farmers began to abandon it in the course of the nineteenth and early twentieth centuries. Mountain pasturage, however, remained an essential element of cattle and sheep raising. As part of a system of transhumance shepherds grazed their animals in the valleys during winter, and then drove them to upland pastures near and above timber line during warmer months.

Mountains provided another resource of incalculable consequence: wood. Over eons of time settlers had doggedly cut down vast expanses of forests that had once covered most of the land mass, save in the near-arctic tundra and in the semiarid south. Hardwood had been used extensively for building material and softwood for fuel. Before the increased demand for coal, Europeans consumed wood for all domestic heating and cooking. They also employed it as a source of energy in metallurgy, after converting it to charcoal, and even the primitive forges of preindustrial times consumed enormous quantities of trees. Huge flotillas of cut logs were floated downstream to saw mills located closer to markets. Apart from building and industrial use, hardwood was needed to build the extensive flotillas of ships that explored the oceans from the fifteenth century onward. As hardwood forests disappeared from the Continent, the search for tall trunks for masts and hulls turned northward to Scandinavia, and came to involve considerable diplomatic maneuvering and sword shaking, in the same fashion as the search for oil in the later nineteenth and earlier twentieth centuries.

Apart from carrying logs to market, rivers contributed the chief means of transport for all heavy goods and were often linked one to another by man-made canals. Certainly one of the most imposing of these man-made waterways was the Canal du Midi, which, combined with the Garonne River, created an all-water transport system from the port of Bordeaux on the Atlantic coast to the Mediterranean Sea. France was particularly well provided with major rivers deep enough to enable animal-drawn, and later tug-drawn, barges and steamboats to carry goods and passengers. Navigable waterways connected the east and west (Seine, Marne, Dordogne, and Loire), as well as north and south

(Rhône, Saône). The German states were also well provided with water communications from north to south (Rhine, Weser, Elbe, and Oder), but only the Danube, arising in the Black Forest, flowed for a long distance west to east, indeed all the way to the Black Sea. It was less useful to the Germans because it flowed only through the rural southern states, but it was essential to the Hapsburg Empire for it was the major means of communication and linkage among its disparate parts. Rivers played another important part in the life of Europeans: They cut valleys along which roads could be built. Barges on the river surface and wagons on the valley roads were the means of a transport revolution.

In eastern Europe where roadways scarcely existed as late as the nineteenth century, river transport was critical to economic development and even political control over such a vast state as Russia. The empire of the tsars would have been condemned to complete local self-sufficiency without its river network, a condition that would certainly have retarded state formation. Fortunately its main water courses linked the central provinces with southern territories, and even though these were hardly developed before 1800, they would eventually provide access to rich agricultural lands. The greatest waterway, the longest in Europe, was the Volga. Its source lay northwest of Moscow, and from there it made its way over nearly twenty-three hundred miles to the Caspian Sea, a fully landlocked body of water, and consequently useful only for trade with the Orient. The northwest, dependent on the more promising Baltic port of Saint Petersburg, was not well served, certainly less well than Moscow in the center. This lack partly explains why the huge empire remained economically retarded for so long.

Spain was not better served. The Ebro was the only major waterway to empty into the Mediterranean; the others, the Tagus especially, flowed westward into Portugal before emptying into the Atlantic. Fortunately for the south the Guadalquivir connected Cordova and Seville to the Atlantic. Italy, like England, depended less on rivers because the major political and economic centers were close to large open bodies of water. London could not have thrived without the Thames whose tidal waters made it a large inland port. Other short navigable rivers were also useful as parts of water transport in the midlands and north, and facilitated industrial development there. Italian rivers, like those of England, were all short, flowing from the Apennines to the seas. An exception was the Po. It arose in the western Alps and traversed nearly all north Italy before entering the Adriatic. It not only provided transport but also irrigation from its numerous tributaries that made the Po Valley the richest region of the peninsula.

Rich were the people inhabiting good farmland under which lay extensive mineral deposits. Such areas were rare. One was the fertile black earth belt of the Donets in southern Russia, happily served by a navigable river of the same name. Far from the center of power in the north, it was neglected until foreign capital and expertise began to exploit its iron and coal deposits. The same was true of the oil reserves in the Caucasus Mountains. Much earlier the English delved into the extensive coal and iron deposits in the midlands and north of their country. Here began the industrial revolution that enriched them beyond the dreams of their rural ancestors. The ample coal fields lying under the frontier between France and Belgium enabled the entrepreneurs of those two countries to initiate significant industrial growth once iron was located in Lorraine, or could be imported from the Rhineland. Somewhat later the Rhinelanders discovered the wealth of minerals and metals that lay under their farms. Agriculture could not create monetary wealth equal to that formed by industrial activity, but the Germans, like the French and Belgians, discovered the benefits of emerging industrial zones amid the rich farmland of the North Plain where food was plentiful for urban workers and transport easy. Apart from these three major industrial regions there were iron and coal deposits on a much smaller scale in many localities. Europe as a whole enjoyed abundant supplies of both ferrous and nonferrous metals, in addition to numerous minerals such as sulfur, potash, phosphates, graphite, salt, tin, lead, zinc, copper, and so on. A serious shortage was not to become apparent until later in the nineteenth century: petroleum. Except for Russia and Romania, Europe would have to import most of its oil. In compensation, many mountain rivers would become sources of power once they were traversed by hydroelectric power dams. As waterways became less vital for transport after the introduction of railroads and paved roads for trucks, their usefulness survived as a major source of energy. Water wheels were never completely replaced by steam engines, especially in regions without coal deposits.

Such was the interplay between man and the environment.

Political Geography

The political geography of Europe in the early 1800s was the result of internal and external policies carried out by ambitious royal families during the three previous centuries. The 1600s were pivotal in the sense that powerful dynastic states assumed more definite form and permanency after a long struggle against local landed nobilities. This trend toward the consolidation of territorial holdings and the legalization of rule over the people inhabiting them was more or less complete in the major states of western and eastern Europe: England, France, and Russia. In each case a powerful dynasty claimed and won rulership after severe political crises involving bloody revolts or civil war. In England the extremely sanguinary internal conflict, the War of the Roses of the late 1400s, led to stronger rule. But the continuing process of legitimacy went again through the rigorous test of the civil war of the 1640s before the existing political institutions enjoyed the full loyalty of most subjects. From their southern base the English conquered and annexed Ireland and Scotland. The end result was a relatively small territorial state with a limited population. Yet this insular realm became one of the richest states of Europe, thanks to its American and Asiatic empire, and its overseas trade that encouraged manufacturing and financial investment. Surrounded by water and protected by an invincible navy, it both stood apart from Europe across the English Channel and yet played an active role as banker to its allies during its numerous wars in the 1700s. England's geopolitics focused on distant lands, and the markets and raw materials they had to offer.

Opposite was France, already a dynastic state far larger in size than England, and far more populous. It was both an Atlantic and Mediterranean power by the seventeenth century and, like England, controlled a sizable overseas empire. But with northern and eastern frontiers on the Continent, it faced the European mainland and was more directly involved in matters there, with the result that it lost to the English most of its overseas empire in the course of the 1700s, a loss that seems not to have reduced its standing as a great power. In a more definite sense than the English, it had many of the trappings of one: a centralized administration, probably the largest population in Europe, a territory second only to that of Russia but far more effectively used, an active economy under the tutelage of the central state, and a very large army. The revolution that broke out in 1789 did not weaken either the state apparatus or its ambitions for conquest and territorial annexations. The kings of the old regime before the revolution had little to show for their aggressive endeavors, but the revolutionaries, and Napoleon who emerged as emperor, were far more successful; during twenty-three years of nearly continuous war, they conquered large segments of the Continent. Napoleon had seized a new crown, but he inherited the human, natural, and administrative resources of the old regime. Unfortunately for him they proved insufficient to carry out his new more expansive geopolitical ambitions. Ignoring the ancient natural frontiers of France, he crossed the Pyrenees and the Alps to conquer both Spain and Italy. Then he pushed beyond the Rhine to conquer Germany, and still not satisfied, he invaded Russia. It seemed that only England was beyond his reach—a grasping arm that could stretch as far as Russia but could not reach over the English Channel. Nor could it crush the English navy in order to block the great wealth that England derived from her overseas markets and colonies. That wealth she distributed to her Continental allies in the form of subsidies. For the English could not allow France to control Europe; in particular, her statesmen would never allow a strong power to possess the Low Countries. In her geopolitical scheme this part of the Northern Plain, which had no natural barriers save the sea, must remain neutral. This tiny flat area had long been a source of contention between the two states. The Low Countries had for centuries belonged to the Hapsburgs, first the Spanish branch, then the Austrian. The English did not fear Austria; half a continent away it posed no threat. But they fought bloody battles to keep the French out of a territory that could become a launch site for an invasion of their little island. Worse, the French generally supported the rebellious Irish, menacing England on her western flank. The unhappy Irish and their island homeland lay menacingly between England and her North American empire, reason enough to refuse absolutely to free the Irish from Anglo rule.

Despite their ongoing conflicts both England and France enjoyed greatness and power in European affairs because they were geographically well situated with easy access to large, open bodies of water that encouraged trade and industry.

Russia in the east was not so lucky within the European context in which water transport was required for development. Like France, the Muscovite polity had been created over several centuries by powerful dynasties overcoming rival families, and by disciplining the old noble class and its tendency toward autonomy to protect their local power. But the struggle between the Muscovite grand dukes and provincial clans incited a period of endemic upheavals bordering on anarchy and aptly labeled the "Time of Troubles" (1604–13). Finally the Romanovs reestablished order and forged an empire stretching from the White Sea in the far north to the Steppes in the south, the land of the Cossacks where no definite frontier line existed. To the east lay the Ural Mountains, a natural boundary until crossed by Russian pioneers forging east into Siberia, just as American frontiersmen and women made their way westward. In the 1700s the empire was still a huge territorial state in the making, even in the north where large bodies of water seemed to provide natural boundaries. In the geopolitical thinking of Peter the Great (1672–1725), the White Sea with its port, Archangel, was not an acceptable frontier because the water was frozen during many months of the year. Peter wanted contact with the West in order to acquire the technology and scientific knowledge he needed to transform his semibarbarian into a modern state, and that required a warm-water port. It also required several wars. In 1703, to crown his success, he built a new city at the eastern tip of the Gulf of Finland, and called it Saint Petersburg, though Peter was no saint.

To complete these geopolitical ambitions, Tsarina Catherine the Great (1729–96) sent armies to conquer the south and gain access to the Black Sea. Although victorious in this endeavor she and her successors readily discovered that this sea, despite its size, was nearly landlocked; the sole outlet to the more promising Mediterranean and the west was through the "Straits of Bosporus," a narrow body of water dominated by Constantinople, the capital of the Ottoman Empire. Henceforth, the geographically driven tsars had before them a major objective: penetration of the Balkan Peninsula and acquisition of the Straits. This goal, not fully clarified as yet, required the destruction of what remained of the Ottoman state. Russia's spacial ambitions, in abeyance during the generation of the French Revolution, resurfaced in the 1820s when the Greeks rose in revolt against their Turkish overlords, and thenceforth remained a permanent part of tsarist Near Eastern policy. It provoked several small wars in the 1800s and was a major cause of the big war of 1914. During the seventeenth and eighteenth centuries England and France had greatly expanded their holdings overseas, Russia overland. Despite the loss of some of their colonies, both western countries had profited enormously from them; Russia benefited far less from her conquests that were in very sparsely populated lands, lacking easy trade communications with the central state and unattractive to Russian colonists save runaway peasants who wanted nothing to do with the northern government. Not until the nineteenth century did the tsarist regime and economy begin to profit from newly acquired lands in the Steppes and Siberia.

Extending west of Russia was a combination of plains, hills, and mountains. This was central Europe, a wide expanse of land divided over centuries of time into hundreds of political entities ranging in size from tiny city-states on the North and Baltic seas to extensive kingdoms like Poland and Prussia. This was a "soft" area, without a powerful overlord to give it solidity, unity, cohesion, and defense. It was open to aggression from the powerful Swedish empire in the north, from ambitious France in the west desirous of acquiring the Germanic lands west of the Rhine, from Russia in the east seeking to expand its coastline along the Baltic, and from two internal powers, Prussia and Austria, each seeking additional territories at the expense of neighboring states. During the Thirty Years' War (1618–48) parts of the Germanies suffered terribly from foreign invaders and internecine warfare between Protestants and Catholics. Small wonder that the Hohenzollern rulers transformed Prussia into a militarized state. The Poles failed in this endeavor with the result that their country was ruthlessly divided, and the pieces were swallowed by Prussia, Austria, and Russia in the late 1700s. What remained in central Europe was a kind of imperial nonstate, still called the Holy Roman Empire. It was nominally under the rule of the Austrian Hapsburgs who were regularly elected to the imperial throne. However, Hapsburgs became less and less interested in German affairs after the Ottoman Turks were halted at the gates of Vienna and then steadily rolled back into the Balkan peninsula. The imperial crown offered nearly empty power; the southeast offered lands to exploit and their Christian populations to tax and, presumably, to save from the Moslem "devils." All three of the major eastern states, therefore, were seeking to expand: Prussia ruthlessly seized Silesia from Austria, as well as her share of Poland; Austria unable to recover Silesia, took a share of Poland and moved eastward; Russia also took her share of Poland and advanced southwestward, on a collision course with Austria.

Spain, compared with the other large states, was geographically satisfied. Her golden age, the sixteenth century, had passed, and her problem now was to hold onto what she had. Although still ruler of a vast Latin American empire her growing weakness at home made increasingly tenuous her ability to hold it much less rule it. The riches from that empire had passed through Spanish hands like sand through a sieve. In a tragic way the several generations of rulers made choices that ignored the rich offerings of geography, and let their kingdom slip into irretrievable poverty and the powerlessness that accompanies economic stagnation, mediocre rulership, and a fatalistic outlook. The geographic formations of land and water provided human societies with advantages and disadvantages; however, it was these societies that decided how to improve or waste them. Spain chose the latter.

The strength of the country lay not with the nobility but with the resolute, long-suffering peasantry. Exploited as they were, the tillers of the soil combined unrelenting tenacity and religious fanaticism. The first attribute saved the population from starvation but scarcely raised the general conditions of life; the second saved the crown from middle class, anticlerical revolutionaries. The rural poor stood by royalist priests even when the church took at least a tenth of their crops.

The inhabitants of the Italian peninsula were not more blessed or enterprising after their apex of grandeur. Like the Hapsburgs of Spain the various Italian princes had benefited from water transport when the peninsula was the center of Mediterranean trade routes between the Levant and Europe; but when these routes declined in importance so did most of the Italian states. Their subjects had little to offer save large numbers of ruins dating from the Roman period, and a vast amount of mediocre religious art of the postbaroque decades. The decline was hastened by political divisions and bitter feuding. Like the German states north of the Alps, the Italian states were unable to achieve unity. They too, were therefore left defenseless against foreign invaders. The French, the Spanish, and, subsequently, the Austrians, all laid claim to Italian lands. The sea that had once brought wealth, now left the land exposed, and the Alps had never been an effective barrier to incursions from the north. Far more than the Germans the Italian states were more likely to be ruled by foreign dynasties either directly or indirectly through families of the local nobilities.

In the far north the Scandinavian countries were past the days of glory that the king of Sweden had brought them. The attempt of Charles XII to expand his power into eastern Europe brought him into conflict with Peter the Great of Russia. The limited population, territory, and sparse resources were not sufficient to support his ambitions. Peter's military success brought him all the land forming the southern coast of the Gulf of Finland and a broad stretch of the eastern coast of the Baltic Sea. The combined state of Denmark and Norway thrived on fishing and other maritime pursuits. Lying on the periphery of the Continent they, like Sweden after Charles's reign, exercised little influence on it.

The political geography of Europe had become more or less stabilized after the Seven Years' War ended in 1763. Relations among the states in the course of the 1600s and 1700s were increasingly dictated by the idea of a balance of power among them, a guiding principle that sought to preserve an equilibrium to prevent any one state from becoming so powerful that it could threaten the existence of its neighbors. Louis XIV had been a major danger to equilibrium, and France was an ominous neighbor as the Spanish, Germans, and Netherlanders discovered. Combinations of powers—the sea power of the English and the land power of France's Continental foes—managed to keep

Louis XIV in check, and he died a frustrated man. However, they did not keep the general peace, simply because emerging states looked on war as an acceptable means of territorial expansion. All of the "gentlemanly" aggressions of the 1700s were violent steps to realign old spacial arrangements to acquire buried minerals and outlets to the sea, capture new populations to tax them, and to extend territory up to a natural frontier.

All of these purely dynastic geopolitical considerations were shaken when the French began a revolution in 1789. New geographical imperatives then appeared, tinged with political ideologies that concealed for a brief while what amounted to the biggest land grab since the ancient Romans carved out their empire.

2

The French Revolution and Europe

The Revolutionary Phase, 1789–99

The hundred years separating the collapse of Napoleon's empire in 1814 and the outbreak of World War I in 1914 are best characterized as a period of unrelenting conflict between the forces struggling to change a society they considered unjust, and those struggling to preserve an old order to which they were both intellectually and emotionally attached. Neither side in this ongoing combat was neatly homogeneous. Among the champions of transformation were moderates who had no desire fully to raze the traditional society but only to repair it where it seemed most abusive. There were also men of more radical temperament who were determined to tear down completely and rebuild anew. On several occasions these two could act together, even to manning the barricades of revolt; however, after their victory, they often fell on each other in bloody combat.

The defenders of tradition were equally divided between moderate conservatives who favored some reform provided their privileges were not threatened and ultrareactionaries who willfully defended traditions they believed sacred. In western Europe, chiefly Britain and the Low Countries, the moderates in both camps found it convenient on several occasions to join forces against the two extremes, and eventually came to form a "third force." Although there were

19

differences among its constituent groups, they became dominant in governmental affairs, became in a true sense a ruling class, and not averse to progress or to enough reform to discourage revolutionaries. Not all Europe was either red or black. In central and eastern Europe, however, the conservatives and the reformers had little in common. The two sides, therefore, were more clearly separated and at daggers drawn. The formation of a third central force proved to be impossible, if only because the moderates on either side were too weak to benefit from coalition. Throughout the century authoritarian conservatives remained in power and even when they made some reforms they acted to increase their hold over public life behind a facade of progress.

In this picture France stands out as an anomaly. Although a dominant element in the West, it was the country in which the two extremes came to grips most often. It was, after all, the home of Paris, and Paris was the initiator of political revolution, in the same way that England was the initiator of industrial revolution. England's economic initiative had little effect on the Continent (Belgium excepted) until midcentury and after. France's first political revolution in 1789, on the contrary, had an immediate influence on all her neighboring states; it created a revolutionary impulse that sent shock waves across frontiers near and far, and that reappeared in France with each succeeding generation until it was extinguished in 1871 in a last frenzy of fratricide known as the Paris Commune.

This tradition of rebellion, a leading characteristic of the nineteenth century, marked its entry into history by inaugurating a quarter century of turmoil that did not end until the final overthrow of Napoleon in 1815. This "Age of Revolution" combined internal convulsions of unprecedented magnitude, as well as foreign wars that annihilated age-old dynasties and frontiers.

In 1789 the French reformers called themselves "patriots," meaning lovers of the *patrie*, the fatherland, the nation. In reality they were "liberals" before the word was coined. The program they wrote into the Constitution of 1791 became the model for Continental reformers after 1815 when the name "liberal" was taken over by them. These patriots were by no means republicans and certainly no economic egalitarians. Rather they erected, with a minimum of violence, a limited or constitutional monarchy to replace the traditional divine right, absolute regime created during the seventeenth century. From subjects, Frenchmen and even Frenchwomen became citizens, constitutionally free from feudal servitude and equal in the eyes of the law. The suffrage, to be sure, was limited to male owners of fairly sizable property—the "active" citizens. "Passive" citizens were men unable to meet the property qualifications. The exact legal condition of women was left unclear, save that they were prohibited from voting regardless of their wealth. This experiment in constitutional monarchy was the most fruitful of the entire revolutionary decade. These moderates abolished the remnants of feudalism, proclaimed to a hostile world that all men are free, equal, and brothers, and that the basic liberties include speech, press, assembly, and religion. Acting on these premises they put an end to noble titles and privileges, terminated the age-old guilds of master craftsmen to remove restraints on industrial activity, replaced the equally age-old provinces by small administrative units known as *départements*, prepared the replacement of ancient regional laws by one all-embracing legal system, and put limits on royal power. Distrustful of the Catholic church as a pillar of the divine-right monarchy, they confiscated ecclesiastical property and offered it for sale to the highest bidders, a process of land transfer reminiscent of the Reformation Era when kings seized church lands to distribute to favorites. To this roster of progressive, indeed, modernizing steps must be added those that proved fatal to the experiment. The Civil Constitution of the Clergy, which required an oath of allegiance from every churchman, alienated the hitherto supportive lower clergy and turned them into ardent enemies. Henceforward priests became the avatars of a sizable counter-revolutionary force with its roots in western France. The moderates also declared war on Great Britain, a decision that began a period of unending war until 1815. They were both unrealistically doctrinaire, and worse, incapable of mobilizing the nation for a successful defense after both Prussia and Austria joined Britain's side. The final act in this political experiment came when the king tried to flee, and when allied armies crossed the northeastern frontier into France.

A loose coalition of determined republicans calling themselves "Jacobins" now seized power, and by early 1793 had initiated the Terror. They beheaded the king, (and the queen, for good measure) proclaimed the First Republic, and organized it as a war government led by committees far more powerful than the absolute monarchs of old. In particular the Committee of Public Safety, headed more or less by Maximilien Robespierre, has won a prominent place in history because it was the prime force behind the Terror. Its agents rounded up, tried, and almost inevitably executed the accused. It became identified with the newly invented guillotine, a superbly efficient instrument for eliminating the numerous persons who either plotted against the Republic, or simply neglected to obey its rigorous wartime measures placing ceilings on prices and wages. Various estimates put at twenty thousand the number of victims who perished by execution from 1792 to 1795 including Robespierre himself and his followers who were sent to the guillotine by other Jacobins who came to fear for their lives. Small wonder that the bloody image of the Jacobin became the bug-bear used by parents of the next generation to frighten their children into obedience.

By 1795 the revolutionary movement in France had brought forth a novel political culture in conflict with old ideas about the proper governance of society. Traditional views looked on the need of authority to control a mass of unruly, immoral, undisciplined subjects. The pillars of order were an absolute monarchy, a privileged nobility, and a dominant religion propagated by an equally privileged clerical hierarchy. The ideal was a society of estates, each functioning in accordance with its given role. The clergy, or first estate, were to pray and teach obedience; the nobility, or second estate, existed to rule, judge, and preserve their honor as a military elite; everyone else, the third estate, must be obligated to support the privileged estates by working and paying taxes.

The English revolutionaries of the 1640s were the first to challenge this traditional structure and to do so successfully. The moderate French revolutionaries between 1789 and 1792 sought to imitate the English by creating a new regime based on fairly flexible classes rather than rigidly segregated estates. The pillar of the new society was to be a government created by a written constitution that limited royal power, provided for a legislature elected and controlled by men of substance, and granted civil liberties to all citizens regardless of income. Implicit in this new culture was the belief that all French people were citizens, not subjects, and bound into a nation by brotherly ties—none but a few feminists mentioned sisterly ties. This experiment failed in practice, yet it brought forth a novel tradition that took hold in France and throughout Europe. Its defenders, at first called patriots, became known later as *liberals*, a term borrowed from Spanish revolutionaries. Most of them belonged to the bourgeoisie, with a few enlightened nobles added for color; as such they included private property as a sacred right and the necessary basis of political power.

The Jacobin founders of the first Republic were, in a sense, forerunners of left-wing liberals in that they, too, considered property as fundamental to any good society, along with personal freedom. Where they differed from the moderates was in their demand for universal male suffrage, and their stress on equality and national feeling. As egalitarians and nationalists they leaned toward an excess of community control that, when caught up in the frenzy of war, led to dictatorship by a few and suppression of freedom for the many. They adopted the tricolor flag as the symbol of a new France, and the *Marseillaise* as its rousing anthem. With these they instilled in their armies the emotive force that transformed illiterate peasants into disciplined soldiers capable of driving back the professional armies of kings and then taking the offensive in the name of the people. In the end the Jacobins' success was their undoing; their republic failed on the homefront, a victim of its inordinate violence against fellow citizens, and the exigencies of war. Yet, it, too, carved in the history of France a tradition that outlived it. Unlike liberalism it remained chiefly an ideal among some lessor bourgeois and the artisan working class. It never spread widely in Europe before midcentury because it was associated with the Terror. By a strange quirk of fate these ardent defenders of the little man opened the way to the "little corporal," Napoleon.

The Imperial Phase, 1800–15

In time the French Revolution followed a course that came to typify all the major outbreaks in Europe. First came the moderate phase, to be followed by a more radical effort to break with the past. As the fervor of this determination acquired the signs of fanaticism, the men who felt that change had gone far enough seized power, only to open the way to a new dictator, Napoleon in the French case, who claimed to embody the best elements of the revolution and to restore order. Although the cycle ended with him there was still the war to win and enlightened ideals and institutions to spread abroad.

These goals became the mission that Napoleon assigned himself when he became the first consul in 1800 and, then, in 1804, the emperor of France. As he moved from one military victory to another, his missionary zeal diminished while his personal ambition grew. Believing himself the embodiment of the revolutionary aspirations of France, he willingly assumed the role of the last enlightened despot as a means both of consolidating revolutionary achievements and imposing them on conquered states. To be sure, the patriotically inspired armies of France had undertaken this mission before the meteoric rise of the Corsican, and were generally greeted as liberators by the middle and lower urban classes in west Germany and north Italy. However, the unlimited demands of both the

Napoleon, undoubtedly a military genius, is surrounded by the generals who led his armies to victory until 1812. The painting is a good example of propaganda art used to give an impression of grandeur, command, and action. This style is "heroic classic."

NAPOLEON,   Surrounded by the most celebrated generals of his ti

French war machine and the emperor soon wore out the welcome mat. When the process of invasion became that of occupation or deeper conquest, hundreds of thousands of armed men required food, lodging, and supplies. In exchange for liberty, they demanded booty; in exchange for equality they demanded recruits; in exchange for fraternity, they demanded obedience. Napoleon's boundless appetite for success doubled and tripled the sacrifices he demanded, to the point where natives were aroused to resistance. Most notable were Spanish peasants whose guerrilla warfare made Spain Napoleon's "open wound." The French had arrived as liberators, they ended as exploiters, and the emperor's systematized exploitation aroused hatred of them. It became out-and-out robbery when Napoleon began taking priceless paintings and statuary from conquered (no longer "liberated") territories. It is doubtful that conquered peoples were jolted into action by the looting of museums and palaces. It was the levy of heavy taxes to finance French armies, and the levy of young males to man them, that stimulated opposition, and this opposition became the cradle in which an awakening nationalistic fervor was nurtured. The patriotism that had worked to the advantage of the French until about 1810 would work for the defeated after.

This was a novel element that was as yet unable to stir the peasantry into action save in Spain and, to a lesser extent, in Russia. The cardinal error of Napoleon was certainly his decision to invade the vast flatlands of the tsar's empire. Leading one of the largest armies then known, about 600,000 men, he began the penetration in 1812. When he entered Moscow he imagined that the tsar, like a conventional commander, would formally surrender, and turn over a city intact and well supplied with food. Instead, Alexander I, by no means a brilliant strategist, retreated, and resorted to a scorched earth policy in the countryside. The French entry into Moscow was a hollow victory; they found no provisions, and almost no lodging. With winter approaching, Napoleon had no choice but to order a general retreat that continued in the bitter cold. His "grand army" of more than half a million was annihilated by "general winter"; barely 60,000 men reentered a Germany that no longer welcomed them but rather prepared to drive them out to liberate the homeland.

This turnabout signaled a change not only in the fortunes of Napoleon, but also marked a reversal in the conflict between the forces of change and those of order. Napoleon had begun this reversal after his seizure of power in 1800. His mission, he proclaimed, had been to restore order. But he also insisted that he was a child of the revolution and called on all Frenchmen to take part in a plebiscite, voting whether or not they approved of his new role. Their affirmation of him was overwhelming; his rule was no longer the gift of God; it was of the people. This was novel, and so was his Concordat of 1801 with the Catholic church. He did not return the church's land; it was by now in the hands of many bourgeois and peasants. Rather he guaranteed to support the church financially and politically—which did not prevent him from kidnapping the pope in 1807 and then transforming the Papal States of central Italy into a Kingdom of Rome, upon whose throne he sat his infant son. He also promulgated his law codes, the most modern in Europe, which were adapted by all the areas of Europe not governed by common law. His Civil Code in particular rejected the feudalistic society of estates to focus on the individual and to sanctify his property.

These progressive steps notwithstanding, the emperor steadily converted his plebiscitary regime into one of divine right. A newly issued Catechism taught school children that their ruler's power was truly of celestial origin. He created a privileged aristocracy from his military and bureaucratic servitors, and steadily reduced the already skimpy role of the representative assemblies he had set up as window dressing to win over flexible liberals. If during the years 1789 to 1815 the forces committed to reform were generally in the ascendant, from 1815 to 1848 those devoted to tradition held the upper hand.

Political-Territorial Settlements, 1814–15: Balance of Power

The final overthrow of Napoleon was made possible by his crushing defeat in Russia. In his retreat westward across the Germanies, however, he was still capable of raising armies, of giving a good account of himself in the decisive battle of Leipzig, but unable to recover the ever-mounting losses of material, men, and morale. His dedicated old guard stood by him, but too many of his generals and marshals were convinced that he must abdicate if only to save the throne for his son, the king of Rome. His wife, after all, was a Hapsburg archduchess, and Austria might not have opposed a regency under her control. Beneath this outward display of devotion to a dynasty they were also hoping to save their own titles and estates. Momentarily disheartened, the emperor finally signed an act of abdication, but he also foolishly sent his wife and son away from Paris. So when the allied leaders entered the capital as victors in March 1814, they were not met by the infant king of Rome but by a very fat old man calling himself Louis XVIII, the Bourbon heir to a nonexistent throne. His return had been carried out by blue-blood nobles determined to eradicate all traces of the revolution. Louis had made himself acceptable to a provisional government by offering a "Charter" that preserved some aspect of constitutional rule, and safeguarded the ranks, titles, and properties of the new Bonapartist aristocracy. Heading the provisional government was the cleverest politician in Europe, Charles Maurice de Talleyrand, one of the few men who survived all the vicissitudes of the revolution and empire, and who now assumed the post of foreign minister and defender of his country's interests in the perplexing world of postwar diplomacy.

In the spring of 1814 the major allies—Britain, Prussia, Austria, and Russia—faced their most pressing issue: what to do with France and Napoleon? On April 14 the fallen emperor reluctantly signed the Treaty of Fontainebleau, named after the majestic palace where he was holding out. That he still had admirers among the victors is evident from the terms: a gift of the Isle of Elba off the western Italian coast, a petty realm where he could once more play sovereign. As for France, the allies were more than generous when they agreed to the first Treaty of Paris on May 30. Although her territory was reduced to the boundaries of January 1, 1792, she still retained some lands along her frontiers that the early revolutionary state had acquired by forced annexation after 1789. Among these was Avignon, formerly the property of the Popes. However, she lost several small island colonies, taken over and retained by the British. The British did not consider these sufficient and put forward the idea of indemnities to pay the costs of war, understandable given that Britain had borne most of the monetary costs through subsidies granted her allies, and her national debt had risen tenfold. But the new French king haughtily declared that he would accept no monetary demands for whatever cause, and the allies, ignoring the British, dropped the notion of reparations. Their armies did not even remain in France. Her soil, nonetheless, was briefly overrun by numerous returning native soldiers, deserters, and liberated prisoners of war, many of them wounded and limping from village to village, begging their way home. These heroes had become pariahs. In contrast, Prussian regulars before departing looted towns and estates, and were rapidly imitated by Cossacks who terrorized the countryside, as though enraged by the lenient treatment of the enemy after all they had suffered. This first treaty, however magnanimous, foreshadowed the general terms of peace, whose final arrangements were left to a "general congress" of representatives of all the belligerents.

It was not until September that this congress met in Vienna where it was hosted by Austria, an overgenerous gesture that seriously set back her treasury. The expenses were so burdensome because the plenipotentiaries and the hungry horde of assistants and dependents spent no time at all in general deliberations and never assembled together in a congress. The only occasions that brought them together were the balls, receptions, military reviews, and tournaments that continued over eight months. Negotiations were kept in the hands of the four major powers, and their main attention centered on territorial arrangements.

These were not at all simple and required patience, tact, and persistence, characteristics shared about equally between Prince Clemens Metternich representing the Hapsburgs of Austria and Viscount Robert Castlereagh, plenipotentiary of Great Britain. Both enjoyed considerable freedom of control from their governments. The Russian foreign minister, Prince Karl Nesselrode, was less fortunate; Tsar Alexander I, often present in person, intervened constantly in unpredictable ways, a result of his complex character. Likewise Prince Karl von Hardenberg of Prussia found it difficult to control the excessively pro-Russian leaning of his sovereign, Frederick William III, a man prone to melancholia. France sent Talleyrand, certainly the most experienced diplomat of those assembled. To obviate any resistance to the Bourbons he came forward with the idea of "legitimacy" as a basis of political settlement; he proposed that only sovereign families reigning before the French Revolution, such as the Bourbons, were legitimate. Upstarts, like the Bonapartes, were *ipso facto* illegitimate, without the right to rule. The idea of legitimacy was an expedient that received nodding approval by the major powers but was acted on only where convenient: the restoration of the Bourbon rulers in France, Spain, and Naples (the Kingdom of the Two Sicilies). No one of consequence proposed restoring the Holy Roman Empire, ended by Napoleon between 1803 and 1806 when he rearranged the Rhineland to create a buffer zone of conquered German states on his eastern frontier. The several hundred petty entities that had enjoyed varying degrees of independence until then were now reduced to thirty-nine. The Italian states, overrun and absorbed by French armies before and after 1798 were simply once more reshaped into a smaller number. Most notable was the emergence of the kingdom of Piedmont-Sardinia, under the house of Savoy, with its capital at Turin in the north-west corner of Italy. It was strengthened as a bastion against France by acquiring the former Republic of Genoa. These consolidating arrangements would later facilitate the unification of both Germany and Italy as national states.

The claims of nationality were scarcely audible in Vienna. The nobles who ruled over the entire population were cosmopolitan rather than nationalist in outlook. Indeed, nationalism was viewed as a dangerous impulse to revolution. In consequence most attention was devoted to the considerably older ideal of a balance of power. Traditionally, rulers of states did not employ the balance-of-power principle to avoid war, an activity they looked on as legitimate and heroic. Rather they used it as a means of preventing one state from becoming so dominant that it menaced the sovereignty of its neighbors. In the sixteenth century the Hapsburg Empire, which then had comprised Austria, Spain, the Low Countries, and much of Italy, had upset the balance by its vastness. From the 1680s the Bourbons of France replaced the Hapsburgs as the menace. Finally the 1789 revolution, which had thrown up Napoleon and forwarded the ideal of nationalism as state policy, had so upset the fragile equilibrium among states that only a vast reordering of boundaries could restore it. Because France was the culprit, the great powers could readily agree on the steps needed to fence her in. To contain her in the north, on which the British were insistent, the former Austrian Netherlands, now known as Belgium, were handed over to the king of the Protestant Netherlands to create a larger bulwark between France and the British Isles. The protests of Belgian leaders speaking for a thoroughly Catholic people, were completely ignored, even by Catholic Austria. Metternich, of course, won "compensation" for this loss by acquiring the Italian-speaking territories of Venetia and Lombardy. His state also regained its Polish possessions taken by Napoleon and expanded its frontier to include land in the Tyrol and Illyria, the latter forming much of the eastern coast of the Adriatic Sea, providing the Hapsburgs with a maritime outlet. Austria was now more consolidated, making for easier administration and defense. Under Metternich's leadership Austrian influence was more extensive than it appeared; in Italy Hapsburg relatives ruled in Tuscany, Parma, Lucca, and Modena.

Entirely different were the situations of Prussia and Russia. The Hohenzollerns, once the commanders of the most efficient army in Europe, had seen their ranks of professional soldiers crumble before the onslaughts of the nationally inspired French troops of Napoleon. To restore the state the diplomats at Vienna readily accorded to Prussia extensive territories in the Rhineland as a means of strengthening her against a resurgence of French ambition. Later, when the Saar and Ruhr valleys became major centers of industry, Prussia's economic base would be considerably strengthened. In central Europe her territorial ambitions coincided with those of Russia but not with the plans of the other plenipotentiaries. Consequently Poland and Saxony emerged as areas of a serious conflict.

In the mid-1790s Poland had simply disappeared from the map, having been absorbed by her three neighbors. Napoleon, when at the height of his power, had partially revived this defunct state as the Grand Duchy of Warsaw. His catastrophic retreat from Russia in 1812 had left the Duchy open to the Russian army as it moved westward. Now, in 1815, Alexander wished to recreate a Polish state, separate from Russia but under his personal rule as its king, a title equally separate from that of tsar. Prussia approved and was willing to let go of her share of the territory if she were allowed to annex the kingdom of Saxony on her southwestern border. The king of Saxony had been an ally of Napoleon; because he had not broken his alliance until Napoleon continued his retreat after his defeat at battle of Leipzig, he was in a weak bargaining position to save his throne—particularly since Alexander was enthusiastic to recognize Prussia's demand. Metternich, however, was strongly opposed to augmenting Prussia's kingdom, for the same reason that he was distrustful of the tsar's plans for Poland, plans that extended Russian power far eastward of its original boundaries. Moreover the tsar, in one of his unpredictable moments, made known his intention to set up a constitutional monarchy in Poland. To Metternich, Russia was already too powerful in the balance of forces, and any statutory limits on a monarch were too revolutionary, a violation of the divine right in which he unflinchingly believed. Castlereagh fully agreed with him, not about divine right but about the menace of Russia.

This situation presented Talleyrand with an advantage he quickly seized to bring France from the outside to the inside of the circle of major powers. He proposed a secret alliance of Britain, Austria, and his state to resist, by force of arms if necessary, Prussian and Russian demands. The separate alliance was signed in January 1815. It was, of course, not kept secret; and since no one really wanted to resume war, the bluff worked. The final arrangements allowed Alexander to take most of Poland, both Prussia and Austria regained some of the land they had annexed in the 1790s and subsequently lost to the duchy set up by Napoleon, and Prussia was ceded only two-fifths of Saxony—not the better part because the Saxon king retained his throne as well as the important cities of Leipzig and Dresden.

Great Britain, although concerned about the claims of Prussia and

Russia, had little cause for alarm. She acquired no territorial gains on the Continent, nor did she request any. Her acquisitions were far-flung strategic and supply outposts taken over during the war, and required by her maritime and naval fleets: Helgoland in the North Sea, Malta and the Ionian Islands in the Mediterranean, Cape Colony in South Africa, Ile de France (Mauritius), and Ceylon in the Indian Ocean, Demerara on the Atlantic coast of Africa, Saint Lucia, Trinidad, and Tobago in the Caribbean Sea. What is more, the French fleet, her only serious rival, had been destroyed at Trafalgar in 1805, and her long-time enemy was now hemmed in on the seas as well as on the land by her strengthened neighbors—a balance that seemed precarious at the time but that proved to be remarkably durable.

At this point it is necessary to note that the term *balance of power* has recently been rejected as inaccurate by several scholars. They argue rightly that there was no perfect balance, that is, equality, of power among the negotiating states: Great Britain in the West and Russia in the East were each more powerful than the Continental monarchies lying between them. What existed was a "hegemonic" balance between the only two truly world-class powers, Britain and Russia. Other states enjoyed merely secondary hegemonies: France in western Europe, Prussia in the north, Austria in the center, and Italy. Peace was sustained, not as a result of equilibrium of power but of cooperation resulting from a general agreement on politics and international law. Cooperation replaced conflict.

This revisionist view has been challenged and rejected by competent scholars who recognize that balance in international relations had never required that all states be equally powerful or equally hegemonic. Even when the two major powers threatened international accord, as Russia did in Poland and Britain did, as we shall see, in Spanish Latin America, balance was not destroyed though it was threatened.

The skeptics seemed correct about the brevity of peace when Napoleon escaped from his tiny realm of Elba. After reorganizing the administration of the island he grew bored and sailed northward to recover the more promising governance of France. In 1814 he had fled from Paris to Marseille in disguise to avoid hostile demonstrations along the route. His "second coming" was quite the reverse. He was wildly applauded in the port of Antibes and along his devious road northward. Louis XVIII sent troops against him, led by the ex-emperor's most favored marshal, Michel Ney, who swore to bring him back in chains. Yet, when he came face to face with his old commander, he fell to his knees in adoration and ordered his troops to join the ragtag forces that had joined the triumphal march toward Paris. When apprised of this, Louis fled to Ghent in Belgium, and the Congress of Vienna declared Napoleon an outlaw. Napoleon undoubtedly believed that his return would divide the major powers, but this belief was as gross an error as his earlier conviction that he could conquer Russia. Nonetheless he collected an army that fought bravely until its defeat at Waterloo on June 18.

After this reverse Napoleon and France found their opponents far less indulgent. The second Treaty of Paris, signed on November 20, took away some strong points along France's northern and eastern frontier, imposed a huge war indemnity of 700 million francs, and an army of occupation for three years, with France to bear its expense. France lost not only half a million inhabitants, she also had finally to pay out more than a billion francs. This was a drain of capital that might have been used to set France on the way to an industrial revolution. The restoration of Louis XVIII, hardly an advocate of the kind of economic and social policies required for rapid economic growth, was a further hindrance. If the old saying is true that a people gets the kind of rulers they deserve, the French must have sinned grievously in their past.

The Concert of Europe

The political and territorial arrangements of 1814–15 formed the basis for peace, not because they were perfect but because none of the powers wanted war. That the balance endured the hard test of time indicates it faithfully reflected the European outlook of the statesman who created it and those who continued it. Even the English, Castlereagh and his successor George Canning, who held their distance from the reactionary policies of continental ministers, supported the idea of an equilibrium among states to preserve peace.

The English, although distrustful of their European counterparts, collaborated with them, because they saw in the "Final Act" of the Congress of Vienna, which contained all the decisions of the plenipotentiaries, the most effective means of containing France, the leading enemy of England since the fourteenth century. In fact, some diplomatic historians refer to the period comprising the reigns of Louis XIV and Napoleon as the "Second Hundred Years' War." What the English subsequently objected to was a tendency that they looked on as a perversion of the concert into an antirevolutionary crusade based on the belief that any revolt was a menace to the status quo created at Vienna. The natural corollary to the idea of balance was that the great powers enjoyed the right to intervene in the interior affairs of any government either to prevent revolutionary change or to crush rebellious subjects by armed force wherever they appeared. This certainly became the policy of Metternich as well as of Alexander who really conducted his own foreign policy. The enigmatic mind of the tsar of Russia could not distinguish between the remarkably liberal regime he granted his Polish subjects, and the reactionary principles he put forward in a document called the "Holy Alliance," a seemingly innocuous call for all governments to rule in accord with the precepts of Christianity. Revolution, of course, was anti-Christian.

Metternich was taken aback by the proposal; in his mind rebellion, without reference to Christianity, was out and out dangerous. For all his belief in divine right, he was not untouched by the rationalism of the eighteenth-century

1815 was the year of the battle of Waterloo, the decisive end to Napoleon's rule. His "old guard" stood by him until the end, but in Vienna the victors were already preparing for the restoration of the Old Regime.

Enlightenment, and the tsar's proposal seemed too obscurantist. Nonetheless he and the king of Prussia, to avoid offending the tsar, signed the document after he made a few amendments by which kings would think of themselves as "fathers" of their subjects, and be obligated to protect "Religion, Peace, and Justice."When this document was issued, there were no queens regnant.

Far more important was the treaty that created the Quadruple Alliance, signed on November 30, 1815. Castlereagh, who refused to join the Holy Alliance, was one of the signatories of this document because in it the four major powers guaranteed to use armed force if necessary to prevent the French from disturbing the tranquillity that had now settled upon Europe. One other provision of the treaty, however, would cause the English to isolate themselves: the powers pledged, not only to keep all Bonapartes from the throne of France but also to safeguard France from renewed revolutionary outbursts against the Bourbon king.

Three years later this treaty was enlarged to become the Quintuple Alliance when France was welcomed as a partner. Louis XVIII was well seated on his throne, and the allied occupation of France was about to end. This occurred during the conference assembled at Aix-la-Chapelle in the autumn of 1818. New agreements removed France as the target of distrust. Alexander now came forward with seemingly new proposals for the alliance: first to preserve

MAP 2–1 Europe after 1815

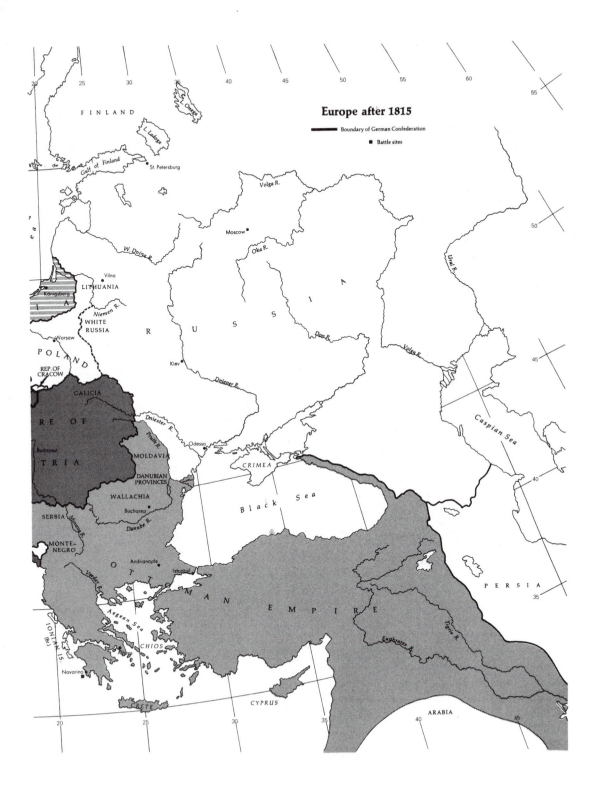

Europe after 1815

▬▬▬ Boundary of German Confederation

● Battle sites

FINLAND

L. Omega

L. Ladoga

Gulf of Finland

St. Petersburg

Volga R.

Moscow

Oka R.

W. Dvina R.

Vilna

LITHUANIA

Königsberg

Niemen R.

WHITE
RUSSIA

R U S S I A

Warsaw

Kiev

POLAND

REP. OF
CRACOW

Dnieper R.

Ural R.

GALICIA

Dniester R.

RE OF

Pruth R.

Odessa

CRIMEA

Caspian Sea

Budapest

TRIA

MOLDAVIA

DANUBIAN
PROVINCES

Black Sea

WALLACHIA

Bucharest

SERBIA

Morava R.

Danube R.

MONTE-
NEGRO

O T T O M A N   E M P I R E

Andrianople

Istanbul

Vardar R.

PERSIA

Aegean Sea

IONIAN IS.
(Br.)

CHIOS

Euphrates R.

Tigris R.

Navarino

CRETE

CYPRUS

ARABIA

33

the territorial arrangements made at Vienna, and logically in his view, to preserve the existing legitimate monarchies. Castlereagh objected so strongly to such a sweeping guarantee that the tsar withdrew it. But in three succeeding conferences between 1820 and 1822, Austria and France, seconded by Prussia and Russia, acted on its intent. Wherever revolutions broke out on the Continent, and 1820–23 witnessed them in the Italian peninsula, Spain, and Portugal, they sent in the army of a signatory state to restore the overthrown rulers. On each occasion the eastern states and France acted in concert, meeting first at Troppau in Polish Galicia during October, then at Laibach in southern Austria where the decision to intervene in Italy was made, over British protest. The final conference met at Verona in October 1822, where the French were empowered to restore order in Spain, which they did the following year, once more over British protest. Verona was the last meeting of the powers because none was called to authorize action against the revolutions that had occurred in Spain's colonies in the New World. This time Canning, the new British foreign minister, warned that his country would oppose any attempts by the powers to restore Spanish rule. Spain could act alone, but Canning knew that the Spanish government, under its incompetent king and demoralized military forces that had initiated the 1820 revolt against the crown, could never overcome the vigorous revolutionary *juntas* in Latin America.

We must emphasize that diplomatic maneuvering, an important component of statecraft, has never taken place in a vacuum. The men who gathered first in Paris to dispose of Napoleon, then at Vienna and subsequent congresses, represented states governed by a noble ruling class whose power rested on the ownership of large landed estates. The populations subject to their rule consisted primarily of peasants, legally free in territories subjected to French occupation, fully servile in some parts of the Hapsburg empire and in the east, recently liberated in eastern Prussia but still heavily dependent on their lords. The exception was Britain, where the lower-landed classes were rapidly declining in number and where the still predominant agrarian gentry were at daggers drawn with merchants and industrialists over tariffs on grain imports. Against this background it is easier to understand why Castlereagh and Canning differed sharply from Continental diplomats who not only remained unconcerned about urban interests, they openly distrusted large cities as centers of discontent, revolt, and atheism. To understand this conservative bias of international relations, we must study more closely the domestic politics of the various ruling classes of Europe from the 1820s through the 1840s. They remained in the ascendent because they enjoyed the support of the major institutions capable of thwarting their opponents.

3

Reaction Triumphant: Policies of the Victor States

The Forces of Continuity

The victor states were those that combined their might to defeat Napoleon and the menace of revolution. They were the great powers of the early nineteenth century, and had expanded their frontiers and populations as a result of their ability to redraw at will the boundary lines that created a balance of power. Apart from the territorial consolidation we studied in the previous chapter, their goal to restore "legitimate" dynasties was never fully undertaken. The disappearance of petty sovereignties was not the primary concern of ruling statesmen; it was the restoration of as many traditional institutions as feasible to link the present to the past, to restore, not lost states but a lost world. For a little longer than a generation they were more or less successful. The forces of change seemed to evaporate like water in sand. The metaphor is not purely literary. The forces of continuity—conservatives, if you prefer—were not unlike a great permeable body stretching over vast space as well as endless time. Their institutions, valued as the preservers of tradition, were both centuries old, nearly omnipresent and yet not unchanging. Unfortunately their champions did not recognize the long, slow evolution they had undergone. The French menace to them was crushed on the field of battle in 1815. The diplomats and their rulers who had earlier gathered at Vienna had as their main goal the extinction of all innovators and their radical ideals in order to restore the institutions that made for a harmonious, organic, and continuous link with the past. The era of revolution had been an aberration of the divine course of history.

The major work of political restoration was carried out by the Continental sovereigns who had never fallen into the dust raised by conquering French armies. They had lost battles but not the war. They were all monarchs, and in their conservative minds not just monarchy, but absolute and hereditary monarchy was now put forward as a major force of continuity. The victor states were all absolute powers save one, Great Britain, where the Crown was limited by the prerogatives of Parliament. During a quarter century not even the most successful of revolutionary armies, although able to force weak kings to flee, had the power to crush out the ideal of kingship. The belief that hereditary right gave the most legitimate claim to rulership was largely based on the image of the sovereign as the father of his subjects. The state, like the family, required the right of succession for its preservation. And, like the family, there could be no doubt that monarchy was the form of government most in accord with divine will. How could His will be expressed through elections, or His voice be heard through the babble of debate among venal politicians? Other forms of rule, including limited or constitutional kingship, divided people, and the violent and bloody class conflicts of the French in the years 1792–95 were ample proof of that. Personal loyalty to a living king, on the contrary, served as the bond uniting society while keeping everyone in their God-given status. To the men assembled at Vienna in 1815 there was no doubt that their final victory over Napoleon was God's will; good triumphed over evil.

Another element of continuity was, as indicated earlier, the official churches. After 1800 there occurred a revival of religious faith, and a renewal of the old alliance between throne and altar. The spread of the romantic movement with its emphasis on emotion and its mystical view of existence undercut eighteenth-century rationalism along with free thinking. Conservative churchmen identified these aberrations with the French revolutionaries. The restoration of the pope to Rome, and the return of Jesuits to their centers of influence, especially in the education of young nobles, marked the high point of Catholic influence. Even Protestant countries such as Britain and Prussia were ready to support the revival of the Catholic Church and papal power in Europe. In fact, the Catholic clergy outside the Italian peninsula dropped their age-old distrust of the papacy. The age of gallicanism, when the prime loyalty of priests had extended to their king above that of the pope, rapidly weakened. The revival of Roman Catholicism not only strengthened the belief in divine right monarchy, it equally strengthened its grip on the rural population to whom its priests and nuns taught patience, deference, and loyalty. In their respective areas of influence, the Anglican, Lutheran, and Russian Orthodox churches played the same role.

These areas of influence were significant. The Catholic Church was strongest in southern or Mediterranean territories such as Spain, Italy, the Austrian empire, southern Germany, and much of France, which combined north and south. We should note here that the Catholic clergy in Ireland, Belgium, and Poland, where natives looked on themselves as oppressed by a non-Catholic power, were not sincerely defenders of the restoration but were more likely to support and even to lead struggles for "national liberation" against Anglican Englishmen, Calvinist Dutchmen, and Orthodox Russians. But this did not mean that these kinds of national resistance implied social or economic revolution. The papacy dealt harshly with priests who took up the cause of the lower classes. Any movement that could be defined as left-wing (later called social) Catholicism was scarcely distinguishable before 1830. Its founder, Félicité de Lamennais, was as yet an outspoken defender of "ultramontanism," or absolute papal power throughout Christendom. Later, when he formulated a creed that placed the church on the side of popular sovereignty and social reform, the Pope excommunicated him. Most of the clergy, whatever their religion, placed a high value on traditional rural ways of life, distrusted cities and their denizens, and preserved its deference toward country notables.

Another defender of tradition was the landed nobility. Whether a large landowner was a titled aristocrat or simply a "notable," that is, a nontitled property owner with enough landed wealth or influence to be esteemed locally, he looked on the local clergyman as his ally, a necessary intermediary between himself and the rural community. This relation had never suffered interruptions in states not overrun by French armies: Britain, and most of central and all of eastern Europe. In Spain the social control of a huge noble class was strengthened by resistance toward the French invasion, a resistance carried out not by upper magnates but largely by the lower classes led by parish priests.

The chief factor that enabled the titled aristocracy to hold on to power was its control of large landed estates. Although Britain differed from Continental countries in that the crown had only limited power, the ruling position of large landowners equaled or exceeded that of its counterpart in Europe. Britain remained under the control of a landed peerage; the House of Lords still provided most cabinet ministers, and the House of Commons was largely in the hands of the landed gentry. Large rural holdings formed the basis of power in all the European states. Although there was wealth to be made in commerce and finance, it was land that carried prestige. In Britain large owners in the early decades of the century quickened the pace at which they took over common land, enabling large estates to grow even larger. Among the victorious states in Europe the aristocracy held on to most of their land, and accepted absolute monarchy at the national level because they enjoyed absolute power at the local level. Where serfdom had been abolished, as in the northeastern territories of the Prussian state, the great magnates took over roughly two-thirds of the land that their serfs had once worked. Like England, Prussia east of the Elbe River and much of central eastern Europe became a zone of huge estates, with the largest in England itself and Poland. The *Junkers* of Prussia closed ranks and became the epitome of a ruling caste, capable of defending its dominant position well into the next century.

Finally, a major force of continuity was the peasantry. French revolutionary armies, wherever they conquered, abolished serfdom among the peasants. By 1815 landed workers in some parts of central eastern Europe and in Russia, untouched by the French, were the last remnants of a servile class. After 1815 the burdens of servitude would arouse them to riot when food crises made their lives too miserable to bear. Yet, throughout Europe, the rural lower classes remained conservative in their loyalty to crown and church, and in their stubborn resistance to change except regarding emancipation from servility. Where they owned land, and about half of them did west of the Elbe River, their distrust of cities and urban dwellers made them defenders of the old order. Many of them in western Germany, northeast Spain, northern Italy, and France itself, where revolutionaries had put confiscated church lands up for sale, were able to buy small plots. But as soon as they acquired some kind of holding they lost interest in reform. The only menace they feared in 1815 was restoration of confiscated land to the original owners. When no government attempted that, they settled back to become a bulwark of conservatism.

With these general observations in mind, we can use them to examine the major powers and their movement along the bumpy road to modernity.

Revival in Central Europe

The restoration in central Europe was both territorial and political. The puppet states created by Napoleon were abolished and their territories included in an entity called the German Confederation. What had previously bound Germans, the Holy Roman Empire, which, as one historian put it, was neither holy, nor Roman, nor an empire, was gone forever. The new formation, consisting of thirty-five hereditary dynastic states and four free cities, was a consolidation of the more than three hundred dynastic entities formerly in existence and therefore a step toward unity. But it was by no means a big step. Each of the constituent states enjoyed almost complete control over its internal and foreign affairs. As before, Prussia and Austria were the largest components, and the latter in particular, exercised considerable influence if not full control over general policies. The restoration under Hapsburg guidance and pressure was more complete than in defeated France. Absolute rulers deposed by French armies were welcomed back by subjects tired of disorder and more deeply attached to authority and patriarchal rule than to natural rights, popular sovereignty, and democracy. The great historian Leopold von Ranke later asked, "What was our restoration...? It consisted in chasing out the foreigners." That is, nothing positive or hopeful followed. Within a new territorial context came back the old bureaucracy, princely extravagance, fiscal oppression, pomp, comic opera armies, and social suprema-cy of the landed aristocracy. Whatever gains the bourgeois had won were swept aside; even their seats in the opera houses and theaters were once more reserved for noble backsides. The major exception was Prussia, probably influenced by her Rhenish acquisitions. The elimination of guild regulations benefiting small producers was preserved, as were middle-class purchases of landed estates once the preserve of *Junkers*. Bourgeois sons even entered privileged occupations in the imperial bureaucracy and lower-level officer posts in the army. The upper middle classes also controlled several municipal councils of major commercial cities. These gains, won during the wars of liberation against the French, remained in effect, but chiefly in the western districts.

The only representative organ of the Confederation was the Diet with permanent headquarters in Frankfurt-am-Main. Just as the Hapsburg emperors had dominated the old empire, so they loomed over the new Confederation by holding the Diet's chair during the rather infrequent sessions. The Diet itself con-sisted of a plenary council, but this body with a high-sounding name seldom met between 1822 and 1847, and not at all afterward. Regular business was put in the hands of a select council in which larger states held most power. As for the Diet it enjoyed little influence. After recognizing the principle of individual rights, it did proclaim that Jews would enjoy equal legal standing with Christians. Although equality for Jews was vigorously resisted by the four city-republics, it was just as vigorously defended by the two major powers, Prussia and Austria. After all, the Rothschilds were in charge of Austrian finances, and the head of that branch of the family was raised to the rank of baron of the empire. This was about the only step taken by the Diet that could be labeled as modernizing. The Confederation, it has been argued, was an improvement over the Holy Roman Empire. The advance, however, was scarcely notable. The new state lacked a common leadership and the means to conduct a common foreign policy. The Diet had neither executive power, nor army, nor a common legal code and unified judiciary—not even a common currency. The Federal Act of 1815 provided for a certain amount of personal freedom and equality of all before the law. But each member state retained full control over its own affairs, and the Diet did not represent people, or even landed constituencies like the British House of Commons. It was a body of men, chiefly nobles, sent by the member states and each representative was under the control of his state. In the final analysis, the Confederation was the creation of Metternich, who looked on it as a defensive league against foreign—read French—foes, than as a step toward German unity.

Indeed, it is difficult to discern any aspect of German union in the Confederation. Diversity was more common than uniformity. Unlike the auto-cratic regimes in Prussia and Austria, there were lesser sovereigns who decided to grant constitutions. The first German state to be so blessed by its ruler was the Duchy of Nassau in 1814, followed by the Grand-Duchy of Saxe-Weimar in 1816.

When nothing untoward resulted from these drastic steps, the southern states of Bavaria, Baden, and Württemberg followed in 1818–19. These middling sovereigns were imitating the French example in that they bestowed a written statement on how their governments would be managed. In all of them the monarchic principle was made clear, particularly that the crown held ultimate sovereignty. The one exception was Baden where French influence had penetrated and remained. Its constitution created the first modern representative organ in Germany, thereby making it the homeland of central European liberalism where the lower chamber was chosen by individual voters who met high property qualifications. Elsewhere membership in representative bodies was by estates, not by general popular elections. The representative bodies were bicameral, with one of them exclusively noble, like the British House of Lords. They were to meet periodically to vote for or against taxes, but not to initiate legislation. This right to vote on taxes was of major importance; it was the only means by which an assembly, whatever its origins, could control the executive, the crown. The English House of Commons had become so strong because it controlled the crown's purse strings, had indeed risen in revolution in the 1640s to preserve this control. That Britain was a truly limited monarchy in 1815 was the result of the Common's control of the treasury and its refusal to approve of tax rights beyond a fixed period. Where parliaments had given up control over taxation, absolute divine right monarchy had grown like a weed in the flower bed of political institutions. This constitutional issue did not spread throughout the German Confederation, because all other states either remained or were restored as absolute monarchies.

Prussia: The Military State

Among the states that survived the French invasion Prussia had come closest to extinction. Ruled by the Hohenzollern family since the Middle Ages, it was the end product of steady expansion from its base in Brandenberg eastward into Prussia, northward into Pomerania, which made it a Baltic power, and southeastward into Silesia where there was an active textile industry and coal mines. It had less than a century earlier supported a professional army considered the most efficient in Europe. When confronted by Napoleon's troops, however, its ranks simply collapsed and for a while the dynasty's future looked bleak. It lost half its territory, taken by Napoleon to carve out new puppet states. It was saved by his catastrophic invasion of Russia, as well as by its revived and reformed army that contributed subsequently to his final defeat. During the wars of liberation, the army was reinforced by volunteer units made up of students and young bourgeois filled with a sense of renewal, of a new national feeling that called for greater freedom within a unified German state. The kingdom was itself not yet fully unified save through personal loyalty to its ruler, Frederick William III, the army and the growing bureaucracy. Both the provinces of East and West Prussia, as well as Poznan, inhabited by many Poles, were not even part of the German Confederation. There were religious differences; the newly acquired Rhenish territories were devoutly Catholic, as were many peasants in Silesia, while the rest of the kingdom was Lutheran, and the Hohenzollerns were Calvinist. Religious freedom, in consequence, was mandatory if only to preserve peace. But that was the only freedom permitted in this autocratic state. When the Rhinelanders, who had welcomed the French revolutionary armies in the 1790s, now called for a written constitution and a Prussian elective assembly, Frederick William saw their demand as tantamount to revolution and rejected it out of hand. To show where he stood, the king brought Prussia into the Holy Alliance. He was fully backed by the Prussian nobility in the East who feared losing their privileges in the army and bureaucracy, as well as their control over the recently emancipated peasant farmers. These *Junkers* made up the most powerful class in the kingdom. Although their estates in the provinces of Pomerania and Prussia were not nearly as large as the enormous holdings of British lords and Polish magnates they were in full possession of the rich lands of the Northern Plain, and also in full possession of the bureaucracy and the army. They equally controlled the local county and provincial Diets. These were purely administrative councils in charge of road building and upkeep, poor houses, asylums, fire insurance, and other such mundane matters. These were essentially the same tasks as those performed by the departmental councils in France, and the county councils in Britain, save that the British gentry were far more independent of central authority than Prussian *Junkers* or French notables.

At the state level the *Junkers* exercised their extensive influence as a ruling class through their younger sons who, unable to inherit family estates, made their careers in the bureaucracy and the military. And it was these two branches of government that acted most aggressively to modernize the state in the interest of efficiency. The absolute need for reform became brutally apparent after the humiliating defeat in the battle of Jena in 1806 and the occupation of Berlin by Napoleon. The "regeneration" of Prussia was urged by Prince Karl Hardenberg in a Memorial sent to the king next year: "Your Majesty! We must reform from above what the French have done from below." The first steps were taken by Baron Karl von Stein as leading minister in 1807. As a native of Nassau, he was not a Prussian noble nor did he possess the autocratic temperament of their class. Rather he undertook to reform the government step by step so as to end with the recognition of liberty for all Prussian citizens. His *Junker* colleagues who continued his work after his fall from grace stopped well short of granting civil liberty and responsible administration, yet their work brought the state out of its old regime and set it on the road to modernity Prussian style. Stein's major achievement was the liberation of all peasants from serfdom. Unlike serf emancipation in France in 1789, the Prussian version of 1807–10 freed peasants from personal servitude but left them without sufficient land to thrive as independent farmers. It also required them to compensate their masters for the loss of personal services and numerous fees. This limited emancipation had been tried in France, but peasants had simply refused to serve and to pay. The Jacobins finally abolished such restraints, thereby fully liberating peasants from the last traces of servitude. In Prussia there were no Jacobins, nor was there a peasantry ready to riot, to burn country houses and their archives, even to massacre lords and their ladies. Prussian peasants, therefore, became legally free as of 1810, but they remained financially bound to the land of their lords. The few acres of soil they did acquire, as part of the land settlement, many of them lost during the economic crisis of the 1820s. In the thirty years after 1816, the owners of large estates added up to 2.5 million acres to their holdings; they absorbed as many as 54,000 peasant farms whose owners became farm laborers or desperately fled to nearby towns. Several hundred villages disappeared as a result. Unlike their French counterparts, they either bowed their heads or fled the land. In this respect they resembled the once-proud English yeomen who also, and much earlier, were the victims of enclosures that deprived them of communally owned land that was taken over by the gentry.

Another reform that influenced the nature of the Prussian state concerned the army. Historians have written that in the 1600s the Prussian state had been recast to serve the needs of the military. Army reorganization after 1815 did not reverse this arrangement; on the contrary, it simply began a process by which the army recovered its efficiency and power. What changed was the composition of the rank-and-file troops. From professionals hired by the king they now consisted of commoners forced into service by selective male conscription—the Prussian (and French) answer to universal male suffrage. The army rather than the state became the focus of peasant life, for after three years of active service, the young farmer, like the young artisan, was obliged to enlist in the reserves for the following sixteen years. The influx of bourgeois officers was limited, and they came mainly from families in possession of former *Junker* estates or in the bureaucracy. This rural and official middle class imitated the ruling stratum. The army, as in the past, remained separated from civilian society, and thrived on its scorn of civilians and the arrogance toward them that had characterized soldiers of the old regime. Prussia became modern regarding efficiency but retained traces of the feudal temperament. That the government expanded the educational system and came close to eliminating illiteracy was another indication of the complex values and political culture of this central European polity—neither fully western nor eastern. Indeed, so complex was it that not even its own natives understood it. All of their subsequent struggles for freedom ended by tightening their shackles.

Among the politically conscious population, a feeling of profound resignation set in. Many of the young men active in the war of liberation withdrew from public life. They turned to religion and the study of history and philosophy. Becoming infused with the prevailing romanticism, they turned from bemoaning the present to idealizing the past, above all, the Middle Ages—from reform to folklore which equally aroused their consciousness of the past.

Austria: The Multinational State

Although Prussia during the years 1812–15 contributed more to the liberation of Germany than Austria, the latter enjoyed a greater influence within the Confederation. This was a curious situation because the Hapsburg empire had an even larger share of its territory lying beyond the boundaries of the new political formation. Just as the Hohenzollern's outward thrust was to the northeast and west, so the Hapsburg's was to the east and southeast, into Hungary and the north Balkan peninsula, as well as southwest into Italy. Unlike Prussia, which was predominantly German in its population and culture except for a Polish minority in Poznan, Austria had already become a multiethnic state combining Germans, Czechs, Hungarians, Italians, and numerous Slavic peoples such as Poles in Galicia, Czechs in Bohemia, Slovaks, Croatians, Romanians, and some Serbs in Illyria. In the opinion of successive emperors, Francis I (1806–35) and Ferdinand (1835–48), such a state could be held together by personal loyalty to a ruler endowed with divine right and by a German-speaking bureaucracy. The army was also one of the few unifying forces in the Hapsburg realm, even though, unlike Prussia's, it included men of different ethnic origins.

Domestic policy was ultraconservative and Catholic. It was mundane in that Francis I and his advisers were blithely ignorant of national aspirations among their numerous ethnic minorities. The emperor was not an enlightened despot, but simply hardworking, overly devoted to details, distrustful of all save the mediocrities he drew around him both lay and ecclesiastical. More competent was his minister of police, Count Joseph Sedlnitzky, who, from 1817 on, became increasingly influential within the government and powerful throughout the state. Under his direction the security police became more all pervasive and alert than before. Among heads of police bureaucracies in Europe Joseph Fouché, Napoleon's argus-eyed cop, has the reputation of being the most efficient with the surveillance technology available at the time: spies, steaming-open correspondence, and gossip. Count Sedlnitzky claimed to be the equal of Fouché. Whether true or not, censorship under his direction, along with espionage of secret and nonsecret societies became so prevalent that even conservatives complained of it. Censorship was extended not only to the arts, it penetrated schools and universities where students and teachers were closely watched. Under such conditions it became difficult for students to go to Germany for study, and foreign students in Austria were kept under scrutiny. Unknown to scholars each librarian was required to present lists of the books professors read. Those who were considered to be rationalists were dismissed, under the urging of Francis's confessor, Father Frent, who conducted witch hunts in the universities. The emperor insisted that faculty teach only old ideas, and he admonished them: "Hold to the old, for it is good, and our ancestors found it to be good, so why should not we. There are now new ideas going about, which I never can nor will approve." As for the press, there was nothing except the official publications of state authorities, and even these were closely supervised by the police, and by Metternich himself.

Throughout the Confederation, however rigorous state control of their subjects was during 1815, it became ferocious after 1817. In that year student societies called *Burschenschaften* organized a festival at the Wartburg Castle where some of their members ignited a fire to burn a corporal's baton, the symbol of oppression. They also threw into the flames a few books, intentionally of conservative writers, but also for good measure a few volumes written by liberals. Only a minority of students were *Burschenschaftler*, and only a minority of them participated in the Wartburg assembly, chiefly those who had taken part in the war of liberation. In contrast most of the several thousand *Burschenschaftler* revealed racist and anti-Semitic tendencies, sentiments widespread in the entire student body. In reality German youths showed little inclination to become involved in subversive organizations, preferring dueling and beer drinking. A few spontaneous outbursts of this sort continued until, in 1819, a feeble-minded student murdered a playwright suspected of being a spy in the pay of the tsar of Russia.

Now Metternich had the reasons he needed to spread Austria's oppressive system to the entire Confederation. He pushed through its Diet the Carlsbad Decrees providing for strict control of universities, prohibition of student associations, censorship of all publications, and the creation of a confederal investigation commission of subversive acts with headquarters in Mainz. The decrees were renewed in 1824 for an indefinite time; in fact, they were not revoked until the 1848 revolution.

This period of oppressive conservatism has traditionally been referred to as the age of Metternich. In reality, as he himself claimed—or perhaps bemoaned—he never controlled Austria's internal policies. In fact he recognized that the bureaucracy functioned badly: There was laziness if not paralysis, redundancy, aloofness, and insolence toward the public, and just downright incompetence. The reforms of his predecessors did not suit him. The emperor had at his own disposal a Council of State for advice, but he rarely sought counsel from the Ministry. The major ministries functioned like watertight compartments. Later steps to produce more coordination among them failed chiefly because Ferdinand preferred to deal with each minister separately, and he intervened too much, burdening himself and his ministers with numerous technical details that could have been more effectively handled by specially appointed experts. As for the empire as a whole, the administration was set up to centralize rule, removing whatever autonomy non-Austrians had enjoyed or sought to achieve. The bureaucratic language was German, a usage intended to achieve uniformity of culture and communication. This limited effort to Germanize the empire became increasingly resented by advanced nationalities, such as Czechs and Hungarians. The German Austrians, however, ignored this as yet nearly unexpressed national sentiment. In fact it was particularly Metternich's policy to preserve power by maintaining disunity both in the Confederation and among the constituent polities of the Hapsburg dominion.

Within Austria, where he was minister of foreign affairs, his chief goal outside Austria was the suppression of political agitation wherever it appeared. He was without doubt Europe's more active leader in a kind of crusade against reform movements whether revolutionary or not, and given the oppressive regimes that prevailed, reformers were forced to resort to secret conspiracies and to revolutionary acts because there was no peaceful way to obtain their goals. The strength of this element of the Metternichian practice of conservatism can be judged by its success. Among the numerous efforts at revolt between 1815 and 1848, there were only three successes. As we shall see later two of them attained their goals with outside help, as in Greece and Belgium. The third, the July 1830 uprising in France, resulted from the incredible stupidity of the last of the Bourbons to rule in Paris, and he was beyond help.

Russia: The Deceptive Giant

Russia, whose vast expanse of land and fierce winters had contributed to Napoleon's downfall, was the most autocratic of the Big Four. And yet, Tsar Alexander appeared the most reform-minded of the lot. Appropriately he has been referred to as the "enigmatic emperor." Unfortunately his unsteady character did not fit him to rule as a reformer in an age of reaction. As the grandson of Catherine the Great he had been tutored by the Swiss, Caesar La Harpe, an enlightened republican who sought to inculcate in his impressionable student the benefits of rationalism, natural law, and hatred of tyranny. So abstract a curricula left the youth totally ignorant of conditions in Russia, and, as an indolent student, not fully learned in the beliefs of the eighteenth-century reform movement known as the Enlightenment. His mentality was also shaken by the death of his father, murdered in order to place the imperial crown on his own head. Having become tsar in 1801 when only twenty-three years of age, he seemed inscrutable. One of his advisers, Michael Speransky, said that he was "too weak to rule and too strong to be ruled." Even so, under Speransky's guidance he set out to lessen restraints on personal freedom, and to modernize the administration. Between 1802 and 1811 he created ten ministerial offices, including one for education, in a time when governments usually consisted of only five, and none for education. He acted the role of enlightened despot, but in the end he was more confused than enlightened. He ignored the advice to abolish serfdom and adopt a constitution. Whatever dreams of reform he still nourished by 1812 he put aside when Napoleon invaded his empire.

During the war he underwent a deep religious disturbance and alteration combining official Orthodoxy and a bewildering mystical version of Christianity that led him directly into the reactionary camp of his allies in the war against France, and it was he who proposed a holy alliance of Christian powers against the evil of liberal revolution. In 1817 he attached to the Ministry of Education the duties of public worship; Christian piety of the most obscurantist sort was to become the basis of all schooling. As in Austria the lay teachers devoted to enlightened rationalism gave way to the mystics and the religious orthodox. There followed regimentation of students, censorship, and the purging of books. The tsar had made a complete about-face. His earlier liberal advisers had long given way to arch reactionaries, whose sway was more profound than that of the reformers.

On the death of Alexander, there was a brief period of confusion in the succession that encouraged two groups of liberal army officers, disgusted with his policies, to attempt a revolt in December 1825. These "Decembrists" were few in number, divided between moderates and radicals, and completely cut off from the lower classes. They fit perfectly into the mold of their ineffectual counterparts of the 1820s in Spain and Italy, as we shall see, and their failure was inevitable. Loyal troops quickly shot or arrested them, and after secret trials five were hanged and the survivors sent to Siberia.

Nicholas I had never flirted with liberal reform; he was a stern disciplinarian, a veritable martinet, believer in divine right, and advocate of the use of force to put down reformers, not to mention revolutionaries. And yet, he learned much from his interpellations of the Decembrists; he recognized the evil of serfdom, but would never take steps to free the serfs on both royal and private estates, or even to improve their conditions. He recognized that the judicial system was grossly inefficient and biased, and that Russian laws were confusing and often contradictory. He created a commission chaired by the ex-liberal Speransky to draw up a new code, a task that took more than six years. The final edition was hardly a major step toward modernizing the judicial system. The code, unlike that compiled in France during Napoleon's reign, and that consolidated many reforms of the Revolution, was nothing other than a more orderly collection of old legislation, not a promulgation of new laws, nor did it offer any reforms affecting civil society. For Nicholas civil society was like the army: Its base must be religion, and its guide a devotion to duty and obedience to authority.

The tsar recognized no private sector of life, only civic duty and military discipline for everyone. When he reorganized the central administration he created the notorious Third Section devoted to police duties. This kind of gendarmerie was created partly to expose and end all abuses of the bureaucracy to gain the confidence of all classes as well as assure them that they had the ear of the emperor. It was also to seek out political criminals, oversee religious sects, foreigners, café owners, and suspect persons. Although not in charge of censorship, it blatantly interfered in literary affairs, and kept a sleepless eye on writers.

It would seem that it was to protect the people from government and the government from people. In reality it concentrated on the latter; it was really a political police. As we noticed, all the reactionary governments established this kind of special surveillance force. However, it would be an error to refer to these early regimes as police states in our modern sense. They lacked the total mastery over widely dispersed rural populations that characterize the recent totalitarian regime, if only because they did not possess the technology of social control that is required. They were without the means of mental and physical regimentation that is the product of mass urban societies, that is, large-scale nationalist education, trustworthy teachers, and mass circulation of propagandistic publications. Finally they lacked an active political party to drum up the mass enthusiasm and collective sense of oneness that nationalism inspires. Russia, like her autocratic neighbors, was a backward rural state, with a huge peasant population too illiterate to be influenced by the official press, indifferent toward conditions beyond their villages, and poorly indoctrinated by a lazy, often immoral clergy, half illiterate itself. These autocratic regimes were able to avoid serious, as distinct from comic opera, revolutions chiefly because the early revolutionaries were as cut off from distrustful peasants as were the autocrats themselves. The tsars of Russia, like all their counterparts, were active building up a huge bureaucracy that became a human wall separating them from their subjects. Until the 1840s too many officials were untrained and aloof or indifferent to the problems of the people, at least the people too poor to bribe them. Such bribes, called "sinless revenues" were taken to supplement the low salaries of lesser state employees. In regard to them, an expression went "any stick will do to beat a thief, but only a ruble will help you with an official." In the provinces every governor was a little tsar with no control on his power. Nicholas, aware of so many abuses, urged his subjects to write in their complaints against abusive officials. But since any complaints ended in the official's bureau, he found means to make life miserable for the complainers. The system had a built-in protection for bureaucrats, not for people.

The tsar was an attentive ruler. Like his predecessor he inherited higher organs of administration, such as the Council of State and Senate, with members appointed by himself. The Council of State was to examine legislative proposals that were usually drawn up by a secret committee known only to Nicholas. Like all other state agencies the council had only an advisory role, and when the tsar sent a proposal it was usually accompanied by an annotation either warning against "superfluous debate," or with a curt order to approve the measure. The Senate fared no better and ceased completely to exercise administrative control, formerly one of its most important duties. After 1840 both these bodies withered as Nicholas relied on his secret committees of trusted advisers. Even the ministers saw themselves relegated to subordinate roles as the tsar attempted to master the massive details of rulership. Unknowingly and unwillingly, he allowed the administrative apparatus to become a huge body of officials, organized hierarchically according to a table of ranks, hardly capable of coordinating their various functions, of increasing efficiency, of avoiding the massive shifting of paper work and red tape. Increasingly the administration malfunctioned, which undermined the ability of Russia to carry on its role as a great power. The army was able to crush a revolt in Poland in 1830–31, and even help the Austrians crush Hungarian revolutionaries in 1849. But these were minor achievements. The Crimean War was to prove how far Russia had fallen from the status of great power. The inability of Austria by itself to overcome the Hungarians is equally revealing of serious internal decay there.

The aid to Austria in 1849 indicates how closely the Hapsburg and Romanov regimes were bound together both in organization and goals. Conjointly they mastered the destiny of much of Europe before 1848. Capable of crushing liberal revolutionaries, as well as influencing if not fully controlling the foreign and domestic policies of central and southeastern Europe, they, like the fabled frog that could blow itself up to tremendous size to frighten its enemies, were looked on as the two greatest of the great powers. And yet, even by mid-century their days of glory were over. The methods they used to crush oppositional forces sapped their strength and locked them into a fading and increasingly unreal world that shut out the thrust of modernization so necessary to survival in a world of power politics based not on suppression but on the release and encouragement of technological progress, economic growth, social mobility, and national aggrandizement.

Prussia, although part of this backward-looking cluster, was drawn from it by its Rhenish provinces as they progressed economically. With the passage of time, power slipped westward toward riverine and oceanic territories, above all those looking out on the Atlantic Ocean and the Baltic Sea. The Prussians found themselves, like Janus, facing in two directions. This was a source of strength; it was also a source of ambiguity that divided not only western and eastern Prussians, but also western and eastern Germans. In fact the dichotomy was even more complex as liberal ideas spread among the southern Germans. The confederal system did not overcome these divisions; neither did the revolts that broke out between 1820 and 1848. The resolution of cultural and geographic divisions was not a pressing issue in the agendas of the dynastic polities. The reigning dynasties had survived divided among themselves for eight hundred years. And yet it was the French who aroused German national sentiment, and the Prussians who started the process toward German economic integration with the creation of a free-trade area that came to include nearly all the confederate states. Conservative in its politics the Hohenzollern kingdom became the most forward looking in its economic goals. In this it differed from both Austria and Russia.

For this reason it is important to bear in mind that Europe, even in its most antiliberal phase, must not be arbitrarily divided between the forces of reaction and revolution, the black and the red. Not only Prussia but much of western Europe was undergoing economic and social transformations that added a slightly pinkish tinge increasingly distinguishable from the black reaction of the east, and the reddish political and social evolution of the British Isles.

Liberalism Triumphant

Great Britain was not merely a continent away from Russia, it was a universe away regarding institutions. Without doubt the British gained the most from the Treaty of Vienna as they took over, not truculent European territories, but colonial dependencies and markets that contributed to her already advancing economic wealth. Even conservatives like Castlereagh drew back from the antirevolutionary policies of their wartime allies and came out flatly against the Metternichean belief that liberalism must be crushed wherever it raised its threatening head. By the 1820s the Foreign Office under George Canning was subtly favoring certain revolutionary movements such as those in Latin America, which further opened rich markets for manufactured goods, in Greece and in Spain where economic profits were also expanding. British economic interests were in contradiction with the purely political concerns of Metternich.

Apart from these differences British politics and society diverged in other respects from those of the Continent. There was a monarchy, but the wearer of the crown had no absolute power. Over the course of the eighteenth century many royal prerogatives had drained toward the Cabinet, and the attempt by George III "to be a king" came too late as his mind steadily deteriorated. Whatever awe still attached to the crown was further dimmed by his successors, the last of the Hanovarian dynasty, whose detestable behavior led many Englishmen to ask whether the monarchy was worth the cost of its upkeep. The ascension of Victoria, a young and engaging woman in 1837, saved the institution, but she could not recover its former power. The true center of policy making and governing had decisively drifted toward the Cabinet as it became more cohesive, recognized the leadership of a prime minister, and as members of Parliament tended toward groupings that became recognized as parties with leaders, some limited discipline, and platforms. The Tories were pro-Crown, Anglican, and dominated by large landowners. The Whigs were pro-Parliament, Protestants all but with many dissenters, and also landed except for a greater concern for urban and business interests.

The true aristocracy, families whose eldest male inherited a seat in the House of Lords, were numerically infinitesimal in the population, less than 150 families, but of huge influence because of wealth and control of the sizable numbers of persons dependent on them. In the House of Commons the membership was largely gentry, that is, nontitled large landowners, or their hirelings with a scattering of businessmen. Some were the younger sons of noble families who inherited little because of laws of primogeniture and entail. Because members of

Parliament were not paid salaries, many of them depended on the largesse of a wealthy patron who controlled an electoral district. The unreformed House of Commons was indeed dominated by agrarian interests who understood little of the changes being brought about by the industrial revolution but were by no means hostile to it.

Between 1815 and 1820 the government was controlled by right-wing Tories. They were inconsiderate toward the terrible sufferings of the lower classes during the economic crisis engendered by the shift from a war-time economy to one based on peace. Their "corn laws," prohibitive tariffs placed on all imported grain except corn (maize), benefited landowners, but provoked hunger and bread riots among wage earners. They responded with brutal repression, the worst occurring in 1819, and equal to the methods of Metternich in the German Confederation. Additionally they passed the Six Acts, similar to the Carlsbad Decrees, which severely limited freedom of assembly, speech, and press.

The 1820s, however, brought a return to normalcy. Moderate Tories, led by George Canning as foreign minister, Sir Robert Peel as home secretary, and William Huskisson at the Board of Trade, blocked the European powers hoping to restore Spanish rule in Latin America, reformed the criminal law along humanitarian lines so that the punishment more nearly fit the crime, dismantled the old mercantilist restrictions on foreign trade, and repealed the Combination Acts, which had outlawed workers' trade unions. Recognizing the folly of religious intolerance they also rescinded the laws excluding Protestant dissenters from holding public office, and, in 1829, granted Catholics the right to sit in Parliament, a step taken to forestall the threat of an uprising in Ireland. This procedure—passing reforms just in time to avoid revolution—became accepted policy by both parties.

When the Whigs became the majority party in 1830 they continued the reform impulse. Their most important step was the 1832 suffrage reform act. It doubled the number of voters among householders: out of a total adult male population of just more than 6 million, 840,000 now enjoyed the right to vote. The act also abolished many "rotten boroughs," that is, it transferred representation from almost uninhabited electoral districts dating in some cases from the Middle Ages to towns with a rising population. This step was certainly justified, but it still left many rural and small-town constituencies with an excess representation. To be precise, the act left 151,492 electors (18%) in control of 331 out of 658 seats (50%).

Granted its limits the act was a major landmark in British constitutional history, and a big step toward modern government. During its passage several maneuvers occurred that completed the rise to dominance of both the Cabinet and the House of Commons. The Whig Cabinet, solidly aristocratic in its membership and headed by Viscount Grey, was able, with the backing of some Tories, to force an antireform king and a hostile House of Lords finally to accept a bill that conservatives looked on as revolutionary. This last term is not a mere figure of speech. The peaceful reform of the electoral system in Britain brought forth a larger electorate than the violent revolution of 1830 in France, as we shall see in the next chapter. It also led Britain closer to popular sovereignty than France between 1830 and 1848. It did not result in a marked change of social class in Commons; most members continued to be "gentlemen" in the elitist sense of that term. Nor was the act seen by its supporters as a first step to contin- ued change. It would, asserted Charles Grey, "afford sure ground of resistance to further innovation." Parliamentary reform, therefore, did not mean that the industrial and commercial middle classes could readily take over Commons; nor were many of them much interested in running in elections; they were too busy making money. However, their growing economic power made itself felt in the next decade when Parliament, intimidated by a massive campaign organized among free traders, abolished the Corn Laws. The immediate effect was to lower the price of bread, uppermost in the minds of northern industrialists who could now restrain wages by holding down the costs of living to compete effectively in foreign markets. As for workers, the still high property qualifications excluded them from the suffrage. Also excluded were women, even those who could meet the property qualifications.

Not more than a handful of candidates calling themselves Radicals won seats in the next elections. In the minds of democratic Englishmen the change was a sham. They therefore managed to put forward five years later a reform movement called Chartism. Their charter was a petition to be signed by millions of men and presented to Commons during a vast and, it was hoped, peaceful demonstration. The document called for universal male suffrage, payment for members of Parliament (MPs), the secret ballot, equal electoral districts, no prop- erty qualifications for candidates, and annual parliamentary elections. Several leaders favored female suffrage, but most argued that it would not be taken seri- ously by the government. In fact the entire charter was not taken seriously, and the effort behind it was weakened by feuding between Chartists advocating peaceful agitation, and those calling for more violent, even revolutionary, action. The latter won a considerable following in northern industrial towns where workers participated in nocturnal meetings and torchlight processions at the end of 1838. Next year, when the Charter was first rejected by Commons, a call went up for a general strike by laborers. There was some violent, localized conflict with the police, but this was as close as England came to revolution. The last serious effort came in 1842 when a petition was again turned down; the move- ment did not survive this failure, except for a very brief ineffective reappearance in 1848. Oddly enough, all the proposals save annual elections eventually became law but not for several generations when the willingness to reform was more deeply rooted. Until then Britain was ruled by a coalition of aristocrats and upper-middle-class men of leisure. This was the Victorian Compromise that broadened the traditional ruling class, a class that enacted legislation favorable to business interests, such as tariff reform, the democratization of municipal administration, simplified legal procedures, and passed a new Poor Law that stigmatized poverty by abolishing home relief and wage allowances, and forcing the poor to inhabit sexually segregated quarters in workhouses.

Yet, the reformed Parliament was not unmindful of labor conditions in textile factories and mines. The Factory Act of 1833 prohibited the employment of children under nine years of age in factories, and reduced to nine hours per day the labor of minors between nine and thirteen years, and to twelve hours per day for all teenagers under eighteen. The acts of 1844 and 1847 further reduced children to half-day employment, the other half to be devoted to schooling. Grown women's hours were lessened to ten, which effectively brought men's working time to the same limit in textiles because the mills could not continue to function after the women and teenagers left; they made up about three-fourths of the work force. Both women and children were also prohibited from working underground in mines. The reasons behind this social legislation varied. It was partly a humanitarian reaction to the vivid exposé of the horrible conditions in textile mills made widely known by a parliamentary commission and social reformers. There was also a shocked puritanical sense regarding underground work in mines when the Commons learned that young girls worked among completely unclothed miners because of the heat and that the girls themselves labored only partly clothed for the same reason.

Factory regulations of this sort were also enacted in Prussia in 1839 and in France in 1841 but, it seems, for different reasons: Children subject to long hours and strain were becoming debilitated and therefore useless for eventual military service. Both armies complained that young men from factory towns were stunted of growth, malformed, and lacking energy as compared with peasant recruits. The differences were that the British were not concerned about the military because they had no standing army or obligatory service while both the French and the Prussians did. It is significant that the Prussians, like the British, made some halfhearted effort to enforce the law; the French did not.

Quite unlike the French the British abolished slavery in their colonies, with considerable compensation to slave owners. This was in 1833. The French would not abolish slavery until 1848. Prussia had no colonies with slaves and had abolished serfdom in 1806. The Austrians and Russians did next to nothing of this sort.

Compared with the victor powers in Europe, Britain emerges as a progressive, modernizing country, still at least a century ahead of the Continent in the recognition of changing conditions and in the initiative to adapt to them.

4

The Revolutionary Powers

Restoration in France

We are concerned here with two kinds of political entities: the aggressor, France, and the victims of her aggression that were to become revolutionary in turn, largely as a result of her influence. Among these were Spain, the Italian states, and the Low Countries. In these latter states revolutions broke out as a result of internal frictions, but success or failure depended on external forces, as we learned in Chapter 2. As we look over the map of Europe we note that two other discernible groups also manned the barricades: Poles who found their national identity through their hatred of Russians, and Greeks who found it in their struggle against the Turks.

Except for Greece, all the previously mentioned territories were overrun either by French revolutionary or by Napoleonic armies from the mid-1790s until 1814. After invasion, Spain became a puppet state, as did the Neapolitan kingdom of southern Italy and Sicily. The remainder of Italy and the Low Countries were absorbed into imperial France. Our concern now is to discover the fate of these territories after the fall of Napoleon.

France, in a class by itself when widely victorious, remained the focus of attention and a center radiating influence even after defeat. It was a common expression after 1815 that when France sneezed, Europe caught cold. We should add that the sniffles always began in Paris. If Russia was an enigma, France was a puzzle, with the key in her capital. Her return to the fold of the Continental great powers as an equal was never complete. Her allies could never overcome the suspicion that in their inner hearts these Gallic people would never be content enough to keep the peace. After all, the kings of France had been perturbers of peace since the seventeenth century, and Napoleon differed from them only in that he was a successful general until 1812. Given this anomalous situation, our spotlight of inquiry will focus more on France than other states before midcentury. Later our spotlight will move to central Europe where changes occurred that finally destroyed the 1815 settlement, upset the balance of power, and reduced the great power pretensions of the French.

In France, the return to the throne of the elder branch of the multinational Bourbon dynasty was the result of a compromise. The nobiliary bourgeois, that is, the wealthy commoners given various titles by Napoleon, and there were some three thousand of them, would facilitate a Bourbon return if the pretender to the throne accepted the social and economic reforms of the Revolution, as well as some constitutional limitations on his powers. This meant the acceptance of land transfers from church and aristocracy to bourgeois and peasant purchasers. It also meant the acceptance of legislative assemblies that would represent and defend the interest of the wealthy since suffrage would be limited to the largest taxpayers. In 1814 the Bourbon heir to the crown, Louis XVIII insisted, however, that he would not accept the constitution drawn up by a provisional government but was willing to grant (*octroyer*) a Charter that, although modified later, endured until 1848. It embodied the essential provisions of constitutional monarchy: the king as executive, a chamber of hereditary peers, and a chamber of elected deputies. There was no provision for an independent judiciary or the equivalent of the American Supreme Court. Several provisions enhanced the king's power. Apart from those that recognized the normal prerogatives of the crown (command of the military, declaration of war, control of foreign policy, and bureaucratic appointments), the Charter also granted the king legislative initiative: He proposed bills to the peers and deputies who could accept or reject them without amendment, but could not propose legislation on their own. This was a modest form of control over the throne. More important were the articles that provided for fiscal control: No taxes could be levied without the consent of the chambers, and all money bills went first to the elected deputies. This partially settled a crucial issue that had provoked the civil war in England during the 1640s, and the revolutions in the American colonies in the 1770s and in France in 1789. Defenders of constitutional government now recognized that parliamentary fiscal control was the only effective means of balancing power between the executive branch and Parliament.

They also insisted that to achieve some kind of balance between the entire government and its citizens, there was need of basic freedoms: speech, press, assembly and religion. On these matters the Charter was rather vague. Louis referred to himself as king "by the grace of God," that is, the Catholic God. This was close to divine right, but did not preclude the toleration of other religions, as well as state financial support for all sects listed in the Concordat of 1801, which ignored the Jews. Nonetheless there was an alliance between altar and throne that allowed the Catholic clergy to recover much of its prerevolutionary control of primary education, at least what there was of it. Educational reform was not an important issue to the Bourbons, so long as most primary schools were in the hands of churchmen and nuns. Illiteracy was still extensive, and therefore the press was not widely influential during the Restoration, except in Paris and the largest cities. The freedoms granted were not only vaguely defined, the Charter provided for their control in case they were "abused" by irresponsible citizens. Personal freedom, therefore, was subject to the whims of the Ministry of Police.

There was one element of the Charter that left open a most important issue, the existence and powers of the Ministry. An article stipulated that the Ministry existed and was responsible, but failed to state to whom—the king or the parliament. This imprecision was perhaps deliberate and, indeed, more in conformity with Continental practice. Britain, not having a written constitution, had no law dealing with this issue. It was historical accident and practice that eventually made the cabinet fully accountable to both houses of Parliament. In central and eastern Europe the matter never arose because there were no parliaments, and no one denied that a council of ministers must be obedient to the Crown. Moreover ministries were not even unified bodies and rarely assembled together; a monarch simply consulted each of his ministers individually, was not bound by the advice he received, and often acted independently. It was not infrequently that rulers lied to their heads of services or fed them false information to act independently. They more often sought the secret counsel of men, both clerical and lay, whose advice they trusted because these servitors were more reactionary than public ministers.

In France the only control the assemblies could exercise over ministers was to accuse them of treason or peculation, and try them before the Chamber of Peers. This was a form of "penal responsibility," according to one historian. But such an act could put the crown in danger, because an attack on a minister was also an attack on the king who chose him. In the West not many politicians still believed that the king could do no wrong. This danger became apparent in the late 1820s.

In every country where kings could claim absolute power, they rarely had the means of exercising it. They simply did not have the manpower to do so. Ministries, compared with those of today, were small. In 1815 Louis had only seven cabinet members: foreign affairs, justice, interior, finance, war, navy, and police. And police was subsequently attached to interior. In 1824 Charles X, Louis XVIII's younger brother and successor, created a Ministry of Ecclesiastical

Affairs and Public Education, which he separated in 1828. Not unmindful of economic matters he created one of commerce and manufacturing, and another for public works just before his overthrow in 1830. What they might have accomplished will never be known.

The overthrow of the last Bourbon ruler was by no means preordained. Louis XVIII enjoyed considerable popular support when he returned in 1814, if only because there was no one else to take up the reins of government. After Waterloo there was no sympathy for the son of Napoleon, and no one even thought of reestablishing a republic. The very word was frightening, associated with the Terror of 1793–94, and young men under thirty had never heard the word mentioned and were ignorant of it. Moreover it was widely accepted that political power should be in the hands of a hereditary monarch supported by an elite of notables. The Charter provided for an elected chamber, but only adult men over twenty-five years of age and paying at least three hundred francs in taxes were eligible to vote. This measure alone excluded 99 percent of adults. And even higher fiscal restrictions limited the number of qualified candidates to roughly 10,000 very rich men, all older than thirty-five years of age. These stipulations, plus a two-tier electoral system, meant that the vote and seats in the Chamber of Deputies would be largely in the hands of the upper nobles and highest bourgeois.

This arrangement brought into the chamber two groups that would weaken the dynasty: the so-called Ultras, or aristocrats who rejected constitutional monarchy unless they controlled it and whose aim was to return to an old regime that predated absolutism; and the liberal bourgeois whose views demanded a figure-head king and rule by a ministry responsible to the deputies. Both extremes opposed the moderate royalism of Louis, who, as he put it, did not want to go on his travels again. That is, he sought to avoid provoking a revolution. This task was not easy, even from the beginning. During 1815 fanatical royalists in the deep South ruthlessly carried out a "white terror," murdering persons identified as Jacobins or Bonapartists. The fury ran on sporadically for several months without any serious governmental intervention.

France was also divided politically by her geography. The South, especially Provence, the Southwest, and the West, were pro-royalist. The Ultras had a particularly large and dogmatic following in Brittany, Normandy, and the Vendée, predominantly agricultural areas in the West, where a major counter-revolution broke out in the 1790s. The middle class liberals, on the contrary, had their supporters in eastern and northern departments where easy communications along with coal and iron deposits encouraged trade, mining, and industry. The French economy was undoubtedly retarded compared to Britain, but well advanced compared to central and eastern Europe. The East and North were more highly urbanized, and the peasant farmers were encouraged to grow crops for urban and external markets. They were more open to new ideas, and the tradition of the Revolution was more deep rooted among them than among the relatively backward, self-subsistence peasants in the South and the West. The two areas were not hermetically sealed from each other, but these tendencies changed only slowly, and if we exclude the lower South, were still present in the twentieth century.

After a brief period of reaction characterized by the white terror, drumhead courts, and a few legal executions of officers who had rallied to Napoleon during his "Hundred Days" reign in 1815, Louis enjoyed a period of fairly peaceful rule for nearly five years. Electors turned away from the Ultras, and the right center made up of moderate royalists dominated ministries until 1818. None of the terms of right, center, or left refer to political parties for none existed. There were, rather, factions that formed and dissolved as issues united or separated deputies and peers. Not more than a handful of politicians acted according to a structured theory of government; most acted out of instinct, and personal and class interest. A sense of class was very strong, and liberal historians like François Guizot interpreted the dynamic of the past as a centuries-old struggle between the nobility and the bourgeoisie. But we must bear in mind that many bourgeois were royalists—there were even royalist cities such as Marseilles, Toulouse, and Bordeaux; whereas some nobles, such as the Marquis de Lafayette, were liberals, a broad term designating the men who, like the Whigs in England, were defenders of parliamentary government and, usually, the civil liberties that they called the "rights of man."

The achievements during the tranquil reign from 1816 to 1820 were significant. Louis's finance minister made the last payments, both for the costs of the allied occupation forces and the indemnity, a sum that eventually climbed to 1.8 billion francs. A more liberal election law was passed, and the army was reformed in 1818. Gouvion St. Cyr created a professional military force by abandoning recruitment through voluntary enlistment and resorted to an annual conscription of about 40,000 young men. Although the conscripts were chosen by lot, it was permissible for well-to-do families to hire a replacement for a preferred son. Therefore the military force consisted mainly of youthful peasants, which probably explains why it was cut off from all contacts with revolutionary movements. The law also provided for a more open system of promotion, and an officer's training college—named after Saint Cyr—enhanced the competence of the commissioned ranks. Moreover promotions were to be based on ability and experience, a rule that hit young nobles who had been advanced without adequate training. Their cause, however, was protected by the king who continued to promote them despite the law, a situation that helps explain the mediocrity of the army when compared with that of Napoleon. A rather large number of sergeants who had served under him remained faithful to his memory, and it was they who began to plot against the monarchy as the decade ended. Their plot in 1820 was a fiasco precisely because the rank and file ignored it.

In the partial elections of 1818 and 1819, the Ultras lost badly, and the liberal left returned stronger in number. However, they were unable to form a stable government. Their ministry, beset by both extremes, revived press censorship and raised the deposit that newspapers had to pay before they could publish. Other laws restricting personal freedom were provoked by the assassination in February 1820 of the Duke de Berry, heir to the throne, by a crazed fanatic hoping to terminate the dynasty. But the duke's wife was already pregnant, and her son became known as the "miracle child." There was also the general situation in and out of France. Revolutions erupted in Spain, Naples, and the Papal States; there were also riots in Paris in May and June in reaction to a new electoral law that weakened the left.

Outside the halls of government, liberals began organizing secret societies in anticipation of violence. This was the era of the *Carbonari*, a subversive international organization with members in Italy, Spain, and France. Although its membership was unimpressive and loosely organized it was responsible for the recent revolts in the Italian peninsula that provoked Austrian intervention. Within France, the Knights of Liberty was founded in the small wine town of Saumur in the Loire Valley. Most of its members were disgruntled soldiers, formerly in the army of Napoleon, but it also drew some professional men of liberal leanings. They initiated several insurrections, but like the Decembrists in Russia, they had no following among the working class and were easily suppressed. With the exception of Spain, seditious societies no longer drew soldiers. After 1822, the military remained persistently faithful to the governments that employed them and henceforth became the chief force used to put down revolts. This change ended the anomalous alliance between Bonapartist soldiers hoping to restore the empire, and republicans who became increasingly patriotic but had no intention of restoring an autocratic regime. This situation lasted until 1851.

After 1820 the Bourbons turned increasingly to the right for support. Moderation had not won over the liberals and frustrated the Ultras. Largely to placate all royalists, Louis in his last years extended the power of clergymen over education. More indicative of the trend was his decision in 1823 to send, at the behest of the Quintuple Alliance, but against the wishes of Britain, an army into Spain to put down the constitutional regime that had been forced on Ferdinand in 1820 by the *liberales*. Napoleonic veterans grumbled about having to fight for monks and against freedom, but the easy victory and restoration of the king wiped out in their minds their humiliating retreat before the crack troops of General Wellington from 1808 to 1811 and the Spanish guerrillas (a term first used for the Spanish resistance).

When Louis's brother, Charles X, ascended the throne, the modest shift toward conservatism took a more decisive turn. He was sixty-seven years old, a legitimist to the core and willingly undertook certain divisive measures that his elder brother had avoided. First, he had himself coronated at Reims, a long-established custom of French kings, and anointed by a blessed oil "miraculously" sent from heaven for French kings since the Middle Ages. This ceremony indicated that the alliance between altar and throne had become an immutable marriage of the two. Second, he undertook to compensate nobles for the loss of their estates confiscated and sold during the Revolution. Since the treasury was already in deficit, his chief minister, Jean-Baptiste de Villèle, simply reduced the yield on state bonds from 5 to 3 percent, while increasing the capital of bond-holders, chiefly members of the middle class. The total sum made available for the indemnity by this saving was to be roughly 1 billion francs, but really came closer to 639 million. Most of it went to upper nobles and was undoubtedly one factor among several aiding the survival of the old regime aristocracy as a class. Only bourgeois bondholders were vexed that they were to pay émigré families who had supported the enemies of the fatherland during the Revolution. Yet, they had one consolation: The issue of confiscated land was finally settled and titles secured. They were also indirectly consoled by the increase in the value of their land.

Third, the Law of Sacrilege was a far less wise—if not downright stu-pid—measure. Recommended by the archconservative Louis de Bonald, the cracker-barrel philosopher of the Ultras, it would punish with execution anyone who stole objects from a church "in hatred of religion," or anyone committing a sacrilege by profanation of the communion host. This statute, which was never applied, when combined with Charles's coronation, aroused all the anticlerical bourgeois who now discerned a pattern of church domination over the govern-ment. Clericals, conversely, praised it as an expiation of the sins of indifference and rapine committed by France since 1789. They wanted the only "true reli-gion" to infuse all the institutions and laws of the state. Like Alexander of Russia, they believed that one religion was necessary for the unity of society and stability in politics. Charles gave every impression that this was the mission of his reign.

Because liberals became increasingly vociferous in their press, speeches, and action, the ministry tried to push through a measure to further tighten con-trol of the press. This was to be a law of "justice and love." The peers rejected it, but Charles set up a council to watch over newspapers and put de Bonald in charge of it. To him "Censure is a healthy establishment set up to preserve soci-ety from the contagion of false doctrines, just like the one that keeps away the plague." Metternich of Austria could not have put it better.

These and other steps aroused liberals, from moderate to extreme, against the regime. In the 1827 elections they created a society called "Help yourself and heaven will help you" for the purpose of organizing voters, making certain that they registered and filled in their ballots. As tension increased liberal moderates deserted the political center to move toward the left. Their animosity had normally been directed against the prime minister, but by 1828 it focused on the king himself as their chief antagonist. In their view he was seeking to subvert the Charter to enhance royal power. This new left was emboldened by repeated victories at the polls, and their determination to stand up to the king made it almost impossible for him to form a viable cabinet. By 1829 the two sides reached an impasse. As a result the issue of ministerial responsibility, which had been evolving in favor of the chambers, was now sharpened as the king flouted a hostile majority.

Charles was a determined old man. He finally called on Jules de Polignac of the far right to form a royalist government. Polignac was not merely a minister, he was a challenge. And one that liberals took up. "Help yourself" became more active to inform the public about the danger to liberty. One leader, Adolph Thiers, founded the journal *Le National* in early 1830 to warn that the country needed a "French 1688" (the bloodless coup d'état in England that deposed James II) and that the Charter must not be subverted. All this activity was carried out by solid bourgeois intellectuals such as Thiers, François Guizot, and the like. Many of them were journalists and professors recently dismissed from their posts. Despite censorship the emerging press entered the fray and would henceforth have to be reckoned with as the "fourth" power.

At a lower social strata politically minded students and artisan workers had been setting up secret societies and arming themselves as best they could. Several riots had already begun in 1827, and brought together the shock troops that were far more ready to build and man barricades than bourgeois liberals. They did not have long to wait.

In July 1830 Charles issued ordinances that suspended liberty of the press, dissolved the newly elected chamber, reduced the number of voters from 100,000 to 25,000 and called new elections. Although he had the prerogative to do this, many Parisians considered the ordinances a violation of the Charter. Legal or not, his decision amounted to a coup d'état. The ordinances were published on July 26, 1830. Charles, who believed himself too well liked in the country for the liberals to act, went hunting. He failed to realize that the mass of provincial Frenchmen would not help him, and his judgment was irreparably faulty for not reinforcing the small garrison inside Paris. The prefect of police, in charge of security in the capital, was equally unforeseeing.

Workers, petty bourgeois, and students, unmoved by news that a French army had just taken Algiers in North Africa, began building barricades on July 27, 1830, and bloody fighting began at once. By July 29 all was over. Charles abdicated and fled, never to return. Now the liberal leaders, not one of whom had mounted a barricade, quickly formed a provisional government lest republicans or Bonapartists seize power. During the night of July 30 and July 31 their agents placarded the walls of Paris with posters calling on the Duke of Orleans, head of the younger branch of the Bourbon dynasty, to ascend the throne.

Meanwhile the street fighters urged Lafayette to become president of a republic. Refusing this dubious honor he joined the Duke of Orleans on a balcony of the City Hall. There he told the crowd below, pointing at the Duke, "Here is the best of republics." And that settled the transfer of power. As Alfred Cobban put it, that transfer was not a revolution, it was a trick. If so, it was a successful one.

The July Monarchy, Another Experiment

Louis-Philippe, as the new king was called, managed to rule for eighteen years, not as king of France but as "king of the French," a change of title that presumably divorced his crown from divine right, from the aura of old regime kingship. He became known as the "citizen king." At times, he even went out walking among the boulevard crowds, carrying an umbrella, looking like a good, solid bourgeois, and he was appropriately called the "bourgeois king." He seemed to be everything save the people's king or the legitimists' king. The latter for whom he was the worst of traitors would have nothing to do with him or his government, and they were swept out of the administration to make place for new men, the Orleanists. The common people of Paris had fought in the streets and some of them had died, but not for Louis-Philippe. The gulf between him and them grew wide over time. However, they would have to wait eighteen years to get their revenge. That this king could survive for about half a generation should make us aware that a regime, to succeed, did not need the love of the people, merely their acquiescence. And this was all that Louis-Philippe wanted.

He had no intention of giving the multitude the vote. The new constitution lowered the voting qualifications and doubled the number enjoying the suffrage. But France remained an oligarchy centered in a newly appointed Chamber of Peers and a newly elected Chamber of Deputies. There was one concession to popular sentiment: The peerage ceased to be hereditary. But once a family obtained a title it retained the particle for its heirs. In fact France was now endowed—or burdened—with three noble classes: that whose title descended from the old regime, that whose title descended from Napoleon, and that whose title descended from Louis-Philippe. Each regime created its own aristocracy. Ultimately a title counted for less but was cherished the more.

To the absolutists of central and eastern Europe Louis-Philippe was an upstart and his peers a gang of arrivistes. His ascent through revolution violated Metternich's efforts to crush revolution wherever its head cropped up. But that was no longer possible; 1830 meant not only a change of regime, it also marked the end of Metternich's beloved policy of intervention. France, after all, was not Naples. Moreover Louis-Philippe was not alone in his success. The insurrectionary Greeks were finally liberated from the Ottoman Empire and given a German to rule them as a constitutional monarch. The Belgians also resorted to rebellion to win their freedom from the Dutch, and were assured of protection from invasion by both France and Britain. In fact Louis-Philippe hoped to put one of his sons on the newly created Belgian throne, but because the British threatened war if he tried it, he abandoned that plan.

The July Monarchy, then, was ambiguous regarding its origins and goals. It sought the friendship of Britain, understandable in as much as it had been put in place by Anglophiles, such as Guizot and Thiers. To them 1830 was the French 1688. But there the likeness ended. The new king could not bring himself to follow the British model of monarchy, nor any other. Although claiming to have been elevated by the people, his government had no communication with the people. Its first five years were turbulent. There were riots, and even revolts in Paris and Lyon, the center of France's silk industry. And there were secret societies, such as The Friends of the People, which actively sought to recruit workers for its cells, even though it was predominantly bourgeois in leadership. Other secret societies appeared, such as the Society of Seasons. It supported an uprising in 1839 led by the socialist agitator Auguste Blanqui, which was a complete failure. The 1830s was a decade of considerable revolutionary activity, but none of it was provoked by an expanding factory proletariat. Those who dug up paving stones to build barricades were skilled craftsmen laboring in shops and petty bourgeois retailing in shops.

The next decade, however, witnessed several factors that were indicative of economic modernization. The July Monarchy was already in power when mechanized production made its entry, chiefly in the Northern Plain. After initial hesitation some entrepreneurs introduced advanced steam engines for mines and textiles. The problem for France was that mechanized industry in the 1830s and 1840s profited from cheap female and child labor; managers, like those of Britain, were not overly concerned about labor conditions. That the government of Great Britain enacted some factory reform and that the July Monarchy did not reveals their different stages of development, and their different social structures: one increasingly urban, the other still mainly rural. It is necessary to remember that France, unlike her channel neighbor already launched on its industrial mission, had still to create an infrastructure of railways and roads; to find progressive managers, foremen, and engineers; to discover what role the state should play in economic growth; and to attract peasants from the land and train a factory working class. Like the British, the French preferred a policy of laissez faire but did not hold to it as doggedly as the British concerning tariffs. Except for some outlays to encourage railroad construction and the rigorous enforcement of trade protection, the state favored a hands-off policy.

In the final analysis Louis-Philippe's regime was more like the unreformed government of Britain. It is curious that the 1830 Parisian uprising which put this "bourgeois" duke on the throne of France, encouraged the British to reform their House of Commons. And yet, once in place, Louis-Philippe acquired enough power over the chambers to block the same kind of reforms that the Whig cabinet felt necessary to save the monarchy.

He managed a self-preserving strategy with consummate skill, partly by adopting the corrupt political practices of the Bourbons and partly by playing off his opponents against one another. Corruption was, as before the revolution, facilitated by the highly limited electorate. Even with lower fiscal requirements, the number of voters was only about 190,000 in 1831 and 240,000 in 1847. The increase, incidentally, is evidence of the growth of wealth in this sixteen-year period. But the increase in numbers did not bring more honesty to the electoral process. This process differed from that of Britain where vote buying was a purely local affair because there was no highly centralized administration. In contrast, French local governance remained in the hands of prefects and their assistants, who were appointed by and responsible to the minister of interior to carry out orders and spend funds sent directly from the capital. They chose the men to be supported as the "official candidates" in each constituency, they paid electors to vote for them, they subsidized friendly newspapers, and openly hired journalists to write pro-government articles. They controlled the electoral lists, willfully struck out or omitted the names of hostile voters, refused to post the list of eligibles until shortly before an election so that a voter whose name was not on the list did not have time to have it inserted. These tactics paid off handsomely; by 1840 the king enjoyed a fairly comfortable majority among the deputies.

He could also split his opposition by offering government jobs to some and not to others. Since deputies were not paid a salary they readily sought positions in the burgeoning bureaucracy and being in the king's pay they naturally voted as he wished. By the early 1840s at least one-third of the deputies held second jobs in the large network of this or that ministry. Such a system had the effect of putting aside the issue of ministerial responsibility by guaranteeing the ministry a safe majority in the Chamber of Deputies.

Corruption as practiced by the king and his ministers not only undermined the basis of responsible government, it was in violation of the spirit of the Charter. In 1830 that document was slightly revised by Guizot and his colleagues to proclaim the principle that the king's power derived from the people, not God. Freedom of the press was strengthened, and the king lost the right to make ordinances for the "security of the state." Moreover, Catholicism was no longer the religion of the state, but simply the "religion professed by most Frenchmen," a wording that probably derived from Guizot's Protestantism and the mild anticlericalism of most liberals.

Guizot's ambitions had led him to the side of the king, and after 1840 he was really the power behind the throne. Marshal Nicholas Soult was the nominal head of the cabinet because, as his friends affirmed, he was a fine "old sword." To his critics he was at best an empty scabbard. Whatever he was he stood above the day-to-day combat in the Chamber of Deputies. It was there that Guizot continued to buy politicians and the men who voted for them, arguing that the ministry was responsible to the sovereign, the king, not the people. What had really occurred was a shift of moderate liberals from the left to the right; they replaced the many legitimists who had refused to take the required oath of allegiance to Louis-Philippe and so abandoned politics. These ultraroyalists were elitists, as were the moderate liberals, but differed in that they believed that ability was in the blood, was hereditary in the family, biologically as well as socially, because it was necessary to acculturate each generation to its duties. They distrusted self-made men as arrivistes, as too individualistic and ready to sacrifice the public good to personal gain out of their ignorance of history and traditional duties. In contrast for Guizot, as for most liberals, government should be in the hands of a financially independent elite consisting of men who had proved their worth and seriousness by hard work and the amassment of wealth, and who therefore would have ample time to devote to public affairs. As for those still disfranchised, Guizot's advice was to "get rich," for only the successful deserved the suffrage. And, he insisted, this was the only way of enlarging the number of voters; therefore he staunchly opposed all proposals to lower the tax qualifications to expand the franchise. Men should rise to the tax requirement; it should not be lowered. He equally stood against proposals that would prohibit deputies from occupying posts in the government.

He headed a group of supporters of the monarchy and the status quo who were called the party of resistance. Standing against it was a loyal opposition called the party of movement. Under the guidance of Thiers the latter managed to win a majority and form ministries in 1834–36, when the army brutally crushed a revolt in Paris, and in 1840 when Thiers, whose body was too small for his ambition, nearly involved France in a war against the major powers. The king leapt at this opportunity, dismissed him, and both saved France from certain defeat, and assured that of his opposition. Quite simply the party of movement did not move when it came to govern, and the king's men enjoyed comfortable majorities until 1848.

Notwithstanding the king's cleverness, this third experiment in constitutional monarchy was not destined to last more than half a generation, about average for governments since 1800. Louis-Philippe, under his bland exterior, was an ambitious monarch more attached to personal power than the naïve men who enthroned him could ever imagine. He not only refused to be a "do-nothing" king, he actively intrigued to divide his opponents and not only separated Thiers from Guizot, breaking up a coalition against his bid for power, he enticed Guizot to play his game according to his own rules. In the short run these intrigues certainly adversely affected France. Compared with Britain, or even to Prussia, the government was slow to respond to pressing social needs. As an active participant in day-to-day politics, the king's mediocre mind, his self-complacency and indifference to domestic affairs except for maintaining order, and his lack of vision were fatal to the regime. It seems natural that he chose Guizot to dominate the ministry from 1840 on. This strait-laced brilliant historian but narrow-minded ungenerous politician was full of scorn for his fellow deputies. These latter, with a few exceptions, were equally limited in understanding social issues. France, after all, was still predominantly rural, and the rural mentality, combined with that of laissez faire liberalism, could not or would not understand or sympathize with the plight of an expanding urban working class.

It was inevitable that such a regime would provoke an opposition more dynamic than the party of movement. Inside the chamber a new generation, led by Alexandre Ledru-Rollin, a lawyer, journalist, and deputy, called for universal male suffrage, a far broader reform than that of Thiers who wished to add several more thousand bourgeois to the electorate. And outside the chamber, a new generation of left-wing liberals also called for a republic, and organized secret societies to prepare to take power, either peacefully or by force. These were the Gallic counterpart of the British Chartists, only while Chartism failed and had no influence on the Continent, the republicans across the channel succeeded in 1848 and unleashed the major revolutionary movement of the century. France sneezed again.

Restoration in the Mediterranean: Spain and Italy

These large peninsula polities had enjoyed great wealth and power three centuries before Napoleon conquered them. Their decay, however, had set in early. With his invasion came administrative and legal changes modeled on his French imperial regime, and there were natives who welcomed him as a liberator from feudalism. Before long, the peasant populations, like the west Germans earlier, discovered the burdens of occupation and began an increasingly systematic resistance led by priests and local notables. Spain, referred to by Napoleon as his "bleeding sore," resorted to full-scale revolt, encouraged by the territorial advance of an English army under Sir Arthur Wellesley, later Lord Wellington, whose final victory occurred at Waterloo, far away from the Iberian peninsula.

During this conflict in Spain, a central Cortes, or parliament, assembled in 1808. Dominated by younger men calling themselves *liberales*, it began the long procedure of writing a new constitution, finally promulgated in 1812. It was modeled on the French Constitution of 1791, with several exceptions; the most telling affirmed that the Catholic religion was to be the only legal one. Spanish reformers do not seem to have absorbed the anticlericalism of their northern counterparts. This document was extremely short-lived; on his restoration in 1815 King Ferdinand VII repudiated it and either imprisoned the *liberales* or drove them into exile. He then based his rule squarely on the clergy and the landed oligarchy. The Inquisition, abolished by the Cortes, was reconstituted, and the Jesuit order, restored by the pope, received a hearty welcome. The church hoped to recover the lands that had earlier been confiscated to pay the debts of the state, but not even Ferdinand consented to this demand. Small farmers had bought some of these lands, but large owners had taken the opportunity to enlarge their estates, and the king needed their support.

Whatever liberal sentiment remained in Spain existed among army officers frustrated by the king's lack of concern for their welfare and his equal lack of appreciation of their struggle against the French. They and civilian Masonic lodges were behind several disturbances between 1815 and 1820. Finally when large army units were concentrated in the port of Cadiz preparatory to the reconquest of Latin America, and then neglected, a broad-based uprising began under the rather vague leadership of a Colonel Rafael Riego. Noncommissioned officers were promised land and release from military service to win over their men. Aided by the Freemasons, the followers of Riego called for the Constitution of 1812. The action, more of a *pronunciamiento*—seizure of power by a minority—than a true national rebellion, nonetheless left the king with no choice but openly to accept the constitutional limits on his power. Liberal *juntas*, or committees, sprang up and seized control of various cities, an indication of the limits of the opposition that barely penetrated the countryside, a typical failing of left-wing insurrections.

This failure was a serious weakness, leaving the new regime without a popular base. An equal weakness was a split among the *liberales* between moderates who wanted no further action and the radicals (called *exaltados*) who favored a republic. Ferdinand cleverly took the moderates into his ministry where the issue of responsibility arose, as in France, from the vagueness of the Constitution. At the same time he sent an appeal to the major powers meeting in Troppau for aid against the "rebels" as he still thought of them.

The major powers, and especially Austria, were more than willing to save the Bourbon ruler of Spain, but the rebellion there had encouraged the Neapolitan liberals to rise in revolt against their Bourbon king, also named Ferdinand. His restoration after the retreat of the French was the most unfortunate for the liberal cause.

The political situation in the Italian peninsula was far more complex than in Spain or France. Italy, as Metternich succinctly put it, was nothing more than a "geographic expression." By that he meant that although Italy had a geographical identity, it was not a unified political state. And he had no intention that it become a "political" expression. In 1815 he had little to worry about on this score. Italian unity had disappeared with the Roman Empire. And German intervention and the rise of the papacy had destroyed any possibility that Italy would follow the pattern of the major dynastic states and become unified. Italy, like Germany, had become a land of combat among stronger, unified states, and by the eighteenth century was dominated by Spain and Austria. Then the French under Napoleon had conquered the entire peninsula, sliced it anew to fit Napoleon's plans, and created republics and kingdoms. Finally, in 1815, the Congress of Vienna restructured it again to carry out a restoration. Disunity returned as displaced rulers recovered their petty territories.

Because the peninsula was so divided these restorations varied in kind and extent. The Kingdom of the Two Sicilies, comprising the southern half of Italy and Sicily, returned to the Neapolitan house of Bourbon. The return of the several branches of the multinational Bourbon dynasty was therefore complete. Complete, in fact, as far as the forms of restoration were concerned. Ferdinand I recovered Naples and the southern peninsula, but the Sicilians were highly distrustful of rule from Naples, insisted on autonomy and never settled down, except to a kind of passive but hostile obedience. Ferdinand abolished all the steps taken by French overlords to model the administration and society on Napoleonic patterns. Feudalism had been abolished and was not reestablished in any legal sense; in fact, most monasteries had been destroyed or disbanded and their huge landed properties put up for sale or lease; as in France earlier, small peasant farmers acquired some of this land. Few of their acquisitions, however, were large enough to provide them a livelihood without their working on the large estates, the *latifundia*, to augment their revenues. As usual, land speculators and large owners purchased most of the land, as had happened in Spain and France. In all three countries legally free peasant farmers soon found themselves bound to their lords by debts.

Rather than disturbing land transfers Ferdinand simply dismantled the efficient administration and civil service of the French, and restored the old regime with its inefficiencies, its brutal suppression of opposition, and its arbitrary police and administrative prerogatives including flogging, torture, and arbitrary confinement of political enemies in the worse prisons of Europe. Without the French there was a breakdown of law and order: brigandage returned to menace travelers, and *banditti* robbed, blackmailed, and murdered at will. From a modernist and liberal viewpoint the Bourbon restorations in Spain and Italy were serious setbacks. This in itself distinguished them from the more efficient Bourbon regime in France but that did not assure the survival of the Gallic branch.

The return of Hapsburg dukes and princes to small northern states such as Modena and Parma did not entail the extensive cruelty of the Bourbons. But Duke Francis of Modena was not a paragon of progress. He too, like King Victor Emmanuel of Piedmont-Sardinia, relied heavily on churchmen and nobles to administer his state. These sovereigns were often well intentioned and not ignorant of the enlightened reformers of the previous century. They all felt, however, that the Napoleonic Civil Code had weakened the family and respect for religion. Like the French Bourbons they reestablished strict paternal control, and ended both civil marriage and divorce. Quite distinct from the French, however, they brought back the laws of primogeniture and entail, which secured the inheritance of large estates by eldest sons, leaving younger siblings with dim futures save the church or army. This undoubtedly explains why so many young men of noble ancestry, as well as sons of upper-middle-class families, became disgruntled army officers or joined the *Carbonari*. It was they who rose in revolt in Naples in 1820 and in Turin the next year. Prussia more successfully opened careers to younger sons of noble families and benefited from the injection of young blood into her institutions.

Metternich, in a knee-jerk reaction, sent Austrian troops to crush the insurrection in Naples when leaders, imitating Spain, called for the 1812 Constitution. A similar uprising in Piedmont came too late to divert Austrian troops from Naples and was easily quashed. These failures reveal the major weakness of the constitutional opposition: internal divisions, regional jealousies, and lack of effective communication. And yet it was among these educated elements that liberal ideas acquired a nationalist dimension, and from this amalgam emerged men like Joseph Mazzini, a *Carbonaro* who called and struggled for a unified democratic state for all of Italy. In 1820–21 theirs was a voice in the wilderness, as was that of their German counterparts. The antiliberal and antinationalist forces of reaction, goaded by Metternich, were in the ascendant.

The New States

The first thrust of France's revolutionary army in the 1790s was northward into the Low Countries. Military success led to their incorporation into the French state. Naturally the victor powers removed this vital area from French rule in 1814. The former Austrian Netherlands (Belgium) were made part of the reestablished Dutch kingdom. The Belgians resented this decision at once, and with cause. They made up three-fifths of the population of the new state, but received only half the seats in the States-General. King William was determined to maintain supremacy for his government and his Dutch subjects. In 1819 and 1822 new decrees made Dutch the official language for candidates to office, as well as all public or official acts. Although French-speaking districts were excluded from the latter decree, Belgians objected because the Dutch managed to obtain all public offices by 1830. To add fuel to the cinders of distrust, resentment flared up from confessional friction between Belgian Catholics and Dutch Calvinists.

By 1830 relations became so strained that a patriotically rousing opera sent the Belgian audience in the streets where the more determined looted gunsmith shops. Once armed, their protest went from arias to action. Groups of leading citizens met in the city hall of Brussels with the aim of recruiting a citizen army to keep order and to appoint a council of regency capable of ruling the Belgian provinces. Not quite prepared for full independence, the well-to-do citizens of the council offered to accept the king's oldest son as administrator of their territories. Instead the irascible William sent in troops, but to his surprise the Belgians drove them back. Further, the Belgians now insisted on complete independence.

At this point the conservative powers of Europe sought to repeat their exploits of 1818–23. Prussia massed an army on her frontier to assist the Dutch, and Russia announced that it was ready to deal with the rebels. But this time the French would not play the game. Louis-Philippe, whose rise to power had angered Metternich, albeit not to the point of intervention, came to the Belgians' aid by insisting that no state had the right to interfere in the domestic affairs of another. Finally the five great powers met in London during November and subsequently recognized Belgian independence. The Metternichian system of intervention came to an end. The new state became a constitutional monarchy under Leopold I. Although William refused to recognize Belgium until 1839, the two polities lived grudgingly side by side; their peoples were prosperous, already actively modernizing industry and agriculture, and expanding foreign commerce as a major source of wealth. Belgium had already become the focus of the Continental industrial revolution.

Quite the opposite was true of the Greeks and the Poles. Centuries earlier the Ottoman Turks had conquered the Balkan Peninsula, as well as North Africa, and the Near East. As the once-mighty Islamic empire began to fall apart in the early nineteenth century, the Greeks as Orthodox Christians grew increasingly restless under Ottoman rule and, hoping for support from Orthodox Russia, began to resist their overlords. When the latter resorted to massacring Greek peasants, Panhellenic sympathizers in Britain and France went off to join the rebels. Politicians were sympathetic and sent squadrons of warships that, without orders to do so, blasted the Egyptian and Turkish fleets out of the Aegean Sea in 1827. For Metternich this was a catastrophe. For the Bourbons and Tories it was an untoward event. For Tsar Nicholas, already at war against the sultan as part of a policy to attract Slavic peoples of the Balkans, it was a success in his crusade to save his coreligionists and advance Russia's boundaries toward the Mediterranean. The outcome was general recognition of Greece as an independent state, set up as a constitutional monarchy, with a Bavarian prince as king. So much for Greek nationalism.

When the Poles rebelled in late 1830 the tsar was of an entirely different disposition; they rose up against *his* rule. Aiding insurgents in the Balkans had paid off in his military occupation of Romanian lands at the mouth of the Danube River, an act that slightly upset the balance of power. But the ungrateful Poles turned to violent resistance when he tried to recruit their young men into the army he intended to send against the government newly established in France. Once more Nicholas could stand shoulder to shoulder with the monarchs of Prussia and Austria who feared rebellion among their own Polish-speaking subjects. They applauded wildly when Russian forces brutally put down the Poles in 1831, that is, put down a rebellion of Polish gentry, for the lowly peasants were as cruelly treated by their native nobility as by the Russians. The Greek rebellion put a strain on the Holy Alliance; it also brought about the first boundary change in Europe since the Congress of Vienna. The Polish rebellion was simply drowned in blood and put a quietus to the liberal regime formerly set up by Alexander. The local gentry, instigators of the rebellion, were lucky to preserve their land. This was no mean achievement since land was the prime source of power and wealth in eastern Europe.

5

Europe's Belly: Agriculture

Traditional Husbandry

Economic revolution is a term signifying the relatively rapid changes that occurred throughout Europe from roughly the mid-1700s to 1914, and refers to the transformation of the methods of production of food, drink, industrial goods, transport, and communications. The word "revolution" has been taken over by historians to denote radical changes within a short time-span—short, that is, when set against the centuries-long context of European history. This usage must be clearly distinguished from political revolutions, whose violent phases lasted only a few days followed by months of debate, and ending in a violent reckoning of accounts. Economic revolutions, on the contrary, went on for generations, and it is a matter of controversy among historians as to when they began, and when, if ever, they ended or simply advanced from phase to phase as ongoing phenomena. Their chronology is far more difficult to establish, and, we must remember, it does not always coincide perfectly with that of political change.

The relationship between governmental policies and the way people earned a living is also a subject of controversy among historians. In particular did economic activity determine the nature and purpose of states or vice versa? Of course the question put this way is simplistic; the relation was highly complex and not unchanging. Far more valid is the view that between political and economic development there has always been a contrapuntal connection that did, indeed, change over time as well as space. Chronologically, from the sixteenth through the eighteenth centuries, absolute monarchs sought to control the industrial and commercial activities of their subjects through a policy called mercantilism. But already in the 1700s there arose a group of thinkers, known in France as physiocrats and in Britain as free-traders. They used the neologism, laissez faire, to sum up their view that the government should leave the economy alone. This intellectual opposition to bureaucratic controls spurred a rising middle class of manufacturers and merchants to challenge royal control of the economy; in France, beginning in 1789, the revolutionaries sought economic liberation as a necessary complement to civil and political liberation of individuals. These goals, combined with the absolute protection of private property, became the program of liberals. Why liberal reformers were strongest and most successful in western Europe is a phenomenon that this and the next chapter will try to elucidate.

The years 1814–15, so important in political and diplomatic history came and went without seriously influencing the way most Europeans earned a living or carried on their daily lives. To be sure many men who had formed the legions fighting for or against Napoleon could, like the poet Alfred de Musset, utter a sigh of relief as peace returned after twenty-three years of war. They could now go back to their homes, to their families, to a normal life. But what was a normal life in 1815 and was it identical to a normal life in 1789? What, indeed, were they going back to?

British soldiers crossing the English Channel after their victory at Waterloo discovered a land that had gone far toward modernizing agriculture. The oldest of the veterans would not have found the same rural landscape that he most likely remembered as a yeoman farmer. Perhaps, like the poet Oliver Goldsmith, he would have been struck by the decline of communal life, and above all, by the many nearly or completely deserted villages, abandoned by evicted or distressed families. The winding dirt road he followed no longer made its way among open fields stretching as far as his eyes could see. Rather they were either closed off from trespass by wooden rail fences and deep ditches, or cut off from view by an endless line of hedgerows. He had spent much of his youth fighting against the French revolutionaries, and yet, his countryside had undergone its own revolution of vast economic and social import. And there was no way he could fight against that. The rolling land, still green and pleasant, had been laid out in large farms and estates whose owners were both rich and powerful, the ruling class of Britain.

All the other troops on the Continent, both victors and vanquished, returned as best they could to their rural villages where both landscapes and economic activity were hardly changed. The French veterans would, thanks to the Revolution, have found many small farms and a free peasantry actively buying minuscule plots of land. But the Austrians and Russians returned to the unchanging rural life of their ancestors. The downfall of Napoleon did not offer them a promising future, merely a return to the dreary yoke of the past. The Prussians did not return to bondage but it was unlikely that they would be able to acquire land, given the terms of the emancipation decree.

Even troops not rooted to the countryside would have found their towns and cities hardly changed. The exception was Britain, where the industrial revolution had made some headway in textiles, especially cotton yarn and cloth; the returned veteran was more likely to end up in a factory tending newfangled machinery. But not even Britain was a fully industrialized country as yet.

All Europe was still predominantly rural in the sense that most people lived on as well as off the land. Admittedly this rural population varied, barely a majority in the west, but an overwhelming element in the center, south and east. Englishmen could still feed themselves from wheat, and even export about 10 percent of the annual crop. The Continental states had to feed themselves. They were, excepting the Low Countries, still locked in an "economic old regime" kept in place by a deep-rooted distrust of change as keenly felt among peasants as among landed nobles and reactionary politicians. Economic systems were compatible with ideals prevailing in royal councils and throne rooms.

Farming methods common to mainland Europeans had scarcely changed since the Middle Ages. The enhancement of royal power by reigning dynasties at the expense of the nobility and higher clergy had not seriously weakened the control of these two groups over most of the arable forest and pasture tended by peasants. It was a common saying that peasants lived off the land, and the nobles and clergy lived off the peasants.

All the land available for exploitation was divided according to ancient usage. Arable or plow land consisted of the best soils. It provided much of the wealth of the nobility, as well as the miserly subsistence of the peasantry. Generally this land was divided either into two fields (common in southern Europe) or three (northern Europe). These fields were open in that they were not enclosed by fences or hedges. And the lands under cultivation were divided into strips, some of which constituted the lord's demesne; the remainder were held by peasants who tilled both their own strips as well as the lord's. Their methods of farming were so inefficient that their share of the crops provided for their basic needs in good years when harvests were plentiful but provoked famines in cold, wet seasons. Most peasants owned a cow or some sheep, and at least one or two pigs to obtain salt pork, the only meat available to them on special occasions. As members of a manorial community they enjoyed several rights: grazing their scrawny animals on the common pasture and waste land, and the gathering of dead wood in the lord's forest. Custom required the setting aside of some land as fallow, a field left untilled for a fixed length of time to allow the soil to recover its fertility. Fallowing could remove one-third to one-half of the arable land from tillage, reducing crops by as much. This practice, plus inefficient broad-cast seeding and lack of manure, maintained yields at a productive level unchanged for centuries. The yield ratio averaged about five bushels of grain for each bushel sown as seed. And this was the harvest of good years! Moreover one of the five had to be kept as seed for next year's sowing. Given that food shortages were fairly frequent, life remained precarious for the post-war generation, perhaps more so than the living conditions of the war-time generation. War, after all, was only one of the four disasters of the Apocalypse, and European statesmen would manage to avoid large-scale conflict for the next hundred years. The three other disasters—famine, plague, and death—were more persistent, and overcome more slowly and incompletely.

Agricultural Revolution in Britain

The break with traditional farming really began in the Low Countries as early as the seventeenth century. But transformation that was massive and rapid enough to be called an agricultural revolution was carried out in England where large landowners borrowed techniques from the Lowlanders; in fact, they even hired Dutch hydraulic engineers to drain their wetlands to expand the arable land. This was a major step in a long process that altered the rural landscape. More important were new methods that required the enclosing of open fields. Beginning as early as the 1500s, but gaining full momentum only in the late 1700s and early 1800s, English landlords divided the village arable land into large consolidated estates that they enclosed either with hedgerows or wooden fences. The village poor folk were forced to give up their few strips in exchange for meager compensation. Surrender of their bits of earth was really forced upon them when they lost the age-old privilege of grazing their few beasts on the communal pasture when it, too, was absorbed into enclosed estates. Given this outcome the poor with nothing left but a cottage and a minute garden patch now had either to hire themselves out as farm laborers or emigrate to the nearest industrial town. In this way their roots in the land were severed as they left their villages to find jobs in factories or in unskilled labor, especially in construction and dock work.

It has been argued that enclosure was a necessary first step toward progressive farming, the only means to put an end to famine. This argument is not without some validity. As we shall discover the French carried out only a partial agricultural revolution after 1815, but it obviated the trend toward enclosure by confiscating church lands and auctioning them in large lots. Eventually much of this land, after wealthy speculators had divided it into small lots, was sold to peasants. Instead of migrating in large numbers to local towns these now "landed" farmers sought to make a living from their newly acquired holdings. This was impossible, and the result was the emergence of a class of owner-workers, men who hired themselves out part-time and whose wives also worked in the fields or as servants in the houses of the local gentry, or did their laundry.

Enclosures, although certainly not unknown on the Continent and fairly widespread in Prussia, were more typical of England. Although the process created great hardships for simple cottagers without farmland and small farmers without capital, it did hasten the introduction of progressive techniques. It made possible the higher yields of grains that enabled the English to feed a rapidly expanding urban population and provided the migrant labor force required for rapid industrial growth. By 1841 British farmers could grow 88 percent of the wheat needed for a population that had nearly doubled in forty years. In the 1700s England had suffered five famines, and four in the previous hundred years. For the nineteenth century, England (as distinct from Ireland where farming remained most inefficient) suffered famine only in 1812, when grain supplies from Russia were hampered by Napoleon's invasion. Not only was there more security from want, there was a rising standard of living that enabled rural people to purchase more manufactured goods, above all cotton textiles.

The greatest efficiency was not always achieved on huge estates managed directly by noble families or gentlemen farmers. Rather it became a common practice for these owners to divide their lands, consisting of thousands of acres, into large farms of a few hundred acres. Then they rented these farms on long leases to well-trained tenants who had access to capital acquired from earnings, relatives, or local money lenders. These landlords were content to live well on their rents, retaining only forests and wastelands for their hunting grounds.

The new agriculture, called "high farming," consisted of radically altered methods. Enclosure brought an end to fallow fields. Henceforth all land was planted and crops rotated continuously. This so-called mixed farming made use of crops that proved beneficial to the soil by restoring nutrients, thereby obviating the need for fallow. For example, Lord Townsend had discovered that turnips returned nitrogen to the soil. Equally useful were mangolds and sugar beets. The potato also spread as a food crop. These legumes served not only to improve soil, they could nourish both animals and people. Rotation involved fodder as well, chiefly grasses such as lucerne (also called alfalfa) and clover. With sufficient fodder on hand it was no longer necessary to slaughter animals at winter's approach because they could be provided with food throughout the year. More important they could be stall fed so that their droppings could be gathered, piled, and spread as manure over the arable land before the spring sowing. Proper manuring enriched the soil and enhanced yields far beyond the wildest hopes of traditional farmers. Wheat crops increased fourfold to fivefold. Another factor aiding higher yields was seed selection. Traditional farmers paid no attention to it, but the observations of pragmatists revealed that certain strains enhanced productivity, so they came to rely on them. Progressive-minded, they were ever ready to change to another strain if it proved superior. They also abandoned broad-cast seeding, relying more on the seed drill to insert each seed separately into the soil after which harrowing covered them. Their willingness to experiment reveals how far these new farmers were removed from their hide-bound ancestors.

Large holding and available capital encouraged the testing of new implements or the broader use of old efficient ones that had been neglected. Among the former was a larger-wheeled plow, made chiefly of wood, with a metal coulter and metal-covered mold board. It required four animals to pull it through heavy soil and was difficult to turn. When iron foundries expanded as part of the industrial revolution, implement manufacturers learned how to turn out lighter, all-metal plows. These were more efficient than the wooden, required only two draft animals, and were easier to turn at the end of a row. As noteworthy was the replacement of oxen by horses as draft animals. Horses were more expensive and more prone to disease, but they moved twice as fast as oxen. What the plowman lost in costs he more than recovered in higher productivity. In fact productivity rose about 1 percent a year, which signaled a "take-off" of steady advance.

The scythe also contributed to higher output. It was by no means a new invention. Its replacement by the sickle resulted from the age-old need to provide work for an excessive rural population; being smaller, it required more hands to harvest cereals. Women were also able to manage it. The scythe, however, was a man's tool and at harvest time, large tenants hired teams of men, lined them in a row like soldiers, and urged them forward. Each worker cut close to the ground and in such broad swaths that they completed their task in a fraction of the time needed by the sickle wielder. Women now gathered the severed stalks and tied them into bundles for transport to a large barn. Over the winter the men assembled to thrash these stalks with flails, a task as exhausting as harvesting but as yet the only means of separating wheat berries from each stalk. As employers became increasingly concerned about labor costs, they began to buy mechanical thrashers. By midcentury they also bought the horse-drawn reaper invented by Cyrus McCormick and manufactured by him in Chicago. Large farmers, trying to avoid rising labor costs, invested in new equipment and made the English farm the most heavily capitalized in Europe.

Inventiveness was not limited to machinery. Farmers as well as animal growers were able to improve the tractive power of plow horses by selective breeding. In fact animal growers on enclosed farms practiced selective breeding for all farm animals, which they had not been able to accomplish when all qualities of beasts cohabited on village pastures. Cattle and sheep, after they were separated and selected, grew larger, while acquiring more meat in relation to bone. Some of them looked grotesque, ill formed by an excess of flesh. However, they brought high prices, enriched their growers, and won gold medals at county fairs. Crops, animals, and farmers fared better under the new husbandry, thanks not only to healthier diets but also because excess humidity, the source of fevers, was decreased as owners and tenants drained low-lying areas. Once more industry aided agriculture when tile makers learned how to turn out cheap, round clay pipe for drainage.

There was, indeed, a mutual supportive relation between agriculture and industry. Before the advent of the railroads with their insatiable demand for iron and steel, agriculture encouraged metallurgy. Apart from metal plows, metal blades of all kinds and metal spikes for harrows pulled by animals over plowed land to level the furrows, there was a need for nails to build barns and erect fences. After 1800 farm needs accounted for 30 to 50 percent of iron production; horse shoes alone consumed 15 percent of it. Animals, along with men, women, and even children, were still the chief sources of energy at midcentury.

Agriculture on the Continent: Western Europe

Before the 1850s the agricultural progress described earlier made an appearance in western Europe, slowly, really very slowly, but could not penetrate the East. Its success or failure depended largely on political and cultural forces: small farmers were viewed in France as the bulwark of a stable, conservative society, a belief shared as much by urban bourgeois as by rural notables. This explains why even free-traders favored high protective tariffs for agriculture as well as for industry. The ideal was a society balanced among all sectors of the economy, a goal requiring peasants to stay on the land. Given this belief, the peasant farmer became increasingly idealized as the decades passed; however, before midcentury the upper classes still looked on the lower-class rural population as brutish and dangerous, best left at hard work over long hours to prevent it from thinking about its condition, and kept in check by religion. Above all the propertied classes did not want peasants migrating into cities; these uprooted people, the upper class was convinced, were the source of violence and crime, the dangerous class, a menace to civilization.

Within the German Confederation, the principalities west of the Elbe River had undergone occupation by French armies, and the most important consequence was the abolition of serfdom where it had survived. Between 1815 and 1848 the remaining serfs were liberated by a series of decrees and the trend toward the creation of small peasant farms continued as it had for several centuries. French conquest had the same effect in northern Italy where numerous small farms thrived in the lush climate and rich alluvial of the Po Valley. This was equally the case in northeastern Spain where the influence of Barcelona was an encouragement to agriculture. In general, husbandry improved where cities offered market opportunities. As in France governments did not devise policies to aid agriculture directly, only indirectly by protective tariffs. This was also true of Britain, but in that island kingdom there were more improving landowners and more investment than in most of Europe.

Geography was also a force that peasants did not fully understand. They had learned over centuries of practice that soil composition, altitude, and climate with its annual weather variations were influences both beneficial and malignant. Even the British, for all their pragmatic knowledge, were able to farm profitably only the most naturally favored parts of their island; no human effort short of a miracle could transform the Scottish highlands into rich farm land. Yet what brought about an agricultural revolution in Britain was the willingness to try new methods. Britain was not more naturally endowed than western Europe. It is true that it benefited from the benevolent influences of the Gulf Stream, but it suffered the negative effects as well. High hill and mountainous formations along the western coast provoked a rate of rainfall over mediocre soils that nearly precluded cereal farming. The north and west were best suited to pasture and therefore land owners raised cattle and sheep for meat, hides, and wool. High farming occurred on the rich soils of the central plain, the east, and south. These latter made up the most densely populated regions until industry drew population northward. And yet, the concentrated people of the east and south were subject to marginal soil and climatic conditions that allowed little safety from the excesses of dry or wet years. It was human initiative that tipped the balance in favor of sufficiency, even abundance. Agricultural productivity, then, resulted from a combination of natural conditions and human initiative. Regarding the former, western Europe was not in a worse state than Britain; it was the latter that was deficient.

The agricultural potential of Continental Europe was severely restricted. The only truly extensive area of high-quality soil, called loess, had been created in varying thicknesses during the glacial period thousands of years earlier. It formed a wide belt extending from the Parisian basin, through Belgium, to the lower Rhineland. Then the belt narrowed in Saxony, Silesia, southern Poland, and ended in the black earth region of central Russia. Elsewhere good soil lay in wide valleys and in river deltas provided they were drained and the river bed controlled. North of the fertile belt the quality of soil declined, varying from heavy clay to sand and gravel, as in Brandenburg. To the south lay thin, generally acid soils that stretched into the Alpine belt from the Pyrenees through the Alps, to the Balkan Mountains and the Caucasus. Only valleys offered arable lands. Between the valley floors and the high slopes lay a zone suitable for seasonal grazing of transhumant animals. Here was a potential for dairy farming, except that the lack of suitable roads made for isolation. Fresh milk, quick to turn sour, could not be transported; so shepherds churned it into hard cheese that they loaded onto animals for transport to lowland markets. Hard cheese not only lived longer than milk or soft cheese—it did not suffer from the journey over narrow mountain trails.

On higher slopes woodsmen chopped their way through forests of deciduous and pine trees to provide wood for heating, cooking, and construction. Thick forests also covered most of Scandinavia where the cold climate offered little incentive to farm because of a growing season too short and uncertain. The Mediterranean south was equally limited but not because of freezes. It was summer drought that restricted agriculture, save for fertile river valleys, to wine and table grapes, citrus fruit, and olives. These, with some vegetables, were exotic produce shipped north by coastal traders from Spain, Portugal, southern Italy, and Greece. Wine was an important element of southerners' diet. Most of it was made for local markets because its staying power after the grape harvest rapidly declined with the arrival of warm weather the following spring. To preserve it, growers distilled it into alcohol for northern people who liked strong drink when they were not consuming beer. Given the high costs of transport grapes were cultivated even in northern Europe, and the nineteenth century witnessed the improvement of the major vineyards of Burgundy, Champagne, and the Rhineland. Everywhere, in Bordeaux, Piedmont, Tuscany, and Rioja in Spain the science of grape cultivation made progress among knowledgeable growers who produced a surplus of grapes capable of making fine wines that entered into national and international trade.

At present I am dividing Europe from west to east. It is also possible to divide the continent from south to north. In general the Mediterranean peoples were poorer, their agriculture less advanced, and their chief money crops were grapes (for wine, eating, and raisins); olives (for oil); and some wheat (for bread and pasta) where irrigation was possible. Northerners, including England, were richer, more progressive agriculturally, more favored by nature with plains and rich soils, and grew cereals of all kinds chiefly for bread on which they spread butter rather than oil. There was, of course, no clear line separating north and south; there were areas of wealth and poverty in both.

Notwithstanding the natural limits of profitable tillage and grazing, western Europeans managed to augment the quantity of food available in various, and chiefly local, markets. In place of a technical breakthrough there was a considerable expansion of plowland. This was not the best solution to the nutritional needs of a modestly growing urban population. And it did not safeguard the entire population from food shortages; the last serious food crisis in western Europe broke out in the mid-1840s partly because of the potato blight, but also because of the inability of farmers, big and small, to overcome excesses of rain and cold.

The weakness of western farming resulted, in large part, from the peasant mentality. Above all it was stubbornly resistant to innovation. From a social point, small independent farmers represented a final and progressive departure from medieval serfdom. From a technical point they were a drag on agricultural advance. It must be borne in mind that only about half of them—if that many—owned enough land to support a family, and most had acquired scattered bits and pieces too small to accommodate modern equipment. In place of a horse and plow they exhausted themselves with hoe and pick; they also harvested with the sickle the low-yielding grains that made up most of their diet. Entirely dependent on their limited crops, they showed no wish to essay different techniques or plants; they used every square foot of land for immediate needs and dared not set aside any for experimentation. Illiterate rather than ignorant, untutored and locked into their village routines, they distrusted change with as much fervor as they believed in God, ghosts, and miracles. Possibly the fact that most of them were Catholic and influenced by traditionalistic priests was a factor of retardation. Was then Protestantism an economically progressive force in agriculture as well as in industry, as some historians have affirmed? Only to a limited extent. Catholic farmers in Belgium, the Rhineland, the Po Valley, Catalonia, and northern France were the most productive in Europe. And there were numerous family as well as large farms in these areas. Lutherans in most of northern Germany and Scandinavia were not in the forefront of rural progress. They were, however, in Denmark. And the Calvinist Dutch were among the best farmers of Europe.

Religion aside, high tillage required a combination of several elements: an open-minded class of sizable landowners; reasonably good climate; fairly fertile soils; capital for investment; and cheap, docile workers. Like England, the fertile plains of northern Europe became a locus of highly productive husbandry. There were also two other elements of major importance: cheap and easy transport to carry food and raw materials to market, and industrial towns serving as expanding markets as their populations grew. Equally necessary was disposable wealth. In England and northern Europe, urban populations found it easier to buy more than bare necessities, and the rural population selling to this market acquired means to purchase industrial goods including new efficient farm machinery. In the eighteenth century, most of the new implements were invented by gentlemen farmers. In the nineteenth century, innovations emerged from the imaginative minds of town artisans and small manufacturers. But they were too expensive for those without capital or credit.

Before the 1840s only a minority of peasant farmers participated in this changing world. For most their access to it was limited by their isolation. It was also restricted by the state of dependency that characterized the existence of numerous crop sharers. They were tenants who received a plot of ground from a landowner and agreed to pay certain expenses as well as surrender a portion of the harvest, usually one-half. These landlords were little interested in new techniques, certainly showed little willingness to spend money on innovations. Neither did the crop sharer, given that his lease was short, one to three years, and without any assurance that he would be compensated for improvements at the term's end. Crop sharing, from both a technical and human perspective, was one of the worst systems of tenure. Not only did it discourage progress, it also created a form of debt peonage. The tenant was legally free, but in almost every case he became indebted to his landlord, which ensured his loss of freedom. Moreover, because the landlord marketed the entire crop, many of them cheated their tenants by deducting fictitious charges and understating prices when calculating net income. The unfortunate tenant, unable to perform simple addition and subtraction, had no means to safeguard himself and ended in deeper debt. He had to borrow to obtain seed and fodder since he rarely produced enough, and too much of his land lay fallow. Small wonder that this form of tenure steadily declined as landlords came to realize that they could improve their incomes by renting land for money. Crop sharing persisted only in the most primitive areas: central France, southern Italy, and nearly everywhere in Spain.

The picture looks bleak for west European agriculture. Perhaps the previous descriptions could lead one to see little save poverty and immobility. The truth is more complex, however. On the one hand, farm practices were progressing in some areas and unchanging in others, with the result that not even France was secure from food shortages until after midcentury when railroads could transport food from areas of abundance to those of penury. But as the population grew rapidly until the 1840s farmers had to bring marginal land under cultivation to provision dynamic urban markets. Even small farms near these markets became more efficient, at least in France, with the result that production of major cereal crops and potatoes grew at an average rate of just over 1 percent between 1815–24 and 1865–74. Such a rate indicates a modest agricultural revolution, thanks largely to the more progressive growers, both large and small, north of the Loire River. Nonetheless there were not enough aggressive farmers elsewhere and the restoration monarchies did little to encourage the loosening of credit and the improvement of transport.

Other than protective tariffs, the Bourbon and Orleanist monarchies did little to stimulate agricultural progress. Investment capital was in short supply so that peasants generally had to borrow at usurious rates from a local notary, or from one or more well-to-do notables who owned estates in their parish. Land hungry as they were, small farmers borrowed money to buy land rather than to improve it. They did not see the need for labor-saving devices or equipment; the heads of households counted on themselves and family members to supply their labor needs. Children of both sexes began tending animals from the age of four or five, adolescents carried out heavy field work, and wives spent almost as much time outdoors as in. And yet, however limited the result, French and western European farmers generally rank as progressive when compared with those of the east.

Eastern Europe

The traveler who crossed the Elbe going eastward traversed not only a river, he crossed into another world, and the liberal-minded could well have believed that he had crossed the Styx on his way to Hades. There lay before him the vast lands of servitude. In Prussia, it is true, serfdom as a legalized form of bondage was ended in 1807. Even emancipated, however, the peasants still owed money and labor services to their former masters. They could commute these by cash payment or by ceding to the landowner one-third of the land they were still entitled to work. Large owners, all of them either *Junkers* or well-to-do gentry, added to their demesnes at least a million hectares (2.47 million acres) as indemnity, or through purchase and appropriation of abandoned farms. More than 100,000 farmers became wage laborers on these estates; others migrated westward to work in shops and factories.

Eastern Europe, unlike the West, was an area of large farms usually owned and managed directly by resident families. Here, too, most land was devoted to cereals, chiefly rye, for the population had to feed itself. Cereals, apart from serving as a basic food source, also provided the ingredients to brew beer, a fermented drink, and most owners willingly distilled some of the beer into a highly alcoholic beverage commonly called "schnapps," consumed in a nearly raw state by urban and rural workers of both sexes to forget their miserable living conditions. This practice was identical to that of large English owners who shared much in common with the Prussian landed class. After all, both had profited enormously by ejecting peasants from the land in order to enlarge their holdings. Both also turned much plowland into pastures for sheep, a more profitable source of wealth after 1815 when grain prices tumbled from their war-time highs. In 1816 there were eight million sheep in Prussia; by 1837 the total had grown to seventeen million. With such huge flocks the Prussians ousted the Spanish from the highly lucrative wool markets and even exported to England where local flocks could not supply textile demands. Not until Australia entered the European market with vigor and aggression after 1850 was Prussia dethroned. In compensation, the *Junkers* grew sugar beets, a new crop that was added to their rotation systems and proved highly useful. Beet pulp and the green tops made nutritious food for livestock. Thanks to chemistry, farmers learned how to increase the sugar content of the bulb, an indication of the future importance of crop chemistry in Germany. Indeed, Prussia and other states of the Confederation led the world in beet production, followed by Russia, Austria, France, and Holland.

Russia was the largest European state in acreage and population. It was undoubtedly one of the poorest if wealth is measured per capita. The vast majority of natives were serfs and, as everywhere in eastern Europe, serfdom was only one step this side of slavery. Nobles enjoyed extensive control over their subordinates, forcing them to work longer hours and more days on their demesne. Most nobles were educated, and they were aware of improved techniques to increase the wheat and rye that was grown chiefly to feed the huge peasant hordes settled on their estates. Indeed, a few brought farm machines from the West, but because scarcely anyone knew how to use them, they sat unused and rusted in the fields. Such estates were truly medieval in the sense that the land was usually divided into three fields and the fields divided into strips, save the one lying fallow. Each village community granted the use of several strips to a family depending on its size; the larger the family, the more strips it farmed until its membership changed.

In a state so large, geographic features naturally made for considerable variety. The central territory comprised the black earth belt, the most fertile soil. Here serfs labored under the *barshina* system: They farmed their own and the master's strips and paid him both in produce and labor service. Because this was an area with insufficient transport, most of the wheat and rye were consumed by the peasants, any surplus—chiefly the lord's—being sold in local markets. Yields were restricted by backward methods and the short growing season, six months contrasted to nine months in the West. Masters and serfs had almost no outside income and therefore depended completely on the annual harvest from mid-July to the end of August.

North of Moscow the quality of farm land declined and climate became an ever-present challenge because of severe winter conditions and spring frosts. Here about half the serfs gave minimal attention to husbandry and worked under the *obrok* tenure. With their lords permission they went to work in non-farm jobs, as laborers and artisans, and paid their feudal obligations in cash. Lucky was the noble who owned serfs with profitable skills because their *obrok* payments were heavier. There were serfs who were managers of businesses, banks, and retail and wholesale outlets, who were traders of the raw materials grown on the estates: hemp, linen, flax, wool, and lard. Towns were the loci of fairs where these goods, plus animals, constituted the backbone of the economy.

In the South were the flatlands of the steppes. This wide band stretched from the Ukraine eastward into Siberia. It was the highway of invasion during past times when Russia suffered from frequent incursions of nomadic tribes from central and eastern Asia. Now it was the turn of the Russians to take the initiative as they expanded south, west and east in this frontier region. Numerous runaway serfs settled here in the eighteenth century, formed into cossack bands until they settled down to cultivate the land. Wheat was the main crop, and the surplus was exported via the Black and Caspian Seas. In the 1840s, when Britain's population was growing beyond the capacity of her food production, Parliament abolished the Corn Laws. The island gave up the ideal of self-sufficiency and became the chief market of Russian, chiefly Ukrainian, wheat. Southern farmers were typical of frontier folk: independent, adventurous, and freedom loving. Here landowners, whether noble or commoner, sought high yields and employed free peasants to till their consolidated fields. Whatever their rank, they were capitalistic in outlook. There were practically no serfs, which explains the greater efficiency of southern farming. Wheat shipments here accounted for 90 percent of all Russian wheat exports. The Ukraine was the feeding end of a kind of umbilical cord that fed the embryonic industrial population of western Europe where industrial growth outpaced that of agriculture.

6

Europe as Workshop

Preconditions of Britain's Industrial Revolution

Significant economic development over a long time has always required harmonious interaction among the four major sectors of an economy: agriculture, industry, commerce, and services. As stated in the previous chapter, farming thrived near urban markets. In turn, urban industry could not go beyond the small workshop stage without a supply of agricultural materials, such as raw cotton and aliments, needed to feed spinning machines, looms, and workers. And then, neither high farming nor mechanizing industry could advance without improved commercial transport to facilitate the movement of manufactures and crops between producers and consumers. We must not rule out services provided by the royal navy: In earlier times it cleared the oceans of enemy ships, thereby opening markets in South America and the Caribbean Sea. The launching of an industrial revolution also had a psychological dimension, requiring a state of mind rigidly self-disciplined, vigorously competitive, optimistic about economic growth but pessimistic enough about human nature to see the need to bring control into the work place and into society as a means of harnessing the productive power of the masses. Most early entrepreneurs believed that without discipline, workers were lazy and uncooperative. Their belief was a cultural factor, as important as machines in the course of development. It seems likely that the stern morality and self-righteousness of puritanical religions were necessary stimulants and explain in part why an industrial leap began in England and Scotland. Even the Catholic Belgians, hardworking as they were, benefited from immigrant entrepreneurs from Great Britain.

Apart from the appropriate mentality there were natural features that stimulated change. Access to large bodies of water and foreign markets served to pull entrepreneurs toward economic innovation. The English in particular laid the groundwork, the infrastructure, during the seventeenth and early eighteenth centuries. By the later 1700s they had improved internal transport through building canals and highways, swept the oceans clear of their enemies, opening wider the markets of the new world and of Europe, created a sound money and fiscal system, as well as a stable government. Apart from the infrastructure they provided educational opportunities for the young men who became inventors and managers, and an open culture that encouraged individual initiative.

The latter statement suggests that the men who initiated industrial mechanization were highly educated. This was not the case. Indeed two caveats are called for here. First, the inventors of the mechanical devices that first enhanced productivity were simple but imaginative artisans. Second, their inventions did not suddenly bring to life an entirely new industrial system. Rather, they put them to use in the cottage textile system and worked them by hand. The fact that Britain was prepared for an economic revolution indicates that the "take-off" into sustained growth had been well prepared long before the period 1760–80, the two decades that are believed to have opened an entirely new era. But how new? There are historians who insist that there was an industrial revolution in the twelfth century; others put it in the period 1540–1640. The term *industrial revolution* is broad and vague enough to grant them some justification. But I think that the notable economic growth and innovation of both these early periods were not sufficiently penetrative of society to merit the title of revolution. The industrial breakthrough that we are concerned with here marked a rupture with the past, a discontinuity. In the words of Carlo Cipolla, "In 1850 the past was not merely past—it was dead"—at least in Great Britain. Certainly the rapidity of change from about the 1750s to the 1850s was unprecedented. So was the extent of change both in the way people earned a living and in the way they thought about novelty. When they readily introduced new techniques affecting the organization of work, when they even began offering both monetary and honorific rewards for original machines, and passed patent laws to protect them as private property, they really invented invention as a public good, a worthy cultural value. Can we, given this penchant, deny that a fresh state of mind in the public at large was a necessary complement to an ingenious machine? In the early sixteenth century Leonardo da Vinci invented some remarkable machines, but not even renaissance society accepted them as useful.

The Industrial Revolution: Textiles

Once the preceding processes began at both the technical and mental levels, they acquired a momentum of their own that carried society with them. More skillful inventors took the hand-driven spinning and weaving devices and adapted them to water power. At this stage producers moved from cottages to factories because they could not bring inanimate power to a cottage, or even to a village of cottages. The geographical locus of production shifted toward the most promising water courses in Britain. And when James Watt improved the steam engine an army of highly skilled mechanics again reinvented the original inventions to adapt them to this new source of power. These steps markedly changed labor conditions in the workplace.

By the early nineteenth century, British entrepreneurs considerably reduced the control that their hired hands had exercised over production. Under the domestic system, spinners and weavers of both sexes had controlled their hours of labor, the tools they activated in their homes, and their leisure time. The introduction of water and, later, steam power, uprooted workplaces by locating mills near their sources of power and by transposing workers from their cottages to the "dark satanic mills." Under the cottage system laborers had worked their tools; in power-driven mills they tended machines. Finally, from about the Napoleonic period forward, they lost control of productive processes as machines became self-activating, and unneeded workers in textile mills, mainly adult men, nearly disappeared from the factory floor. Conveyor belts rather than human hands turned spindles and activated looms, while special gears and axles directed their whirling and reciprocal motions. These new generations of machines were made of metal because wood could not stand the severe shocks and vibrations to which productive equipment was now subjected. The simple artisan inventor had given way to the highly skilled machinist and the mechanical engineer. For the hands who remained—increasingly feminine and teenage—the workplace was transformed from a locale silent enough to allow singing by operatives to one of intense noise where they were fined merely for conversing above the din.

The new mills and the mill towns were, as far as one can determine from early descriptions, unpleasant places to work. Their geographic location, being determined by the need for coal after steam power was introduced, shifted to the Midlands and the north where coal deposits as well as iron ore could be found. Coal and ore were too bulky to be shipped to traditional production centers in the Southeast. Population, along with industry, also moved northward, and as mines were worked more intensely, and high smokestacks spewed smoke, the land became covered with high piles of slag and discard, the air filled with fumes and soot. This was the cost of industrial modernization, a process that concentrated on increasing productivity and total output at the expense of all other considerations. Entrepreneurs paid little attention to these human and environmental costs as distinct from the cost of manufacturing goods. Agreeing with them were all the persons in the upper layers of society who enjoyed the power of decision and rule. Most of them were environmentally illiterate even though they included the governing groups made up largely of a rural class whose wealth came primarily from land. Although proagriculture, and disdainful of ambitious urban capitalists, they profited from the high demand for food crops to nourish an expanding urban population. Except for wool and timber they had little to offer as raw materials, unless coal and iron were discovered in the subsoil of their estates. Only the romantics, with their worship of a green nature, denounced the uglification of a once verdant, tranquil countryside where one could hear the birds sing. In their view early industrialists were obtuse materialists. Conversely, the early entrepreneurs were original, pioneering, imaginative, and aggressive. Only the last adjective, however, is pejorative. Most of these men were narrow in their values because they were untutored parvenus.

Early entrepreneurs were self-trained or learned their profession while apprentices in a business. There they acquired the basic methods needed to manage an enterprise, such as bookkeeping, pricing, production methods, capital formation, as well as the moral code for success: self-discipline, an abstemious life-style, use of reason and profitability in decision making, the benevolence of self-interest, and the dangers of feeling guilty about pollution or pity for employees or anyone else including themselves. For many, their model was Mr. Gradgrind, the heartless, logic-driven character in Charles Dickens's novel *Hard Times*. But Gradgrind was a caricature, the stuff of which fiction is made. In contrast there was Robert Owen, a highly successful manufacturer who transformed a factory town, New Lanark, into a pleasant place to live. Probably most entrepreneurs stood in between these two ideal types. They were harsh toward their workers, but harsh toward themselves and their families when starting out and short of capital.

The need for start-up capital was serious in the later 1700s and early 1800s. A textile mill was rather inexpensive to build, but unfortunately there was little cheap capital available during the long belligerency against France when government bonds paying high interest drew most of the surplus wealth to pay for military operations. After 1815 when interest rates fell there was a burst of capital investment in plant, which was followed by another in 1832–36. But well before these periods, budding entrepreneurs used every method to acquire investment funds: borrowing from relatives and friends, pooling their limited resources with a few others to form a partnership, selling shares in large denominations to a few wealthy landowners willing to speculate as sleeping partners, tapping the treasuries of merchant manufacturers—the wholesalers grown rich exploiting cottage spinners and weavers—and, in many cases, plowing most of their profits back into their small enterprises to expand them. This was fixed capital, a long-term demand needed for operations. Their working capital was more readily available from local bankers who saw less risk in these short-term loans. It is now generally recognized that bank loans played a larger role than previously believed in the early phase of industrialization. What is also recognized now is the rather large number of small and medium landowners who shifted into textiles; they literally outgrew the cottage system in which they had begun their industrial careers. The sale of a farm provided start-up capital, and a barn, from which animals were driven, became a shell to house new machines and operators hired from neighboring families. Early mills were not expensive because so many were modest in size and operation. Yet, they housed the most up-to-date mechanical devices that foreigners both envied and feared.

The British government, seeing itself as the embodiment of national interests, hoped to keep these industrial accomplishments for the country's own profit. Until 1825 it was against the law for skilled workers, especially mechanics, to leave the country. It was equally illegal until 1843 to send textile machines to foreign markets. Such prohibitions, like those against alcohol drinking, were impossible to enforce. Thousands of Englishmen and Scots carried their knowledge abroad and spread industrial innovation; when they could not export machines they "exported" themselves and built the devices on foreign soil. The major conduit for both mechanics and equipment was Belgium, as it became the hub from which the industrial revolution radiated south and east, and revealed that the Catholic religion, in this setting, was not an impediment to economic growth. The leading instigator was William Cockerill, a Lancashire carpenter. With his sons he started building cotton textile mills in Belgium, a land occupied by the French in 1799 when they arrived. Eighteen years later his most famous son, John, started a large enterprise in Seraing, near Liège, to construct textile machines, steam engines, and locomotives. From there his business, which included foundries and coal mines, spread to Liège itself and other parts of Europe. From his headquarters he gathered information about markets and new inventions that he transmitted to his other plants. British craftsmen came to work for the Cockerills, and from there many set off to set up their own companies, profiting from skills as yet unknown on the Continent. They built the models that were eventually duplicated by native entrepreneurs.

In France the initiators were mostly small men, former local merchants who shifted from trade to industry, or overseers ambitious and self-taught, coming from the artisanate, borrowing capital from one or more trusting bourgeois. The shift from workshop to factory began very cautiously in the 1830s and acquired revolutionary dimensions only during the 1840s, a decade later in the Rhine Valley and other west German lands. Had the French middle class invested its resources more ambitiously, it could have, perhaps, caught up with the British, for France was the wealthiest nation at the beginning of the nineteenth century. Her population was three times England's, the only country with substantially higher levels of per capita income. But the French people of all classes invested most of their money in land speculation. Also the French banking system bequeathed by Napoleon was a hindrance to industrial expansion and modernization because of its tight credit policies, its restricted issue of banknotes and their excessively high denominations that limited exchange, the simple buying and selling indispensable for economic growth. And the situation was even worse in the provinces where the paucity of specie stifled both industry and commerce. Many British immigrants built highly mechanized textile mills in backward areas, using cheap labor, with the result that their undercapitalized units went bankrupt during the depression of 1829–30 when their markets dried up for lack of credit and cash. Such limited markets were best served by local cottage producers who were able to survive periodic crisis by part-time farming. They turned only slowly to cotton because their chief tissues were wool, and the making of woolen cloth thrived in Languedoc where sheep survived on the thin dry soil. Army contracts kept the industry alive there until the 1870s. Silk also thrived in the region around Nîmes and Lyon where highly skilled artisans labored in shops fulfilling orders for merchant manufacturers. Then the spreading use of Jacquard looms in the suburbs of Lyon raised productivity without other technical changes.

The revolution in cotton textiles in France came in the north on the Belgian border, and also in Normandy and Alsace, where transport was easier in the plain, coal available for steam engines, and British know-how more accessible. Here merchant-manufacturers had begun concentrating spinners and weavers in large buildings before the introduction of power-driven machines, and found it easier to mechanize precisely because of earlier rationalization. They cleverly resorted to new styles of fabric combining a warp of cotton and a weft of wool to turn out *circassiennes*, a material that looked more expensive than plain cotton. Meanwhile Alsace grew famous for its ginghams, cheap to produce and easy to sell. Costs went down when they introduced power looms, thereby widening their markets. Unlike the British manufacturer who sold more than half his cottons to a widespread international market, his French counterpart had to prosper in the national, even regional, market, and could only compensate for his higher costs by charging higher prices. The producer's most serious problem was to induce wholesale buyers with limited resources and near absence of credit to buy his wears for distribution to retailers. He solved the difficulties of distribution and merchandising partly by maintaining good quality and attractive appearance. He also relied on aggressive retailers in direct contact with individualistic and often choosy buyers. But given the expense of manufacturing and transport, the producer needed more lucrative sales outlets.

He was aided by a new middleman, the *marchand de nouveautés*, who retailed all kinds of cheap goods on a fairly large scale. Although only a "five-and-ten" operation, it was more efficient and survived on large turnover at low prices. His emporium was the forerunner of the big department store. On a far lesser scale he was both a purveyor of cloth and of ready-made clothing, catering to the lower bourgeoisie and higher-paid workers. Such markets encouraged the clandestine importation of power looms from Britain until the late 1830s when

British immigrants and then native mechanics began to construct them in the North and around Lyon. But these looms turned out cloth of the plainest sort, middle-grade cottons not attractive to the special tastes of the French. More so than in Britain, fashion markedly influenced the textile industry in France. The whims of fashion were constantly changing and demanding different kinds of cloth. Cotton weavers were more flexible and adapted to new modes. Woolen weavers, however, whether in cottage or workshop, were traditionalistic and reluctant to learn new methods. Since their turnout was difficult to sell, merchants lowered the prices they paid, and in the crisis years, 1827–32, rates fell to eight francs for work of 130 meters, that is, a mere two sous per meter. As William Reddy put it, weavers preferred to beg. Sometimes they resorted to strikes as they did in Languedocian woolen mills. Because they were making woolen cloth for army uniforms, the government could pressure employers to make concessions. But neither begging nor picketing could guarantee the survival of an industry gradually withering in the face of mechanization, a growing preference for cottons, and changing political conditions.

Governments were not neutral observers of the economic vicissitudes of their subjects. Their mercantilist traditions called for an active role in both industry and trade. By 1815, however, both political organization and policies had been shaken to their foundations. Although the restoration in 1815 had placed kings back on their thrones, it had not endowed them with acumen and foresight. They were particularly deficient in the latter because they were, given the context, more eager to recover the past than prepare the future. Traditions, then, strongly influenced the relation between state and economy. For this reason the last Hanovarian sovereigns of Britain were the least active. It was Parliament who safeguarded big agrarian interests with the Corn Laws, because most politicians were part of the landed gentry. But the history of British tariff policy is full of paradoxes, mainly because so many landowners also had interests in manufacturing and commercial activities that thrived on free exchange. Heading the Board of Trade, William Huskisson (1770–1830) understood the needs of businessmen, and although a Tory, he began the dismantling of the remnants of mercantilist policies hindering commerce. Far ahead of his time he believed in a world division of labor, "leaving to every part of the world to raise those productions for which soil and climate are best adapted." In 1820 a petition from the merchants of London revealed that they did not fear foreign competition. What they did fear, rather, was government intervention. British businessmen carried out their industrial modernization with the least governmental involvement and financial aid. Across the Channel, however, the idea and practice of absolutism remained solid, too deeply rooted for rulers to stand aside, indifferent toward the activities of their subjects. In Belgium, France, and Prussia, various official agencies felt called on to act in the state's interest. As it happened, that interest was particularly tied to the improvement of transport as a means of binding together either recently acquired or older but culturally distinct territorial segments of the state: the Rhineland to Brandenburg, and Brittany and Languedoc to Paris. But policies intended to tighten political controls had in the long run a positive influence on transport and metallurgy.

Traditional Transport

Until about the 1820s, textiles were the leading sector of industrial development. But then as cotton mill owners required more machines, they expanded the market for iron. As yet their demands in the aggregate were modest and would fade in comparison to those of transport. Beginning in the late 1700s overland shipment of goods and people by wagons and carriage grew significantly, as did the river and overseas carrying trade. Formerly carriages, barges, and ships were made of wood; that material was perfectly adequate for horse traction and wind power. Merchant companies had amassed great fortunes relying on wooden hulls and square sails in overseas trade, more modest fortunes relying on wagons and canal barges drawn by animals. But these forms of shipping posed serious obstacles to entrepreneurs in need of lower freight costs to reach markets spreading over greater distances. Older means of haulage could stifle a young enterprise in its infancy. To be successful, an economic revolution required not only innovation and dynamism in banking and manufacturing, but also in transport. There was no sense in producing huge quantities of cloth if the bales could not be carried quickly and cheaply to far-flung national and world emporiums.

In Great Britain there was a mutual interaction between manufacturing and transport. Well before cottage industry of wool and cotton gave way to water-driven mills, the volume of imported raw cotton and shipments of finished cloth depended on cheaper means of haulage. There was ample motivation, therefore, for capitalists to use the initiative they had brought to industrial concentration in the effort to modernize transport. Beginning in the mideighteenth century they constructed hard-surface turnpike roads. Their companies, of course, charged a toll; however, because their roads were open all year, they profited from ever increasing use of stage coaches for passengers and wagons for light goods such as raw cotton and cloth. By the turn of the century hard-surface highways had reduced travel time by a third. Less rapid was the carrying of bulky, heavy commodities such as timber, coal, and iron, which were moved in canal and river barges drawn by animals at a walking pace. Whatever its drawbacks, this form of overland traffic made an industrial revolution possible but limited its scope. British textiles also benefited from overseas trade—most of which was carried in British bottoms, at first powered by wind and sail, later by coal and steam. Clearances rose fivefold from just under two million tons in the 1820s to just over ten million in the 1860s.

Continental producers faced more difficult problems. At the time of Napoleon's defeat, France was not the equal of Britain for all-weather roads, but was fairly well endowed with main arteries usable in dry weather. The Restoration government, in the tradition of absolute monarchy, undertook to repair some of the highways ruined by warfare and overuse. Unlike Britain, governments on the Continent were more active in the field of transport. The July Monarchy, more attuned to the needs of business, resorted to France's excellent corps of transport engineers, the *Ponts et Chaussées*, to repair and then to double the mileage of royal roads. The expense would have been enormous had not the regime made use of the *corvée*, a labor system that allowed peasants, unwilling to pay the public works tax in money, to labor three days out of the year on nearby roads. This, however, proved to be a most inefficient method of highway maintenance, especially since peasants carried away many stones from old bridges and buildings with the intention of improving their own houses. Greater progress was made in bridge construction and repair because bridges were especially vulnerable to heavy traffic. The road law of 1836 enhanced the state's contribution to highway maintenance and to such good effect, that it possibly discouraged early railways development. France also had an excellent system of navigable rivers (4,000 miles in 1814) and canals (750 miles). Between 1820 and 1840 an additional 1,600 miles were added to both, an enterprise that encouraged the growth of heavy industry in the North, where transport was easiest. Waterways, however improved, remained closed to traffic when the water froze, as it could in northern winters, or the water level rose too high during floods or fell too low during droughts even for shallow draft barges. As in Britain there was active coastal shipping, but it, too, was dependent on both weather and port facilities. The French could do nothing about the former, but government engineers improved ports and expanded their facilities.

Transport in France made considerable headway without, however, lowering costs or increasing speed significantly before the 1840s. It is doubtful that the less-than-ideal means of transport prevented an industrial revolution from occurring; rather the major hindrance was a lack of venture capital, resulting largely from a middle-class psychology that valued land above industry. The decision of peasants to remain on the land also involved a governmental policy to keep them there, and to protect both agriculture and industry behind high tariff walls. Liberal economists were never able to organize a pressure group comparable to the free trade movement in Britain.

The poor condition of overland transport was a far more serious problem in the German Confederation where political conservatism was a drawback. During the twenty years following the Congress of Vienna, German rulers did little or nothing to aid economic development by compensating for the absence of investment capital, inefficient transport, and low-income markets. Even in the most economically progressive part of Prussia, pioneering industrialists found it hard going to start businesses. Friedrich Harkort created an iron works in the Saar basin during 1819, but found it too costly to haul in iron and coal to build machines and then to ship them to market. He could not compete against lower-priced British imports shipped upstream on the Rhine River. His works foundered; he was ahead of his time for Germany.

Metallurgy and the Transport Revolution

The British determined the tempo of European economic progress, and rounded out the industrial revolution by elevating iron output to a level equal to that of cotton textiles as a leading stimulant of modernization. In doing this they not only discovered that iron was essential for fabricating steam engines and looms, but also that it was the ideal material to modernize transport. Certainly cloth manufacture would have remained a cottage industry far longer without the use of iron steam engines, so much more reliable than water power and a more lucrative investment. Its ever-growing efficiency made possible the complete mechanization of all steps in textiles. Until the midnineteenth century woolen weaving was hardly mechanized and not all the processes of cotton manufacture had been improved by machine application: Harvesting, combing, bleaching, finishing, and printing had to await new inventions adaptable to the new power source.

Steam power enjoyed at least two advantages over water: It did not freeze during winter, nor dry up during summer. Within the general category of power it was the steam engine that became the workhorse of modernization. From about 1800 onward it not only drove spindles and looms, it moved locomotives, river boats, and, finally, ocean-going vessels; additionally, it pumped water from both coal and iron mines. However, the use of steam depended on the cost of machines, and this cost depended on advances in the processes of smelting iron ore and the strength of the finished product.

Fossil coal replaced charcoal in the later eighteenth century at about the time that Britain came close to depleting her usable forests. The next major step in converting coal to industrial use came when Abraham Darby of Coalbrookdale discovered the means of smelting iron ore with coke rather than coal. Then in 1783 Henry Cort patented his smelting process consisting of raking or puddling molten iron to remove impurities, such as sulfur, and then of rolling rather than hammering it to achieve a higher state of strength more cheaply and rapidly. This technique spread through England and Wales where it greatly speeded the process of iron production as the machine-making industries multiplied their demand for a strong metal.

The age of iron, however, began after 1815 with the application of steam to transport. Britain's lead in the production of coal and iron resulted in part from increased demand for both in textiles, from the inventiveness of her technicians and engineers, and from the luck of having coal and iron deposits lying in close proximity, and neither very far from cheap water transport. Once more both geology and geography were on her side.

Man and his use of nature put the steam engine at the center of the industrial revolution. Water power was not abandoned but was steadily replaced by the predictable power of vapor under pressure. James Watt's contribution to improving the engine was considerable, but as with the devices used in textiles, the continued perfecting of engines was the work of numerous technicians. Many of them had acquired their knowledge of precision technology in light industry, chiefly in clock making. George Stephenson, inventor of one of the first practical locomotives, learned much about mechanics by studying clocks. Of equal importance was the lathe, a machine needed to shape objects and bore holes. It was given greater precision by John Wilkinson, who applied the techniques of light industry to heavy to improve methods of boring cannon, and then of boring cylinders for steam engines where inaccuracy had reduced their efficiency. Britain undoubtedly turned out the best mechanical and civil engineers in the world. Not only did they excel as inventors, they improved methods of mining, and tunneling for canals and railroads. Continued progress of industry after 1800 demanded a far greater knowledge of scientific theory and mathematics, and how they could be applied to mechanics. Since traditional universities paid little attention to science and its practical use, training was centered in technical high schools, created oftentimes by associations of industrialists. But inventive abilities were not limited to the educated. George Stephenson was a self-educated genius, a trait that continued into the next generation of the family. His locomotive, the *Rocket*, built in 1829, when added to the *Royal George* of Timothy Hackworth, put an end to horse-drawn wagons for long-distance carrying.

The railroad age began in the 1820s, following that of canals and highways. British rivers, turnpike roads, and canals made an industrial revolution possible. But with the increased reliance on such bulky commodities as coal and iron, further economic advance required even cheaper, faster transport. The railroad came to the rescue. Not only did it lower costs, it attained unheard-of speeds when in the 1830s Stephenson's locomotives attained velocities of 35 or more miles per hour. This was an advance of tremendous import, comparable with the invention of the wheel. Since man had domesticated the horse, he had not been able to travel or haul goods over long distances and for hours on end at more than five or seven miles an hour. Improved steam locomotives ushered in the age of persistent, untiring speed—much to the annoyance of country folk who condemned the noise and soot that spread over their crops. No one paid attention to their complaints or to their fear that when locomotives replaced horses no one would buy their oats.

The early 1840s was a period of frenzied rail laying of strengthened iron tracks to withstand greater speed. Between 1844 and 1846 Parliament authorized 400 new lines, representing the high point of the railway mania. Company shares sold at sky-high premiums as speculation spread. Before long, panic seized the stock market, and there was a collapse of prices and many sorry investors. In compensation there were also nearly 5,000 miles of track in 1848, and the financial setback was short-lived. Britain was well supplied with transport when the great boom years began in the 1850s for the Western world.

What is essential to understand is the continuous interplay among industry, transport, finance, and government policy. Metallurgy was certainly encouraged by conversion from water to steam power, but engines and the metal used in spinning and weaving never offered a very large demand for iron. Railroads, on the contrary, constituted the pull that brought iron and later steel production into the limelight. Locomotives furnished an ever-growing market, and iron tracks formed an even more dynamic demand as they were laid from one end of the country to the other, and eventually from one end of Europe to the other.

On the Continent governments played a far more active role in transportation than they did in the general economy. In Britain, many short lines were built from the 1820s through the 1840s with private investment and ownership. Parliament simply passed laws authorizing company formation and geographical right of way, but did not plan for a national network, nor even standardize track gages. Order was brought into an anarchic condition when large companies bought out smaller ones and consolidated scattered networks into a few sizable ones and profited from the short distances between places of production and places of consumption, as well as from the dense traffic created by industry. In France, distances were greater, and commercially important centers more widely spaced, with population too disbursed to generate dense traffic. Under these conditions investors were less certain of enjoying high profits and hesitant to advance funds. Land seemed a more solid placement, unless, that is, the government would guarantee them an adequate return. From 1832 to 1842 debate on railroads, often acrimonious, continued in the press and the Chamber of Deputies. Progovernment forces wanted to follow the British model. The political opposition, however, wanted the state to build and own the railroads, and manage them in the public interest. They feared the emergence of big capital and the power over society that it would acquire by controlling in its own interest the main source of transport. Whoever controlled railroads would hold industry and agriculture at their mercy. The railroad law of 1842 was a compromise: The government would buy the right-of-way, provide land and roadbeds, dig tunnels, build bridges, and guarantee interests for private investors. These latter would lay track, build stations, purchase rolling stock, and provide capital and management. Finally state engineers laid out a uniform network of trunk lines for all of France. They made Paris its hub with the main lines extending like spokes in all directions, connecting major cities, and continuing to the frontiers of the hexagon-shaped nation.

Railroad building in the German Confederation was hampered by political divisions and rivalries. The first line built in 1835 was hardly more than a convenient connection of eight miles between Nüremberg and Furth. But its financial success led to a building mania in the 1840s when German mileage surpassed that of France. Most construction was carried out by private companies financed with foreign, largely British, capital. In fact, most of the engines and tracks also came from Britain. But the English were not able to preserve this lucrative market, for at last, when barges and river boats were equipped with steam power, the time arrived for German industrialists to take over national needs. Most big machine companies—and Harkort was back with his own—appeared in the Rhineland and near large cities elsewhere. In 1837 August Borsig opened an ironworks in Berlin and put out his first locomotive four years later. By the 1850s native works were equipped to supply the totality of German demand and even to begin exporting.

Rail linkages not only stimulated metallurgy and mining, they also were part of a unifying process that aided the ultimate formation of the German nation. Until then, however, the Prussian monarchy reluctantly entered the economy by laying down rail lines in her eastern agrarian territories where private capital saw little chance of profit. Initiative did not come from the king who complained about the cost of laying track and snapped that it did not make any difference if he arrived in Berlin a few hours earlier or later. Yet, in 1871 when Prussia unified the German territories into an empire, the new state held title to more than half the national network. In contrast, the French government had paid heavily but owned nothing.

Governmental intervention in economic development was more active in central Europe because of the persistence of fully or semifeudal retardants of economic growth. In the West absolutist monarchies had just about cleared away the numerous local dues and tolls that had hindered the movement of goods over long distances, and abolished guilds and their privileges that defended traditional modes of production at the expense of modernity. Commercial codes, copyrights, property rights, and free internal movement were in place by 1800. In the middle of the Continent, in contrast, they were only gradually brought into existence.

German entrepreneurs, like Italian ones, were disadvantaged by tariff walls separating the numerous small political entities that reappeared after the fall of Napoleon. The more restricted the state boundaries were, the more limited the market. The Prussian government was particularly concerned by the separation of its newly acquired Rhenish provinces from its traditional eastern locus; between them stood Hanover and several small principalities. From 1819 to 1834 Prussian bureaucrats worked out a series of tariff treaties with these small entities as well as with larger ones such as Baden, Bavaria, Saxony, and Würtemburg. The culmination was the *Zollverein*, a free-trade union that marked another step toward unification by creating a far larger German market and linked economies among the major states.

Prussia took the lead in the long march toward unity by modernizing its industrial economy, and it accomplished this by following an old tradition of state initiative. In Germany it was widely believed that civil servants devoted to the general interest could manage government-owned enterprise of all sorts. The

French left leaned toward this view but never found the opportunity to practice it since the governing classes, like their British counterparts, vehemently believed in laissez faire. But in Prussia and much of Germany the governing class was the bureaucracy, and Prussian tradition favored state ownership and management as part of royal policy. Absolutists like Frederick the Great had looked on the state as a servant of the military that must create the wealth that a modern professional army required. After his acquisition of Silesia he set up the Seehandlung, a state-owned organization in charge of the sizable array of royal properties and also in control of much foreign trade. By the 1830s the Seehandlung managed numerous nationalized industrial enterprises in Silesia and elsewhere including nearly all the coal and mineral resources, foundries for casting cannon, a workshop to produce gun powder and small arms, textile mills, as well as railroads and ships. Although many of these enterprises were gradually sold to private companies, the Prussian state remained a strong force in the economy and a social force as well. When hand-loom workers were displaced by machines, the state set up cotton mills that employed them at current wages. The British government, faced with the same problem, built poor houses that segregated families by sex and stigmatized poverty. For all of its reactionary politics, the Prussian monarchy attracted able and progressive civil servants. Friedrich von Motz initiated the steps leading to the creation of the *Zollverein* when he became minister of finance in 1825. He overcame the resistance of small states fearful of Prussian domination by building roads benefiting them as well as Prussia. He also concluded a treaty with the Dutch that opened the Rhine to free navigation by ending the transit dues formerly charged at the river's mouth. Peter Beuth, head of the Department of Industry and Trade in the Ministry of Finance, actively disseminated the technical information he gathered during his tours in Britain and France. As head of a technical commission he subsidized textbooks on scientific and technical topics. Christian von Rother, when director of the Seehandlung, built 600 miles of highways, financed railroad companies, and modernized the banking system.

Already present was that strange combination of political conservatism and economic progressivism that would transform Prussia, then Germany, into both a mighty power and a menace to European stability. From a firm defender of the balance of power during the restoration era, Prussia, under the influence of economic growth, became the most dangerous perturber of balance. Of course, production and trade made up only one element in this evolution.

Eastern Europe hardly fits into this chapter save as a convenient contrast. Russia in 1815 was economically a different world, a realm of serf labor both on the land and in the little industry that existed. Servile labor was still dominant in the Ural Mountains where mining and smelting operations were carried out on a large scale since the late 1600s. But primitive transport severely inhibited output, as did the lack of capital and commercial initiative. Nearly all Russian external trade was in the hands of foreign merchants and carried in for-

The trade fairs of former times gave way to industrial exhibitions as manufacturing gained ground. Many of the displays consisted of artistic and artisan creations, but new mechanical inventions fostered the idea of progress among thousands of milling spectators.

eign ships. Already the country was too big to link the peripheral locations of natural resources in the east and south to the location of population in the center and northwest. As noted in chapter one, rivers did not always link produce and markets, and roads were impassable in rainy seasons. In fact, the best time to move people and goods was winter when horse-drawn sleighs traveled over frozen surfaces. Until the end of the century, Russia was frozen, not only in harsh winters, but in the past, and only the warmth of foreign capital and engineering skills let her flow into the modern age.

The Economic Conditions at Midcentury

By the 1840s Great Britain had completed the first phase of economic modernization. As yet her dominant position in textiles, metals, and mining was uncontested. Given that half the population resided and worked in urban centers is ample evidence of the major changes that had occurred. Agriculture was sacrificed to industry, and commerce enjoyed world markets. The British merchant marine, backed by a vast navy, had even before 1815 dominated foreign centers. Her textiles and metal products were the cheapest and her naval gunners the most accurate. The two went together in a time of buccaneering competition. A more tranquil and orderly international market was not created until 1815, when peace became indispensable for manufacturing centers like Britain with a productive capacity far exceeding domestic demand. By the 1840s ocean-going steamships were beginning to out-tonnage sailing vessels. Only the beautiful, slick, and rapid clipper ships could compete with steam, but they, too, like dying swans, lost out by the 1860s. Yet, while they lived they contributed to Britain's sea power. In 1801 British foreign trade had a total value of nearly 67 million pounds. In 1845 it had leapt to 295.8 million.

On the Continent there were pockets of industrial and commercial growth: The Rhine Valley was a center line of their geographical foci, which included Belgian and French Flanders, the Rhineland-Westphalia, Alsace, and parts of Switzerland. Secondary pockets were located in a belt of valleys stretching across Saxony, upper Silesia, and Bohemia. All these were the most technically advanced. Prosperous, although still using traditional technology, were centers near and in Paris, Lyon, Saint-Etienne, Barcelona, Milan, the Danube Valley below and above Vienna, and around Saint Petersburg and in the Urals.

The emergence of these pockets had a marked effect on their surrounding rural territories, both positive and negative. Positive in that many employment opportunities appeared in mills, foundries, and mines. Negative in that cottage industry diminished or disappeared, forcing rural folk to leave home and village, to uproot themselves, and to submit to the harsh discipline and regimentation of capitalistic mills. This transition did not always occur peacefully. Wherever their livelihood was threatened, artisan shop workers rioted, broke machines, and, on occasion, burned factories. But theirs was a hopeless cause.

Not all artisans or home workers felt compelled to resort to violence. For not all segments of production were affected by mechanization and concentration. Woolen and linen textiles were far slower to be modernized. The clothing industry, leather, wood products and forestry, tobacco, wine making, beer brewing, construction, and dock work were among the many activities where traditional processes lived on. Wherever a high degree of skill was called for, as in carriage and furniture making, fine clothing, jewelry, printing, and bookbinding, new processes were generally ignored, even resisted more successfully. At midcentury the Continent from the Atlantic to the Urals was predominantly rural and agrarian. The not-so-fine clothing industry as well as hat and cap making (everybody wore head covering of some sort) created a vast enterprise of seamstresses working alone or in sweat shops for miserable wages. The local smith, like the harness maker and whip maker, continued their trades as individuals or petty craftsmen because the number of draft animals rose, not only for agricultural tasks but also for short haulage to railway depots, rivers, and seaports. Urban transport, in the few cities where it existed, was still horse drawn, and men gathered manure in the streets for sale to farmers. At midcentury only the main railway trunk lines serving large centers were more or less completed; secondary lines to small towns would come much later and those east of the Elbe would come very much later.

The service sector began to grow in response to the urbanization of western Europe. The number of domestic servants steadily increased in cities, accompanied by medical doctors, veterinarians, lawyers, notaries, teachers, entertainers, clerks and general office workers, barbers, and hairdressers. Their numbers added to the general increase and complexity of Europe's population.

7

Society in Transition

Population Explosion

The two generations that lived and worked in the first half of the century laid the foundations of truly modern societies. In 1800 the most progressive state administrations were still closer to 1700 than 1900 in many of their functions, and most people, in their private lives, had witnessed little or no change in the conditions of their housing, diet, work, and entertainment. Not even clothing fashion changed sufficiently to symbolize modernization save that men of the French middle class began wearing long pants rather than knee britches and silk stockings; they also gave up wigs.

What was different was the larger number of people in Europe, despite the high mortality of war. In addition there was a growing desire on the part of governments to count them. As yet, however, practically none of them was equipped to count accurately the number of persons living inside its borders, nor to distinguish them by age groups or sex. The most active bureaucracies had just set up divisions to begin taking census counts, but the results were far from satisfactory. And yet, the movement of population was in a sense the pulse of society. Even before the French Revolution speeded the heart beat of all Europe, demographic changes indicated the beginnings of a new age.

One of the few uncontested generalizations among students of the past is the fact that Europe's population grew at unprecedented rates from about 1750 to 1914. They differ, however, about rates of growth as well as exact numbers. Quite simply there are no exact numbers until about the 1840s when census bureaus had finally put in place the personnel and procedures capable of enumerating the population by head rather than by hearth or family, as in the past; they were also able to provide a good deal more information about males and females including their ages, marital status, family size, birth and death rates, and even their professions. A mounting number of official investigations provide all kinds of data including their wealth or, alas, their lack of it.

The best head counts put the total number of Europeans of all ages at about 140 million in 1750. Half a century later their total rose to 187 million, and by 1850 attained 266 million. On the eve of World War I they had surpassed their parents and grandparents to reach 468 million. That made an increase of 234 percent in less than two centuries. By fifty-year stages, the rate of growth was 34 percent from 1750 to 1800, 43 percent from 1800 to 1850, and 79 percent to 1913. As population became more dense, so did the rate of growth.

The peopling of Europe before 1750 had evolved far more erratically, depending on disease, food, and weather. In bad times deaths exceeded births and totals fell; then as conditions improved surviving couples produced more children as though to make up the losses, and totals rose. Premodern demographic movement was cyclical and varied widely from place to place. In the modernizing phase, population movement took the form of an S-curve, with the sharpest climb occurring roughly between 1800 and 1913, after which came a leveling caused by falling birth rates. Early societies were characterized by high levels of maternity and mortality. Infant deaths were so frequent that couples had to produce many children to be assured that two or three would live to adulthood. That women accepted such a heavy physiological burden was indicative of their conditioning from childhood, and their willingness to suffer the pains and dangers of numerous pregnancies out of duty to family and society. Given the medical conditions of these early decades many women died during or soon after delivery. Undoubtedly many wives would have preferred to limit the size of their families and those of the upper classes often had the knowledge to do so; however, husbands' insistence on having at least one male heir, and the churches' pronouncements against birth control, made it very difficult for women to avoid pregnancy. In a sense women not eager to produce numerous offspring were better off in former times when delayed marriage reduced their years of fertility.

Now we come to the difficult question: What caused the transition from the pattern of cyclical ups and downs, to one of fairly steady and uniquely rapid increase of people? The industrial revolution does not offer a fully satisfactory explanation; in fact, it is possible that population rise was one of the forces causing rapid industrial development. But this was likely only under the conditions that prevailed in the West where arable land was limited and already occupied; expanded population in eastern Europe did not provoke industrial growth there, even though the demographic upsurge in Russia was of an order nearly equal to that of Western industrializing countries. Population patterns were surely related to economic conditions, but the relations were not causal in one direction only; they were very complex, even elusive.

For a long time, it was commonly believed that rising birth rates brought about the demographic revolution; more recently a new generation of demographers has pointed to falling mortality rates. In reality the number of births per couple had usually been high, even with delayed marriage, and this continued until the later nineteenth century. That more babies lived, thereby increasing life expectancy, was the novelty and undoubtedly a prime cause of population growth, but for the numbers to mount ever higher in a short time required the maintenance of the age-old maternity level. There was even a slight increase of births owing to the domestic system of production; it allowed rural couples to marry at a younger age because they no longer had to await the death of a parent to inherit land. Particularly rural laborers were able to augment their income by marrying early. The husband worked the land for a wage, and the wife spun cotton yarn; also, both could weave rough cloth, providing additional earnings for the family.

This development explains why population growth pre-ceded the first cotton mills by a few decades in Britain and by many decades on the Continent. When the mills began to dot the river banks, young workers drawn to them continued to marry early, a proclivity extending the wife's years of fertility. The old virtue of prudence gave way to the delights of procreation. Industry, whether cottage or factory, had some effect on population size but a much greater effect on the locus of population as transport improved.

An equally important factor was the decline of mortality. Improvements in medical science came too late and spread too slowly to have contributed significantly to the survival of infants and young children, not to mention mothers, before midcentury. Inoculation against smallpox was known to be effective since the eighteenth century but was largely practiced by the upper classes. And yet, at all levels of society infant mortality remained dangerously high until advances were made in medical science. It is very likely that improved living conditions generally contributed to the falling death rate. An increase of food supply, especially the gradual spread of the potato, promoted better health and therefore greater resistance to disease. There was also a contrapuntal relation in that the rising demand for food by more hungry bellies encouraged efficiencies in agriculture.

Nature seems to have helped in that average annual temperatures rose just enough to increase the number of plentiful harvests, without, however, fully eliminating the years of shortages, distress, and death. The "little ice age" came to an end by the 1820s. With several notable exceptions extremely cold winters were less frequent, which helped human survival, and drought or excess rain were rarely so widespread that they destroyed food crops everywhere, save in the 1840s. Improved transportation now made it possible to ship grain from areas of plenty to those in need. And when this occurred, more efficient bureaucracies acted quickly to make provisions available to the hungry public. By the 1850s food riots were no longer a menace in the West. The last major famine there resulted from the potato blight of the mid-1840s. Although the blight was widespread, the Irish suffered the most pitifully because potatoes had become their main staple. British relief efforts were unable to save the masses weakened from undernourishment that led either to outright starvation or such physical weakness that about a million died of disease between 1846 and 1851. Given the massive emigration following the famine, Ireland's population declined absolutely, the only country to experience this phenomenon. The last major famines caused by nature rather than by war or revolution swept over Russia and Italy in the early 1890s, but they were mild compared with that of Ireland.

These isolated events remind us that demographic trends, although generally upward, varied in time and place. Perhaps the most notorious aberration among the western industrializing states was France. Most likely the half-generation of warfare from 1792–1815 took its toll on French manpower; some 860,000 men were killed or maimed or simply disappeared, leaving an unbalanced sexual ratio and therefore many women without men to marry. France's birth rate fell from 32.5 per thousand in 1790 to 26.7 in 1850, the lowest among her neighbors. In 1821 there were 30.5 million French people, in 1846 there were 35.4, a less than spectacular rise of 16.2 percent, given that the European average was more than double this figure. A combination of two factors provide a more cogent explanation than war casualties for this lethargic advance: At least three-fourths of the population were farmers, and about half owned land; the Napoleonic code required equal division of property among all heirs including females. Given the land hunger of peasants and their desire to augment the family's holding, a large brood splintered the estate with the death of each family head. So this vast mass of illiterate farmers, most of them Catholic, restricted their fertility, and undoubtedly used the traditional methods of restraint, semi-abstinence combined with *coitus interruptus*. This trend did not abate after 1850 when their population increase was the slowest in Europe, a mere 2.2 percent.

The French model was not unique. Wherever there were large peasant populations owning family farms, and the attraction of the land strong enough to keep them on it, and partible or equal inheritance the norm, population growth was limited. Southern Italy, including Sicily, where few peasants owned sizable farms, was plagued by an excess of rural dwellers. Unlike the French, however, birth rates retained their age-old high levels because mortality rates retained theirs.

Rural overpopulation was usually indicative of the lack of opportunity for redundant farmers, chiefly younger sons and daughters, to move elsewhere, mainly to cities that required their physical strength. Italy had many cities, but they were filled with unemployed immigrants. What made the demographic revolution an integral part of the modernizing process in western and northern Europe was the capacity of nonagricultural economies to absorb the burgeoning population, to give them work and incomes, and successfully to alter the space in which rural newcomers lived by herding them into small territories known as towns, cities, or even neighborhoods. Modernization involved extreme concentration because of intensive growth and lack of room. In the West this crowding was partly relieved by large-scale migration overseas. Eastern population increase was far more extensive in the sense that Russians unattached to an estate were able to spread themselves over vast, nearly uninhabited lands, and were scarcely drawn toward urban centers until later in the century.

Early Urbanization

The nineteenth century was a pivotal one in the long history of cities. The population explosion we noted earlier led to overcrowding in many western rural areas, leaving younger people little choice than to emigrate toward the nearest town. Between 1800–1846 a list of the most densely populated areas indicated the rapidity of urban concentration. Belgium, England, and Wales stood high in the list. Persons per square mile is not a perfect indicator, however, as shown by the extremely high density of Lombardy in north Italy as well as Ireland. Save for Milan and Dublin neither territory became highly urbanized or industrialized; rather, overcrowding on the land was unrelieved by migration because birth rates were so high. These exceptions apart, high densities characterized industrializing states in western Europe and low densities the rural ones of central and eastern Europe where fairly large capital cities stood out from the cultivated fields dotted with villages and small market towns. This was also the Mediterranean pattern where a town thrived chiefly as a main place serving the commercial, administrative, and professional needs of satellite peasant communities. Any industrial activities were carried out by artisans catering to the local market.

The link between industrial and urban growth was early established in England and then in Belgium. The enclosures in England were just about complete by the 1830s, reducing the rural population drastically and ultimately destroying domestic spinning and weaving. The dispossessed sought jobs in early textile mills located along the numerous streams. As mill owners resorted to steam power, however, they relocated near coal fields, and drew with them enough workers to transform hamlets into villages and then into small towns as jobs and population grew. There appeared a wide scattering of settlements in Lancashire, none very big. After 1800 there was also migration into older urban centers such as Manchester where machine building and metallurgy were important, supplying textile mills in surrounding towns. In 1824 only 24 percent of its population were in textiles. Manchester became a focal place profiting from its role of commercial and service center to surrounding towns. Above all, its middle class made available a resource indispensable to entrepreneurs: information about prices, markets, and world conditions. Its rail and road linkage to the port of Liverpool opened European and transatlantic urban markets. It was both a main place serving satellite towns and a link in a network of growing cities over Europe and beyond the seas. As such its size grew exponentially from 90,000 to 303,000 in just fifty years.

Given a more footloose migration toward towns, and particularly toward larger cities, the population of Britain doubled between 1810 and 1851, from 10 million to nearly 21 million. In this latter year, half the population lived in urban centers of more than 5,000 people. This phenomenon, unique in the world, resulted from the near doubling of the people of major industrial and commercial centers as well as significant seaports. Almost every decade after Waterloo cities such as Birmingham, Edinburgh, Glasgow, Manchester, and Sheffield grew with industry and services; Liverpool and Bristol expanded along with foreign trade. London, like most national capitals, more than doubled in size, from 1.2 million to 2.69 million, partly from natural birth rates but also from immigration, much of it from Ireland. It was not a great center of new industry. Rather it was still dependent on persons with special skills in service trades, professionals, and highly qualified artisans serving upper-class tastes in housing, furniture, clothing, and the arts. The British Isles created a model of intense urbanization not followed elsewhere before midcentury, or even before 1914.

On the Continent, urban growth was limited except for capital cities that attracted the educated and skilled to perform the paper work of expanding bureaucracies, and the desperate unskilled to sweep streets, remove garbage, and lift heavy objects. As yet, even in the West, domestic industry prevailed as an adjunct to farming, a combination that kept even the young on the land. The major exception was Belgium where machine works enticed peasants. But not very many because, with the quadrupling of Brussels, farmers could thrive on the land by growing food and raw materials for the future capital after liberation from the Dutch. The diminished economic role of the Dutch was evident in the stability of the city population. Amsterdam required the entire century merely to double its human size. This curve of growth was about as moderate for German North Sea and Baltic ports. There were Rhenish towns that doubled in size, such as Essen, but it rose from merely four to eight thousand. Like other small manufacturing centers its explosion came after midcentury.

France, like her eastern and Mediterranean neighbors, remained a predominantly rural country. In 1851 her farming population stood at 64 percent of the total compared with Britain's 25 percent. These figures refer to persons actively engaged in agriculture or forestry, not to the numerous artisans and retailers inhabiting and serving the large villages and small burgs in which most peasants lived. There was out-migration but in thin lines, not vast waves, even though the countryside was overcrowded. The first to leave were laborers and tenants, usually departing for the nearest town where employers, in an age before machines, wanted their brawn. Most migrants had no skills needed in communities save lifting, carrying, and digging. The result was a slow process of urbanization. From 1810 to 1850 Paris doubled in size, from 547,000 to just over 1,000,000, for the same reasons that London did. None of the textile or metallurgical centers matched this rate: neither Lyon, Lille, nor the port city of Bordeaux. Marseilles did better because of the growing importance of Algeria across the Mediterranean. But Algeria did not attract many continental Frenchmen, a people reluctant to leave their familiar soils for overseas adventures. Because nearby provincial centers offered few opportunities, migrants remained in them briefly before moving on to the next largest. Paris grew by drawing in footloose provincials from a rather broad radius north of the Loire River. Only later did it suction the uprooted from farther afield. But by 1851 it stood far above all other cities in the realm, which added to its power to make and unmake governments.

Population growth in eastern Europe did not lead to high densities. This vast land mass was both chained to the past by serfdom, which bound peasants to large estates, and by the Russian conquest of land north of the Black Sea, a part of the Steppes to which runaway serfs had been fleeing for two or more centuries. Serfs avoided cities because they could not find freedom there; when they ran away they migrated to the South and Southeast along the Volga Valley. In the far north Saint Petersburg doubled in population as an industrial city and major port; Moscow grew more slowly for without the imperial court and its large bureaucracy it had less to offer save the overcrowded tenements, narrow filthy streets, and winters as hard as those on the Baltic. By 1851 Russia's urban population came to only 7.8 percent of the total of roughly sixty-seven million.

Life in Urban Communities

It is difficult to generalize about the conditions of life in human agglomerations where agriculture was not the main activity. There were new towns brought into existence as though by enchantment of marvelous machines. They fell under the administrative control of narrowly elected councils presided over by a mayor, most often elected in Britain, customarily appointed by a minister of interior, or chosen by the local notables on the Continent. There were also old cities whose origins date from the medieval period, or from the Roman conquest. The most prominent of these old centers became the capital cities of royal and princely dynasties seeking to carve out territorially large states. When they were successful they fortified the town, surrounding it with high, thick walls. Only in the nineteenth century did rulers and municipal councils begin the complete demolition of these massive ramparts, leaving space for circular or "ring" boulevards open to an increase of traffic. All they preserved were toll gates at which incoming goods paid a rather expensive entry fee. Before midcentury these ancient cities such as London, Paris, Berlin, Vienna, Milan, and Rome with its rule by priests, were filthy, disease ridden, overcrowded with horse-drawn carts by day, and deserted except for thieves by night.

Old regime municipal administrators who survived the upheavals of revolution and war were not all of a piece. If we limit ourselves to Paris and London, the western neighborhoods inhabited by upper-class families were far more open to air, thanks to broader boulevards, than the eastern ones inhabited by the lower classes including both resident, respectable workers and the "dangerous classes," the term Louis Chevalier used for new immigrants whose personal and public morals left much to be desired. Not all immigrants into old or new towns were necessarily dangerous. Most of them traveled to a town because a relative was already settled there and was ready to help the newcomers find work and to take them in as boarders. Family networks undoubtedly eased the sudden transition from village to town and, as the urban center grew larger, created family and ethnic space within the city for newcomers who generally did not even speak the municipal language, assuming there was one. It is an error to believe that cities were homogenous accumulations; on the contrary there were ethnic neighborhoods just as there were professional streets, such as the street of bakers, watchmakers, butchers, goldsmiths, and so on. Even today one can find traces of these special streets where shop after shop housed artisans of the same craft. In western Europe craft guilds were outlawed as restraints of trade because they fixed wages, hours, quality, and other aspects of production. Yet their traditions survived them, and in Germany they even enjoyed a revival. But they no longer controlled labor conditions or any other conditions of life, least of all municipal governance as they had in the past.

In relatively new and rapidly growing towns it is very likely that living standards of people suffered a decline between roughly 1800 and the 1840s. This is a difficult subject, and there is no universally accepted definitive statement that can be made about it. First of all, it is evident by now that the initial phase of rapid industrialization brought about human suffering as old skills became useless, work discipline grew harsh and life more regimented, hours of work became regulated by clocks rather than by the sun and the seasons, and overcrowding destroyed whatever sense of privacy and human dignity people still possessed. These characteristics occurred in west and central Europe in the early and midnineteenth century, in eastern Europe before and after the Bolshevik revolution of 1917, and are commonplace in Third World countries today.

When trying to understand the conditions of life and the degree of sensitivity felt by Europeans to those conditions, we must try to put aside our own prejudices and accept the past on its own terms. By standards of today, life in even the recent past seems nasty, brutish, and short. Cities like London and Paris before the nineteenth century were divided between the rich, the better off, and the poor. The rich lived upwind to avoid the foul smells that pervaded the neighborhoods of the poor. In between were quarters of mixed classes, the better off inhabiting the lower floors of apartment buildings, the poor relegated to unheated and often unventilated attics and cellars. Streets, save for a few broad, paved boulevards, were muddy, filthy with garbage, narrow, and winding— streets that had been there for centuries. By day they were damp and shadowy because the sun's warmth rarely entered them. In winter they were whipped by frigid winds; in summer they were stifling with airless heat. Rainwater carried off the garbage from high places only to deposit it at low points where it accumulated. The water rose several feet, flooding surrounding buildings and often carrying several cadavers of animals, even of humans, especially of babies abandoned during the night.

As cities grew in size, chiefly through immigration, their denizens inherited all the defects of centuries of indifference by oligarchic magistrates, and both created and compounded their own problems.

Certainly one of the major problems for all urban communities was, first, to bring in sufficient food and drink for the human population and work animals; second was to remove the animal and human excrement that resulted. Even overburdened city councils improved the first so that urban food shortages diminished, and prices tended to decline after 1815 with the end of war-created shortages. The second remained a problem: Only a few main streets in better neighborhoods had underground sewers capable of drawing off discards of all sorts. These large pipes dumped all their gathered filth right into the main waterway, the Thames, or the Seine in the case of London and Paris, the Rhône for Lyon, and Mersey for Manchester. Surface garbage depended either on rain to be swept away or scavenging pigs to devour it. This accumulation also ended in nearby waterways to such an extent that major rivers became part of one vast open sewer. By the 1840s the stench of the Thames was such that politicians sitting in their newly built House of Parliament began to complain of it. Horse manure was too precious to waste so it was shoveled into wagons and sold to nearby farmers. Human waste, before the spread of flush toilets, was emptied into buckets, placed after dark on street corners, and gathered by men who sold it as "night soil" to vegetable gardeners within or just without the city walls. Small wonder that disease was rampant.

City people were a sickly lot. French military doctors regularly found it necessary to reject for physical weakness large numbers of young men from industrial cities while accepting the greater part of country lads. But such a stark differentiation has recently been challenged by scholars arguing that filth and disease were also rampant in rural areas, and farmers' sons were not always healthier than young men raised in cities not highly industrialized. Life in terms of health was far more precarious in urban than in rural habitats. In both, families were crowded into small spaces, but the difference had nothing to do with cleanliness or housing or food supply. The difference resulted more from the greater magnitude of unhealthful conditions, a rapid juxtaposition of ever larger numbers of city people in small spaces. This difference was first experienced in Great Britain because of the rapidity of urban growth. In 1801 there were about 1,500,000 persons living in towns of more than 20,000. Five decades later this total had leapt to 6,300,000 or nearly 1,000,000 each decade. Industrial cities were doubling their inhabitants every ten or twelve years. Many urban problems resulted from the sheer density of people packed within limited room too rapidly.

Before the advent of cheap public transport, most laborers as well as their employers, sought to live near or even in their place of employment. Most merchants inhabited the floors above their shops. Those inhabiting tenements had to walk to factories and workshops; given the insecurity of streets after dark, they desired to reach home quickly after work ended, usually after sundown in winter. Housing was inadequate and expensive. Construction was in the hands of small builders, craftsmen themselves who hired other craftsmen, whose methods were not all modernized and would not be until the late invention of the cement mixer. Under these conditions rents had to be high to provide a decent income to the contractor. More often these structures were rented to middle-class families. Workers found one or two rooms to rent in rundown buildings that were either renovated slightly or jerry-built by speculators out to profit from a greater demand than supply of housing. Most fast-rising towns underwent a building boom of row houses, wall to wall, all the same dull red brick facades, and "back to back," that is, two stories of one room each without back or front yards, with merely a narrow band of land, always piled with junk and garbage, separating one row from the other. Lodging like this took about one-third or more of a factory worker's wage. To cover expenses, families took in a lodger with the result that as many as five or six persons of both sexes lived in one room. Sometimes only a bed was rented, slept in during the day by a worker on the night shift, and during the night by one on the day shift.

Under these conditions disease spread easily and quickly. Dank humid apartments combined with excessive crowding encouraged airborne maladies: Tuberculosis, influenza, and pneumonia were permanently present. Cholera assumed epidemic proportions in the early 1830s and 1840s. Worsening the lack of public hygiene was contaminated water drawn from polluted rivers. There was no running water save in the dwellings of the rich. The worker's wife or able-bodied children had to carry buckets to the nearest well or fountain and haul their contents back. Well water was often contaminated by seepage from the external out-houses provided for apartment dwellers. Since dozens of families used the same facility, the hole filled quickly, was rarely emptied, and the contents seeped into the water table and into wells, as well as into basements inhabited by the poorest of the poor. Small wonder that child mortality was so high that city populations could hardly grow by natural births but relied on immigrants to replace the dead.

The near absence of building codes allowed constructors to erect tenements on all the once-open spaces. What made the new cities so dreary to new-comers from the country was the absence of greenery. Without parks and beset by overcrowded interiors people took to the streets. Such a practice in Mediterranean cities was common; now northern cities became the settings of an active street life. Children played there, indifferent to the piles of garbage into which old people poked their filthy fingers looking for anything of value, even old food. The listless simply stood or sat; women did their spinning or sewing; artisans made wooden objects for sale or fashioned little figurines with a pocket knife. Butchers cut their meat, hung it on hooks, and ignored the swarms of flies that immediately converged on it. Any part of the animal that they could not sell they simply tossed into an open corner where dogs and pigs soon pounced on it. If the lower classes did not take to the streets for air they went to local bars for alcohol, beer in the North, wine in the South, brandy everywhere to help forget the spiritual barrenness of life.

The narrow streets were filled with the grating sounds of hand saws, the whir of spinning wheels, the gossip of women and oftentimes their singing, the verbal arguments of disgruntled men, the cries of children, and, above the din, the shouts of vendors. The wandering sellers of small objects cried their wares: water, cakes, bread, vegetables, firewood, dogs, chocolate, or alcoholic drinks of dubious origin, hats, ribbons—any and everything they could carry on their backs. Women—single, married, or widowed—often made extra money this way when unemployed. The more elderly among them worked full time collecting rags that they sold to paper manufacturers; the use of wood pulp had not yet appeared. Paper was, in consequence, of superior quality but expensive, which influenced the price of reading material from books to newspapers.

Did then the industrial revolution lower standards of living? Left-wing historians see the rise of industrial capitalism as the cause of urban poverty and exploitation of workers. Their right-wing colleagues exculpate capitalism because its spread led to rising standards of living once technological problems, like cheaper pipe for sewer drainage, were solved. A general analysis must recognize that life for the "working poor" and the jobless poor was deplorable in the eighteenth-century city before the rise of capitalist industry. Perhaps the major change lay in the fact that by midnineteenth century poverty was no longer seen as a state of grace, but as a social evil to be ended; economic development, whether capitalist or not, appeared the best way to eliminate it. Unpropitious for the lower classes, there was a time lag between the introduction of new technology in building and sewer construction, and the social benefits derived from it.

Conditions of Labor: Management Level

The "first" industrial revolution occurred in Britain, and it inevitably changed the conditions of labor. Usually the term *labor* refers to the methods of work among men, women, and children who were employed in the early textile factories. The root term, however, has a far broader meaning if we accept it as including both mental as well as physical effort. The number of families that thrived without working was extremely small: in England the high nobility and the wealthiest gentry, on the Continent the far more numerous noble class that inherited titles and land, and employed agents to collect their rents. By no means did the Revolution of 1789 decapitate the aristocracy as a class, or deprive its most hostile members of all their land. In Europe, after 1815 many titled families bemoaned parents and grandparents who had perished either in the Terror or the French invasions that followed. After 1815 the church did not recover its confiscated land wherever French armies settled as an occupation force and revolutionary law was enforced. Its fields and forests had too often fallen into the hands of noble or upper bourgeois families. Conversely, many nobles either never lost their land, because they registered it under another non-noble name during their exile, or repurchased it through an agent when the land was put on the auction block, or by recovery after 1815. In Britain, rulership and wealth were shared between the lords— blue-bloods—and the squirearchy: large estate owners with only the honorific title of "sir" or "gentleman." Their equivalent on the Continent were the numerous petty nobles who lived on their lands and usually oversaw the planting and harvesting of their crops if their heritages were small, or who hired land agents to look after their interests. They and their ladies then spent their time hunting, gambling, eating, drinking and, sometimes, in amorous adventures. This style was that of the court nobility of the eighteenth century, the libertine century. The highest ranks sought to preserve this style: the last Hanovarians, Louis XVIII despite his age and obesity, and Metternich himself, who saw no reason to change, provided one kept up a public facade of religious devotion and decorum.

Values, however, had changed, at least on the surface. The blood-lettings of the Revolution, the wars of Napoleon, had sufficiently shaken nobiliary licentiousness to make way for a new kind of heated-up religiosity. Tsar Alexander and Charles X were the ideal representatives of revived faith in religion as well as in mystical cultism. To them, the revolution and all the horrors that followed were the punishment of God. Their labor, then, consisted of restoring the values of the old regime. It did not involve creating wealth through entrepreneurship, but the recovery of family estates if they had been confiscated and preserving them for succeeding generations, the only means of guaranteeing the purity of noble blood. They labored also at ruling: They filled cabinet posts, managed administrations and bureaucracies, officered the military, and in the West where parliaments existed, exercised their electoral or inherited functions. This essentially landed class also managed their estates, because court life was no longer the wasteful attraction it had once been, nor royal subsidies as generous. Family survival required more efficient farming; in this endeavor enlightened landlords from England to Russia were still the chief supporters of agricultural societies and the most active to experiment with new implements, seeds, and methods of soil culture. A good example of these productive activities was the work of the Accademia dei Georgofili of Florence where gentlemen landowners like Bettino di Ricasoli, who collaborated with Camillo di Cavour of Piedmont to unify Italy, continued the empirical practices that brought about the eighteenth-century agricultural revolution in England. Only after midcentury did professional scientists and state-sponsored agricultural bureaucracies overshadow these learned amateurs in the modernization of husbandry. Of course not all aristocratic families were blessed with hardworking heads. Many were the sons who were more interested in milkmaids than dairy herds. Eventually they turned to the far more expensive pleasures of wine, women, and song after inheriting, and ended by losing the estate, often to a wealthy bourgeois ready to acquire nobiliary acres as a source of social esteem and ascension.

Middle-class families underwent the same ups and downs of fortune. Theirs was the world of business with all its vicissitudes, and the men who brought about the industrial revolution displayed a great variety of talent and temperament. Their existence was precarious; many failed as the result of business recessions, which began to occur with some regularity after 1815. If they had borrowed they went to debtors jail until they or a more affluent relative paid their creditors. Those who succeeded, starting up companies that outlived them, were men of talent, imagination, self-discipline, industriousness, and, in many cases, ruthlessness. They took risks but planned carefully to minimize them. As stern moralists they believed in demanding schedules for themselves, their partners if they had them, their families, and their hired help. They were religious because they were self-righteous, believing God to be on their side. They hardly went along with biblical admonitions against the pursuit of wealth; among the Protestants, as many of them were, they welcomed clergymen who agreed with them. If Catholic, as they were in Belgium, most of France, and the Rhineland, they participated in charitable societies but, like their Protestant counterparts, were cautious if not stingy, lest excessive charity lead to idleness among recipients.

Idleness was the devil's helpmate. Long hours of work, even the forcing of child laborers to clean textile machines on Sunday morning, led not only to profits, but preserved the weak-willed from drunkenness and fornication. Needless to observe they were equally stern with their families. They married women as serious-minded as themselves, hardworking as wives and stern as mothers. They had no use for the frivolous women or the life of lust they associated with the landed nobility. As strong family men, they believed in business as a family enterprise. Therefore they sent their sons to technical schools and took them early into their business where their offspring learned on the job as apprentices. It was not uncommon for them to place a son in another firm to broaden the outlook of an heir who might end up marrying a daughter of his mentor. This was often the destiny of younger sons if they had no inclination toward law, science, or the clergy. The founding generation of what became over time industrial dynasties were often culturally limited, especially if the founder rose from the independent artisan class and had little time for formal schooling beyond the primary level. His main sources of reading were account books and the Bible, perhaps in time some of the financial and technical periodicals that began to appear in the early decades. Successful entrepreneurs needed information about new machines, prices, markets, and much other data to make rational decisions. For, indeed, these men believed in reason and were scornful or ignorant of romanticism. The downfall of manual laborers, they were convinced, was the result of laziness and thoughtless extravagance, like drinking in bars. There was a certain hypocrisy here. Numerous employers paid their workers in bars on Saturday night, and the barman naturally encouraged workers, especially dock workers, to buy drinks. In fact many barmen acted as employment agents and offered jobs only to their most libacious customers. This practice continued until it was abolished by law in Britain later in the century.

Conditions of Labor: Manual Level

Usually the term *labor* is reserved for those who earn money by performing various kinds of physical tasks, from working a loom to digging ditches. In fact, the English language even provides two terms to distinguish two distinct types of work and pay for nonproprietary employment: *salary* for the remuneration of professional personnel, from hired managers to various specialized office workers. The term signifies a certain genteel occupation, clean hands, and white collar. *Wage* refers rather to manual laborers hired on an hourly or daily basis to perform jobs from handling complex machinery (honest work) to sweeping floors and cleaning latrines (nasty and cheap work). There was a hierarchy of employment just as there was a hierarchy of society, and it was easier in the fluidity of these early decades for a foreman to become an entrepreneur than for a dock laborer to marry the foreman's daughter, especially if the foreman was English born and the laborer a poor Irish immigrant, or the former a German and the latter a Pole. The nastiest work was the preserve of half-starving outsiders who more than likely came from a province with an old ethnic identity and that was now ruled by a people of a different ethnic identity.

The wage-earning working class in textiles was in the process of transformation since the late eighteenth century. Linen spinners and weavers were being displaced by the spreading use of cotton cloth. Home workers in woolens would suffer the same fate, but at a slower pace, and those in silk hung on until after midcentury, save the myriad Irish in the east end of London who nearly were put out of business by cheaper European competition. They and the miserable wool weavers of Belgium suffered terribly from declining wages. Many of the early reports on the horrible working and living conditions in industrializing cities described the misery of these poor wretches rather than the standards of factory hands, the people who became known as the proletariat.

Most of the early factories were textile mills. Persons accustomed to the domestic system or those whose skills were put to use in workshops specializing in quality yarn and cloth looked at factories with loathing. They worked hard as a family team, and women lost none of their modesty while spinning at home. Both sexes enjoyed extensive time off inherited from the generous calendar of saint and feast days of medieval Christianity. Well worshipped was Saint Monday, a jocular reference to the Monday that was spent recovering from the carousing of Sunday. Above all, laborers in workshops and home controlled both their time and work schedules. They enjoyed a quasi-independence that they prized highly, that gave them a sense of their individuality, of their human and social worth.

Factories, in contrast, functioned according to rigorous schedules. Employers, seeking a rationalized work day synchronized with water or steam power, demanded that all workers start and end their routines at fixed hours. How could hired hands be paid by the hour if they did not all start and stop at a given hour? Women, although reluctant to abandon the security of domestic labor, which allowed them to combine professional, domestic, and maternal activities, finally found no alternative save the factory. Their entry into large mills was facilitated when employers began hiring entire families to fulfill specific tasks; parents were left in control of their offsprings' functions, such as tying broken thread or assisting to set up looms for turning out specialized cloth such as fustians when they became the mode. Parental discipline could be more forceful, even more brutal, than that of an overseer. Small children, exhausted by long hours, were beaten into wakefulness by mothers or fathers rather than a paid employee.

Under the domestic system hours were long but irregular, and the work day broken by rounds of drink and joking. The factory system was as stern as a teetotaling Baptist. The day began early, six or seven in the morning, with the ringing of a bell or a steam whistle, was interrupted for a meal at midday or thereabouts, and did not end until seven or eight in the evening, with the sounding of a signal. Workdays of fourteen hours, not counting time for a meal, were normal for adults and youngsters. Because cotton fibers required a warm humid atmosphere to preserve strength and flexibility, textile interiors were closed, heated and damp, filled with cotton fluff—a perfect condition to encourage the lung and respiratory maladies that were widespread.

Early factories were environments far less desirable than home or workshop. Filled as they were with rapidly moving machines, their interiors were noisy. No longer could the women sing as they worked, nor gossip as was their custom. Workers of both sexes, the men chiefly in machine-making plants, gradually lost control over the work floor. The foremen, under orders from employers, hastened the pace of operations by accelerating the speed of steam engines. Conversations during work hours, if not drowned by noise, were absolutely forbidden and fines levied against violators. In France, employers enjoyed a special privilege thanks to Napoleon who was determined that foundries turn out the weapons he needed; he issued a law requiring all workers to carry a *livret* or kind of workbook that was taken over by employers who noted in it their opinion of the workers' conduct. Actions considered unproductive—such as complaints about labor conditions—or subversive—such as trying to organize a trade union—were noted in the *livret* and the worker was fired. With such comments, the worker was not likely to find another job in industry. He had no recourse except turning to farm labor where the *livret* was not required. It is not difficult to understand why proletarians were reluctant to organize or to strike. Both activities were outlawed everywhere. Only in Britain were trade unions tolerated by law in 1824, but their right to strike was severely limited the next year after an increase of work stoppages. Elsewhere serious labor protest was left no recourse save revolution.

8

Midcentury Crisis

Forms of Collective Action before 1848

Before midcentury there were numerous outbreaks of collective violence for various reasons. The term *collective violence* means turbulent acts carried out by groups of people, usually to protest against changes or conditions affecting their way of life. Revolts were sizable uprisings by many people; riots were most often local and limited in scale and objective. The so-called Luddite protests that began shortly after the restoration of peace were destructive riots initiated by small textile producers, either artisans or home workers distressed by competition from larger mills able to lower costs and, therefore, prices. Unable to compete and reduced to wages that scarcely kept them and their kin alive, they formed bands to attack the early factories and the mechanical devices housed in them. A good many machines and buildings fell under the blows of iron bars, hammers, and torches. These attacks were generally fairly well planned in advance, but were economically reactionary in goals and doomed to failure. Employers often fled for their lives, or hired armed guards because local police authorities were either nonexistent or friendly to the machine breakers. Shortly after the attack the mills were rebuilt and new, more efficient machines installed, thanks to insurance compensation. Traditional outbursts of anger and desperation continued until midcentury. Food riots were desperate protests against the high prices that adversely affected the lower classes as a result of a poor harvest. It was inevitable that they would break out in 1847, like those in Berlin and Vienna where workers plundered food shops. They were widespread because the lack of adequate transport hindered the movement of food items from areas of plenty to those in want. These kinds of actions were centuries old and would not disappear until economic modernization obviated traditional forms of spontaneous violence by eliminating their cause. Antifiscal riots were of the same character, acts of rage by poor populations resisting the modernizing state with its need of funds to pay its expanding bureaucracy, its professional army, and its territorial ambitions. On the whole, this type of unorganized, spontaneous protest was not successful; the absolutist states had become too powerful to be resisted by such crude tactics.

The successes of the English revolution in the 1640s and the French in the 1790s are indicators of new trends of collective violence: action based on organization, discipline, and planning. When occasions were propitious, as in France in 1830, members of the society, Help Yourself and God Will Help You, instigated the revolution of that year. But effective or secret organization and even considerable discipline among members were often not more successful when rulers acted to defend themselves. Two organizations in France, the Friends of the People, and then the Society for the Rights of Man, each with a sizable following, led violent insurrections against Louis-Philippe in both Paris and Lyon in 1831, 1833, and 1834, none of which succeeded. The latter two were put down with considerable bloodshed, even downright massacre in 1833. Failure dogged the *Carbonari* and their actions to unify Italy, the Chartists in Britain, and, finally, the various youth movements like Young Italy, initiated by Joseph Mazzini. Other youth movements attracted mainly frustrated exiles. All of these existed underground because repressive legislation prevented democratic opposition groups from organizing openly. Moreover it was extremely difficult to control and maneuver clandestine bands; they were infiltrated by police spies and their leaders often arrested, leaving the scattered followers powerless. Yet, the fact that persons with grievances—whether political, social, or economic—recognized that success depended on organization and rational leadership were signs of a modernizing tendency.

The model for nonrevolutionaries became the Anti-Corn Law League and its ability to call up the urban masses to pressure politicians for a particular objective. This was possible only in Britain where large demonstrations were permitted. Continental governments forbade meetings of more than a handful of persons, and sent the army to deal with street demonstrations. When monarchs lost their thrones it was usually because they lost the will to resist or had no advisers or generals capable and willing to crush insurgency.

Changing of Revolutionary Goals

The crisis of the midnineteenth century came two hundred years after that of the midseventeenth century, and reveals the extent of social and economic change over time. In the 1640s revolts broke out in England, France, Scandinavia, Russia, and southern Italy. The common goal, although not always clearly expressed, was to check the aggrandizement of royal power within the confines of dynastic states. The leaders were powerful noble families that were losing much of the local control and autonomy that they had once enjoyed. Save in England they were not successful, and there it took a second revolt to limit the Crown's power. Elsewhere threatened monarchs both crushed the rebellious nobles, and granted their lands to more obedient servitors. In the end, the upper nobility was domesticated, if not to say housebroken. The lower aristocracy and gentry were left in control of their landed estates and continued to enjoy extensive if not full rulership over their peasant tenants and hired labor.

The middle decades of the nineteenth century witnessed a similar revolutionary crisis. This time, however, the adversaries were, on the one hand, powerful monarchs supported by most of the aristocracy, and, on the other hand, a rising middle class that sought to limit royal power and participate more actively in the management of the state. Just as the nobles and gentry received support from urban people in the 1640s, the bourgeois received more active support from urban wage workers suffering from a serious economic depression, support that professionals at first recruited but then found too active—indeed. a menace to their own property and prerogatives.

Over two centuries of time the class structure of Europe, as already explained in chapter seven, had undergone significant modification. A once weak and subservient middle class that had generally supported the growth of royal and princely power to make society safe for business, now found that absolutism based on aristocratic privilege was more a hindrance than a help to their interests.

Now it is important to bear in mind that the 1848 revolutions were not conflicts between reactionary and revolutionary classes. Not all nobles were opposed to modernizing reforms, nor all bourgeois opposed to strong rule by crowned heads. The same is true of numerous artisans who were master craftsmen; in the two most industrialized countries, Britain and Belgium, the huge mass of male factory workers did not build barricades. At most, the Chartist movement breathed its last in a nearly moribund demonstration and then ceased to exist. The great mass of peasants were, with few exceptions, either quiescent, indifferent, or hostile to urban troublemakers. The upheavals of midcentury were primarily urban and broke out initially in a few capital cities on the Continent.

The Revolutionary Impulse in Latin Europe

The first revolution of the year occurred in Palermo in western Sicily, the island half of the Kingdom of the Two Sicilies. The outbreak had widespread support, but its leaders were feudal-minded nobles, owners of vast estates who called for a Sicily independent of Naples, the capital of King Ferdinand II. He had begun his reign in 1830 as a mildly liberal man, but had become increasingly close to Metternich, and over the 1840s assumed the mantle of absolutist. There remained a streak of enlightenment in his ideals; his plans for Sicily, as for the mainland, called for railroads, economic encouragement, and centralized rule from Naples. His accomplishments, however, were minimal; his bureaucracy was imperious toward local notabilities and very costly. The Sicilian nobles, in contrast, could not lay claim to enlightenment, even to the pretense of it. They simply wanted for themselves the power emanating from the capital, and the taxes that were sent there. The lower classes that had joined the revolution in the eastern cities as well as Palermo, wanted an end to the hated grist or flour tax that raised their cost of living. The peasants, tenants of the landed aristocracy and gentry, were no longer serfs, but they were still held to the land and labor by debts they could never extinguish. And local leaders had no intention of relieving their condition. This was hardly a model revolution. In fact, once the neapolitan imperium was removed the natives found themselves subject to gangs of bandits (the *banditti*) who terrorized both urban and rural subjects unless paid off. Much of western Sicily fell into a state of anarchy. Nonetheless the revolt did provoke the liberals of Naples to threaten Ferdinand with similar action, whereupon he promised his subjects a constitution based on that of the July Monarchy of France. The grand duke of Tuscany followed his example several weeks later. As it turned out, however, these constitutions were stillborn, never really put into effect. The Italians were seeking what the French liberals were on the point of repudiating.

It was not Palermo but Paris that ignited the 1848 crisis. The lower classes in France, as everywhere, suffered severely from the bad harvest that had begun in 1845 and, added to the rotted potato crops, continued into the next year. Food prices shot up because of shortages. Urban workers not only had to pay more than half their wages to feed their families, many of them became jobless when an industrial crisis followed the agrarian. Because peasants could no longer buy industrial products, employers simply dismissed vast numbers of shop and factory laborers. The number of men and women out of work, large enough among Parisians, was augmented when small-town workers made their way to the capital in search of jobs or charity. Conditions began to improve in 1847 but readjustment required time. Although this was the last farm crisis to provoke an industrial depression, it had repercussions beyond the economic sphere. The jobless, both native and immigrant, formed the huge contingents of street fighters who built and manned the barricades.

This human suffering was not the primary cause of the revolt that occurred in late February; it simply made a truly violent outbreak a possibility. Workers were the kindling to which a lighted match had to be applied. And it was well-fed politicians who took that fatal step. The "dynastic opposition," although loyal to the crown, was out of power and saw no hope of capturing the ministry save through a broadening of the franchise and parliamentary reform to prohibit deputies from holding jobs in the royal bureaucracy. Because every bill brought forward to reform the system was defeated, largely with the adverse votes of "deputy-bureaucrats," the opposition resorted to gastronomic demonstrations. In July 1847 they began holding a series of banquets as a palatable form of protest, but according to Gustave Flaubert, the food was indigestible and the speeches endless. These moderates, charging ten francs per meal—about four times a worker's daily wage if he were working—feasted and toasted their reform proposals with local wines. Their main goal was roughly a doubling of the electorate by lowering property requirements. Although influenced by the tactics of the Anti-Corn Law League of Britain, they had no intention of arousing the urban masses whom they did not even want to enfranchise.

Before long, middle-class radicals in the Jacobin tradition took up the idea, organized banquets at two francs a plate, and paid this sum for a few of the workers who were known to them. Here banqueters toasted, not the king and not a limited reform; they drank to the republic and universal male suffrage. These were the goals they also extolled in their newspapers, *Le National*, and *La Réforme*, which leaned somewhat toward social as well as political democracy. The more determined members of the liberal opposition finally agreed to collaborate with radical deputies to hold one last banquet on February 22, 1848 and to locate it in Paris, the other banquets having taken place in provincial cities.

At the last minute Guizot forbade both the banquet and the protest march planned before its beginning. Large crowds gathered to witness the march and when they learned of the refusal they became incensed. Without visible leadership workers and Jacobin bourgeois began building barricades. The next evening a cortege moving along the Boulevard des Capucines and threatening Guizot was scattered by a deadly volley from troops, and soon more barricades went up and a full-scale revolution began. Louis-Philippe certainly had sufficient army units to recover the insurrectionary eastern quarters. Yet he grew discouraged when battalions of the National Guard sided with the revolutionaries, abdicated, and, like Guizot, fled to England.

On February 24, 1848 a rump meeting of reform deputies chose members of a provisional government that immediately departed for City Hall when a mob of angry workers and petty bourgeois invaded their Chamber. City Hall had been taken over, as had become customary, by armed insurgents who demanded a republic. To placate them the deputies, more or less guided by Alphonse de Lamartine, Alexandre Ledru-Rollin, and François Arago, accepted into their council the socialist Louis Blanc—made popular by his book,

Alphonse de Lamartine was the romantic poet who briefly won European fame in 1848. He is a good example of the moderate statesman who was unable to exercise effective power in a time of troubles, excited crowds, and frightened property owners.

Organization of Labor—and an artisan, Alexandre Martin, popularly called Albert. With this task completed, the violent phase of the revolution was over, at least for a while.

This makeshift and disparate group functioned as a provisional government. Its majority consisted of moderate republicans who, uncomfortable with Jacobins and socialists, considered their main function to be the preparation of elections for a constituent assembly, and as quickly as possible. They had represented provincial constituencies and feared the Parisian crowds. Ledru-Rollin as interior minister replaced the Orleanist prefects with his own men, his "missionaries," who were to win male voters over to republican candidates. On the left were Blanc and Albert. They received no ministerial posts; Blanc's request for a ministry of labor was rejected. Rather they were shunted over to the Luxembourg palace to set up a kind of workers' assembly for studying the problems of labor. As one cynic put it, they were sent off to tell the poor that they were poor. This Luxembourg Commission, as an assembly of labor delegates, was without a budget and could do little more than debate, listen to lectures, and select candidates for the coming elections. Meanwhile workers and middle-class republicans, both in the capital and provincial towns, were actively creating political clubs where meetings were called periodically so that improvised orators could enlighten urban men on a broad variety of topics. In Paris most of them became part of a supreme advisory body known as the Club of Clubs. It collaborated with the Luxembourg preparing for a decisive electoral battle. One of the great errors of these inexperienced men was to choose as candidates too many workers hardly known even among the laboring class.

The provisional government faced several serious problems. Almost immediately after it met, a large turnout of laborers forcefully entered its meeting room, pounded rifle butts on the floor, and demanded both jobs and the right to work as a law. In reply the ministers created a public works project called the National Workshops. Put under the direction of an antisocialist it paid its workers two francs a day, and set them to planting liberty trees, removing barricades by replacing the street paving stones torn up to build them and, when these tasks were completed, to digging holes during the morning and filling them during the afternoon. As costs grew the ministry levied an additional land tax of forty-five centimes, which bore heavily on the peasants. They in turn resorted to France's last antifiscal riots, requiring thousands of troops to restore order. Undoubtedly this move alienated much of the rural population, and Paris, always suspect, was more than ever the enemy. Oddly enough these same rural disturbances frightened the provincial notables who decided to support the new regime as a safeguard against both peasant anarchy in the country and renewed violence in the capital.

The ministry was like a fragile ship in the turbulence of Paris. On two occasions, in March and April, huge demonstrations gathered menacingly before it with demands. One called for substituting the red flag for the tricolor as the national symbol. Lamartine, romantic poet recently turned republican, proclaimed in his golden voice that the red flag had triumphed only in the streets of Paris, the tricolor in every capital of Europe. Such exalted patriotism sent the crowd home shouting *vive Lamartine* and *vive la patrie*. More serious was the second demonstration, this time to demand the postponement of elections.

To republicans, postponement seemed necessary for the simple reason that most of the rural population did not even know the word "republic," and if they did, they associated it with the republic of 1793 and the Terror. As Flaubert wrote in his novel *Education sentimentale*, "the specter of 93 reappeared, and the blade of the guillotine vibrated in all the syllables of the word Republic." For the Parisian left, these country bumpkins had to be taught the virtues of government by the people. For centuries peasant life had been dominated by parish priests. Although they were critical of Orleanist anticlericalism, they were equally fearful of its republican brand. On the surface they seemed to have accepted the liberal Catholicism that even the new pope, Pius IX, embraced for a while, but they were basically conservative. Blanc expressed well the apprehension of republicans: "the people of the countryside are submissive to the ascendancy of the rich by their needs and to that of the clergy by their ignorance." Finally, elections were postponed until April 23, and on that Sunday manhood suffrage on a national scale was exercised for the first time in Europe. Nine million men over twenty-one years old were entitled to go to the polls. Only a quarter of them lived in urban centers. Most were illiterate, yet 84 percent turned out, many led to the ballot box by the local priest or landlord. The provinces turned massively to local notables. There were 876 seats to fill, and most of the victors were men of wealth and property, many having served in previous regimes. Most, however, were first-time officials, including the mere eighty-five radicals and socialists whose political careers were to be very short. Political titles often meant little because many monarchists running in unsure circumscriptions called themselves republicans, especially in large cities. As it turned out the contest was not primarily between town and country. Only a few truly radical candidates won in Paris; the list of worker candidates presented by the Luxembourg Commission was a drastic failure. Regional differences were more important: The West and much of the North voted conservative; the East and the South voted republican and often radical. The central districts were largely conservative with pockets of voters opting for "les rouges," the reds, as left republicans were called.

Despite its large delegation of men of property, the Constituent Assembly drew up a constitution that proclaimed France to be a republic, enjoying universal adult male suffrage, governed by a unicameral legislature and a president, both to be chosen directly by all men. Astonishing was the law granting a salary of twenty-five francs to deputies. In Britain members of Parliament received no stipend.

Having lost at the ballot box the extreme left was prepared and even determined to win in the streets. Its leaders were a new phenomenon—professional revolutionaries who spent all their time organizing secret societies and laying plans for insurgency. Such was Auguste Blanqui. During the course of a long career he spent about half his life in prison because he was not a particularly successful revolutionary. Unlike most early socialists, he did not believe that a revolt involving great numbers of people could succeed. Rather he organized secret groups divided into cells, or what he called "weeks" and "months"—hence, the name of one of his creations, the Society of Seasons. Well armed, highly disciplined, and fully committed, members were limited in number and sought not to win over the masses but to capture the real source of power, the state, and that by a *coup de main*. He looked on the likes of Louis Blanc as traitors who sold out to the moderate republicans. He was active in the May 15 invasion of the assembly when he announced that it was disbanded and then took off for the City Hall to set up a kind of dictatorship of the proletariat. There he and his conspirators were arrested, and thrown back into the prison from which the February revolutionaries had rescued them. He had tried a *coup de main* in 1839, with the same results. But the May 15 insurgency had far greater results: It provided conservatives a reason to jail as many radical leaders as possible.

Part of the reactionary impulse was perhaps deliberately planned as a means of eliminating the left-wing menace once and for all. That menace was most visible in the National Workshops. The Executive Committee of the Constituent Assembly, after the May 15 invasion of the Assembly's chamber, decided to abolish it, especially because several thousand of its workers had taken part in the coup. That step so aroused the laborers that in late June they resorted once more to the barricades. Only this time the army under General Eugene Cavaignac and National Guard regiments from the more affluent west end of Paris, met the insurgents head on with artillery. At least 1500 workers were killed, another twelve thousand were arrested and either jailed or sent to labor camps in Algeria. The June Days marked the end of the social aspects of the revolution, and the Second Republic that came into being when a new constitution was completed late in the year was not destined to be long-lived either.

The course of the revolution in France incited upheavals elsewhere, but then nearly ceased to be of great consequence beyond her frontiers. Lamartine, the foreign minister, informed Europe's rulers that his country, although it repudiated the 1815 Treaty of Vienna, had no ambition either to conquer territory or topple crowns. The days of romantic crusades were over.

Revolution in Central Europe: Hapsburg Empire

The upheavals in central Europe were ignited by Paris, but at once assumed a different character. Austria, and Vienna in particular, emerged as the main focus of power: Since 1815, whoever controlled the Hapsburg seat of government controlled central Europe and from there influenced the Continent east and west. This ancient dynasty had assumed a leading role in the German Confederation despite its failure to prevent southern states from joining Prussia's *Zollverein*. Within its imperial frontiers it combined Germans, Hungarians, Slavs, and Italians. It dominated them by playing one ethnic group off against another: Slavs against Hungarians, or Czechs against Slovakians. It was not above using class war: When the Polish gentry in Galicia rose in revolt in 1846, the Austrians incited Polish peasants against them, resulting in the massacre of 2,000 gentry. These serfs expected their emancipation to come from Vienna, and it did but not until 1848–49. A monarchy centuries old was not in a hurry.

Ruling such a motley empire was made easier by two factors: The ruling classes in critical parts of the Empire believed that Austria was a needed center of power to safeguard their privileges, and also it was needed to preserve a balance so that no one nationality threatened the others. It was even said by a Czech that if Austria did not exist, it would be necessary to create her. Equally important was the weakness of national feeling among the illiterate population.

Whatever nationalism there was stirred urban students and professionals, and they were too few and weak to initiate viable movements for ethnic independence.

Just as the demonstration in Paris to remove Guizot led to a violent uprising, so in Vienna the revolution can be said to have been directed against Chancellor Metternich in its initial stage. Even before 1848 there was a conspiracy against him in the highest circles of the imperial court. But events moved rapidly when news of events in Paris reached Vienna on February 29. As yet the liberals were without a clear-cut program except the removal of the chancellor and the recognition of civil liberties. When the Diet of Lower Austria met on March 13 many liberal bourgeois and radical students, some five thousand strong, sent petitions to express their limited goals. As in Paris, a well-dressed and well-behaved crowd gathered on the main square. They were soon joined by an assembly of workers led by students from the industrial suburbs. Now the government sent troops to clear the area, and because they were greeted with sticks and stones (which could indeed break bones) the soldiers let go a volley. This event, although on a smaller scale, was like the massacre of the Boulevard des Capucines in Paris. The dead were carried about the city, and then the barricades went up. But the Austrian troops, consisting largely of Slavic Croatians, succeeded in an attack on the barricades. At this point, late in the day, the emperor dismissed Metternich and accepted a truce. All became quiet within Vienna's walls.

Beyond those walls, however, a different kind of group action was occurring, indicating that, as in Paris, there were two insurrections. Within the walls the liberals wanted a reformed imperial regime, and, as men of property, might use workers to carry out the street fighting but feared them as a menace to order and property. In the *extra muros* suburbs where both artisans and factory hands lived in squalor and poverty, the population resorted to traditional and archaic types of protest: attacks on food shops, tax bureaus, and factories and machines. Political goals were not at all clear in their minds.

On the fifteenth, students led by a young medical doctor, Adolf Fischhof, who was familiar with the workers' poverty, reoccupied the main square and called for a constitution. After the emperor promised to summon a constitutional assembly, the crowd dispersed. This was not much of a victory; it left the students and workers without any real control over the government save a kind of committee of public safety under Fischhof, who was no Robespierre. However, the true source of decision making lay in the imperial court, the bureaucracy, and finally, the army. Indeed, it would be Field Marshal Alfred Windischgrätz who would save the monarchy.

The first step toward recovery occurred on March 20 when a preliminary decree abolished forced labor (the *Robot*) and all other manorial obligations. The government would compensate landlords for lost labor and then tax the peasants up to an amount not specified to recover its disbursement. Peasants, as was usual, having attained their immediate goal, now lost interest in the revolution. That they should continue supporting constitutional reform was beyond their understanding. An important source of strength was thus lost to the students and workers.

The greatest threat to the Empire came less from Vienna than from its non-Germanic holdings. The Sicilian uprising of January 12 threatened the Bourbon dynasty that Austrian troops had restored in 1820. The Hapsburgs loomed like a watchful shadow over all of the peninsula, but ruled directly only Lombardy and Venetia. Foreign rule had aroused a higher degree of national sentiment that cut across all classes of the native populace. Even the rebellious Sicilians wanted to sever ties with Naples in order freely to join a confederation of mainland states and create an Italian nation. But it was the north Italians who took the initiative to drive out the German-speaking conquerors, the impediment to union. When news of Metternich's dismissal reached the main cities of Italy there were shouts of joy and celebration. Then came a series of insurrections. In Venice the move for freedom was led by Daniele Manin on March 17–18 and Austrians were expelled a few days later. Manin then assumed the presidency of a provisional republic for he wanted to tie his action to the past when Venice had been an republic, albeit an oligarchic one. The glory and much of the wealth of Venice was also gone with the past and in Manin's view its future looked promising only if it joined an Italian nation.

The Milanese of all classes were far more vigorous in their effort to oust the Austrians. In January they had launched a boycott of the Austrian tobacco monopoly, which led to brutal violence by occupying troops. Anger built up until March 18 when news of the Vienna revolt arrived. A demonstration turned into an uprising that drove the troops from the central city. Hastily liberals and radicals formed a coalition government under Carlo Cattaneo. In this situation Marshall Joseph Radetzky chose withdrawal into the four fortresses in Venetia known as the Quadrilateral, there to await events. One event was the decision of Charles Albert, king of Piedmont, to declare war on the Hapsburg Empire. Although his dynasty had also been saved by Metternich in 1820, he had recently granted a constitution to placate his liberal critics. His goal did not include a united Italy but a northern kingdom wrenched from the Austrians.

Had he tried to expand his kingdom south of the Po Valley he would have encountered Tuscany whose grand duke had recently promised a constitution to his subjects. An even greater obstacle would have been the Papal States stretching laterally across the middle of the peninsula. Pius IX had also granted his subjects a constitution, but he would not, and could not, become a sovereign who "reigns but does not rule." The pope was not only a head of state but also the revered leader of all Catholics throughout the world including Austrians. He could be neither a true liberal nor an Italian nationalist.

A far more serious revolt broke out in Hungary where the gentry were led by Louis Kossuth, a fiery, patriotic liberal who managed to induce the landowners to give up their manorial rights to win the Magyar peasants to their cause. Magyar nationalism had been growing for several decades, nurtured by the Diet, and numerous intellectuals who created a mythical past focused on the Kingdom of Saint Stephen when Hungary had been a free nation with its own language and culture. Self-centered as they were, the Hungarians wanted freedom for themselves, but opposed it for the many thousand Slavs living within their borders.

Finally the Czechs in Bohemia wanted a grant of autonomy. They were not opposed to the imperial regime so long as it did not try to Germanize them. They preferred self-governance within the multinational empire as a means of preventing their total absorption into a unified Germany. When the bourgeois of Prague came to believe that the Hapsburgs were unwilling to accept their demands, they, too, rose in revolt and took over the city. But unlike the Italians and the Hungarians, where all classes stood united, at least during the struggle, the Bohemian aristocracy was German and encouraged the imperial army to put down the Czech rebels, which it did.

Central Europe: Germany

News of events in France spread rapidly among the villagers of western and southern Germany. The subsistence crisis had adversely affected them, and they resorted to rioting in late February. Their grievances were directed against the landed aristocracy that extracted money, fees and labor services from them, and against the local Jews to whom they owed money. In Baden, Württemberg, and Hesse-Darmstadt, where conservative constitutional governments already existed, there was an excess of rural population, and tenant holdings barely supported a large family. Maddened by hunger because of crop failures, the villagers attacked landlords and their agents and burned the records of their debts and obligations. None of this had political overtones, save that some pamphlets were passed about calling for abolition of the noble class and rule by an elected president. "Then the taxes will immediately fall away, like rotten apples off a tree," proclaimed an anonymous pampleteer.

Although these *Jacqueries*, a common term for peasant revolts, were isolated from urban middle-class and worker concerns, the rulers of southern states formed liberal ministries in early March. In Bavaria, King Ludwig was widely condemned but not for incompetence. Under the spell of a dancer, Lola Montez, he flouted her too openly. When the bishop urged him to banish her, he is said to have replied, "the bishop has his stola, I want to keep my Lola." He was shortly forced to abdicate, the only ruler in all central Europe to lose his crown and for reasons entirely irrelevant to politics.

When peasant rioting spread north, rulers there also appointed liberal ministers, and even sent liberals to represent them in the federal Bundestag.

Mass demonstrations in capital cities rather than bloody revolutions sufficed to bring these changes—or at least promises of reform.

Prussia was the exception. Berlin's economy had not yet begun to improve. When the Borsig works fired four hundred workers who now joined a mass of jobless, unrest increased, and on March 15 a motley crowd demonstrated before the royal palace. As was almost inevitable, a few shots rang out, infuriating the crowd, and barricades went up as by magic. The large reinforced garrison dealt with these summarily. On March 16, however, news of insurrectionary events in Vienna reached the Prussian capital, raising the fervor of people from all classes. Beer halls near the Brandenberg gate had become centers of lively political discussions and the sources of every sort of rumor. On March 18 the municipal council called for the dismissal of the ministry it believed responsible for the brutality used by soldiers against Berliners. The king, after promising to end censorship, gave orders to clear the crowds gathered around the royal palace. As the soldiery began to push people with their accustomed brutality, two shots were fired. Cries of treason rose above the din, and more barricades went up, leading to eight hours of grim fighting.

Frederick William became despondent. In his mind he was both ruler and father of his subjects. The next day he issued a proclamation to his "dear Berliners," offering them forgiveness and withdrawal of troops. Far more soldiers departed than he intended, and he was helplessly forced to view a macabre parade of his "dear Berliners" carrying their dead, wounds exposed, and pay his respects to those killed on the barricades. Further, he now promised a constitution and called on Ludolf Camphausen, a Rhenish businessman and liberal, to form a ministry. But he was no more suited to the role of constitutional monarch than was Louis-Philippe in France. He continued to issue orders to his administrators without consulting the new ministers, and, more important, he retained absolute control of the military. The army had fought for him, but it had not "saved" him, because he was never in danger. The crowds gathered before the royal palace were not republican; they merely wanted reform and the king to initiate freer rule and lead the march toward a united Germany. The crown itself could hardly be saved when its existence was never seriously threatened. Camphausen's liberal cabinet was not a beginning, only an interlude. So was the constituent assembly that convened in Frankfurt on May 18. By this date the so-called "springtime of peoples" was about to give way to the summer and autumn of reaction.

Waning of the French Republic

While the Frankfurt delegates formed committees and orated, the forces of order steadily acted to recover their dissipated powers. Just as France had opened the liberal revolutionary era, she was in the forefront of the recovery of power by the forces of order. The new constitution provided for the direct, popular election of a president. Perhaps its framers had in mind General Cavaignac, almost dictator after he effectively crushed the workers' revolt of June. In the December elections, however, Cavaignac, like Ledru-Rollin, ran far behind an unknown, Louis-Napoleon Bonaparte, nephew of the celebrated emperor. His was the only name that had stirred the peasants, and they voted for him in masses. In the May 1849 elections to a Legislative Assembly, there was a resurgence of the left, and especially of the Jacobin left, whose members won a third of the seats. Since the moderate liberal middle was badly defeated as voters chose either monarchists or radicals, the defenders of order felt particularly triumphant. So did Catholic churchmen.

The church was deeply involved in this gradual weakening of the democratic features of the Republic. To profit from the resurgence of religious faith in a time of troubles, Louis-Napoleon sent a military expedition to Rome to crush a rebellion there. The recently elected Jacobins condemned him for violating the constitution and tried to stir up popular opposition in Paris. But since the June Days of the previous year the lower classes were both weak in numbers and discouraged. Led by Ledru-Rollin the uprising was easily suppressed and its leaders imprisoned or exiled. The result was serious; there was to be no democratic left worth noting for nearly a generation. In 1850 the monarchist majority induced the president to sign two bills, which he did reluctantly. The first restricted the suffrage by means of residence requirements, thereby depriving one third of the workers of the vote. The second, the Falloux Law, gave the church the right to operate secondary schools in competition with those of the state, and it increased church supervision of state elementary schools. Clearly anticlericalism was out of fashion; Orleanists made their *mea culpa*. The liberal Catholicism that had made headway in the 1840s was also outmoded.

Most probably Louis-Napoleon went along with this current because he wanted the assembly to revise the constitution and allow him to run for a second term. The legislators accepted a president but wanted no dictator and their fears of Louis-Napoleon grew. In turn he gave way to advisers urging that old and tried Bonapartist tactic, a coup d'état. He was fortunate in that the army officer corps, although neutral in politics during four decades, disliked the Republic and backed the seizure of power on December 2, 1851. The only physical resistance came from established left-wing districts in the south and east, and center. These were small-town and rural areas, rather heavily given over to wine growing, that provided more than 100,000 men to resist the illegal confiscation of power, the largest uprising outside of Paris in the nineteenth century. Paris, exhausted, remained quiescent. Those unfortunates who were taken arms in hand were arrested, and many of them were sent to penal colonies in Algeria. When, a year later to the day, Louis-Napoleon staged a coup that transformed the Second Republic into the Second Empire and himself into Emperor Napoleon III, there was no opposition worth noting. The new ruler claimed that he was carrying out the wishes of France, and he was right. After his coups of December 1851 and 1852 he restored male suffrage and, in plebiscites, won almost universal approval. He opened the eyes of other rulers, especially Benjamin Disraeli of Britain, to the conservatism of the lower rural classes.

Restoration in Central Europe

After the flight of the Austrian imperial court to Innsbruck, radicals like Fischhof, backed by students, set up a pale replica of the French Committee of Public Safety. It had very little power to begin with because it could not command the army. On the contrary, when the Czechs rose up in Prague on June 12, Windischgrätz, governor of Bohemia, bombed the city into submission. He anticipated Cavaignac and the June Days in Paris by a week. Austrian radicals now faced a serious dilemma: side with the army or the nationalist insurgents. Earlier, Fischhof, like most romantic nationalists, believed that all nationalities were equal and deserved both respect and autonomy. But faced with Czechs distrustful of Germans both in Austria and at Frankfurt where the Constituent Assembly insisted that Bohemia would remain part of the German empire, they sided with the army. Their position vis-à-vis Italians and Hungarians was the same. The honor of Austrian arms was at stake and must be upheld. This ethnocentric outlook divided Germans, Slavs, and Magyars, a situation ideal for the old Hapsburg strategy of divide and conquer. Distrust among the nationalities wrecked the Constituent Assembly when it met in Vienna on July 22. Its first task was to create a ministry capable of holding the empire together. As it turned out, no ministry had either the cunning or the power to do that. The empire was held together by the army and its marshals who acted largely on their own initiative to accomplish a counterrevolution throughout central Europe. Marshal Radetzky duplicated the work of Windischgrätz when his victory at Custozza on July 23 forced Charles Albert to sign an armistice. Piedmont and Italian nationalism suffered defeat for the same reason that the Czechs did: absence of unity. Not only did Slovakians and Moravians fail to aid the Czechs, in Italy the rulers of Naples, Tuscany, and Rome refused to continue the struggle—the first two out of jealousy and distrust, the pope because Austrian bishops pressured him. After all, Austrians were faithful Catholics and the pope was their vicar.

To Italian nationalists the pope's recall of his troops was treasonable; however, they did not understand the pontiff's dilemma. To them Austria was the enemy, and the France of Louis-Napoleon an accomplice in evil. It was probably inevitable that Roman extremists would revolt and proclaim Rome a republic. The pope fled, leaving his capital to Mazzini and Garibaldi. Now leadership in the struggle for liberation and unity fell to Rome and Venice. Mazzini asserted that Italians would now reject their despicable rulers and that a war of the people would accomplish what the war of kings could not. In February 1849 a

Constituent Assembly met in Rome, but without the support of Tuscany, where country districts remained loyal to the grand duke, even though he had joined the pope in exile, or of Piedmont, which sent no delegate to Rome. The national cause was severely weakened. Although Charles Albert would have nothing to do with republicanism, he nevertheless renewed the war against Austria on March 20. In six days Radetzky crushed his forces at Novara. Humiliated, he fled to Portugal where he died four months later.

Since June 1848 the tide of republicanism and national liberation had been ebbing. In 1849 it receded to its lowest level, leaving a vast stretch of dead martyrs and drowned dreams. Radetzky finally recovered Venice and Louis-Napoleon's troops restored the pope. In both cases, the republican defenders fought heroically until overwhelmed by superior numbers and arms. However heroic its defenders, the republican cause went down with them. Mazzini and Garibaldi fled, and although they would return later, it was monarchy that would finally triumph in the peninsula.

Equally heroic were the Hungarians. In fact, they were the only national group to resist the Austrians successfully. In the winter of 1848 Windischgrätz had captured Budapest but could not hold it. The Hungarian parliament declared its independence in April 1849 and elected Kossuth as governor. Freedom lasted only a few weeks. Tsar Nicholas believed, as had Metternich, that monarchs must aid one another, and concerned that a free Hungary might incite another Polish revolt, he sent an army into Hungary that finally restored Hapsburg rule in August. Kossuth, like nationalists everywhere, fled to England.

In October 1848 Windischgrätz crushed the democrats in Vienna as decisively as those in Prague. Some 3,000 Viennese were killed in the fighting, and twenty-five radicals were executed. Under the ministry of Felix Schwarzenberg, brother-in-law of Windischgrätz and adviser of Radetzky, the feeble-minded Ferdinand was forced to abdicate in favor of his nephew, Francis Joseph, only eighteen years old. Determined to restore the prestige and military power of his dynasty, he encouraged the reconquest of both Italy and Hungary in 1849. He and his ministers were equally determined to prevent the unification of Germany.

Austria's policy of division was aided by conflicting views among the members of the Frankfurt Assembly. One group demanded the inclusion of Austria, along with Bohemia, in a united German state. That the Czechs were vehemently opposed made no impression on them. Bohemia had a German minority and that made the land German. Opposed to these exponents of a "greater Germany" were those favorable to a "smaller Germany," that is, an Empire without Austria. The latter finally won out and in April 1849 offered the crown to the king of Prussia. By this time Frederick William had recovered all his power and wanted no crown that was offered from the "gutter." His refusal ended the assembly but not unrest. When revolts broke out in Baden, Bavaria, and Saxony, he sent troops to quell them. This action aroused Schwarzenberg, who became concerned about Prussian ambitions. When disturbances occurred in Hesse-Cassel in 1850, he sent an Austrian army there. Prussia mobilized in reply, and a few clashes occurred. But the king gave way and in November agreed to the pact of Olmütz, dictated by Schwarzenberg. Prussia was humiliated, and it was Austria that restored the Confederation and dominated it as of old. Now the restoration was complete.

Conclusions

It would seem that the revolutions of midcentury were, like those of the 1640s on the Continent, an unmitigated failure. Thousands of men full of hope had their dreams crushed and their lives either snuffed by death, or curtailed by imprisonment or exile. Was so much given for so little in return?

Certainly if the gift of life and freedom can be considered a short-term investment in the stock of modernity, then returns were distressingly meager. But as a long-term commitment, the returns were far more lucrative. The restoration in its Hapsburg dress lasted only half a generation. Austrian generals could win battles, but they could not win the war because the real war about which their military manuals told them nothing consisted of changing social structures and the growing power of new ideas. The upheavals in Germany have been called by Louis Namier the "revolution of the intellectuals," a term not meant as a compliment. It contains some truth, but if we think of this revolution of the intellectuals as a force suffering only a setback rather than a defeat, we can recognize that the ideas of liberalism and nationalism survived 1848–49, and served as an ideological framework for the general processes of modernization.

The revolutionaries failed largely because they ignored rural problems and the needs of the lower classes. Their temporary successes were limited to the largest cities, usually with a population of more than 100,000: Paris, Vienna, Budapest, Prague, Berlin, Rome, Milan, Naples, Palermo, and Turin. Their attempt to rally the vast peasant hoards was undermined by the fear of change among semi- or fully-illiterate peasants, and by timely rural reforms of conservative governments. Serfdom disappeared, along with the last traces of manorial obligations. Having achieved their immediate goals, farmers were more likely to stand aside, or line up with traditional rulers and the church.

The revolutions were not wholly sterile. In France manhood suffrage survived, as did payment of a salary to deputies, which lessened eventually the monopoly of power by the wealthiest classes. In Belgium the king doubled the number of voters while his counterpart in the Netherlands granted more power to parliament, and the rulers of Sweden and Denmark issued constitutions with provisions for bicameral legislatures. In all of these countries, the sovereigns limited the suffrage as well as parliamentary control. But absolute monarchy was nearly moribund; reform had staved off revolution. This was particularly the case in Prussia and Piedmont-Sardinia where newly established parliaments won some control over the fiscal powers of kings.

The Jewish populations profited slightly; many of them had sided with revolutionaries, and some had even assumed leadership—Daniele Manin in Venice and Adolf Fischhof in Vienna, to mention two. Where constitutions were issued Jews acquired civil rights, and increasingly the younger began to adapt to modernizing influences.

The revolutions left untouched the conditions of two social categories: workers of both sexes and women in general. Workers had manned the barricades while their wives and daughters procured powder, loaded muskets, and nursed the wounded. The heartier among them also mounted barricades and fought and died with their men. At a higher social level some women wrote pamphlets to abet liberal or radical goals; the novelist Georges Sand sent dispatches to Ledru-Rollin's commissioners in the provinces.

It is likely that the initial success of revolutionaries opened the eyes of rulers to the shortcomings of their heavy-handed bureaucrats and inefficient regimes. Reforms improving administrative recruitment, promotion, and practice, already underway before 1848, were hastened as a result of general, albeit temporary, breakdowns of governments during a time of crisis.

Conversely, liberalism, in central Europe particularly, underwent a transition from its idealistic, romantic phase to one in which its ideals of liberty and human equality were sapped by an increasing devotion to nationalism of a fairly exclusive sort. This trend would entice these liberals to disengage their spiritual roots to Western concepts of freedom in order to enhance the power and will of the nation. The result was the emergence of a more authoritarian liberalism in the central states.

9

Transformation of Central and Eastern Europe

Austria: Key to Central Europe

The restoration of conservative states in 1849–50 offers numerous similarities with the restoration of 1815. Most striking was the crucial position of the Hapsburg Empire; once more it was the director of an orchestra of lesser powers observing the maestro to discover their parts in a larger arrangement. Having crushed all opposition to the dynasty, loyal but disgruntled generals helped put on the imperial throne a young, seemingly intelligent, tradition-bound successor named Francis Joseph. The length of his reign just surpassed that of Queen Victoria, sixty-eight years. During this remarkably long time-span the emperor aged in the comforting belief that his dynasty would reign forever. As it turned out he was the second to last of the line to govern, and the decline of his power was most rapid during his first twenty years as sovereign. In 1850, after the humiliation of Prussia at Olmütz, Austria was a major power; in 1870, however, the empire had slipped to second rank. What had happened?

Quite simply central Europe was drastically transformed. For centuries the small- and medium-sized states there were a great temptation to major and ambitious powers: Spain and France on the west and Russia on the east had absorbed land and peoples by invasion and occupation. The final defeat of

Napoleon in 1815 brought relative tranquility and balance until the upheavals of 1848. Once the midcentury crisis passed central Europeans hoped for the restoration of order. This could be accomplished by the revival of a less dogmatic Metternichian system, with the Hapsburgs once more in command. However it turned out, the situation in 1850 was only superficially similar to 1815, and the old maestro, Metternich, was no longer around. Over the next twenty years the focus of power shifted northward, and the Prussian Otto von Bismarck took up the baton. The music of power politics became increasingly Wagnarian and teutonic; the maestro's baton became a bayonet.

Italy: A Model of State Making

In 1849 the unification movement was in a shambles. Piedmont's defeat at Novara dug the grave, not only of the dead on the battlefield, but of the hopes of all patriots still living. Many of the latter were in exile: Mazzini, whose writings had inspired them, had fled to foreign lands dragging with him his bag of mystical beliefs about Italian greatness. Garibaldi also beat a retreat, to wander in foreign lands where he further perfected his knowledge of guerrilla tactics by participating in revolutions in Latin America, as he had before 1848. The days of the *Carbonari* were over.

Secret societies and uprisings staged by a handful of ardent idealists gave way to power politics, *Realpolitik*, as the Germans called it. Mazzini had vehemently insisted that in the struggle for liberation the Italians would go it alone and serve as spiritual guide for oppressed peoples. But to a new generation of patriots, it became apparent, given the debacle of 1848–49, that Italians could not attain their goals on their own. Failure of the old tactics called for entirely new ones.

Most influential among the men who became aware of the need for change was Camillo Benso, count of Cavour. As a radical in his youth, he had represented the identification of the aristocracy with the national cause. Italy was unique in that most aristocratic families, save for those of Sicily, Sardinia, and Naples, descended from businessmen who had formed the ruling oligarchs of urban republics during the Renaissance and who had assumed noble titles when the republics gave way to autocratic rule. A sizable section of liberal, progressive Italians, perhaps a majority, came from these noble families. They were joined by the scions of business and the professional classes of Piedmont, Lombardy, Tuscany, and duchies in the Po Valley. It was this upper class that finally achieved liberation and unity, under the leadership of Cavour, who was not at all moved by the mystique or abstract belief in the creative role of the masses. Italians could not go it alone; they needed first to reform their economies, reinforce parliamentary government without chopping off crowned heads, secularize society, and promote individual initiative by ensuring individ-

Unification of Italy, 1859-1870

Legend:

- Kingdom of Sardinia before 1859
- To Kingdom of Sardinia: 1859, 1860
- To Kingdom of Italy: 1866, 1870
- Italia Irredenta
- Battle sites

SWITZERLAND

AUSTRIA

FRANCE

SAVOY

Magenta
Novara

Turin

Po R.

PIEDMONT

To France, 1860

Genoa

NICE

Nice

"THE RIVIERA"

LOMBARDY

Milan
Solferino

Trent

Custozza
Verona
Villafranca

Venice

VENETIA

Trieste

PARMA

MODENA

ROMAGNA

Bologna

Po R.

"THE MARCHES"

Leghorn

Florence

TUSCANY

UMBRIA

PAPAL

Rome

STATES

CORSICA
(French)

KINGDOM OF SARDINIA

SARDINIA

Tyrrhenian Sea

Adriatic Sea

D A L M A T I A

ALBANIA

KINGDOM

OF THE

TWO

SICILIES

Bari

Naples

Taranto

A P U L I A

C A L A B R I A

Palermo

SICILY

Strait of Messina

M e d i t e r r a n e a n   S e a

Tunis

A F R I C A

MALTA

(Br.)

Tripoli

0   100   200
Miles

Map 9–1 Unification of Italy, 1859–70

ual rights. This was his program to bring about the *Risorgimento*, the title he used for a newspaper he founded in 1847 before he assumed office in Piedmont, and that became the title of the movement for national revival and liberation. He brought together a parliamentary alliance of moderate liberals and conservatives that carried through his proposals for domestic reforms.

In the early 1850s he was appointed minister of agriculture and commerce in the government of King Victor Emmanuel. He was already a keen admirer of England, its political setup, and above all, its economy. He had traveled extensively on the Continent as well as in England and had come to recognize that the future, first of Piedmont and eventually of Italy, required modernization by following English precedents. The geographical situation of Piedmont was promising. She had access to the Mediterranean Sea as well as to the Po Valley; by entering the world market her farmers and producers could prosper and invigorate society. He began by stabilizing the currency and improving the tax structure. While funding the national debt, he borrowed heavily to create model farms to improve agricultural practices; he built highways, railroads, and port facilities, and he encouraged industry. He also negotiated a series of trade agreements with France, Britain, and Belgium, reducing import tariffs to a minimum, while opening new markets to Piedmontese exports, mainly agricultural, and raw materials. Cavour was a liberal disciple of Adam Smith and read extensively in the literature of Smith's disciples, including those whom he had visited during his travels.

Although the kingdom began to prosper, the treasury suffered losses from lower tariffs and the costs of economic modernization. Undaunted, Cavour took over the finance ministry, floated an internal loan for immediate needs, then borrowed heavily from English bankers to pay off the balance of the indemnity owed Austria. Nothing changed when he became prime minister in November 1852; he was really imposed on Victor Emmanuel by the Chamber of Deputies, a recent addition to the government and created by the royal statute of 1848.

He continued the earlier goal of his predecessor, Massimo D'Azeglio, in the effort to reduce the hostile influence of the clergy. In 1850 the Sicardi bill passed the Chamber of Deputies by 130 to 26 and the Senate by a two to one majority. The law abolished ecclesiastical courts, the right of asylum for criminals in churches, and subjected the clergy to secular courts and punishment if found guilty of crime. The pope, standing firm on an earlier concordat, refused to recognize this modification of clerical privilege. He also persuaded the king to refuse to accept a bill legalizing civil marriage and to prosecute anyone speaking against the belief in eternal damnation as taught by the church.

Cavour, however, was convinced that if Piedmont was to become truly modern in the liberal sense, the powers of the church had to be curtailed. To this end he put forward a general program of disendowment. His bill dissolved all religious corporations not directly engaged in teaching or caring for the sick. Their property was to revert to the state. A kind of *coup de grace* was the capital levy imposed on all other religious houses, the richest benefices and bishoprics. The funds collected were intended to compensate the impoverished lower clergy. Neither the prime minister nor the king sought outright disestablishment. Italians of all classes were Catholic, even if they were anticlerical. This the pope never comprehended. Pius IX, imagining himself still a power to be reckoned with, excommunicated every politician who voted for these bills. This he believed was a necessary step toward securing his shaky papal throne, but it had little effect. Secularization of life was spreading rapidly through industrialized and urbanized Europe; it inevitably penetrated northern Italy as the economy grew there. This does not mean that people stopped going to church, but only that religion ceased to be their major concern.

Cavour, well before 1848, was sympathetic to the cause of unification. What changed in his mind was his concept of the means to achieve it. He had lost whatever faith he had in the "people." He was at heart a constitutional monarchist and the binding together of the peninsula sovereignties would be brought about by princes, not people. He had no trust in democracy. As a good liberal he planned a broad educational program; economic progress depended on an enlightened public devoted to individual initiative, hard work, and laissez faire. The ignorant stubbornly followed routine; only the educated dared try new methods of agriculture, industry, and commerce. But their efforts would prove beneficial only in the broad market of a united Italy.

For the romantic Mazzini, Italians were a nationality martyred by history—divided, weakened, and dominated. Only in their mystical souls could they identify themselves with their God-given mission: the salvation of all humanity. Italians were a Christ-people; their glorious humanistic mission would require many sacrifices—even crucifixion on the cross of alien rule—to accomplish their universal mission. And this was the role of the masses; it was they who must go it alone.

To the rationalistic mind of Cavour, Mazzini's verbal ramblings were unrealistic. The people, illiterate peasants, understood nothing. Not even Piedmont had managed to expel the Austrians, the main bulwark to the creation of a nation. Domestic policy could bring about their material progress, but foreign policy was the instrument to bring about unification.

Cavour's foreign policy was simply an extension of his ambitious plans for Italy's future. He recognized that the Piedmontese army lacked the strength to expel the forces of the Hapsburgs, yet the unity of the peninsula would remain an idle dream without their expulsion. Because his resort to foreign loans to modernize the economy was a palpable success, why not bring in a foreign army to deal with a foreign occupation? In 1851 and 1852 he applauded the coups of Louis Napoleon, now emperor and master of France. He knew that France's new ruler was partial toward national movements, and had, indeed, joined the *Carbonari* when a young man in exile and had nearly been killed in one of their Quixotic invasions of Italy in the 1820s.

The decision to woo the emperor of a Catholic country, and one who had sent troops to restore and protect the pope in 1849, was a calculated risk. Yet, there was no other choice, save perhaps Britain. The British had aided the Greeks against Moslem Turks, and being a Protestant people, had no religious sympathy for Catholic Austria. Cavour therefore allied with both states during the Crimean War of 1855–56, a step that won their gratitude and put the problem of Italy before Europe.

Napoleon vacillated until 1858. On July 20 he and Cavour met secretly at Plombières and agreed on an alliance against Austria. Their goal was the creation of a north Italian kingdom under Victor Emmanuel, with recompense for France. They also laid plans to provoke Austria into declaring war so that their aggressive alliance would take on the appearance of a defensive one. Inept Hapsburg diplomacy led Austria into their trap, and when hostilities broke out, incredibly inept generalship led the victim to defeat at Solferino. Cavour, elated, wished to carry on the war, but Napoleon, troubled by the casualties he witnessed at the scene, by the outrage of French Catholics at home, and the massing of Prussian troops on the Rhenish frontier, secretly arranged an armistice with the enemy. Cavour was furious; so were the Italian patriots who had rapidly taken over the duchies in north central Italy.

Neither Napoleon nor Cavour had planned on such popular uprisings that precluded a return of the pro-Hapsburg sovereigns who had governed the duchies. And they certainly had not imagined that Garibaldi would reappear. Really a highly skilled professional soldier, resourceful and full of energy, he sailed to Sicily with roughly one thousand red-shirted followers, took over the island, moved onto the mainland, captured Naples, and then moved toward Rome. Everywhere he was greeted and reinforced by enthusiastic crowds. Fearful of the consequences if he attacked the papal city, where there was still a French Garrison, Cavour sent the royal army to meet him and absorb his northward thrust. In this he succeeded; the irregulars were disbanded, and Garibaldi reluctantly bowed out. In all the captured territories, north and south, plebiscites were held, and opinion favored annexation to Piedmont. Excluded was the city of Rome and its coastal holdings, and Venetia, where the Austrian army and rule held on. In February 1861 a national parliament convened in Turin where, in March, it proclaimed Victor Emmanuel king of Italy. Cavour did not live to witness the final acts of unification. Exhausted from the pressures imposed on him by events, he fell ill and died in the summer.

The new kingdom acquired Venetia in 1866 when it sided with Prussia and her successful war against Austria. The remainder of the papal lands literally fell to the new state in 1870 when France, having gone to war against Prussia, pulled out of Rome the troops needed on another battlefield. On the entry of Italian soldiers the pope withdrew behind the walls of the Vatican and from there continued his fulminations against the "satanic" new regime.

After the acquisition of Rome and the establishment of the national government there, territorial unity was complete. There were a few extremists who claimed more land in the Trentino from Austria, as well as the city of Trieste on the Dalmatian coast; to them, these lands became *Italia irredènta*, unredeemed Italy. But few people shared their ambitions. The major problem was not to conquer more land but to create an Italian nation. As one activist put it, "We've made Italy, now we must make Italians." That was not to be an easy task. The methods of Cavour, diplomacy laced with duplicity and war, had achieved his immediate goal; the peninsula was no longer merely a "geographic expression" as Metternich had mockingly asserted. But it was not yet a true nation.

Germany: The Giant with Feet of Steel

Austria's destiny was determined by conditions on all her frontiers. Hapsburg misfortunes in Italy were rivaled by those in Germany that were far more destructive of her great power status. It would appear that Austrian leaders learned nothing from the events of 1848, or from the changes that were transforming the economy, society, army, and government of her northern rival. Her quashing of overt Prussian claims to leadership in central Germany, resulting in the humiliation of Olmütz in 1850, was due largely to the support of Russia. This was a reenactment of her weak confrontation with Hungarian nationalists in 1849 when the tsar's army vanquished Magyar resistance to Austrian rule.

Just as Cavour proved to be the nemesis of Austrian policies in Italy, Bismarck played a similar role in the German Confederation. And he used the same strategy as Cavour—resort to duplicity and war to achieve his goal. But here the parallel ended. Cavour, with a rounded face and small metal-framed eyeglasses, was a man of iron determination. But the iron in his character was part of an ideological alloy in which liberalism was a major component. He was a businessman of noble extraction and never a true militarist. His legacy was that of a free citizen in a free state.

Bismarck, on the contrary, was a *Junker* conservative. His strong features, bush mustache, and deep-set eyes suggested an authoritarian antiliberal grudgingly willing to work with the middle classes because he shared their desire to unify Germany. As in Italy this goal necessitated the forceful expelling of Austria from the Confederation, the only means of ending her domination of it. Since he was a Prussian patriot rather than a German nationalist his legacy was a Prussianized German empire in which the professional army played a major role in the formulation of foreign policy and the spread of social values. He successfully put military priorities at the root of subsequent German history. This became clear during the constitutional crisis of the 1860s.

A constitution had been granted by King Friedrich William in 1850. It provided for an upper house consisting of hereditary members of the royal dynasty, the heads of certain noble families, as well as a few men appointed for

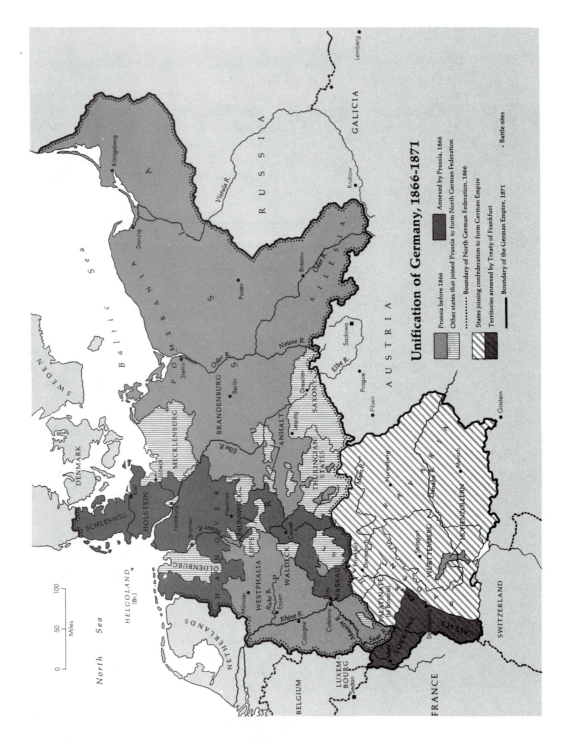

Unification of Germany, 1866-1871

Prussia before 1866

Annexed by Prussia, 1866

Other states that joined Prussia to form North German Federation

•••••••• Boundary of North German Federation, 1866

States joining confederation to form German Empire

Territories annexed by Treaty of Frankfurt

Boundary of the German Empire, 1871

• Battle sites

Map 9–2 Unification of Germany, 1866–71

life by the king. The lower house, in contrast, was elected but by a system that severely limited its link with the people. All adult men enjoyed the suffrage. However, to limit the influence of the lower classes, the electorate was divided into three orders according to each voter's taxes. The first order was the richest, the second the well-to-do, and the third everyone else, the vast majority. Each order voted separately to elect an equal number of delegates to a district convention, which then elected the district's deputies to the lower house of the national parliament. There each order collectively had one vote, and the vote of each order counted equally, an arrangement that lasted until 1918. Although designed specifically to limit decision making to the noble and higher bourgeois, it did not always produce the results the crown desired. Some kind of constitutional conflict was inevitable.

In a sense, the constitution promulgated in 1850 was already out of date by 1860 because of the rapid growth of industry, cities, and a liberal-minded bourgeoisie. Its inadequacies, like those of French constitutions, were evident in the ill-defined concept of sovereignty. As might be expected a crisis resulted from immediate financial problems affecting the army. But far more than the army budget was at stake. The new ruler, King William I, was an ardent devotee of tradition, believing his sovereignty resulted from divine right. As an authoritarian he also embraced the well-established privileges of the military. Before 1848, no one had questioned the king's power or the sacrosanct position of the army. But by 1862, when William became king, the liberals had made notable progress as a political force, an indicator of how rapidly Prussia was industrializing; most of them represented the western provinces and other economically advancing districts. Despite the complicated electoral system, the elections of 1858 had returned a sizable majority of them. Old-line *Junker* conservatives fell from 224 to 60. Most liberals, despite their unexpected strength, did not directly challenge royal power; however, they were determined to attain two objectives: enhance parliament as a legislative branch of government and unify Germany.

By this time conditions of the army had deteriorated. Albrecht von Roon, minister of defense, and Helmuth von Moltke, chief of staff, set out, paradoxically, to modernize it by reviving its old regime status. Since the wars of liberation against Napoleon the military had incorporated elements closer to a militia in which common soldiers elected their officers. William looked on himself as a soldier-king in the tradition of his Hohenzollern ancestors. Like his military advisers he wanted to remove the civilian elements; they were lax in discipline and weakened the morale of professionals. What the military wanted was both an enlarged army, equipped with new up-to-date weapons, as well as a strictly professional force obedient to king and country rather than to the parliament. The army must again become the school of the nation; the Jacobin nationalism of the war of liberation of 1813–15 must give way to military nationalism. The army and its noble officer corps must become the basis of the nation. So the constitutional conflict was a struggle between two cultures that were uniquely Prussian.

There was no parallel in any other state. The army bill that von Roon presented to the lower house did away with the reserves whose officers were small town gentry, lacking spit and polish. It called for the recruitment of Prussian peasants loyal to crown and landlord. The army bill was crucial, more important than appropriations as such because it would remove the army from parliamentary control to place it directly under the crown.

Liberal politicians were fully aware of the danger of this threat. On June 6, 1861 a majority of them founded the Progressive party as a means of organizing the defense of parliament. They roundly voted against the bill, but granted nine million thalers, thereby authorizing a temporary trial of military reform. When the king used the money to implement the rejected bill, the opposition refused further appropriations. Furious, William dissolved the house and called for new elections in 1862. Progressives increased their numbers, an outcome that made them more determined to transform Prussia into a limited, parliamentary monarchy like Britain. Above all, the lower house must not give up its control over taxes.

In September, von Roon urged William to appoint Bismarck as chancellor. The new minister was in a quandary. He was determined to strengthen the army, but he did not want to urge war against the Progressives. Most of them represented the dynamic business and professional sectors of society, with their strength in the Rhenish districts. Their voice was that of industrialists, merchants, bankers, and scientists. They also represented intellectuals; however, the chancellor was less interested in them, unless he could buy them to further his aims. He recognized, quite contrary to his Austrian counterpart, that economic progress was the basis of a strong state and strong army. He differed from most *Junkers* in that he was not sentimentally attached to Austria. Rather he was convinced that German unity could be achieved only by forcefully expelling the Hapsburgs from German affairs. The new state would be *Kleindeutsch* or it would not be. In his mind the Austrians sought to preserve a past that was not worth preserving because it had no future. As it turned out only liberals were prepared to accept such drastic measures. In the end, Bismarck understood them better than they understood themselves. When he confronted them and proclaimed that great issues were decided, not by endless debate but by "iron and blood," he touched on their split personality: They were prepared to wage war to unify Germany but refused to pass legislation that created the kind of army capable of success on the battlefield.

With incomparable boldness he simply ignored them, collected the taxes needed and left it to von Molkte to create the military force required for the ultimate goal, a unified middle European empire. His interpretation of the constitution differed from that of the liberals. There was no clause stating what procedure to follow in the event of a deadlock between executive and legislature. This, for him, did not mean open conflict. Fundamental powers embedded in the crown required it to carry out its duties until the conflict was resolved. William accepted this view, reluctantly to be sure, but the crisis revealed that a ministry in control of the army and the bureaucracy could act as it wished.

Events played into Bismarck's hands, with help from himself. First, he wooed Russia away from Austria by applauding the tsar's crushing of the Polish rebellion in 1863. He wanted no free Polish state on his east lest it stir up the Poles residing in Posnan and Silesia. The Danish king then willfully, and for Bismarck obligingly, annexed the province of Schleswig into his kingdom, in violation of earlier international agreements. The province was inhabited by a majority of Germans who desperately called on the Confederation for rescue. Prussia and Austria joined forces, easily defeated the Danes, and incorporated the two territories into the Confederation. This arrangement lent itself to Bismarck's plans. It enabled him to bring about a quarrel with the Hapsburgs over the spoils, and the two powers went to war in 1866. The south German states, fearful of Prussian domination, sided with the Austrians. It was now that the Prussian army proved its mettle and its metal. Von Molkte and his general staff had successfully planned for a war of swift movement. Using the railroads Prussian troops were far more mobile than their enemy who lacked rapid transport. And once engaged in combat the infantry, equipped with a new breech loading rifle, was capable of firing faster and farther than the Austrians using muzzle loading weapons. When Italy sided with Prussia, Austrian troops had to be sent to deal with them, which they did as effectively as they had in 1848–49. But they were not able to return as reinforcements to the main regiments that held out only a few weeks. Hence the name, the Seven Weeks' War. William and his generals wanted to appropriate land both from Austria and her south German allies. Bismarck would hear nothing of it. He looked on the Hapsburgs as future allies, and the southern Germans as future fellow countrymen. Austria simply paid an indemnity and lost Venetia to Italy. In contrast Prussia grew to cover almost all of north Germany. The annexation of Schleswig, Holstein, the kingdom of Hanover, and several duchies united the western and eastern parts of the kingdom into a consolidated state, the North German Confederation.

Not only did Prussia win 27,000 square miles of fertile land and 5 million new subjects, Bismarck gained the support of most of his parliamentary opponents. Their patriotism overcame their constitutional ideals; they even approved wholeheartedly a new bill legalizing the unconstitutional actions of the chancellor. Most liberals, who now looked on him as a hero, abandoned the Progressive party and organized the National Liberal party to further the cause of unity. The chancellor's bet had paid off handsomely.

Luck and cunning did not abandon him as he laid plans to unify the north and south under one crown. During the next three years he steadily encouraged a distrust of the French as a menace to German integrity. When the Seven Weeks' War was raging Napoleon had hoped to play the benevolent broker to both sides, for a price, such as Luxembourg, the Saarland, or the Rhine's left bank, perhaps even Belgium. His foreign minister, the Duke de Gramont, unwisely stated these aims in a written document. However, the war ended before the French could intervene or win concessions. Bismarck now used this document, discretely made known to high-placed persons who wittingly or unwittingly divulged these imperialist goals. In time Bismarck openly informed Napoleon that the German people would never tolerate the loss of their lands.

Luck had it that the Bourbon line of Spain ended with the overthrow of Queen Isabella II in 1868. A provisional government in Madrid then offered the crown to Prince Leopold of Hohenzollern. On July 2, 1870 the prince announced his acceptance. Immediately the Duke de Gramont excitedly informed the Chamber of Deputies in Paris that France could not tolerate the presence of German rule on its eastern and southern frontiers. William, sensing a growing tension among his western neighbors, deferred to their feelings and insisted that Leopold renounce his candidacy. After this gesture of good will he considered the matter closed. But the French ambassador, on orders, demanded a guarantee that the candidacy would not be revived. This the king firmly refused to do. He then described this meeting in a telegram to Bismarck who released it to the press, after sufficient editing to make it appear that the ambassador had been snubbed, even humiliated, by the king.

Now the war of the German and French press began, with mutual insults and recriminations. In Paris, excited crowds shouted "on to Berlin." Pressured by mobs and the war-crazed chamber, the emperor declared war against Prussia on July 19. The Prussian army, joined this time by those of the south German states, moved rapidly westward. The French fought bravely, were well armed, but their generals were better prepared for the parade ground than the battle field. They allowed themselves to be surrounded, and, along with the emperor, were taken prisoners. The Germans, after laying siege to Paris and defeating the untrained recruits rallied by Leon Gambetta, leader of a provisional government to carry on the war, were masters of the situation. Gallic resistance ended in January 1871. Hastily a new government was elected, headed by Adolf Thiers, who signed an armistice and finally the Treaty of Frankfurt in May.

Triumphant everywhere, the Germans, north and south, were now ready to unite. The king of Bavaria, persuaded by the chancellor, invited William to assume the crown of a new realm. On January 18, in the Hall of Mirrors in the Palace of Versailles, he became head of the Second German Empire.

What is interesting to note is that war, always an instrument of state policy, had now become an instrument of revolutionary, or at least radical change. Russia had ended serfdom after defeat in the Crimea; Austria was reduced to a second-rate power; Napoleon's empire was destroyed; and both Italy and Germany unified—all as results of war. Map makers probably grew rich as a result of so many territorial changes. What the maps could not reveal were the novel implications of military defeat. Save for the upstart Bonapartes, the loss of wars had not normally resulted in political changes; deep-rooted dynasties had suffered defeats, even loss of lands and subjects, but survived unchanged. That was no longer true: War had become a form of revolution, no longer waged between reigning dynasties but between national states; the dynasty that could not prevail in battle was doomed to destruction.

Austria: The Dual Monarchy

Military defeat in 1867 left the Hapsburg state cut off from Germany; it also left it with a host of non-German peoples clamoring for recognition of what they considered their historic rights and national identity. In response Francis Joseph and Schwarzenberg, his premier, were more determined than ever to bury the aspirations for autonomy aroused in 1848. During the 1850s official policy called for absolutism, centralization, and Germanization. Local diets were abolished, replaced by predominantly German-speaking bureaucracies directed by the interior minister, Alexander Bach. The civil agents he sent everywhere were widely hated, as was Bach himself, whose "system" certainly did nothing to draw the loyalty of the several ethnic groups as they became increasingly frustrated.

Defeat in Italy in 1859 struck a blow, not mortal but crippling, to the Hapsburg government. Bach's system was seemingly abandoned, provincial diets revived and the Imperial Council offered a large role as a consultative body with delegates from all parts of the empire. In reality, the Council was dominated by loyal German-speaking aristocrats and ethnic Germans. Greater change came only after defeat in 1867. The thoroughness of the military rout made it evident that not only the imperial army needed reform, the entire government was in need of a profound renovation. Francis Joseph's limited foresight did not prepare him to go that far. Rather he came to an agreement with the people he most feared, the Hungarians. What resulted was a "compromise" (*Ausgleich*) that created the Dual Monarchy, composed of the two equal states more or less independent of each other, and held together by the person of Francis Joseph, emperor in Austria and king in Hungary. Each was endowed with its own parliament, separate ministries, civil service, and administration. However, foreign affairs, war, and finance were carried out by joint ministries supervised by separate committees meeting in Vienna and Budapest, but rarely in joint session.

The two dominant minorities resolved their differences at the expense of the others. Czechs, Poles, Romanians, Slovaks, and Slovenes remained frustrated and incapable of winning autonomy. Their very frustration led them to extend their wish for autonomy to a longing for complete independence. Since most of them were Slavic, they turned their gaze from Vienna and Budapest eastward toward Russia. But their reaction to a Pan-Slav movement emanating from there stirred mixed reactions, perhaps because it never really put forward clear-cut goals. Were all Slavs equal or were those of "mother" Russia to dominate all others? The question concerned chiefly politicians and intellectuals who were most concerned with ethnicity. Some looked on Russia as the protector of Slavdom, others as a menace to their purely national aspirations.

Russia: A Brief Era of Reform

During the third quarter of the nineteenth century central and eastern European governments passed through a transition from old to new regimes. This does not mean that they all became fully modernized, but that they were drawing farther away from their medieval traditions. Germany moved the farthest and fastest; Austria-Hungary and Russia responded more hesitantly to the lure of modernity, and of these two, Russia kept at least one foot in the past, her foot of clay.

After 1848 Russia was as yet a territorial state in the making. Borders were uncertain because they were still expanding. Eastward lay the vast continent of Asia where the tsars had ambitions. However, few Russians shared those ambitions, showing little inclination to go east, far less so than Americans to go west. Conversely they went south into the steppes, and along the northern shores of the Black and Caspian seas, a vast stretch of a land peopled first by runaway serfs, eventually by free settlers. It was in this direction that the imperialist ambitions of the tsars turned as early as the eighteenth century when the Asian dwellers, who had conquered this land centuries earlier, were themselves conquered. After the restoration of 1815 the tsars' interest turned not only to the Black Sea, on which they built a navy and a small merchant marine, but above all to the Straits of Bosporus, a narrow strip of water offering access to the Mediterranean Basin. This was their southern warm-water outlet to the west and the large markets in need of Ukrainian wheat as countries like Britain came to rely increasingly on imported food for their urban populations. What the Russian government wanted, of course, was control over the Straits. That this precious neck of water belonged to the Ottoman Turks and that their capital, Constantinople, dominated it, was an unfortunate arrangement to be changed. It was the leading factor determining Russian foreign policy throughout the century.

To control the Straits Russia had either to destroy the Ottoman Empire, or to dominate the Sultan, a more likely aim. To legitimize an expansionist policy, the tsars claimed to be protectors of the Orthodox Christians living under Turkish rule in the Balkans as well as in Jerusalem. This was why Nicholas, a fanatical enemy of revolution, decided to aid the Greeks in the 1820s and in subsequent hostile encounters, and to encourage the Orthodox in the Balkans to look to Russia for protection. By midcentury and after, Russian statesmen were referring to the Ottoman state as the "sick man," and believed that by hastening his demise, his body could be carved and distributed among the major European powers, the Straits and the south shore of the Black Sea going to Russia, along with other sectors of the Near East.

These ambitions were not at all acceptable to three other states: Austria, which feared that the rise of Pan-Slavism fostered by conservative Russians would stir up the Slavic subjects in her empire; then Britain and France were both concerned about the commercial markets they were developing in the Near

East. The British in particular relied, before the Suez Canal, on free passage of their exports to India and China via Syria and other lands under the Sultan. If the complacent Ottoman state had not existed they would have created it. The proposal that it disappear was absolutely unacceptable and to be resisted, even by military action if necessary. The French agreed. Napoleon III had his own plans for rearranging national frontiers to enhance France's power. Given these conflicting ambitions a negotiated settlement over a trifling issue was not acceptable.

A quarrel between Orthodox and Latin Christians over the use of the Holy Places in Palestine was the spark that set off the Crimean War (1854–56). Britain reluctantly and France more willingly allied with the sultan to resist tsarist ambitions that coveted Jerusalem and also the Danubian Principalities, occupied arbitrarily by Russian troops.

During the siege of Sevastopol in the Crimean Peninsula, the armies of the major powers revealed personal courage but gross inefficiencies of supply, lack of coordination, deplorable command, and disgraceful hygiene. More men died of disease than battle wounds. It was during this campaign that Florence Nightingale, remarkable for her strength of will and foresight, set about reorganizing the British medical corps, a branch almost neglected by the generals of all armies. The Russians lost because they were simply more inefficient than their enemies, and lacked supplies and reinforcements because of poor communications. The Treaty of Paris ended the fighting, forbade Russia to reenter the Danubian Principalities and all the area north of the Danube estuary, and neutralized the Black Sea, which eliminated the Russian navy and fortifications on all shores. More important than this minor war were its unexpected results. The animosities that intensified during its brief span delivered "a catastrophic blow to the precarious international stability established after the Napoleonic wars and the Concert of Europe," according to Norman Rich. The traditional belief that national interests were adequately safeguarded through treaties negotiated to maintain international order and peace was seriously weakened. The conflict opened the way for the *Realpolitik* of Bismarck and Cavour who looked on war as a valid instrument of policy, not as a last resort. The war was such a minor conflict; its results much greater. It saved the Ottoman Empire from domination by the Russian bear but not from its internal decay that went on apace. The regime was indeed a "sick man," but victory turned out to be little more than a Band-Aid.

It was, on the contrary, Russia that was more seriously affected. The tsar's regime, too, was sick, and more and more educated Russians came to realize it and to conclude that the disease was serfdom. This was also the conclusion of the new ruler, Alexander II, who succeeded his father during the war. The opponents of reform had argued since 1815 that autocracy based on serfdom had defeated the first Napoleon; Russians had no individual freedom, but they were loyal to a strong government. They warned against trying to imitate the West. Autocracy, orthodoxy, and nationality distinguished Russia and gave it a soul and mission; serfdom, along with aristocratic rule, were the products of historical growth, part of God's will. This kind of Slavophilism contended that Eastern Orthodox culture was not only different, it was superior to Western culture. To their discredit they were blind to the fact that defeat in the Crimea, at the hands of Western powers, made evident that Russia was not strong but inefficient, decaying, and corrupt. Alexander, more sensitive than his Slavophile advisers, felt that reform would have to come, and if it did not come from above, it would come from below, from the peasant masses, and as revolution. Indeed peasant riots spread widely.

The reign of Alexander II forms a watershed in Russian history. Reforms put off by his father were implemented rapidly within a decade. The most far-reaching and permanent was the abolition of serfdom, carried out in 1861 for serfs on private estates, and 1866 for those on state lands. Emancipation in Russia differed from that of France in 1791, which transformed peasants into free, "inactive" (nonvoting) citizens, free to leave the land, or to buy it if they had the means. In Prussia in 1807 serfs became legally free, but remained subjects (there was nothing to vote for), and could leave the land if they gave up claims to the acres they and their forefathers had worked. In Russia the peasants also became free, and remained subjects as in Prussia. But they were not allowed to leave the land. Rather, they continued to be attached to the *mir*, the village in which they dwelled. The tsar wanted no landless proletariat as had been created in the Baltic provinces when serfs were freed there early in the century. He wanted peasants to remain in place so they could be recruited into the army and pay their heavy taxes.

When receiving freedom the peasants also wanted ownership of the lands they had worked. In their view, they had belonged to their masters, but the land had always belonged to themselves. The decree rejected this argument by placing peasant land under the control of the *mir*, and the *mir* continued to function as always, distributing strips of soil to each family according to its size, and deciding on crops and methods of cultivation. The entire village continued to be responsible for collecting taxes, and also for collecting redemption fees. The peasants were now personally free, but their labor was not; they had to make redemption payments not to the lord but to the state because the state compensated the lords. Therefore peasants were indebted to the central authority and were to make payments over forty-nine years.

Peasants were not given the choice whether or not to buy the land they had worked; they were compelled to but only as a village community. Worse, the value of the land they received was usually assessed roughly one-third higher than its market value, a means of granting landlords "hidden" compensation, not for land transferred to the *mir*, but for lost dues and services. In addition, the division of land between lord and peasants often left the latter with less fertile, less accessible arable, forest and pasture. This same inequality usually applied to water rights. Given these conditions the ex-serfs found that they could not live on the crops and income from their small allotments. They were compelled, therefore, to labor for wages on the lords' land.

To the degree that emancipation did not bring freedom of movement to peasants, it enhanced the power of the *mir*. Apart from its role as money gatherer, the village preserved traditional usages, which meant that Russian agriculture remained backward, hardly affected by scientific and technological discoveries. Because lords hired peasants very cheaply to work their holdings, they had little incentive to innovate. In addition the commune now assumed the police and judicial powers once wielded by landlords. This made for a rough egalitarianism because heads of family elected communal leaders who formed a village assembly. Cantons also became more important. They consisted of several villages and were governed by elders, assessors, clerks, and judges, all chosen by an assembly of delegates from each *mir*. This created a kind of peasant democracy within the autocratic empire but a very limited democracy; police officials and outside bureaucrats could intervene to prevent any actions considered dangerous to the national regime.

Emancipation certainly did not solve the "peasant problem." This problem had little to do directly with politics but with economic survival. Vast numbers of peasants, now legally free, were unable to produce sufficient crops to live above bare subsistence and in years of poor harvests, not even at that level. Before 1900 rural society did not move beyond the menace of famine. Peasants were beset by insufficient lands, inefficient farming, rural overpopulation, and excessive taxes and payments.

There was also a landowner problem. The upper levels of rural society did not fully benefit from emancipation. They were compensated for lost land, but only indirectly and inadequately for lost labor, and many could not afford to hire peasants. Most of them found the government's compensation inadequate: All were reimbursed in state bonds that soon began to lose value, and owners had to cash these bonds because their yield was not equal to a landlord's needs. Therefore they lacked capital to improve their land; most of them also lacked the energy. Serfdom had vitiated their initiative; they had earlier lost interest in agriculture and had lived off the labor of serfs. With the ending of that source they sold their acres and moved to cities in search of a livelihood in the bureaucracy or to find a wealthy widow. Gone were the days of champagne and caviar, unless they were lucky in their quest.

Their lands were readily bought by the minority of aggressive, knowledgeable owners who became gentlemen farmers. Most of them were located in the black earth regions; they introduced improved farming methods and machines, hired peasants, kept accurate accounts, and lived well. It was unfortunate for Russia that they were not the majority, or that they did not become the equivalent of British squires, or of the Prussian *Junkers*. They did not have a great impact either on the economy or the social structure, and least of all on government policy before 1906 when agrarian policies underwent far-reaching changes. Official agrarian policy was a sort of x factor in the modernization equation. Alexander II has been called the "liberating" tsar because he ended serfdom. But the role of government was minimal and capricious in the modernization of the east. The tsar was not an agronomist, nor an economist, nor particularly forward looking, save out of necessity. And the emancipation decree obviously did little to bring Russia abreast of the major powers of the West regarding all aspects of human life. That Russia produced great writers and composers did little to enhance the quality of life save for the small minority of the educated. All reforms were hedged. Alexander deserved the title of "tsar emancipator," provided we do not remove the quotation marks as an indication of the novelty and limitation of his decrees. This became apparent in all his reforms.

These limitations become apparent in his educational program. Russia was one of the few states to have a ministry of education. Nicholas I had begun the process toward more open school curriculums, which Alexander II continued. The remarkable, albeit narrow, expansion of education, increasingly freed of bureaucratic restrictions, was a major move in the direction of liberal learning. Censorship of textbooks and teaching were relaxed. But no decrees emanated from Alexander to create a free, compulsory, secular system of public schooling. Neither he nor his more progressive advisers even approached the Prussian and Western education systems.

Local instruction, where it spread among the lower classes, was the task of the Zemstvo, a district assembly of educated gentry, small-town middle class, and some peasant members, created in 1864. Voting in elections to them was weighted in favor of noble land owners. Alexander, whose permission was required to set up a school, used these bodies to eliminate two abuses in local administration: corruption and excess centralization. Their task centered on primary education, road and bridge construction and maintenance, welfare and poor relief, veterinary supervision, and public health. Their revenues derived from limited taxes on real estate and business enterprises. District Zemstvos elected representatives to provincial Zemstvos, and remind one of county councils in Britain, Diets in Germany, and similar bodies in most European states. They both increased the number of schools and improved welfare, public health, and medical services. They were an enormous advance over the former serf owners who sometimes provided local services.

It was also in 1864 that the tsar issued legal reforms made necessary by his emancipation decree. The old legal system left much to be desired from a modernist viewpoint. Trials dragged on endlessly, and the accused remained behind bars for months, even years, before a verdict emerged. Trials were held in secret, and the victim might never learn why he or she was condemned to some kind of medieval punishment. The accused had no defenders because there were no lawyers, and judges, appointees of the state, had their ears attuned to bureaucratic demands. The reform, therefore, partially separated the judiciary from other branches of government, providing for more independence. Judges were appointed for life, and their salaries raised to obviate corruption; no one expected it to be eliminated. Finally, trials became public and a jury was introduced to provide, it was hoped, more impartial judgments. Those chosen for jury duty had to be literate, and their shrewd common sense, it was believed, would temper the harsh punishments that a still antiquated legal code imposed on the condemned. As in England before penal law reform, when sentences imposed years in prison, exile, or even death for minor offenses, the juries simply acquitted the accused. The Russians still had no penal code based on the notion that the penalty should fit the crime. Peasants were not beneficiaries of legal reforms. They remained under the jurisdiction of communal and cantonal courts.

The Crimean War, stimulator of so much reform, inevitably provoked a reform of the army. Under General Dimitry Milyutin in 1874, a system of compulsory military service was introduced for all men of about twenty years of age. They served actively for six years, then joined the reserve until the age of forty. As everywhere, only about one-third of eligibles were called, and the illiterate were provided with an education. Milyutin abolished corporal punishment and organized new military academies to improve officer training. It was hoped that officers would treat their men with more consideration, without undermining discipline. The army decree was the last of the major changes, and it was issued belatedly partly in response to a crisis.

In 1863 the Polish gentry rose in revolt against Russian rule and attempts at Russification of the people. Alexander moved against them, supported by Bismarck, and belatedly by Austria. Although there were pro-Polish outcries in France and Germany, not many individuals were ready to die for Warsaw. An as yet unreformed Russian army crushed the revolt—the Polish gentry could not rally their peasants whom they had exploited mercilessly. The result had social ramifications. Alexander confiscated many gentry estates and gave the land to the peasants, placing them in a position far superior to that of their Russian counterparts.

The revolt provided Russian reactionaries with the excuse they needed to condemn the reforms. In their minds, Alexander was trying to westernize holy Russia. Their leading spokesmen were Michail Katkov, editor of the *Russian Messenger* and *Moscow News*. An attempt on the life of the tsar in 1866 caused the tsar to question the wisdom of his own program of moderate modernization. Inspired by the Slavophile Katkov, he appointed Count Dimitry Tolstoy as minister of education. It was he who purged schools of progressive-minded teachers in order to make schools a bulwark against change and a defender of autocracy, orthodoxy, and nationality—the sacred triad of the Slavophiles. He came close to abolishing science and technology courses—really all studies not centered on religion, Greek and Latin languages, and rhetoric. Political intervention went on to involve the courts of law; prisoners considered dangerous were brought before special police or military courts without juries. In 1878 the law code was revised to include acts considered treasonable, that is, open political opposition to the regime. Russia now had two legal systems: one modern and based on trial by jury; the other arbitrary and repressive and based on political needs.

Liberals deplored this reversal, and emerging radical and revolutionary groups, having denounced the reforms as inadequate, now set out on a program of political assassinations. Grouped in an underground organization, Land and Freedom, they provided Russian annals with numerous martyrs, as terrorism of an anarchic nature took hold of the early extreme left. Finally they succeeded in their effort to kill the tsar who fell victim to a bomb thrown on March 13, 1881. So ended a very brief era of reform. The modernization process that had emerged in the west, then had partially penetrated the center, had made no more than a dent in the wall of eastern autocracy.

10

Liberalism on the March: Slow Step

Bonapartism: A French Malaise

Undoubtedly the great majority of French voters, when they elected Louis-Napoleon president in December 1848, prolonged his presidency in December 1851, and finally approved his ascent to the majestic rank of emperor in December 1852, were convinced that they had saved society from the "reds" threatening private property, sanctity of the family, Christian morals, order, and peace. Louis-Napoleon campaigned during the 1848 presidential elections as the "Napoleon of peace." Unlike his uncle, he put forward the impression that tranquillity at home and abroad was more compatible with a new age of scientific discovery, economic progress, and social justice. Had he not written a pamphlet optimistically titled *The Extinction of Poverty*, his claims to be a man of the new age would not have been supported. There is reason to doubt that the hoards of peasants voting for him had ever heard of his pamphlets; their notion of Bonapartism, if they had one, was a combination of law codes sanctifying property, and the opening of Continental markets for their crops. Their collective memory was short, fuzzy, and easily misled. They conveniently forgot about the military ruler who took from them taxes and sons; rather they were reminded of the victories, the glory of French armies, the invincibility of the "little corporal" as Napoleon I's men called him, all of which contributed to a semimyth spread among them by many of the emperor's noncommissioned officers retired from the army at half-pay in 1815, and who were reduced to vegetating in rural villages where living costs were minimal. Accepted into the peasant communities, they had numerous occasions dramatically to embellish their victories, especially if they spoke the local dialect in a society, largely illiterate, that preserved an oral tradition of past events, and greatly admired the *raconteur*, the teller of tales. Apart from this advantage, the new emperor enjoyed massive rural support until the end, thanks to a general era of prosperity in farming which outlasted that of industry.

Louis-Napoleon took the title Napoleon III. There never was a Napoleon II, for the first emperor's son, half-Hapsburg, the *Aiglon* (eaglet) hero of the playwright Edmond Rostand, died young in exile. The journalist Henri Rochefort later wrote—France never had a better ruler: no oppression, no taxes, no wars.

Napoleon was certainly the strangest ruler of a major state. His knowledge of France was limited; he had lived most of his life in exile, and spoke French with a German accent. Before 1848 he seemed more fit for roles in comic opera as revealed when he attempted on two occasions to invade France with a motley gang, once by land at Strasbourg, and once from the English Channel at Boulogne where his seasick followers were rounded up, including the live eagle accompanying them, and Louis-Napoleon was condemned to prison in perpetuity. He soon escaped to England where his actress-mistress supported him. Once elected to office, however, he put her aside, and after his seizure of the throne, he married a Spanish noble lady, as Catholic as he was indifferent in religion, save that he bowed to clergymen who led peasants to the ballot boxes, and who, some anticlericals asserted, stuffed them after crossing themselves.

During the 1850s it is doubtful that they found it necessary to resort to electoral trickery. The prefects and their subordinates were more skilled at that task; after all, many were hangovers from the July Monarchy. They chose "official" candidates, loyal men of wealth, avid of social advancement via politics, and willingly backed the throne. These men were the basis of the "authoritarian" empire. The new constitution provided for an hereditary crown, a Senate chosen by the emperor and a *Corps Législatif*, Legislative Body, elected by universal male suffrage, and which met simply to debate bills but possessed no legislative initiative. Even its right to vote on the annual budget was limited. Its title, in consequence, seems hardly appropriate, but then, the Bonapartes, both uncle and nephew, created all kinds of political bodies with high-sounding titles that were utterly devoid of any meaningful functions. The Council of Ministers was chosen by the emperor, and responsible to him. The emperor, not the people, was sovereign.

Napoleon was called the "good" because he hoped to reconcile the rural and urban lower classes, on the one hand, and the wealthy classes, noble and not, on the other. His strong support among peasants especially opened the eyes of other rulers to the fact that manhood suffrage, their bugbear before 1848, could be fashioned into a solid basis of conservative government. Gerrymandering so as to give rural electoral districts a preponderance over industrial districts by sheer numbers was part of this system. Both Bismarck, as chancellor of Prussia, and Benjamin Disraeli, premier of Britain in the third quarter and after, recognized that the farm vote, although diminishing in numbers, was nonetheless still significant, especially on the Continent. The French middle class, divided in 1848 between left and right, also rallied to Napoleon during the following decade. And many workers followed them, as their real wages steadily went up, and unemployment went down.

Most of his supporters knew very little about him; even those closest to him were mystified by his character. One of his female cousins casually remarked, jokingly, of course, that she would like to split open his skull to see what was inside. She would have found the brain of a complex being, far more complex than voters realized. In a sense, they backed an unknown leader to protect their property and homeland. Given the prosperity of the 1850s, his authoritarian style fit the public mood. There was no opposition worthy of the name: Jacobins, socialists, as well as many moderate republicans were dead, in jail or penal colonies, or living penuriously in exile. Their journals had been crushed, their nonconformist presses closed, censorship was fairly strict, large assemblies forbidden, and the police active, although the gendarmerie, responsible for order outside of the Parisian area, numbered only 24,000. And yet the Second Empire did not become an authentic police state; neither the emperor nor large segments of the bourgeoisie insisted on going that far. Nor was there need to; opposition candidates managed to win only five seats in the *Corps Législatif*. Their electoral campaigns ran into many obstacles: names of sympathizers were arbitrarily removed from voter roles, their posters torn down, public meetings disbursed, even their personal safety was in danger when traveling among villages. These were all the old tricks of previous regimes, and elections in Britain were often more violent and corrupt. The so-called Five (the opposition) were very moderate anyway, center left liberals at best. By 1854 the regime, resembling in many ways the July Monarchy save for manhood suffrage, seemed solidly rooted for the present, and for the future after the empress gave birth to a male heir. Given Napoleon's age, forty-five, his lucky star shown bright. It was even more brilliant after 1856 when his army, allied with the British, defeated Russia in the Crimea. The war was hardly a glorious one, and it put an end to the pacifistic claims of the emperor. It was, at least, a move in line with traditional foreign policy: Shore up the sinking Ottoman state, preserve the neutrality of the Straits, and keep Russia's foot, even if made of clay, out of the Balkans and the Near East. His conquest of Cochin China later in the decade was in keeping with the invasion of Algeria by the Bourbons in 1829, a political ploy. Apart from these successes, his foreign policy became increasingly erratic and ultimately led to his undoing.

As a statesman he stands well below Bismarck and Cavour, but well above Francis Joseph, Alexander, and other Continental rulers. In comparison he stands closest to Cavour in that he actively encouraged industry and agriculture, and was sympathetic to movements for national liberation. What he lacked was an authentic command of power politics, simply because he lacked Cavour's ability to plan his decisions, and Bismarck's genius for arranging events to suit his ends. In short he was too near-sighted to foresee the most likely results of his policies, and too weak willed to act when the situation called for action. Finally, he was not skilled enough in parliamentary processes to create the political force he needed to defend his regime even in moments of adversity. Perhaps he inherited these weaknesses from his uncle, without the military genius. Like the first ruler of his line, he did not form a Bonapartist party. The first Napoleon did not need a party; he had an thoroughly devoted army. Within the imperial court of his nephew, the true Bonapartists could be counted on the fingers of one hand: Baron Victor Persigny was the most devoted but of limited capacity; Eugene Rouher was an old-line conservative and never understood that Napoleon III had at one time been simply Louis-Napoleon, dreamer, would-be maker of new worlds, disciple of Claude-Henri de Saint-Simon, who was the very ancient forerunner of the advocates of a "managerial revolution." He had proposed a society in which civil servants, high-level technocrats, bankers, and the workers, organized in cooperatives, would share in rulership via their representatives. As emperor, Napoleon still retained his affection for the hard-pressed peasants struggling to survive in a rapidly changing agriculture. The empress shared none of these aspirations, being an admirer of Marie-Antoinette and pro-Bourbon. Duke Charles de Morny, illegitimate half-brother of Napoleon, was the cleverest of the inner circle; however, he was an Orleanist by temperament and fortune. Having helped organize the original coups that brought Napoleon to power, he took over as chair of the Legislative Body where his skill disarmed opponents and assured the passage of imperial budgets. A shrewd businessman he speculated in the schemes for urban renewal and made a fortune. His death in 1865 weakened the emperor's control over the legislative at a most critical time. Critical because Napoleon had, on his own initiative, undertaken the projects that would destroy him. His most determined enemies, the republicans, were impatient but impotent. As it turned out, he was his own worst enemy.

Uppermost was his intervention in Italy where Cavour induced him to wage war against Austria as part of a plan to liberate north Italy from Hapsburg rule. In 1859 he made the decision to join the kingdom of Piedmont in a war to set up—what?—he was not quite sure: perhaps an Italian federation under the pope or, more likely, a north Italian kingdom under Piedmont. For a ruler so heavily dependent on support from the Catholic church, and given the ferocious papal opposition to such projects, his decision was, to use the kindest words, an egregious folly. As noted in the previous chapter, he withdrew from bloody hostilities before accomplishing his goal, which infuriated the Italian nationalists and won him no gratitude. Indeed, national pride, where it existed, was further enraged when he annexed from Piedmont the provinces of Nice on the coast and Savoy in the Alps, and this after rigged plebiscites. Catholic opinion, at least that of the clergy and the upper class, was highly critical if not alienated. His use of French troops to safeguard Rome did not appease them; it merely further enraged Italians. He retaliated in 1860 by appointing less ultramontane bishops, limiting religious orders, stressing secular education and suppressing *L'Univers*, the extreme pro-papal newspaper edited by the bulldog of reactionary Catholicism, Louis Veuillot. The only proponents of a war policy to unite Italy were his opponents. His attorney general warned him, "To find partisans of a war in Italy you have to go find them in the centers where people lay plots to overthrow the empire." When his more moderate opponents, as well as the more determined, increased their vote in the elections of 1863, he reversed his crackdown on outspoken Catholics.

In fact, two years earlier, when the Americans were slaughtering one another in a civil war, he launched his incredible scheme to found a puppet Catholic regime in Mexico, also mired in a revolution. Perhaps he sought to turn attention away from his Italian misadventure. As in Italy the French army sent on this anachronistic mission to Mexico could win battles, but the native anticlerical forces of Benito Juárez were as elusive as the Spanish *guerrilleros* who resisted the French armies of his uncle in the early 1800s. The man Napoleon destined for the bayonet-supported throne was later captured and shot. He had been deserted by the French in 1867 when the successful Union army began to mass troops on the Mexican border to enforce the Monroe Doctrine. Napoleon's combination of ineptitude and cowardice seriously undermined his standing in France and Europe.

The Second Empire is remarkable more for internal improvements that, in part, were a response to foreign policy failures. Domestic reforms were equally influenced by rapidly changing economic conditions. The emperors' defenders usually refer to the 1860s as a time of major innovations leading toward a liberal empire. These innovations were the freeing of parliamentary debates and their publication. One had to be a true believer to wade through the myriad words that characterized the florid, bombastic style of political speeches, but the left wing press was competent at summarizing them. Only now did opposition deputies enjoy the right to question government policies. Not only did the unpopular Italian policy come under hostile scrutiny, mainly by Catholics, but also Napoleon's free-trade treaty with Britain, which middle-class industrialists, well represented in the lower house, began to blame for a national economy losing its momentum. It was widely believed that the emperor had bought off British opposition to his Italian policy by betraying French producers. Orleanists, like Theirs, now began a systemic but by no means threatening opposition to Napoleon. Orleanism was recovering and sought to remake the empire into a constitutional monarchy responsive to protectionist businessmen.

Napoleon, for all his faults, was far more innovative and open-minded.

He conceived of Bonapartism as a dynamic force carrying France along the road to modern ways of life, and that called for a competitive economy, easy credit, daring entrepreneurship, and increasing wealth more widely spread over all of society. Orleanism, although not opposed to progress, was far more a system of slow growth, conservative investment in the hands of the *haute banque*, distrustful of too active a state, equally distrustful of the growing working class, and unmitigatingly upper-class elitist in its outlook. They were as protectionist as they were pacifistic and, fearful of Napoleon's foreign adventures, they sought to curb him by controlling the national budget. The liberalization of the empire was not a tendency toward a republic but the penetration of Orleanism into the empire.

The elections of 1863 revealed how far this penetration had affected the voting population, especially its growing urban segment. In every city with a population more than 40,000, liberal monarchists and republicans won a majority. Official candidates won in smaller towns and the countryside, receiving just over 5,000,000 votes compared to the combined opposition's 1,900,000, an increase of 1,300,000 for the latter since 1857.

Napoleon, advised by Morny, recognized the need for additional reform. In 1864, to win town workers, he allowed them to strike, but did not grant them full freedom to picket, and when a wave of work stoppages occurred in the later 1860s as a recession began, local authorities acted to prevent or squash them. The emperor's Saint-Simonian views scarcely penetrated his civil service and left the police untouched. Moreover Napoleon tolerated unions, but he never legalized them. Nor did his government tolerate the French section of the First Workingman's International that had been set up in London in 1864. As the economy declined the policy of toleration and prosecution aroused worker opposition in factories and shops, putting proletarians on a collision course with the regime.

Within the Legislative Body deputies won increased freedom to question and openly criticize the ministry, and to block certain plans the Catholics among them opposed. Napoleon's blueprint to improve education came to little. Victor Duruy, minister of education since 1864, sought to modernize the system by introducing more lay teachers, raising their salaries, and founding new faculties in the universities. When he called for free and obligatory schooling, Catholics feared a reversal of their near monopoly of primary and secondary instruction, and when he proposed equal education for girls, he was sent packing.

The election of 1869 was a heavy blow for the emperor. An opposition consisting of Catholic legitimists, Orleanists, protectionists, and republicans— who had little in common save their opposition—reduced the government's majority to a million votes. The time had clearly come for a change. Napoleon was losing his grip; he suffered from kidney stones and other ailments; merely to ride a horse was torture. He finally called on a *rallié* republican, Emile Ollivier, to organize a reform ministry, revise the constitution so as to create a liberal state, and put it to a referendum in the spring of 1870. More than 7,000,000 Frenchmen voted *oui*, an overwhelming victory that both weakened and safeguarded the throne.

The new regime, however, lasted only a few months. The Franco-Prussian War brought it down on September 4, when news of defeat at Sedan reached Paris. Leon Gambetta, a newcomer, elected on a radical republican platform in 1869, led an invasion of the City Hall where a government of national defense was quickly set up. Gambetta's hastily formed cohorts could not defeat the Germans who laid siege to Paris. Those Parisians who had not fled the city earlier now passed a horrible winter; they were reduced to eating animals in the zoo and rats were rated as fine cuisine.

In February 1871 the Orleanists in the legislature took the initiative, arranged for an armistice and the election of a new legislature, the National Assembly. Voting was on the issue of war or peace, and because most Frenchmen wanted peace they chose conservatives who promised it. Republicans, the war party, lost badly.

In the spring occurred one of France's most tragic outbreaks, the Paris Commune. The government elected on the war issue chose Thiers as its provisional leader. Fearful of Paris and its half starved people, representatives met at Bordeaux, declared an end to the moratorium on rents and debts, when no one

Emperor Napoleon III is shown here at the 1867 exhibition inspecting cannons made by the Krupp Company of Germany. He lost his throne three years later when those cannons were turned on his armies.

had any ready cash, and worse, put an end to the daily wage of 1.50 francs paid to national guardsmen who had no other income because of the siege. This step had the same effect as the abolition of the National Workshops in 1848. Meanwhile there emerged in March a Central Committee of the National Guard, fiercely patriotic, republican, and determined to resist the restoration of monarchy, as well as peace on German terms. The men remaining in Paris also elected a Commune to govern the city; thirty-five of its eighty members were artisans, not simple factory laborers. There were, as in 1848, numerous republicans, chiefly Jacobins, socialist followers of Blanqui (still in jail), and anarchist disciples of Proudhon. As a result the Commune lacked an ideology save decentralization through communal autonomy throughout France, and a federalist republic. It was too short-lived to advance far beyond issuing verbalized programs that were often in conflict.

Thiers and the monarchists in Bordeaux viewed it with horror, and created the myth that it consisted of thieves, drunks, vagabonds, the dangerous classes, and their prostitutes. The first duty, then, was to crush it, and so thoroughly that the piles of its corpses would serve as a lesson to the rabble elsewhere. Thiers sent troops who took the city in late May. It is curious that these soldiers, so ineffective against the Prussians, became ferocious warriors against the Communards. No quarter was given by either side. During the fighting, street to street and house to house, prisoners were shot on the spot by both sides. The army had the better of it, and when at last in control of the city, rounded up hundreds of Communards, lined them against a wall in Père Lachaise cemetery, and shot them all. By then much of central Paris was in flames including the Tuileries Palace and the City Hall. The retaking of Paris left 100,000 Parisians dead, jailed, or exiled. The June Days revolt of 1848 was a minor skirmish compared to the 1871 revolution. Of much lesser importance were the communes that were set up in Lyon, Saint-Etienne, Le Creusot, Narbonne, Toulouse, and Marseilles. In these cities middle-class radicals retained control of the rebels and were subdued with far less bloodshed.

With republicanism moribund if not entirely dead the monarchist majority was in control of France. Bonapartism, responsible for these terrible years, was swept away, once more unable to survive military defeat. The royalists, fully triumphant for the moment, were not to enjoy the fruits of their bloody victory. Bonapartism died on the battle field; monarchism, as we shall see, committed suicide in the National Assembly.

Great Britain: Rock of Stability

Having avoided the continental political upheavals of 1848 the British pursued their placid evolution toward a more democratic society. During the 1850s, after the Crimean War, the Whig party ruled with an easy hand. Palmerston, as its leading statesman, was remarkably complacent. He made no attempt to tighten party organization. Primarily interested in foreign affairs, he ignored domestic matters. As late as 1864, when queried about additional legislation, he replied, "Oh, there is really nothing to be done. We cannot go on adding to the Statute Book *ad infinitum*. Perhaps we may have a little law reform, or bankruptcy reform; but we cannot go on legislating for ever." These words can be read as a kind of death wish for the party. Indeed, by midcentury new political groupings were gradually emerging. Robert Peel's decision to abolish the Corn Laws in 1846 had split the old Tory party. The right wing of the Whig party, gentry for the most part, comfortably drifted toward the Tories. Their concern had more to do with the preservation of English control in Ireland and the preservation of the Anglican church in that predominantly Catholic country. They were also opposed to further broadening of the suffrage. This combination of Tories and Whigs came forth as the Conservative party. In contrast the reform minded Whigs eventually united with the rising Liberal party. The conservatives came under the leadership of Benjamin Disraeli, the liberals under William Gladstone. These were two of the most brilliant statesmen of the century.

Both party leaders recognized that society had evolved and that the progressive changes of the 1830s were no longer sufficient. The factory working class had grown beyond Palmerston's imagination and were demanding the vote; towns had grown into cities and cities into metropolitan areas, yet they were either not represented or grossly under represented. Gladstone, like Peel before him, had been a staunch conservative and had almost become an Anglican clergyman. His keen mind, perceptive powers, and long political experience led him to put aside the ideals of his youth: By the 1860s he stood for free trade and lower taxes, which he achieved when chancellor of the exchequer. He also modified his intransigent Anglicanism to recognize the rights of Protestant dissidents and Catholics.

Disraeli, called Dizzy by his friends, was a converted Jew, a fact that put obstacles in his political advancement, but not insurmountable enough to prevent his rise from a mere curiosity, because of his rather colorful dress and his social novels, to become leader of the Conservative party and prime minister. He had, as he put it, climbed the "greasy pole." His grasp of society as being divided between rich and poor, which he vividly described in his novel *Sybil*, was superficial, but he neither condemned the poor nor condoned the rich. Rather he looked to the gentry of his party as the natural guardians and protectors of the lower stratum, endowing them with a kind of updated *noblesse oblige*. He favored enfranchising the town workers, believing that they would vote conservative out of hatred for their industrial employers in the Liberal party. His Conservative grouping was fairly homogeneous, consisting primarily of the rural landed classes, Anglican divines, the officers of the military, with a mixture of wealthy bourgeois who planned to buy land and enter the gentry. It also attracted numerous retailers and men in the services, all of them dependent on the upper classes socially and economically. There were also workers distrustful of middle-class Liberals. Like the defunct Tory faction it was for church, country, and Crown—small wonder that Disraeli enjoyed friendly relations with Queen Victoria.

Gladstone's party was far more complex. Reform-minded gentry, dissident manufacturers devoted to free trade (led by Bright), and political radicals clamored for both political and social reform. The parties, in consequence, became more distinguishable, debates more heated and insults more cutting when exchanged between the two tiers of bench's on which MP's rested their bottoms. By the mid-1860s the debates centered on the suffrage. They reflected the social changes mentioned earlier that helped create a situation of political imbalance. Five out of six adult men, mostly wage workers, were without the vote. The northward thrust of population had changed the locus of its voting segment, enhancing distortions of representation since 1832. Half the urban dwellers of Britain sent to Parliament thirty-four members; the other half, rural by origins, sent three hundred. Only Chartists had condemned such blatant discrimination, and memories of Chartism, unlike the movement itself, had not died. On the contrary, trade union leaders reminded their followers that their voice in Parliament was needed to discourage judges, the constabulary, as well as local officials, from undermining the legal recognition of trade associations and intimidating strikers.

When the Liberal cabinet under Lord John Russell presented a bill in 1866, as he had in 1832, to broaden the franchise, workers responded with considerable enthusiasm, organizing public meetings and debates. When the police denied them the use of Hyde Park, the metal railings surrounding the park were pulled down with the vigor that artisans had put into Luddite riots thirty or more years earlier. History seemed to be repeating itself, for the main orchestrator of popular agitation in the North and Midlands was John Bright. When he appeared on the moors, huge masses of workers came out to hear him, and then, by torchlight, parade past him shouting for the vote. Nothing like this was possible in any Continental country. The British organized demonstrations; Continentals made revolution. There were at least two distinct political cultures on either side of the Channel.

When a combination of arch Conservatives and unreformed Whigs defeated the bill, the latter now leaving the Liberal party in droves, the Russell cabinet fell. Rioting spread. At this moment Disraeli persuaded the moderates of his party to steal Liberal thunder and make the bill their own, in the expectation of winning workers' gratitude as well as their votes. His reform bill of 1867 went farther than Russell's and Gladstone's by granting the suffrage to every male householder in towns. He specifically excluded lower-class rural males; the gentry had no intention of enfranchising their field hands and shepherds. The reform added half a million new voters, most of them from urban centers. The countrymen who met the lower qualifications were village notables. There was also a geographic redistribution of seats: boroughs of under 10,000 inhabitants lost one member. Yet the countryside and small towns remained overrepresented, a phenomenon that existed in all states where there were parliamentary and local elections.

Disraeli's belief that conservatives could win over the town laborers was not entirely correct. New elections returned the Liberal party, and Gladstone, now its leader, entered on his greatest period. Lasting from 1868 to 1874 he successfully pushed through bills that established the secret ballot, improved the rights of native tenant farmers in Ireland, disestablished the Anglican church there, removed restrictions on trade unions, ended the Test Act that had prohibited non-Anglicans from attending Oxford and Cambridge, and reformed the army by the termination of the purchase of commissions. Such a step aroused a storm of protest among the gentry who had bought places for their younger sons either in the army or the church. Apart from the major act that, at the least, opened the door to military modernization, there were several improvements in military command. Compared with the German army, however, the British were at least a century behind. To be sure, armaments were brought up to date with breech-loading rifles; ordinance officers, however, actually insisted on using muzzle-loading cannon! No general staff was created. The Duke of Cambridge, as commander in chief until 1895, "obstructed progress in the central direction of the fighting machine," according to R. C. K. Ensor, which created one among many obstacles to British soldiers during the Boer War at the end of the century.

The Licensing Act, which sought to control alcohol consumption, may or may not be looked upon as a reform, depending on one's drinking habits. It raised a loud and riotous protest among "publicans" (bartenders or bar owners), and in the liquor trade. The bill's passing in Parliament led to rioting in various towns, so insistent were the British on their "God-given right to drink"—and presumably to get drunk. This act had a marked effect on politics. Before 1872 many publicans—who exercised enormous influence of their client's political inclinations—were generally Liberal. The Licensing Act, however, brought a reversal of fortune to the Liberal party. Formerly distillers tended to favor the free trade that liberals stood for, but when the Liberals sought to limit the hours of drinking, every public house became an "active committee room for the conservative party." What was significant and perhaps inevitable was that the party of the heavy-drinking gentry and "two-bottle parsons" now received financial support from the expanding liquor trade. When Liberals had won over the laissez faire business classes, they had absorbed the nonconformists and Quaker business community, the entrepreneurs who had banished alcohol from their factories, and severely limited it in their company towns, the men who helped create a skilled workingman's cult of abstinence and regular chapel attendance. The marriage of liquor and conservatism in Britain would be matched by that between iron and wheat in France and Germany, an alliance of conservative metallurgists looking for army contracts, and large, equally conservative cereal growers, both eager to obtain protection and subsidies.

Far more effective was civil service reform which introduced competitive exams for all government posts, save those in the Foreign Office. This house cleaning of many unqualified sons of influential fathers demanded that candidates have an education and pass examinations to prove it. The broadening of the suffrage also made it clear that the mass of voters should be educated. This was the reason behind the Education Law of 1870. It resembled in some respects Guizot's education law of 1833 in France. It provided state subsidies for existing voluntary, usually denominational, schools, and created national "board" schools, nondenominational, but offering instruction in the Bible. As yet education was neither compulsory nor free. However, many British families had saved to provide their children with primary instruction and in ten years school attendance jumped from 1.1 million to four. This remarkable burst of reform came to a pause with the Judicature Act of 1873. It attempted to bring reason and order into a judicial and legal system, much of which dated from the Middle Ages. It combined the formerly separate courts: common law, whose judges decided cases that set precedents, and equity, whose judges could override common law in the name of justice. The number of courts with often conflicting or overlapping jurisdictions were united into one Supreme Court of Judicature, with various specialized branches. The House of Lords remained the highest court of appeals.

By 1874 Gladstone and the Liberal party had pushed ahead on many fronts, but had also aroused many antagonisms because each reform adversely affected some special interest. When he proposed building a nondenominational university in Dublin he angered all denominations because most people did not want learning separated from religion. The vote went against him, and he resigned along with his cabinet. This was by no means the end of his career; he led two more cabinets over the next two decades. During those years he offered a solution to the Irish problem, home rule, but only a few party faithful went along with him. In the 1874 elections the Irish returned sixty advocates of home rule but to no avail. Indeed, by now it was apparent that his land reform act was not successful in improving the lot of Irish tenants because it failed to offer them effective protection against arbitrary eviction from the land they rented. The British were little moved. Whether rich or poor, they could hardly convince themselves that the Irish belonged to the human race. The British were not alone in displaying such a national prejudice based on ethnic differences. The French felt the same about the Moslems in North Africa, the Germans about the Poles in Silesia and Poznan, and everybody about the Jews. The British also had a rather low opinion of the Spanish, dating at least from the sixteenth century when Spain sent the great Armada against their island fortress.

Spain: Endemic Malaise

Spain is certainly one of the European exceptions to modernization theory. When French troops put Ferdinand VII back on his throne in 1823, they were acting in concert with the major continental powers. They restored a ruler capable now of preserving order, save for the white terror of the extreme conservatives, the *apostolicos*, more royalist than the king, more Catholic than the pope. Even Ferdinand sought to curb their excesses but he was as impotent as Louis XVIII in France during the white terror there eight years earlier. His brother, Don Carlos, was the darling of the right and next in line of succession since the king had no son. Hoping to avoid this succession Ferdinand married a fourth time, but given his age, well beyond that when men sire sons, his wife produced a daughter, Isabella. The *apsotolicos* denied her the right of succession on the death of the king in 1833. The queen mother, acting as regent, turned to the liberals. A civil war then broke out and although the liberals held the upper hand—purging the Carlists (as the right became known) from the royal court, universities, and army—fighting continued, indeed, became endemic. Neither the queen mother nor her daughter nor anyone else could find a solution satisfactory to both sides. The Liberals themselves soon split into Moderates and Progressives. Their new constitution, promulgated in 1834, was stillborn, and further revisions in 1837, 1845, 1852, 1855, and 1876 punctuated the dismal political history of this period. As each constitution failed to win support, respect for law weakened, and power shifted from the Cortes to the army. There were only two really national institutions, the church, which was mainly conservative, and the army, which shifted sides and proved incapable of preserving order as Spain suffered from a kind of "constitutional disease." Only strong monarchs had managed to hold the country together in the past, but Isabella was neither strong nor admirable. Her lusts were egregious, and she lacked any talents outside the royal bedroom. In the peninsula, anarchy could be tempered only by absolute rule based on the church and the military. Isabella controlled neither. The *fueros*, specifically the regional laws and rights of Basques, but by extension the local self-government of other provinces such as Catalonia, militated against administrative centralization. Civil war therefore tended to be conflicts among *guerrilleros* fought out in mountainous regions where familiarity with terrain was decisive. This troubled and bloody situation was worsened by foreign intervention: The Carlists were backed by Austria, Prussia, Russia, and France; the Liberals belatedly by Britain. The revolution of 1848 did not bring change; there were minor uprisings in the major cities where radicals hoped to seize power. These all failed, as they did throughout Europe.

Despite the violence there was economic development during the 1850s. About 15,000 miles of railway track were laid and foreign commerce doubled. The population at large, however, hardly benefited. In other countries railways spurred economic growth where industry and agriculture were already making progress. This was not the case in Spain. Rails and rolling stock were imported with borrowed money enabling natives to export mainly raw materials, especially fruit, vegetables, and wine. Most peasants were desperately poor, and wars impeded industrial growth. The middle classes showed little initiative; they did not even take part in the violence or seek to end it; nobles, peasants, soldiers, and priests were the perpetrators. Isabella and her ministers were incapacitated by factional rivalries and local feuds, but also by lack of money. At one point she tried to sell Cuba and the Philippines but found no buyers because of the risk.

Isabella was the greatest risk because she was incapable of finding a solid basis of support in the political quagmire. When the liberals turned against her, General Prim led a *pronunciamiento* on September 18, 1868. She fled, leaving behind the issue of succession. It was Spain's vacant throne that led to the Franco-Prussian War.

The Balkans: State Making, Small Scale

In 1800 the Balkans were an integral part of the Ottoman Empire. Southeast Europe below the Danube was the last Continental possession of the sultan, the Spaniards and Italians having expelled the Moslems from their Mediterranean strongholds centuries earlier. In the Southeast two movements were taking place simultaneously: The Ottoman state was growing progressively weaker because of the sultan's preference for the harem to energetic government; and the Balkan peoples were growing increasingly restless to free themselves of rule by political and cultural foreigners.

Ottoman rule was lax in some respects, yet highly exploitative. To Moslem administrators, the Christian natives were allowed to exist to pay tribute into which local officials dipped greedy fingers before they sent the remainder to Constantinople where the sultan resided. The life of the *rayahs*, the non-Moslem masses nearly all of whom were Orthodox Christians, with a minority of Jews, was hardly enviable. They were not only taxed by their Moslem overlords, they had to pay fees and labor dues to native landlords, as well as to the Orthodox clergy who were as rapacious as the Moslems. Almost all of them were farmers, and even those who owned land still had to work the large estates of local lords and the church. The term *rayah* signified their status, meaning herd, little better than animals, really beasts of burden. To find similar cases of mass poverty, we must turn to Ireland, Central Spain, southern Italy, and serf-bound Russia.

Generally peasants of such low estate did not make revolutions; they rioted in order to correct specific abuses. The Balkan peasants, however, became a revolutionary force led by their own or by a petty gentry one level above them. Their initiative was motivated partly by their continued control of village management; the Turks left them to govern themselves, and village governance became their school of politics. The Turks also left them their religion; their priests, even when venal, served sometimes to rally Christians against Moslems. I have not included Balkan revolts in previous chapters on revolution precisely because they differed from the bourgeois working-class rebellions of the West.

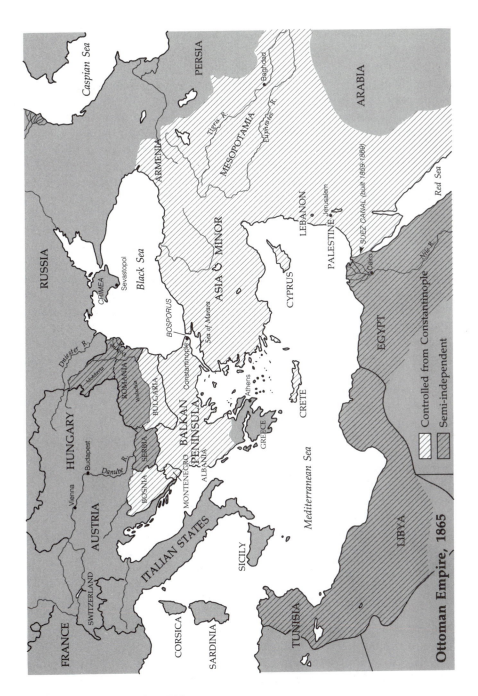

Map 10–1 Ottoman Empire, 1865

With few towns to dot its countryside, the Balkan population was predominantly rural and peasant. Its upheavals sought to end Ottoman exploitation and win some control over land, taxes and spiritual beliefs. They were closer to the *Jacqueries* of the west, but without urban support and with broader aims. State making in western and central Europe was the work of kings aided by prosperous bourgeois and enlightened nobles; in the Southeast, it was the work of self-governing peasants who fought to preserve their autonomy, even against the men they put in power. Part of their inspiration was the oral traditions that kept them aware of an oftentimes mythical past of freedom and warrior heroes.

Certainly the natives of mountainous Montenegro were the most warlike of the Balkan people. The Ottomans had never fully conquered them, and in 1799 they won limited freedom. What emerged was a theocracy under a prince-bishop. However, the Turks were not fully reconciled to freedom and fighting continued along the borders. Their success was contagious, but so was the French Revolution and Napoleon whose conquests extended into Illyria and Egypt. The Serbs, influenced by those events, decided to take up arms against the abuses of the Janissary corps stationed in Belgrade. The major part of Serbian peasants were small land owners, primitive in their life-style but rarely hungry for want of crops. They had arms and found a leader in George Petrovich, called Karageorge because of his wild black hair. In 1804 simple resistance to Janisssary depredations became a war for freedom. The Russians gave some assistance because the tsar was at war against the Sultan until 1812. The native campaign was continued under Milosh Obrenovich and was aided by the Greek revolt. Backed by France and Britain the Greeks won complete freedom; by ricochet the Serbs managed to obtain autonomy on condition they continued payment of tribute to the sultan. Serbia now became a principality with Milosh as hereditary prince. Also liberated was the Serbian Orthodox church from Greek domination. Subsequent Serbian history was more troubled than neighboring territories. Milosh proved to be autocratic and greedy, too much like a sultan for these village-minded peasants. He was overthrown, to be followed by several leaders who were no better. After his recall to power in 1859, he was soon followed by his son Michael who successfully negotiated the retreat of Turkish garrisons from Serbian lands, a step that made his country independent for all practical purposes. He was in the process of organizing all southern Slavs for one last onslaught upon the Turks when he was assassinated, a fate rather common among Balkan rulers. His successor was a frivolous man, bent on the pursuit of pleasure. In this he resembled the sultans.

The people known as Romans or Rumans lived in Moldavia and Wallachia, two principalities at the mouth of the Danube River. However they hardly benefited from the commercial opportunities afforded by water traffic. Their local leaders were landlords ruling over peasants, many of whom were serfs. Although their geographical situation could have aided them economically, it was less favorable politically for they stood on the pathway the Russians followed in their drive toward the Straits. Had the Romanians been a stronger force they could have played the tsar against the sultan, but they were really ill organized and subject to both pressure and occupation by the Russians, their would-be protectors, as occurred during the Russo-Turk War of 1828–29. In 1848 the natives rose in revolt against the local administration imposed by the tsar; as was to be expected, his army crushed such insubordination and fully occupied the two principalities. Austria did not oppose this move. With many Romanians under its rule, the Hapsburgs wanted no Romanian state nearby lest it stir up those living in Transylvania under Austro-Hungarian domination.

But in 1859 the elected assemblies of the two territories chose a common ruler, a native boyar, John Cuza. What he acquired was limited power and rule over a very backward society. The best land was owned by a few lords for whom the peasants worked like serfs. There were few towns, very little commerce, most of it in German hands, and none but handicraft industry. Cuza was a man of 1848, eager to create a landowning peasantry, and as a first step he abolished serfdom in 1864. He also set about dissolving monasteries and planned to establish a school system. These actions frightened the nobles who overthrew him in 1866 and invited a German prince to replace him.

The Romanians were well off compared to the Bulgars. No *rayahs* were so dominated and brutalized by the Turks. During the Ottoman advance they had lost their native leaders, and did not have recourse to a native clergy. Their church, the most important bond within and among villages, was subjected to the Greek patriarch whose policy was thorough hellenization and Greek bishops shared that goal. The Bulgar tongue was replaced by Greek in religious services, and the Bulgar past was obliterated, leaving no history, however mythical, to infuse a sense of identity. Only after the liberation of the Greeks and Serbs did they awaken to a national consciousness. And only slowly did an educated class emerge to teach the natives a national goal. Finally, in 1870 and under pressure from Russia, the Turks allowed the formation of a Bulgar church, and from this time Bulgar history became inextricably interwoven with that of Russia.

In reality all of Balkan history was interwoven with the foreign policies of the major states. Britain usually wanted to preserve the Ottoman Empire by reforming it, and particularly Disraeli stood in opposition to the Panslavs of Russia who encouraged Balkan states with the intention of dominating them. Concerned with the rise of nationalist fervor, Austria acted to isolate her Slavic peoples from contamination and that usually involved taking steps to keep Russia out of Balkan affairs. These conflicting postures came together in July 1875 when the peasants of Bosnia rose against their Turkish overlords. The next summer Serbia and Montenegro declared war on Turkey, still their nominal suzerain, in support of Bosnians. The Bulgarians also rebelled, so the Ottomans resorted to a massacre of some 12,000 natives. European opinion was outraged, but only Russia sent in troops. A peace treaty, signed at San Stefano, would have made Russia master of the Balkans, a condition absolutely unacceptable to the major powers. So they met in Berlin where they drew up another treaty. It finally granted full freedom to the newly formed states, but it also returned East Roumelia (southern Bulgaria) and Macedonia to the brutalities of Ottoman rule, and kept Bulgaria itself under nominal Moslem suzerainty. Not until years of strife did the Bulgars win freedom in 1908. To protect their interests Austria occupied Bosnia and Herzegovina, Britain Cyprus.

The Balkans were by the 1870s balkanized: broken up into small entities with uncertain borders, scarcely modernized economies, governments dominated by nobles, and a populace highly filled with nationalist aspirations largely untouched by Western liberalism. Such conditions made these states collectively the "tinderbox" of Europe. As they attempted to modernize with only limited success, the shadow of tragedy waited in the wings.

The Northern Periphery

Compared with the tragic events of the Southeast the history of the northern periphery seems rather dull but more hopeful. Life was far more stable and comfortable. Belgium's economy kept pace with Britain's, and her standard of living became one of the highest. Perhaps this progress in comfort explains why there was so little pressure exerted for political reform. In 1830 Belgium was a bourgeois oligarchy, with a highly limited franchise comparable with that of Great Britain before suffrage reform. Industrial growth did, however, produce a sizable laboring population that organized trade unions and joined a socialist party, and it was these two institutions that finally won the vote for all men older than the age of twenty-five, after a general strike paralyzed the country. The upper classes only partially gave way; apart from the higher than normal voting age, additional votes were given to university graduates and the men most heavily taxed.

The Dutch Netherlands, chiefly agricultural and commercial, lagged seriously on the road to democracy. The first written constitution appeared only in 1849, and William III retained considerable power, most notably an absolute veto over bills emanating from parliament. The suffrage remained extremely limited; the "reform" laws of 1887 and 1896 left only 14 percent of the male population with the vote. Like Catholic Belgium, the Protestant Netherlands provided state aid for both private denominational and public schools where religion was part of the curriculum. Such close church-state relations usually—but not always—were a sign of a conservative society.

Denmark was a prosperous country but not a lucky one. In 1815 she lost Norway to the Swedes because of her close alliance with Napoleon before his final defeat. Then Prussia and Austria seized Schleswig and Holstein in 1864, using the excuse that the Danish king had violated international law regarding the provinces. The king was not wise but the peasant majority did not suffer from the loss of Germanic lands. They enjoyed the property of their up-to-date dairy farms and foreign markets.

The Swiss were sufficiently isolated in the Alps to avoid dangerous entanglements. Besides, their neutrality was guaranteed by the Treaty of Vienna of 1815. Their worst enemy was their religious prejudice, a set of mind that led to a civil war in 1847 between the highland Catholic cantons and the lowland Protestant ones. The latter were victorious, and used their victory wisely. In the following year all the cantons drew up a federal constitution modeled on that of the United States, and then, we might say, lived happily ever after. Switzerland was a rare state where patriotism was not based on language; in fact, the natives were allowed to use four different tongues. Most used German, but French, Italian, and Romanche enjoyed official standing. This was an exceptional situation, when the culture of Europe was moving forcefully toward national differentiation based largely on language. Initially the constituent cantons enjoyed a large degree of autonomy. Later constitutional revisions shifted a little more power to the federal state. With a growing economy, universal male suffrage, and the right of recall and legislative initiative enshrined in the fundamental law of the land, the Swiss were among the freest and, one can assume, the happiest people of Europe. This is a pleasant note on which to end a chapter describing so much war, duplicity, and human suffering.

11

Economic Prosperity

A Golden Age: Financial Innovations

The term *golden age* can be simplistic, but it is appropriate for the third quarter of the century if only because the discovery of gold in California and Australia put vast amounts of the precious metal into circulation, made more money available for private and state enterprises, and encouraged a modest inflation that was more helpful than harmful for business. With capital more easily attainable and rising prices, entrepreneurs were encouraged to found new industries, expand older ones, and innovate in the technology of production and distribution. It was a time remembered after its end because it came between the "hungry forties" and the depression of the fourth quarter.

The benefits of the age were not due solely to gold mining. On the Continent economic growth had started earlier, at least in the 1840s, a decade combining at first good and then bad years. The latter began with the crisis of 1846–47, when there was not only privation but real starvation. The depression was gradually coming to an end when the 1848 wave of revolutions submerged it and prolonged the agony. The bloody crushing of insurgents had a double effect. It restored confidence to the landed and monied classes; it also dealt a heavy blow to the many small craftsmen who were in revolt not only against arbitrary government but also against an even greater menace to them: capitalism based on large-scale factory production. The new or restored regimes made the world safe for investment and profits in agriculture, industry, and, above all, finance, the oldest branch of the capitalist system.

Financiers, after all, were needed to distribute the new sources of wealth to entrepreneurs. This function was less attractive to the older banking houses that traditionally invested in government bonds and served as agencies for their public sale in large coupons. Therefore continued economic growth required a new type of bank and state action. As it happened the revolution in France had thrown up a new ruler, Napoleon III, and he had earlier absorbed ideas that looked to a more intimate and stimulating relation between state and economy. He was much taken with an early thinker named Claude-Henri de Saint-Simon who envisioned a state run by bankers and scientists who would use their wealth and knowledge to promote industry as a means of increasing the well-being of everyone who worked. Napoleon surrounded himself with some of Saint-Simon's disciples, Michel Chevalier, a free-trader, and two brothers, Isaac and Emile Pereire, who founded in 1852 the Crédit Mobilier, an investment bank organized precisely to invest in industrial enterprises. It reinforced the Comptoir d'Escompte, founded in 1848 for the same purpose. At about this same time the Schaaffhausen Bank of Cologne, as well as a deposit bank in Darmstadt, opened their doors to industrialists in need of working capital.

In fact, a sizable network of banks emerged, with interlocking directorates crossing state boundaries. They were all joint stock in form, managed by dynamic men of vision who made capital available for building and also consolidating railroads throughout Europe. The Crédit Mobilier was as active in Austria, Prussia, Spain, Italy, and Portugal as in France. More bankers began to sit on the boards of companies they financed, and in this capacity the heads of the Crédit Mobilier reorganized the mines of the upper Loire Valley coal field, united the omnibus company of Paris, set up insurance and gas companies, shipping lines, and big construction firms. In 1855 it paid a dividend of 40 percent; in 1867 it crashed, having overreached itself. Napoleon could have saved it, but at this late date, as noted already, he was suffering both political and physical maladies and submitted to the pressure of the Rothschilds who distrusted the Pereire upstarts even though they were all Jewish.

By the 1860s, even the more traditional houses had entered the field of industrial development. Their main business remained the servicing of state loans, but they also bought shares in the banks that were actively financing new enterprises. Even the Bank of France, the avatar of conservative finance, became more active and, equally important, its directors founded numerous branches outside of Paris to make credit available in the provinces. Discounted bills rose from 1.8 million francs in 1847 to 14.6 million in the period 1861–75. It was now evident that money had to circulate as rapidly as goods, a feat made much easier by new technologies of communication such as railroads and telegraph lines. The demand for capital was constantly rising among entrepreneurs who were in competition and made more combative by new means of transport. International markets were the battleground—at least until business leaders later curbed competition by means of monopolies.

During the 1870s several results became clear: Money was more plentiful and, therefore cheaper, which made possible the lowering of interest rates; there was lesser demand for owners to rely strictly on profits to expand. This in turn made more money available for even higher profit distributions and higher wages, although the rate of profits surpassed that of wages. Borrowing was no longer seen as a stigma, a sign of weakness, but rather as courageous entrepreneurship, as dashing management. With so many dull generals around the innovative businessman could become a kind of heroic model, encouraged by the far more dynamic organization of finance on an international scale.

The geographical spread of financial modernization did not move outward evenly in all compass directions. The area it covered was still limited to northern and western Europe, with some limited impinging on other regions already favored, where local businessmen and politicians, like Cavour, encouraged modernization with government loans and other stimulants. There appeared as a result a distinctive geographic division of labor. Western and northern industrialized zones living on commerce, manufacturing, and service industries such as banking, shipping, insurance, technical and engineering skills developed most dramatically. Other zones, southern and eastern Europe in particular, profited from this concentration, which contributed to urban growth, by providing the food stuffs and raw materials the North and West required. It would be too simplistic to allege the existence of an industrial-urban Europe fully distinct from an agricultural-rural Europe. There was too much interpenetration between the two, and there were areas of economic backwardness within the more modernized zones. Yet there were differences, and the histories of each zone followed fairly well-demarcated and separate paths into the twentieth century. The successful move toward freer trade during the quarter was inspired by the notion of regional specialization, first European wide, eventually world wide. Urban mouths, after all, had to be filled. People cannot eat machines, nor drink industrial lubricants. An imaginative writer of the eighteenth century had published a book entitled *Man the Machine*, but not even he believed that humans could do without food. Men and women often labored like machines, and were treated as such by their employers; however, they still required food and drink.

Agriculture: Feeding More Mouths

Farming did not fit neatly into the rose-colored picture of the age, partly because landed interests were reluctant to borrow, partly because their access to loans was limited. Napoleon encouraged the founding of a mortgage bank, the Crédit Foncier. As it turned out, however, its loans went mainly to rebuilding cities, above all Paris, and it encouraged the more speculative activities of urban renewal.

Some large landowners managed to gain access to credit as a means of modernizing. Small farmers more often eschewed banks as banks eschewed them. But there were exceptions, particularly numerous in Germany, and more so in Prussia. Small growers in the Rhineland and the South were able to set up cooperative lending institutions by pooling their resources. Two men were leaders and innovators in the spread of rural cooperatives. Hermann Schulze-Delitzsch came forward with the plan of a communal collective group sharing unlimited liability and acting as creditors and guarantors for each other. There were 174 such cooperatives in 1874, but they were weakened by the crash of the previous year. They learned that unlimited liability was dangerous for their treasuries. More viable was the work of Friedrich Raiffeisen who proposed the idea of single village cooperatives that would provide credit, but, as important, purchase collectively fertilizers and fodder for distribution at wholesale prices. The peasants managed these institutions themselves with considerable efficiency. Unfortunately there was hardly any move in this direction elsewhere, and without doubt German industrial expansion owed much to the rising standards among the rural population. Long without extensive foreign markets, German industrialists served the rapidly growing domestic market, largely a rural one until the urban populations grew sufficiently to enhance their purchases of manufactures. There was, behind German dynamic growth, a contrapuntal relation: Farmers equipped themselves from urban factories to improve their methods and enhance yield, and in turn supplied a growing urban population with food and raw materials. In eastern and southern Europe, where most of the rural population were too poor to buy manufactures, industrial progress was confined to a few regions in or near the largest cities and seaports.

In western and northern Europe farming techniques underwent significant improvement, pulled ahead by blooming urban populations. Rapid, cheaper transport facilitated exchanges over large spaces and opened new markets formerly closed by the high costs of shipping. Railroads especially but also rivers and canals, when steam engines replaced animal traction on barges, were the arteries along which flowed both local and exotic goods.

Agricultural cooperatives provided credit and the chemical industry discovered the fertilizers and insecticides needed to augment yields, particularly of wheat to feed cities. Soil chemistry, pioneered by Justus Liebig, discovered how plants drew nourishment from the earth, and their need for nitrogen, potassium, and phosphorus. British knowledge of how legumes, if plowed back into the soil as green manure to enrich it, now became widely accepted on the Continent. Frenchmen were somewhat slower than Belgians, Germans, and Danes to adopt new techniques and to mechanize. Limited industrial growth and the persistence of small enterprises failed to reduce costs significantly and therefore prices of

farm machines were often too high to capture large rural markets. But everywhere fallow land was taken over for permanent culture. Large estates, formerly
rather backward save in Britain, became more efficient and more profitable, perhaps less so in eastern and central France where crop sharing was practiced and
owners too stingy to modernize. About half of France's farmland was tilled by
tenants either as croppers or renters. Their farms, like those of most peasant
owners, were both small and fragmented into plots often not even an acre in
size, and widely dispersed over a large area. This situation made it impossible to
use heavy machinery. After the very bad harvest of 1855–56, the last that caused
starvation in the West, there was progress resulting from greater consolidation
of holdings. But fragmentation remained a common inhibiter throughout
Europe; in Germany, however, cooperatives were fairly effectively used to overcome it, as well as to encourage plot exchanges as a means of consolidation.

Save for the mid-1850s, food production just about tripled, yet all industrial countries had to import wheat to feed the rapidly growing cities. Where
farmers could not compete with grains from the Ukraine, and later North
America and Australia, they turned plow land into pastures for raising cattle.
Beef, along with mutton, appeared as a fairly common article on the tables of
industrial workers. Milk made into cheese also became a source of rural wealth
and some localities became famous for their specialties, like Gorgonzola in Italy
or Roquefort in France.

Fast trains brought another product to mass markets: table wine. Before
railways only the most expensive wines were shipped far beyond the vineyards.
This was why grape vines were cultivated well to the north of their recommended growing areas where cold and damp made grapes and their wines excessively acid, and low in alcohol. Such wine was often homemade and home consumed; only small quantities entered town markets where it was dispensed in
lower-class taverns and competed with beer. It was swept from the market when
mass-produced wines could cheaply travel northward from lower Languedoc in
railway wagons and sold in taverns and groceries right out of the barrel. Only
expensive wines were sold in bottles. This turn of events was delayed for a few
years when mildew struck southern vines. A scientist at the University of
Bordeaux found a sulfur compound that destroyed the malady and for two
decades, 1855–75, southern France both deindustrialized, abandoning woolen
textiles, and grew rich on oceans of common jug wine. Lucky were the growers
who saved their profits because a tiny aphid, the phylloxera, began its invasion
in the late 1860s and in two decades simply destroyed the entire vineyard of
France and then of all Europe. Spain and Italy benefited for a little more than a
decade by quenching the thirst that had been created for wine; however, by the
late 1880s their vineyards, too, succumbed. French scientists once more came to
the rescue; they grafted vinifera vines onto American rootstock that was resistant
to the aphid. By the 1890s Languedocian vineyards were again in full growth. The
cultivators and shippers, however, hardly benefited. In their frenzy to increase

yields they literally flooded their markets with thin, acid beverages that no one wanted, prices dropped and massive failures followed. The cheap wine industry had its golden age; it would not have another before 1914. Even fine wine producers were adversely affected because consumers were turned away by the adulterations that had become common practice during the shortage.

Italian farmers benefited from political unity, especially as the new government energetically sought to tie the disparate regions of the peninsula, Sicily and Sardinia included, with railway track. After 1860 all crops grew in output save wheat. Grapes and citrus fruit exports leapt up as transport went ahead. Silk cocoons produced in Lombardy and Piedmont were shipped to Lyon where the silk industry recovered for awhile. Silk, raw or thrown, made up one-third of all exports. Credit cooperatives, encouraged by Luigi Luzzatti, a disciple of Raiffeisen, provided capital for modernization in the north around Milan and Cremona. Before and after 1870 agriculture made a greater contribution to gross national product than industry. The picture was more grim in parts of the center, and absolutely bleak in the south, the *Mezzogiorno*, as well as in the islands. The lack of industry left a large unemployed and underemployed labor force, a situation depressing wages and more encouraging of banditry than modernization. Crop yields were even below those of the Balkans and Russia. Largely at fault was the crop sharing system, the *mezzadria*, widely practiced on the dominant large estates. With such cheap labor there was no incentive to buy machines. When three-fourths of an estates' income went into the absentee owners' coffers the peasants faced a life as hopeless as that in Ireland, and they, too, had to emigrate to foreign shores. Tools were of the simplest; plows were made of sticks with metal points forged by the village blacksmith. This, combined with lack of fertilizer, meant that yields barely exceeded medieval levels. Even in the richer north, meat consumption was only one-half that of Germany; in the South it was one-seventh.

Spain and Russia, poles apart, were typical of the peripheral economies. The Spaniards were too busy fighting one another, the so-called Liberals fighting the very authentic Conservatives. A grossly ignorant and indifferent aristocracy, owning huge estates, was absentee and concerned only with milking the land and the wretches who worked it. Our comments about Italy emphatically apply to Spain. Even woolen exports, once a major source of wealth, steadily declined as a result of the loss of foreign markets. The fine wool of Merino sheep, once a Spanish preserve and widely bred in the south and center, was now grown extensively in Germany, France, and Italy for the shrinking number of buyers. Cotton was king, wool at best a lowly prince.

Russia offered little relief from this dreary picture. The emancipation of peasants hardly affected farming techniques. The explanation is not complex. When in 1862 the serf was freed from both lord and state, he was not freed from the village (*mir*). The tsar and his ministers had no intention of creating either a rootless urban or rural proletariat, so each individual remained bound to his commune, which remained collectively responsible for his payment of taxes as well as the sums he owed the state for the land—redemption payments that were to stretch over forty-nine years. Therefore no peasant could leave his commune save with permission that was not readily given; worse, land was retained in strips, with those of peasants widely separated from the core village and from one another. With more than 80 percent of the population still classed as rural, industry and trade were tortuously slow to grow, and relied heavily on foreign capital by the 1860s and after. Russians encountered, for the time, insoluble difficulties: vast distances and no railways; terrain, much of which was barren; climate, hardly improved over the centuries, the so-called "little ice age" hardly abated in the East, whereas the West enjoyed a slowly moderating climate since the 1840s. Progressive culture was hindered by the peasant's inability to buy land outright and set up for himself.

Civilly free, each peasant remained an economic serf. There were no rich, large peasant landowners until the next quarter. Families with many children received more land from their communes, but as children grew up, married, and formed their own households, the original family holding declined in size. Unless, of course, several generations continued to live under the same roof, a situation despised by young wives everywhere because mothers-in-law treated them as servants. The few "well-off" peasants, called *kulaks*, were not typical. And they were "well off" only in the Russian context.

Probably most peasants of both sexes were content to remain in a village community and only a few complained of the near-collective system of tillage that the strip system imposed. They were not tempted by machines, at least no more than the large owners. Yet, peasant discontent did not lessen, and riots broke out with traditional frequency, caused not by communal organization, but by heavy taxes and redemption payments. Protest usually led to a refusal to make these payments. In the peasant mind they, as serfs, had once belonged to a master, but the land had always been theirs. So why should they have to pay for it? And most of them, either willfully or not, fell into arrears. And official collectors could do little to coerce them, especially when prices for commercial crops tended downward. The poverty of Russia's peasant class was hardly a stimulant for industrial development. The absolute state of tsarist Russia could hardly solve this problem as long as its restrictive policies were part of the problem.

Industrial Development: Rich Western Nations

By midcentury Europe was economically divided into rich, less rich, and poor areas. The north, west, and center were the most prosperous; the Mediterranean was far less well off, and the east was still mired in poverty. The view of the third quarter as a golden age must therefore be tempered by the recognition that growth was not universal. It was not even ubiquitous within the richest areas because there were backwaters where industrial growth did not penetrate, where it was openly damned as disruptive of a healthy artisan economy. In the third quarter domestic production of coarser textiles was still active, although on its last legs, not in backward but in progressive economies.

Even progressive economies suffered weaknesses. There was excessive optimism about profits and productivity. Railroad companies whose shares had become highly speculative in the 1840s, continued to attract capital investment. Everywhere in progressive Europe, laws encouraged growth simply by facilitating joint-stock business organization, as I pointed out earlier.

The industry easiest to set up and control was still cotton textiles. Britain led the way, deriving much to its profits from foreign markets made even more active by the many British immigrants in North and South America. Iron and steel production spread to the Continent as rail lines demanded greater and greater output. This was an era of major innovation in metallurgy. Increased speed demanded steel rather than iron rails, and British inventors were not lacking the skills and technical acumen to meet demand. The Bessemer converter (1855), the Siemens-Martin process (1865) and that of Thomas-Gilchrist (1878) provided means of removing impurities such as carbon and sulfur from iron ores, enabling producers to lower prices for a refined end product. Demand for locomotives and rails bypassed textiles as the stimulus of industrial growth. British engineers built railroads in Europe and all over the world. France and Germany were still actively building their national networks, first the main trunk lines, then the secondary arteries so essential to local manufactures.

The European network had attained about 14,000 miles at midcentury; twenty years later it had grown to 78,000 miles. Much of the recently laid track was made of steel, stronger than iron and needed to stand the pressure of trains going more than forty miles per hour and faster as locomotives became more efficient.

Another stimulus to iron and steel was the conversion of maritime commerce from wood to iron. Coastal shipping was very slow to change, but overseas transport shifted rapidly, the last great sailing vessels, the clippers, dying out in the 1860s, replaced by ships built of iron and driven by steam. The invention of the screw propeller in the 1850s and improvements of engines in the 1860s made steam power far more efficient. The opening of the Suez Canal in 1869 really made steam obligatory. It is odd that the French who built the canal were the slowest to abandon wind power, probably because the Third Republic subsidized equally all ships of French flag, whether of sail or steam power. Another encouragement to both steel rails and ships was the declining price of metal, the natural result of superior new furnaces using the Bessemer converter that removed impurities by blowing air through molten iron, and then the Siemens-Martin open hearth that was even more efficient and permitted the use of scrap iron and low-grade ore. German industrialists had to await the Gilchrist-Thomas process because it was the most efficient in the smelting of their highly phosphoric ores. With adequate financial backing they constructed bigger works and brought in the latest equipment. Metallurgical dynasties were the driving force: the Stumm family in the Saar, the Krupps in the Ruhr, the Borsigs in Berlin.

Equally important was coal, the only efficient fuel before oil and electricity. Britain retained her prime position, both in the national as well as the international market. In fact, the increasing number of steam-driven ships not only increased consumption but also lowered the costs of exporting coal to countries lacking it such as Italy, or short of it, like France, or nearly devoid of it but with important iron ore deposits in need of coal for smelting, like Sweden and Spain. The third quarter witnessed the near depletion of forests, so there was a rapid transition to coke as charcoal became too expensive.

Mining operations benefited from the lowering of taxes on coal, relaxation of government controls and supervision, save in Britain, and cheap labor as peasants, formerly part-time underground workers, became full-time miners. Mining engineering probably improved the safety of working conditions as mine shafts went deeper under the earth. In France the École des Mines trained young men for this work.

The resort to coal and coke as fuels enabled the Ruhr Valley to become a major center of metallurgy. By 1871 the newly unified German Empire became the second coal-producing country, still far behind Britain, but ahead of France and Belgium. Old medieval towns became factory centers as the Ruhr surpassed upper Silesia, mainly because, as in England, coal and iron ore lay in close proximity. Also Western financiers invested heavily in coal mines. To protect their investments, they encouraged the consolidation of small concerns. The economic crisis of 1857 furthered their aim by putting many small companies out of business. The same process occurred in upper Silesia so that during the 1860s six large firms controlled two-thirds of that province's coal production.

The third quarter witnessed a marked transition in textiles as well. In Britain, hand spinners and weavers were nearly an extinct specie, whereas in France and Prussia their numbers were on the wane. In all these countries, textile production, manpower, and exports were second in volume only to agriculture, but no longer the major producer of wealth. By now cotton had far surpassed wool, and linen was seriously on the decline, unable to compete with cheap cotton cloth. For this reason the American civil war, when the Union navy cut off cotton exports from the southern states, provoked a crisis for four years in Europe. The prosperity of the 1850s gave way to plant closures and unemployment. There was some relief when raw cotton began to arrive from Egypt and India, but it was a different kind of fiber requiring adjustment of machinery and insufficient in amount for the high demand. Many of the smaller mills using antiquated machinery went out of business. Consolidation began in textiles just as it did in coal and metals. In the German states mills tended to be larger than their British and French counterparts, hiring usually more than 500 workers.

They used the latest equipment and all processes were now mechanized. Yet they could not meet all the needs of the domestic market, at least for finer fabrics that were imported from Lancashire. In textiles the Germans learned and borrowed from the British, but they could not surpass them either in the quality of cloth or in exports.

Industrial Development: Poor Eastern Nations

Russia was the largest national state in Europe both territorially and demographically. Before the coming of railways its very size was a disadvantage; it was isolated from Europe, and its manufacturing areas were too distant from major markets. In 1852 the regime had laid less than 400 miles of track connecting Moscow to Saint Petersburg. By 1885 there were 17,000 miles of track. This was an important expansion but still left vast areas with nothing but bad roads to supplement the rivers and canals. The first sign of mechanized industry came with the introduction of cotton textile factories in the central region and in Saint Petersburg during the 1840s. Spinning and weaving machines were imported from Great Britain, as were mechanics and engineers. Capital came either from state subsidies or loans from some liquor tax concessionaires. These companies were either joint stock or partnerships. As for the entrepreneurs, most of them came from merchant or gentry families. These early enterprises did not make much of an impact on general conditions in the third quarter. Industry was so little developed in 1860 that between 80 and 90 percent of the population still lived most of the year in rural areas. Serf emancipation the next year did not help industry. On the contrary, emancipation struck a blow to old serf artisan manufacturing. Iron ore production fell 15 percent during the sixties after serf miners were freed in the Urals. The only industries that showed any life were those devoted to consumer goods. Had the Crimean War effort depended on samovars, washboards, and oil lamps, Russia would have won.

This tardiness was largely the result of tsarist policy. Leading officials, as well as the tsar, were favorable to the Slavophiles, conservatives who looked on industrialization as a Western import that would undermine the traditional class structure and rural way of live of mother Russia. As well-to-do romantics, they completely distorted the realities of Russian life. The *mir* was sacred to them and must be preserved—as it was—to the detriment of agricultural progress. Russians had to wait until the last decades of the century to experience the first signs of rapid economic growth, and the state would have to take the initiative after it acquired the resources to do so, chiefly by borrowing capital from the West.

In the Southeast none of the Balkan states had or would acquire the resources to "jump start" their terribly backward economies. What resources they garnered they invested primarily in industry to the neglect of agriculture, a policy that wasted resources of societies not yet mentally prepared or with natural resources to modernize rapidly. Romania was blessed with oil, but it was used for lamps and of little generative value until the invention of the internal combustion engine for automobiles. The energies of Balkan peoples, as indicated already, went into state building, a process that gave scant attention to wealth building.

Commerce: An Era of Free Trade

Although the third quarter of the century was an active period for production, it was also a time of rapid growth of transport and commerce. After all, the mass of goods issuing forth from factories and workshops had to be sent to market and sold. Population growth continued at an accelerated rate and therefore more people had not only to be fed but also clothed, housed, and provided with the vast array of household furnishings and tools needed for daily life in industrializing and urbanizing societies. Peasant farmers in traditional societies made at home many of the objects they needed; apartment dwellers (the vast majority of urban inhabitants) had to buy everything. As more and more of them improved their incomes they were able to purchase a greater number of objects.

Most people made their purchases in small retail outlets, family owned and operated. There were advantages in this: Buyers and sellers often knew each other, credit was available, and even bargaining and sometimes wrangling over prices added some relief from the monotony of everyday life. But prices were always high because low turnover increased the costs of doing business. And prices were particularly steep for articles made by skilled craftsmen such as tailors, shoe, hat, and furniture makers, to mention only a few.

From the 1850s on retailers in large cities began to suffer from the appearance of large department stores, new ventures pioneered in Paris by a mercantile genius named Aristide Boucicaut. These were virtual emporiums with names suggestive of low prices, like Au Bon Marché of Boucicaut himself and La Samaritaine, or luxury with Le Louvre or Le Bazar de l'Hôtel de Ville. In these one did not bargain over prices, and paid on purchase. By 1870 these large outlets represented only 17 percent of sales, so they did not put many small merchants out of business nor seriously lower prices. Besides, until urban transport was improved and tramway fares went down, few people—mostly middle-class women—could travel to them. This was unfortunate because the limited sales and high prices of retailers formed a bottleneck in the commercial chain between manufacturer and final buyer. Mass factory production lowered the cost of production per unit, but the savings tended to become absorbed by wholesale middlemen and retailers. Cities, especially those in the provinces, remained honeycombed with narrow twisting streets lined with small shops.

In industrial cities, working-class families, especially susceptible to avaricious shopkeepers, began to set up consumers' cooperative stores. The Rochdale Equitable Pioneers was founded in 1844, and as its name states, it was a pioneer in this movement. Start-up conditions were primitive: The first store was located in the home of one of the founding weavers. The few staple groceries carried were sold at prevailing prices to avoid the animosity of private merchants, but members was credited with a share of the profits according to the amount of their purchases. Within three decades membership grew to 8,000, with the volume of business at about £300,000. With the formation of branches, handling a wide variety of merchandise, the consumers' cooperative movement really got under way. The Rochdale plan was adopted elsewhere, and spread to foreign countries. It called for incorporation under limited liability laws. Just as precious as returns on purchase prices was the practice of cooperatives to offer pure produce in a time when petty retailers proffered watered milk and sand in the sugar, as well as their thumbs on the scales, to name only a few of the abuses. Fortunately wholesale and retail prices were moderated when the costs of transport steadily declined, thanks to railroad expansion, subsidized by all states, partly through mail contracts. Even cheap goods could now travel over long distances at low rates. The British government, although it interfered little in the economy, set maximum rates both for freight and passengers. Other states soon followed. Because all European networks, save those of Spain and Russia, used the same gauges for track spacing, freight could travel over national boundaries even if locomotives could not.

Equally important was overseas trade between Europe and the world. The commercial revolution of the eighteenth century had prepared Britain for an industrial take-off. Foreign markets continued to prod industrialists to achieve greater productivity by improving techniques, organization, and management.

With the growth of foreign trade there arose movements to lower the tariffs that had long hindered exchange among nations attached to the old mercantilist tradition. The British led the way, as noted earlier, by abolishing the Corn Laws. An even greater step toward free trade was taken in 1860 when Cobden for Britain and Chevalier for France drew up a treaty that reduced tariffs on most goods to a nominal level, just enough to provide revenue rather than protection, and for gathering statistical data on imports and exports. For the next twenty years other countries signed similar treaties, all of which contained most-favored-nation clauses, creating a veritable free-trade regime among the more advanced states. The countries benefiting most from these exchanges were the British and the Germans in general, and French wine growers and luxury producers in particular.

A few numbers are enlightening. In 1844 clearances from British ports came to just over 10 million tons. As railroads connected ports to productive hinterlands, clearances increased dramatically, attaining 36.6 million tons in 1870. France too benefited. In 1860 her share of European exports was 19 percent; then her exports of manufactured goods rose 5.3 percent annually until the 1870 war, placing her a far second behind Britain. The British made up the chief market for Gallic high-value exports: wine and silk textiles especially. But French manufacturers and merchants were much less interested in overseas than in European markets. This position put a damper on industry. It also limited her merchant marine; most trade was carried in foreign bottoms, all the more so after Napoleon III reduced taxes on foreign ships entering French ports. He subsidized both shipping and ship building. But after 1870 German industrialists and merchants forged ahead and surpassed France for exports in the early 1880s, and the gap widened thereafter, never to be closed.

Taxes: The Inequality of Life

The roughly twenty-odd years when international commerce was freer of impediments than it had ever been since the Roman Empire, consumers should have enjoyed the benefits of lower prices. Of course, they did. But at the same time that governments lowered tariffs on foreign objects, they raised domestic taxes on virtually every item available for sale. These were excise taxes, also referred to as indirect taxes. They made up a major part of government revenue and, being regressive, burdened the poorer classes rather than the wealthy. Only Great Britain had a mildly progressive income tax, a direct tax on fortunes. Established in the 1840s by Peel, it exempted small incomes, the vast majority. Most states also had land taxes, calibrated according to the estimated value of land. There were taxes on doors as well as windows, which induced landlords to wall window space, and cut off light and fresh air in the already dim and damp interiors of lower-class tenements. But it was sales taxes that most adversely affected lower-class standards, since they were levied on grain, meaning bread, the staple of life. In times of short grain harvests, ministries had lowered duties to encourage imports and control prices. This tactic had as its object to prevent bread riots. As we noted earlier, bread riots ceased to trouble authorities after 1850, and there were no tax revolts in industrial countries either. Nonetheless taxes of every sort went up after midcentury as costs of government mounted to pay for economic subsidies and investment on infrastructure, for more numerous civil servants, and for modernizing armies and navies.

It is interesting to note that parliamentary debate on taxes had little to do with their social impact, but with political concern: Liberal politicians wanted to control the crown's taxing power as a means of controlling the crown. That the majority of the population was inequitably taxed in relation to income did not become an important issue until the later years of the century. Meanwhile, it was not a question of the people eating bread or cake; taxes ate the people. Especially city people.

Cities: Patterns of Growth

During the first half of the century the urban communities of western Europe began to grow at an unprecedented rate, both in space and inhabitants. Over the course of the third quarter this phenomenon became more pronounced as it spread to other parts of the Continent. Meanwhile national administrators, having themselves become victims of filth, pollution, and disease associated with urbanization, began to take measures to clean the environment, to renovate the urban setting where they were forced to live. They slowly became aware that cities, especially capital cities, had become the habitat of a far larger segment of the nation's population than at any time since the Roman Empire. The general pattern was physical expansion, rising density with more people per square mile, increasing grime, and an almost superhuman effort to renovate and clean up streets, sewers, and water supplies.

Before midcentury textile factories had transformed squalid hamlets into squalid villages and these into even more squalid towns, usually strung, like dirty beads, along strong flowing rivers. Eventually steam power attracted entrepreneurs to coal fields. River towns enjoyed relatively unspoiled air, but their water supply soon became little more than a sewer; coal towns raised the level of grime to a new high for which there is no historical precedent. Where coal attracted metallurgical plants, there resulted an enormous increase of foundry workers, intense population density, overcrowded habitation, all the features that worsened air and water pollution. How was it possible for people to increase in this poisoned environment? Either the deplorable living conditions have been exaggerated by contemporary observers, or—more likely—immigration was of such magnitude that it overcompensated for local death rates. And this was what really happened. Older cities were often spared these results because of another factor: Many factory owners did not settle in them. At first factory owners avoided setting up in established cities where occupied land was scarce, expensive, and heavily taxed. In addition the cost of living was dearer for workers, making it necessary to pay higher wages. They preferably built their mills in rural communities that became satellite centers of production, separate but in constant contact with the larger regional cities that provided legal and other services, particularly information about markets and prices, as well as financial support through loans and stock issues after limited liability was legalized. These older cities, often nearly dormant, came back to life as "central places," connecting factory towns to the outside world via advanced means of communication and transport.

Certainly industrial development led to increases in the size and number of urban communities. Early in the century coal-fired steam power in Great Britain drew cotton mills to a ring of small towns or even villages around Manchester, which served as a central place for them and was in direct contact by rail with the port of Liverpool. It became a way point in a far-flung network linking mill towns to itself, then to Liverpool, and finally to transoceanic markets. In eastern France Lyon performed the same function for a sizeable array of silk spinning villages, and also for the iron smelting firms in Saint-Etienne and Le Creusot. But Lyon, unlike Manchester, had a dynamic of its own, at first

Traditionally, cities were built upward to accommodate more residents in a limited space. Cities of the nineteenth century, however, were also built downward to lay vast underground sewers. As street traffic increased they also began constructing the Paris *Metro, which* was begun a decade later.

spurred by its own silk production. In time, however, the Lyonnais relegated silk to the outskirts and adapted new technologies in photography, artificial fibers, and electrical equipment.

In the North, where a large coal basin crossed the Franco-Belgian frontier, cotton textiles created new towns that doubled and even tripled their populations almost every generation. In 1800 the Ruhr in western Prussia was an impoverished region of retarded farming and domestic manufacture. Its few small towns, dating from the Middle Ages, were almost evenly spaced along an East-West trade route. Then, in midcentury, came railroads and coal mining. Entrepreneurs in the iron industry moved in rapidly: Friedrich Krupp in Essen, Jacob Mayer in Bochum. Old towns grew rapidly into sprawling cities like Gelsenkirchen. By 1900 half of the Ruhr's two million population lived in its five largest cities. Two kinds of settlements accounted for significant urban growth at midcentury and after: mining operations scattered over coal fields and places devoted to metallurgy that were usually dominated by one very big firm. Roads, canals, and railways brought in iron ore (as well as food), and brought out finished products via the Rhine to Rotterdam and beyond, linking the Ruhr to a vast international network of great urban markets. In general, the truly big cities with more than a million in population by the third quarter, were not major industrial centers. The settlement of factories in mining areas led to rapid industrial and demographic growth, but because population in the initial phase was so small, even very high growth rates did not produce the largest cities. For example, Essen in 1850 had nine thousand inhabitants, in 1880 it attained 57,000, a growth rate of 533 percent! In contrast, Berlin grew from 419,000 to 1,122,000 for a growth rate of only 168 percent. Yet Berlin was an imperial metropolis, and Essen a middling town specializing in one industry. It could not become more than a satellite dependent on a central place to link it to outside markets. The truly eminent cities were all regional and national capitals. These places benefited from the "economies of agglomeration." That is, big producers eventually found it worthwhile to locate in a large population where they readily found workers, professionals, and customers near to hand. Producers who earlier had located away from cities because of the high costs of land and services, now relocated usually in a suburb because the available services and customers were worth the price. These cities' expansion was undeterred by the absence of nearby iron or coal, or good canals and river routes. The biggest grew bigger, partly by annexing surrounding villages and by extensive immigration. And a large proportion of the newcomers were not peasant men and women come to work in factories or in well-to-do homes as servants; they were persons with education and professional training, with mental capital, who joined native professionals, technicians, and managers to expand the indispensable, skilled assistance that these great cities provided to entrepreneurs in the satellites. These people were lawyers, teachers, journalists, economists, librarians, archivists, civil servants, and office staff, people fleeing the provinces and drawn to capital cities where their talents were needed. Thus arose the white-collar class that soon made up nearly half the population of central places. As their number grew there arose an entirely novel urban culture, quite different from that rooted in the countryside. The rise of an urban population influenced not only how people earned a living, the social background of politicians and government policies, but the way people thought, their sense of values.

12

A Conflict of Cultures: Rationalism versus Romanticism

The Quarrel of Ideologies

Throughout the first three quarters of the nineteenth century there were two broad cultural or ideological styles: one supportive of industrialization, the other generally hostile to the modernism that rapid economic growth entailed. This does not mean that Europe was divided between the forces of light and those of darkness, the red and the black as Stendhal put it. Within each style there were numerous variations: Liberal thinkers looked on the capitalist economy as a progressive stage of human history; Karl Marx looked favorably on it as an historically necessary stage in a further evolution toward socialism. What both had in common was the belief that the physical world was the only real one, that metaphysics, the world beyond matter, was pure myth. The critics of laissez faire ran the gambit from Joseph de Maistre, the most reactionary defender of clericoroyalism, to de Lamennais, the precursor of the worker-priest movement of postwar France. What both had in common was the insistence that laissez faire capitalism was a demonic evil. It is clear that culture was not a hot-house creation, protected from the cold and heat of economic and political developments. On the contrary, ideas were an integral part of human events, combative in support of varying activities. These were fighting ideologies not at all lost in cloud-coocoo land, or isolated from real life.

At this point it is important to recognize that the ideologies involved here were part of what is called "high culture," that is, the lucubrations of learned thinkers expressing themselves for a literate audience, and more than merely literate but educated as well. For the vast majority of Europeans these ideologies were unknown, part of a world they could not enter because they were illiterate or even if literate had no time for philosophy. This culture was the creation of bourgeois and aristocratic persons, who were, like the *philosophes* of the eighteenth century Enlightenment, full-time thinkers, the early intelligentsia. In western Europe, where universities were generally closed to new ideas, they either inherited wealth, or had the backing of a patron, or earned an income from their writings. There were, of course, exceptions: Adam Smith, the father of laissez faire as an economic program, was professor of moral philosophy. Many of the Germans also were salaried university professors or churchmen.

Economics: The Dismal Science

In the West the bible of liberal thinkers was Adam Smith's *The Wealth of Nations*. He was a product of the eighteenth-century belief in natural law. The physical universe, created by a divine being whose talent was that of chief mechanic or clock maker, had brought into existence a vast system of matter that functioned in accord with divine or natural law. These laws were not revealed to man; he had to discover them. The great Newton had performed that service when he worked out the law of gravity, the supreme force that held the universe together and kept it functioning with the accuracy of a clock. These laws could not be violated. If one held an apple and released it, it fell to the ground at a prescribed speed as worked out by Newton. If on release the apple shot upward, that would be a violation of nature's law, a miracle. But miraculous events were merely part of ancient mythology devised by ignorant priests to fool the people. In time laissez faire liberals developed their own orthodoxy and mythology. As individualists they rejected any intervention of the state in economic life. Industrialists, merchants, and financiers must be left alone to follow the laws of political economy, each acting on his own and for his own interests. This license might seem like anarchy, but nature provided a system by which all the independent and competitive pursuits of profits by individuals were somehow, by the benevolence of a "hidden hand," brought into harmony and the end result of this egotism was higher production at lower costs. For Smith, "the whole art of government lies in the liberty of men and things."

Smith's disciples continued to discover other truths they insisted were as valid as his law of supply and demand. The French economist, Jean-Baptiste Say even "discovered" a law that posited a natural adjustment between the quantity of goods offered and the level of their consumption. The appearance of subsequent crises resulting from over production or under consumption left him undaunted. Before long liberal economics became known as the "dismal science," thanks to the contributions of David Ricardo and the Reverend Thomas Malthus. Together they turned the school away from an optimistic outlook to the darkest pessimism. Ricardo was a successful financier turned economist who discovered the "law" of the wage fund. The total amount of capital available for workers' wages was fixed and could not be augmented without driving all manufacturers to bankruptcy as they would lose their competitive advantage. Therefore if one segment of workers by means of strikes raised their wages, another segment would have to suffer declines of their pay. This conclusion was hardly one to cheer wage laborers. So to make the literate among them aware of their fate, the skillful fiction writer, Harriet Martineau, published short stories to enlighten them. In one, a labor strike succeeded and increased the pay of the strikers, but the factory owner then found it necessary to fire some of them. Thus, Ricardo's law could not be ignored. In another story she explained that public expenditure on the impoverished raised taxes, which discouraged capital investment, slowed economic growth, and, finally, led to unemployment and more poverty.

This was a not very subtle attack on the 1834 Poor Law, and was closer to the views of Malthus. The good reverend claimed to have discovered the law of population, which resulted from his calculation that all living creatures, including humans, were destined for extinction. Population naturally grows at a geometric rate of 1, 2, 4, 8, 16, and so on, whereas food supply rose at only a mathematical rate of 1, 2, 3, 4, 5, and so on. The number of mouths to feed, in consequence, outgrew supply and starvation would result. These figures, as we shall see, gave Charles Darwin his idea of the struggle for existence as a cause of evolution. Neither Malthus nor Darwin offered much encouragement to the weak and the poor. Malthus, at least, offered one ray of hope: the will to curb population. The number of people to feed was naturally controlled by war, famine, and plague. If, however, society could voluntarily control birthrates by sexual restraint or even complete abstinence, there would not be so much human suffering; however, Malthus was a true pessimist and did not trust much in human nature. He really believed that humanity was caught in a bleak cycle of birth, privation, and death. His conclusion was not novel; numerous eighteenth-century thinkers had reasoned along the same lines, at least regarding the lower classes. Malthus ignored classes and was concerned with all society. His ideas had a wide influence and explain both why the British Poor Law of 1834 not only drastically limited public charity and made its acceptance degrading, and why the sexes were segregated in poor houses.

Laissez faire economics was readily taken up by the industrial and commercial business community in the West; the French, after all, had coined the term that the British loosely translated as *free trade*. The activities of John Bright and Richard Cobden blessed the cluster of ideas supportive of economic freedom with the name, Manchester School. Under their guidance there emerged a certain class conflict between, on the one hand, the struggling middle class of industrialists, often nonconformist in religion, and on the other hand, the squires, landlords, and Anglicans of various intensity who ruled England. Dominant in Parliament, they ignored Manchester economics to pass factory acts violating free-trade principles. Perhaps they were influenced by a thinker who formed his own school.

Jeremy Bentham was one of the most eccentric of men in a land of eccentrics. He propounded a philosophy called Utilitarianism. It was not an economic theory but a proposal for legal reform, and he claimed to offer a new science of law confined to one simple rule: "the greatest happiness of the greatest number." Bentham reflected the optimism of the eighteenth century. He even proposed a "felicific calculus" to measure the greatest happiness, to provide an external and logical standard for judging the law. He coined the words "maximize" and "minimize" to measure pleasure and pain. The sole purpose of government and law was to prevent acts that caused pain to society and to punish offenders. Government, like punishment, was an evil but a necessary one. In his role as a law reformer he rejected the theory of natural rights as a basis for a civil code. There were no rights—only pleasure and pain; he equally rejected traditional usages and customs as a basis, which left him open to a far more radical turn. In 1818 he followed the logical course in favor of a democratic and secret vote, annual parliaments, and going beyond the later Chartist movement, women's suffrage. He now concluded that individuals were the best judges of their pleasures and pains, and should vote accordingly. In this way freedom would be assured without recourse to natural rights. Unlike Adam Smith who justified the free play of self-interest by invoking the guiding hand of providence, Bentham did so by calling on utility.

Bentham's appeal was to middle-class liberals who found the unwritten common law of England lacking in justice and the historic criminal codes too brutal. His followers, called utilitarians, set out to make the law more humane, and to find an ideology other than natural rights as a basis to win control of political life. They differed from most liberals before midcentury in that they favored universal male suffrage; not many of them unequivocally came out in favor of the vote for women.

The most forceful and coherent proponent of women's rights was John Stuart Mill, but he espoused this cause somewhat late in life. For a while he was a utilitarian, and picked up his ideas from Bentham via his martinet of a father. The person who truly converted him to women's rights, however, was Harriet Taylor, whom he long befriended while she was married and subsequently took her as his wife after her husband's death. Mill had a deep admiration for her intelligence and saw no reason why females should be subordinate citizens. Indeed women, although none of them assumed leading roles in philosophic literature, went further in participating in debates on political economy than the "blue stockings" of the previous century. We have already mentioned the role of Harriet Martineau who, with Mrs. Marcet, popularized the recondite explanations of Malthus and Ricardo, but took them at face value and left the working classes with as hopeless a future as ever.

Rather it was John Stuart Mill who broke away from strict laissez faire doctrines. Perhaps this change resulted from an elevating transition that marked his life. Identified early as a genius his father, James Mill, had him reading Latin and Greek by the age of three or four, and soon plunged him into the texts of British political economists, as well as Bentham and major Continental writers. The result was a nervous break down when still a young man, and he saved himself from the dry logic of his mentors by turning to the romantic poets, Wordsworth and Coleridge. In them he found the elation, passion, and depth of irrational feeling that had been absent in his strictly utilitarian education. They could not, however, turn him against the doctrines of his early training; he remained attached to reason, utility, and individual liberty, in short, to a liberal creed.

His major contribution was to provide a democratic basis for the creed. On the whole liberals favored free trade and constitutional monarchy, with the franchise limited to property holders. Mill did not oppose limited monarchy, and while he contributed to the current of thought that eventually led to universal male suffrage, he wanted the educated to enjoy more than one vote as a safeguard against mob rule. And in his famous textbook, *Principles of Political Economy*, he proposed separate standards for production and distribution. Manufacturing, he wrote, must continue along laissez faire principles; competition and individual initiative were requisites for efficiency and progress. It was distribution that must be rearranged to satisfy the physical needs of society. With this distinction Mill laid the ethical justification of the welfare state; however, he remained a liberal, not at all eager to strengthen the central government, and he never really clarified the system that could be used to enforce a more just distribution of wealth without augmenting the state bureaucracy. Yet, his textbook remained popular and went through several editions until the rise of a new generation of economists, preaching marginal utility, made it obsolete. Mill's writing fathered not a new economics but a new liberalism more concerned with freedom *from* pain, that is from hunger, rather than freedom *of* speech or of assembly. He never abandoned the basic rights of man, however. On the contrary, he published in 1859 his essay *On Liberty*, the most compelling defense of a maximum of individual freedom. He had a deep hatred of censorship and intolerance. Resorting to his utilitarian heritage he argued that no person or group of persons, however exalted their station, were infallible. Different doctrines, therefore, might be correct and must not be suppressed lest society perpetuate an error; or they might contain some truth and therefore useful. Even if they contained no truth, their dissent was necessary to ward off mental stagnation. It was during debate among differing proponents that truth would emerge.

Modernization, Technocracy, and Authority

Liberals were not the only advocates of general progress in accord with natural law, and their voices were most commanding only where capitalism was in the ascendant. Where individual freedom was not deeply rooted either in politics, society, or the economy, there emerged sects devoted to the emancipation of men from the outmoded traditions of a feudal past, but they, in the tradition of "enlightened despotism" of the previous century, called on an all-powerful leader to spearhead the thrust toward a rational society based on the ideals they claimed to have discovered. Unlike liberals who inherited the mechanistic universe governed by unchanging laws and therefore static save to the extent that society was reformed to be in accord with timeless law, the new *philosophes* were historical minded, convinced that society, or at least the "mind" of society, evolved from a primitive past and was ineluctably moving through time toward a predetermined future. It was not static laws that needed to be discovered, but the inner dynamics of ever changing society. For this new generation, their predecessors were too negative in their attack against the old regime, too cynical to provide the spiritual awakening of post revolutionary society. It is evident, as we shall see, that the romantic movement with its organic and historical base, had a marked influence on the new thinkers who imagined themselves to be guided, not by metaphysics but the hard facts of science.

The distinction of this intellectual current, and its parentage with other trends, can be found in the voluminous works of Claude-Henri, Count of Saint-Simon. Although an aristocrat of ancient lineage he, like Lafayette, fought in the American Revolution. During the revolutionary upheaval of his own country he made a fortune in financial and land speculation, then barely escaped losing his head to the guillotine; he did, however, lose his wealth and he died impoverished in 1825. While he lived he was a continuator of the utilitarian facet of the Enlightenment: His new society would result from a complete reversal of the social hierarchy of the old regime. In a brilliant parable he condemned as parasites the nobles, priests, and everyone who did not work and contribute to the wealth and well-being of society. He did not call for their brutal elimination. He was a man of a kindly disposition. Rather, he concluded, they would disappear as a class when they could no longer leave inheritances to their offspring. Their place would be taken by the *industriels*, a word he coined to designate those who managed economic activities.

The productive elements would make up a new, fairly fluid class, ruled by the most competent and educated among them. In his book, *The New Christianity*, he treated these rulers, scientists, and technicians, as a new priesthood. Unfortunately he was not always consistent as regards the elite; at times he enthusiastically gave dominance to bankers and large industrialists. Beneath the all-powerful elite—Saint-Simon was no democrat—were layers of lesser technicians and his hierarchy went down to simple workers who could, if capable, rise through the ranks, just as those in high places could descend if their competence faded. A son did not inherit a father's position unless he proved competent to fill it. There was no equality of wealth or common ownership. There would, he was sure, be wealth enough for everyone, and therefore, no poverty.

Before his death Saint-Simon attracted an extraordinary collection of followers including bankers, scientists, engineers, mystics, Napoleonic veterans, and *Carbonari*. More decidedly than their master they had strong leanings toward communal collectivism. In fact, they and their lady friends set up a kind of collective not far from Paris. To emphasize their mutual relations they designed clothes that were impossible to put on or take off without the aid of others. Like most communal sects it soon acquired some habits strange for the times. One of the leaders named Prosper Enfantin wore a kind of T-shirt with *PERE* (father) written across the front; he was in search of the *MERE*, (mother) preferably an Asian lady, and the consummation of their marriage would signal the unity of East and West. After the commune was dispersed by local authorities, the denizens being accused of practicing free love, the cult split, and Enfantin traveled in the Near East still looking for the *MERE*.

The rapid spread of Saint-Simonism, chiefly among the educated, can be attributed to its flexibility and eclectic dimensions. It sought to fuse the Enlightenment with romanticism, faith with reason, mysticism with science. It became the cradle of feminism, pacifism, philosemitism, Europeanism, and Christian socialism. It attracted numerous students in the Polytechnical School and young men like Enfantin, who after their youthful escapades, became heads of engineering firms that built France's main railroads; one of them, Ferdinand de Lesseps, planned and carried out the digging of the Suez Canal. Louis-Napoleon was also under their spell when he penned *The Extinction of Poverty* in the 1830s, and, when emperor, hoped to implement some of their proposals, as we noted already. Its appeal was strongest among persons who favored the industrial revolution but rejected laissez faire economics.

August Comte, who served as Saint-Simon's secretary for a while, fits perfectly into this latter category. He was a *polytechnicien* who published between 1830 and 1846 his *Course of Positive Philosophy* in six volumes. He was an extremely wordy writer and certainly borrowed heavily from his employer. He, too, emphasized the importance of science, only his concern was less with the physical and natural sciences than with the use of scientific methods to study the history and condition of people. He set out to found a new science of society and coined the word "sociology" to define it. Human development had passed through three stages: over thousands of years the theological when people worshipped blindly; the metaphysical of the seventeenth and eighteenth centuries when they sought to understand what they worshipped; and, finally, the positive when social science would banish the mysteries and myths of the past, and people would live rationally and harmoniously. He divided each of these major phases into subphases and became increasingly obscure and repetitive. The nineteenth century, he asserted, was one of laissez faire anarchy that was destined to evolve into the positive phase with a highly organized society and state, as well as a new religion, the worship of mankind, the only true god. The positive stage was to be one of order, of authority; its bible the sociology of Comte himself. He was the high priest. No wonder John Stuart Mill, who admired the scientific basis of positivism, was highly distrustful of its political implications.

The scientific basis was gradually eroded by Comte himself. As he grew older he fell under the romantic influence of a sickly young women whom he cast as a kind of Virgin Mary of his cult. He confused the roles of social scientist, social reformer, and religious prophet when after her death he idolized her as the feminine and mystical agent of his religion of humanity. As a new religion positivism appealed to bourgeois disenchanted with Christianity, and they were as numerous in predominantly Catholic countries in Latin America as they were in Europe. Some of his early European disciples, like Emile Littré, the lexicographer, and Hippolyte Taine, the literary critic, remained faithful. Littré published a massive etymological dictionary of the French language; Taine sought to create a scientific literary criticism that transcended the critic's emotions and therefore would be as unprejudiced as a scientific treatise. For him, vice and virtue were like chemical products and could be evaluated as such.

Other disciples dropped away. Ernest Renan was studying for the priesthood when he lost faith in the church, left the seminary in 1843 and eventually published a *Life of Jesus*, using methods of research and evaluation of documents based on scientific techniques. His Jesus lost all divinity but emerged as a humane, sympathetic human being, worthy of admiration but not of worship. His disappointment with the spiritual deviation of Comte was revealed in his simple statement that his former mentor had not really created a new idea and, worse, wrote in a deplorable French style. In the final analysis he was right.

Romanticism

The intellectual movement called romantic was both a revolt and a reaction. Coeval with the early and somewhat primitive scientism recorded above, it was a revolt against the emphasis—perhaps overemphasis—that the Enlightenment had placed on rationalism and materialistic utility. But early romanticism was more than a philosophic revolt; its original creators were hostile critics of the Old Regime in all its aspects. The German dramatist Friedrich Schiller wrote *The Robbers*, an attack on brutal aristocratic rule, and Wordsworth and Coleridge hailed the French Revolution until the Jacobins began cutting off heads. There emerged, then, a left-wing romanticism which survived the Terror and regained its fervor after 1815. In contrast there appeared a conservative romanticism that supported Napoleon without enthusiasm (he was the last "enlightened" despot) but that felt at home with the royalist restorations.

Was there, then, really a romantic phenomenon? What did the various romanticisms have in common, if anything? These are difficult questions to answer. There certainly was a romantic phenomenon; it revealed itself in literature, in art, and in history. In fact, romantic concepts of time deepened the field of history and this was one characteristic that not only signaled a new style of culture but helped to distinguish it from the Enlightenment. The *philosophes* believed that the Great Clock Maker had created a universe that functioned according to natural law. He (they never thought of a she-god) then went off to do other things. History, therefore, consisted of the gradual discovery of these natural laws over human time. History was essentially an unfolding of human knowledge about the universe. Not all scholars so limited themselves; several German academics, in particular, ignored the traditional royalist chroniclers who thought of the past in terms of dynastic periods. Historians at the University of Göttingen were even concerned with economic and social developments. But these men were professionals and it was the amateurs, traditionalists like Edmund Burke and his Continental disciples with their grandiose schemes, who attracted public attention and laid the intellectual groundwork for the romantic style.

Romanticists, then, tended to be historical minded, and undoubtedly the profession gained enormously from an increasing emphasis on a temporal dimension in philosophy. The field of history grew up as a justification for gradual as distinct from radical change. As Burke argued, societies evolved over eons of time; they were bound together from one generation to the next and could not be uprooted according to the whims of revolutionary reformers, but must evolve as driven by an inner spirit or "soul." There were no natural laws, only the impulse to evolve by each people in accord with traditions. Sudden breaks with past roots could only lead to terror, as witnessed in France, and a desperate search for salvation, which brought forth illegal tyrants like Napoleon.

The German idealist school of philosophy put forth a far more complex view of history and religion than Comte or Burke. Georg Friedrich Hegel sought, like Comte, to eliminate the dualism, the absolute distinction between God and man that Christianity had introduced at its founding. He merged divine with human reason. He depersonalized God and substituted the notion of a Spirit that created the material world and human society as the dialectical antithesis or opposite of itself. The Spirit became, or rather becomes conscious of itself, its absolute reality, progressively by means of gradual self-realization through the thought and action of humans as Spirit and humanity move toward a synthesis of themselves. Spirit becomes man and man Spirit. There was emerging a new God, one of becoming as well as of being, a material universal whole. Hegel, therefore, made a significant contribution to romantic and German thought, fostering the historicism that could be summed up in the stanza of Alexander Pope: "Whatever is, is right." History was a totality and the unfolding of reality, the mind of the universe. History was no longer chaotic or aimless, without meaning because each event had a place in the vast scheme in which all actions had a purpose.

Hegel's followers, called the Young Hegelians, went one step beyond their master when they fully humanized God, as Comte was doing in France. Ludwig Feuerbach wrote that "what was formerly contemplated and worshipped as God is now to be perceived as something *human*." The Young Hegelians created an even newer religion based on the Spirit that was not separated from but was the essence of mankind. Hegel did not venture quite this far and carried much greater influence than his young disciples. He ended as the court philosopher, less for his theology than his politics: He concluded that the Prussian monarchy was the perfect synthesis of absolutism and constitutional government!

The past inspired romantic writers to revive an interest in the Middle Ages. Classical authors of the Renaissance and Enlightenment had heaped scorn on this period as one of ignorance, superstition, and ugliness. Above all they disliked Gothic architecture with its strong perpendicular lines as part of a design to lift men's thoughts upward toward the Godhead. The discovery of ancient monuments led to the Renaissance emphasis on horizontal lines to remind man of earthly life and human creativity in his own lifetime. The Gothic revival, in contrast, was inspired by romanticism, and can be seen in medieval-like castles and churches constructed between 1810 and the 1840s, the high time of this religious impulse. In literature Sir Walter Scott published many novels glorifying and romanticizing the knights and their ladies of the Middle Ages; Alfred Tennyson wrote extensively about the mythological King Arthur and his knights of the Round Table.

A religious revival also occurred, spurred by René de Chateaubriand's imaginative evocation of the pure beauty of medieval architecture in *The Spirit of Christianity*. He recalled the inner joy, the spiritual uplift one felt in the candle-lit and colonnaded interiors of Gothic churches, the brilliant stained-glass windows casting their multicolored rays across the stone floor, the sweet sound of chant-song mingling with the light and shadows; how could one not adore God in this setting?

There was also a tingling attraction for the horrible, as seen in the ghost stories of Mary Shelley, and for the grotesque, as revealed in Victor Hugo's *The Hunchback of Notre Dame*. German romantics went in particularly for the somber and macabre. In the words of Sir Isaiah Berlin, one finds in Wachenroder, Schelling, Tieck, and Novalis a "new and restless spirit, seeking violently to burst through old and cramping forms [of classical rules], a nervous preoccupation with perpetually changing inner states of consciousness, a longing for the unbounded and indefinable, for perpetual movements and change, an effort to return to the forgotten sources of life." British and French romantics displayed similar characteristics but seem almost moderate when compared with the Germans, perhaps because the Enlightenment never quite penetrated central

Europe, save in the form of enlightened despotism, a generalization that can be applied to Russia where romanticism was derivative.

The Germans most emphatically rejected the mechanistic and sensationalist concepts of the *philosophes*. As followers of Immanuel Kant, the true founder of Idealism, they denied the assertion that the human mind was a blank at birth and acquired knowledge by means of the senses and reasoning. The fullness of reality did not lie in the matter discerned by the senses. Through them the mind could comprehend the surface of things, and this it accomplished by understanding (*Verstand*), but beyond the visible surface lay true reality and to penetrate to this depth, to the "thing in itself," the mind needed both understanding and a kind of vital spiritual insight (*Vernunft*). Man was no longer the measure of all things, but enveloped in vast cosmic forces that were infinitely greater than himself even though he was a part of them and through his actions participated in their evolution over time. This kind of thinking must not be confused with the enthusiastic rejection of reason, outright delight of irrational responses to the beauties and mysteries of forests, sunsets, stormy oceans that elicited turbulent passions. The Idealists considered themselves rational, only their's was "pure reason."

Hegel had a wide appeal because he taught that all elements of the universe were parts of a whole that evolved through interaction of the parts. Such a view insisted that both philosophy and science must describe the individual not in Benthamite isolation, but in relation to a larger whole of which he is a part. Knowledge meant fitting things together, including individual persons, into a totality that was alive and growing. The test of an institution was no longer its reasonableness and utility but its origin and history. The rational became the traditional rather than the useful. This sounded very antirevolutionary, and indeed it was. But it is important to bear in mind that for Hegel and his disciples—who drew from him what they wanted, as we shall see—social and political life was not static. On the contrary, life was a process, growth, and movement toward a higher goal, a synthesis, the final stage when the essential goodness of human nature, no longer alienated by traditional Christian worship, would emerge.

This was not the view of dyed-in-the-wool conservatives such as Joseph de Maistre, an aristocrat from Savoy, a Francophile, and both a comfort and an embarrassment to Louis XVIII because he was not a compromiser. That he was not a French citizen was a disappointment to him but of minor importance. He was to France what Burke was to Britain: the defender of tradition, only more so. For de Maistre, society was "organic," written in capital letters. Like all the returned émigrés, he rejected liberal individualism. The society that God created, and he had no doubts on this, was an organic society that had no place for individual liberty. Society was like a vital organism in which the life of the whole depends on that of the parts, and the life of the parts depends on the whole. Society was primal, the individual secondary. The trunk of a tree could lose a branch and survive; however, the branch, detached from the rooted trunk, had no chance of survival. The symbolism of the tree, incidentally, was very important to romantic conservatives as an image of rootedness and survived into the twentieth century.

De Maistre, as a returned émigré from Savoy-Piedmont, was vindictive against the Revolution that had so upset his world. Far more than the German Idealists he was a brilliant advocate of an authoritarian, integrated society. Not really a romantic—he displayed none of their exuberance for primitive nature—he was rather a dour type, too bitter to be gay, too experienced in distress to be hopeful. To him, individual liberty was anarchy of the most dangerous sort, and the solution against liberal revolution consisted of the creation of three pillars of stability: a strong monarchy supported by a hereditary aristocracy capable of firm rule; a Catholic church with a pope supported by a dynamically religious clergy; finally, a system of punishment with the executioner as its final arbiter.

Romantic Individualism

The romantic reaction was never a clear call for a return to the Old Regime; even de Maistre recognized that the past was a phase of tradition and therefore was, indeed, the past. Although romantics delved into the supernatural, as in the works of Samuel Coleridge, and reveled in the exotic and old with Scott and Chateaubriand, many of them looked to nature for liberation of the spirit from the bonds of natural law. They practiced a cult of genius, especially poetic and artistic genius, that must be free to create, must throw off the shackles of the old aesthetic formulated by the ancients, and revived during the Renaissance and Enlightenment. In contrast to the eighteenth century disregard of everything not universal, they emphasized individuality and distinct personality. Inspired by the revolutionary pedagogy of Jean Jacques Rousseau and the Swiss Johan Pestalozzi, they called for the fullest encouragement of the unique potentialities of every person. The whole aim of culture and life was to create the conditions favorable to freedom, individuality and self-expression. Johann Wolfgang von Goethe, as much a classicist as a romantic, urged self-reliance, the essence of classical liberalism. Although often a skeptic he was not without hope and belief in the value of life, traits he retained from the Enlightenment. He would surely have agreed with Victor Hugo who once affirmed that romanticism was liberalism in literature. What he, Goethe, and others envisioned was the striving after richer experiences, a fuller life, the embracing of all knowledge and sensation. This was cultural revolution, the counterpart of the economic, social, and political revolutions that were transforming European society from top to bottom.

This rebellious side of romanticism was a move to speed up the attainment of goals laid out in the eighteenth century. Rousseau and Schiller taught that man is naturally good, but everywhere he is in chains. Their individualistic urges drove them to a form of artistic anarchy; the essential move was to resist literary oppression, to destroy superstition and prejudices that made man into a willing slave. Such was the message of Percy Shelley, of Hugo's character Hernani, of George Sand in her way of life. Even the heroes of authors not recognized as romantic were at war with the restored political order: Alexandre Dumas's Antony, Honoré Balzac's Vautrin, and Stendhal's Sorel rejected conventional standards as well as religion as a form of quiescent consolation. Their truculent ambitions would not be consoled.

Romantic Socialism

The most intransigent rejection of liberal economics and the individualist concept of human relations came not from Saint-Simonians (many of whom became capitalists), but from authentic socialists, a word coined in the 1820s to identify a quite new intellectual movement, one calling for the full abolition of private ownership of the means of production. Until midcentury there were three main factions composing this variation.

The earliest was the revolutionist. It emerged in 1795–96, created by a small group of desperate men organized in a Conspiracy of Equals, who planned an uprising to overthrow the plutocracy that had seized power in France after executing or disbursing the Jacobins. Their plot was discovered and those who could not escape the country were promptly executed. The affair was of minor importance, and forgotten until Philippe Buonarroti published a history of the conspiracy in the late 1820s. He has been called the first "professional" revolutionary, and indeed, he and his companions founded a tradition of conspiratorial action that took its deepest root in France, chiefly Paris. By the 1830s there emerged a particular type of activist, the *révolté*, the full-timer who made a career of insurrection. Auguste Blanqui, whom we have already observed in action in the 1840s, was the archetype, having assumed the mantle from Buonarroti. The initial step was to organize a small band of fully committed followers, then seize the center of governmental power, and finally call on the "people" to rise up, transforming a *coup de main* into a mass revolution. Blanqui did not have a clear idea of class; he thought in terms of a combat between the masses against the upper element of society, somewhat along the same lines as Saint-Simon's distinction between the idlers and the industrious. Blanqui, of course, had no use for captains of industry. The revolution he longed for—and never carried out successfully—was to result in a dictatorship of the conspirators. Lenin would have something similar in mind, but was critical of Blanqui for his overly narrow views and lack of political theory.

The second contingent consisted of the dreamer of egalitarian communities. The pioneer in this endeavor was Robert Owen, the successful textile manager already discussed in chapter six. After making a fortune, buying out his partners, and transforming the manufacturing town of New Lanark into a model center, he decided to carry out his dream of founding a completely egalitarian community. Abandoning Europe he chose the United States as the land of promise and in 1824 he set up New Harmony. It lasted five years but was already a costly failure before its demise. Although ingenious as a factory manager in Scotland, he was a complete failure as the leader of a collectivist group. Long before he left England, he became convinced that land tillage by use of the spade was a source of great agricultural progress. In consequence New Harmony was an agrarian experiment foisted upon its population of city dwellers almost totally devoid of farm experience. Soon hostile cliques appeared, and verbal conflicts became physical conflicts. Had Owen remained in residence he could have perhaps overcome many handicaps, but he was rarely present. The failure considerably diminished the fortune he invested in his dream.

His dream faded, but not his example or fame as a social reformer. Although he never actively sought a mass following—he appealed to the rich to set up reform societies—many skilled workers adopted his notion of cooperation and at least one idea he borrowed from Adam Smith: the labor theory of value. Smith, like Ricardo, used this concept to defend the owner's right to property; the value of a commodity was created by the managerial labor of the capitalist, not the physical labor of the workers. A group of early social theorists, known as "Ricardian socialists," reversed Ricardo and argued that workers created value and were therefore entitled to the commodities they made. Owen accepted this view, and his working-class followers took it up as they organized trade unions to defend themselves from exploitative factory owners. Between 1830–34 about half a million members enrolled in Owen's Grand National Consolidated Trade Union. This effort also failed. By 1836 union members had already turned to Chartism, that is, sought to make Parliament responsive to labor's plight. In his last years Owen, earlier a near atheist, turned to the consolations of mysticism. He has suffered ridicule for this, but during his active career he had transformed religious faith into secular humanism, a direction that was followed by the Saint-Simonians in France.

France was the classic land of revolution, and Blanqui was a product of that environment. He was a utopian of *putchism*, illegal seizure of power by a minority. But he was only one prophet in a land of them. Voltaire had once remarked, comparing culinary expertise, that England had a hundred religions but only one sauce, whereas France had only one religion but a hundred sauces. Comparing socialist imaginings, one can assert that England had only one true utopian but a hundred reformers, whereas France had a bevy of utopians but only a few reformers. Perhaps this condition helps explain why the English avoided revolution while the French went from one to another.

Utopian or cooperative socialism was so widespread in the land of Gallic fervor largely because there was an active, discontented artisan population, fairly literate and resistant to labor in large factories. The idea of a community of limited size, of social solidarity and mutual aid, appealed to their workshop experience.

The man closest to their ideal was Charles Fourier, an eccentric like Bentham, and who indeed sought to combine individual proclivities with general welfare. Fourier believed himself an observer of people's psychology and in his mind each person was motivated by passions. By giving these passions free play, which required a minimum of central authority, it would be possible to create a community, a phalanstery, in which individuals were both free and yet bound to all other members. A phalanstery was an association of about 1,600 members of both sexes, or, I should write, of three sexes since Fourier considered children a separate sex. The most important passion of the human psyche was the "butterfly." Each person was drawn toward a preferred activity but enjoyed it for only an hour or two, and then was drawn toward another pleasing task for an equally limited time. Thus, members working in small groups would belong to different teams and act harmoniously because of a passion shared even if only fleetingly.

A group of his followers tried to put his ideas into practice in a small community in Texas, and a few other places in the old and new worlds. They all failed.

The last of these utopians worth looking at is Etienne Cabet if only because he attracted a large following estimated at 100,000 in 1846. He differed from Owen and Fourier in that he was not philosophically a communitarian; he described in his book, *Voyage in Icaria*, a national state, France, entirely collectivized. No one owned anything, and the only outward, as distinct from biological, difference between sexes was in the design of the work clothes distributed by the state. There was equality between men and women, marriage was for love and for life, and the family sacred. Perfect harmony had been secured after a revolution created Icaria. For this reason there was no proliferation of newspapers or books with differing opinions: Why bother because no one was dissatisfied? Moreover Cabet's Icaria was a large industrial state, not the bucolic ideal of Owen and Fourier. As a second generation utopian, that of the 1840s, Cabet was far more aware of industrial growth and more patriotic than the first generation of the 1820s. Icaria as he described it seemed far too uniform and conformist to be anything but a popular dictatorship. In his political activity, however, he was active in the democratic movement and his journal, *Le Populaire*, contributed to its revival. It is odd then that in 1848 he encouraged his disciples, called appropriately, Icarians, to set up a small settlement in the United States. And of course it failed because of some acrimonious disharmony. Save for this dismal experiment Cabet had much in common with the rare pre-1848 socialist who rejected utopian communes. Louis Blanc also believed that socialism could only flourish in a large state. With the publication in 1839–40 of his short brochure *Organization of Work* he founded the school of Jacobin socialism, that is, a collective economy combined with a government emanating from manhood, not universal suffrage. He was not antifeminist, but like nearly every democrat he feared that most women, religious as they were, would vote as reactionary priests dictated. Women would participate in elections only after public education liberated their minds from the clutches of superstition and obscurantism.

The state, meaning the central power, must be free of these retardants to carry out its mission: the provision of free or very cheap credit to artisans' cooperatives, a policy that would enable workers to own collectively the means of production. Blanc used the term *workshop* (*atelier*) in his small book, but he really had in mind large enterprises specializing in a product, earning a profit, and therefore amortizing their loans and becoming free of state ties. He has erroneously been called a "statist," but in fact he looked forward to the withering of all central political power as cooperatives grew into worker-run factories that traded harmoniously with one another. Blanc, although an admirer and defender of Robespierre and the Jacobins as saviors of the revolution, was hardly a dictatorial type. Conversely, he did not rule out violent methods if they became necessary. In his way he contributed to the 1848 revolution and, as described already, became part of the provisional government in the Spring. His moment of triumph seemed to have come when he was chosen president of the Luxembourg Commission set up to study the labor question. The Luxembourg Palace, as it turned out, was at first a forum to spread his ideas, and the phrase Organization of Work was on every worker's lips, but it was also the tomb in which his socialism was buried when the workers' uprising in June, and its bloody suppression, brought down the socialist movement that was part of the romantic era. The ideology about the goodness of man, the peaceful road to reform, the emergence of a humanitarian society based on love and fellowship—all this idealization of society came to an abrupt close throughout Europe. Gentle ideology gave way to brute reality. The imaginings of romantics made way for the harsh eye of scientifically inclined materialists. Before the 1840s everyone wanted to smell a rose; afterward everyone wanted to dissect it.

13

The Culture
of Materialism

Culture and Society

John Donne once wrote that "no man is an island, entire of itself." To para-
phrase, no culture is either. There were romantics who lived, if not on an island,
then in a world of their own. Their love of nature often led them to live or at
least dream of living in places of natural beauty where they would be isolated,
but thrilled by mountains, lakes, stormy seas, and sun light. Their interest in
human society appeared slight; they stood above the material interests of the
commonalty. John Keats came closest to this type, but he scarcely survived long
enough to have matured politically. For most romantics, however, indifference
to worldly matters was not typical. Thomas Carlyle was, like Keats, of a laboring
family and he, who spent much of his life in near poverty, became a conservative, a critic of economic liberalism and Benthamism, the "pig philosophy" as he
put it. Like him, most romantics did not advocate art for art's sake but believed
that literature must have some moral purpose in addition to its aesthetic value.
In their own way they were fully conscious of changes taking place in their time,
and they reacted against large-scale industrialization and the economics of the
marketplace. They were, in large measure, the products of the landed classes
whose sense of *noblesse oblige* was awakened by the poverty and squalor of

industrial cities. The most prominent writers were nobles or sons of nobles and squires: Lord Byron and Percy Bysshe Shelley in England, Alfred de Musset, Alphonse de Lamartine, René de Chateaubriand, and Alfred de Vigny in France, Friedrich von Schlegel, Heinrich von Kleist, Novalis (pseudonym of Friedrich Baron von Hardenberg) and Johann Goethe in Germany, Michael Lermontov and Alexander Pushkin in Russia. Samuel Coleridge was the son of an Anglican vicar, George Sand (pseudonym of Aurore Dupin) in revolt against the landed class from which she came for forcing her into a disastrous marriage. In contrast William Wordsworth came from the petty bourgeois and as a Francophile greeted the French Revolution of 1789 with "Bliss was it in that dawn to be alive, but to be young was very heaven." Romanticism was not merely an intellectual revolt against mechanistic rationalism, it was also a protest of the refined landed classes against the social and aesthetic results of the Industrial Revolution.

The humanitarianism, aestheticism, and ruralism that it ardently championed steadily faded in the 1840s before a new intellectual style brightly aglow with the challenge of a materialistic interpretation of nature, man, and the universe. As such, it was more in tune with the politics of power, the accelerated rate of economic growth, and the further expansion of cities and urbanites. It was a culture that expressed the increasing power of the bourgeois, of monied wealth, of middle-class man's genuflection before the world of matter. This assertion does not accuse the European bourgeois of crass materialism, of a grasping desire for wealth. Many of the readers of the romantics were middle class while many nobles and landowners spent their lives hunting, drinking, and carousing. There has never been a sharp line between cultural styles of authors and artists who create them and those who admire them. Rather there were intellectual tendencies that reflected changing conditions in society and at the same time contributed to them by making the public think.

The romantic impulse had passed its prime by midcentury but it left a legacy in John Ruskin who vehemently denounced the ugly cities of industrial England. He was the prophet of a Gothic revival with *The Seven Lamps of Architecture* (1849) and *The Stones of Venice* (1853). He was convinced that great art came from a sound society; the Gothic stemmed from free medieval craftsmen, but only Jerry-built ugliness from workers who were merely the degraded appendages of machines. He carried on Carlyle's fierce hatred of modern industrialism and unregulated capitalism that had turned London into "a ghastly heap of fermenting brickwork." His successor was William Morris, who also attempted to revive the craftsmanship that factories had destroyed. In literature Matthew Arnold sought to combat the philistinism of bourgeois taste, to create a "certain temper of mind," more cultured, broad, refined. He was equally critical of the crude manners of the gentry. Morris and his like were aesthetes, and although fairly widely read by the public were not much heeded. Dickens, in contrast, had a huge audience. He was no romantic but, as noted already, vehemently hostile to bourgeois materialism.

What is interesting to note here is that none of these writers were socialists. Rather they were of middle-class origins, and indicate that the bourgeois was now taking over from the landed classes and producing its own critics. On the whole, however, the rising bourgeois class paid little attention to them. Rather it gloried in its success, wealth, and growing political power. Financial security and respectability became its watchwords. It still felt comfortable in the world it was creating, and increasingly came to believe that this world consisted of matter, not spirit, and the nature of matter became a passionate preoccupation, challenging traditional interest in religion. I am not suggesting that the middle class turned away from religion. Of course many did, but certainly Victorian respectability involved church going. A large number of businessmen were Quakers and held to the conviction that God was on their side. Yet, an increasing number became negligent about church attendance, insisting only that their wives and children go. These men were satisfied to believe that God smiled upon their progress, their material well-being. Religion was useful, but its creeds offered little knowledge about the world of matter.

Matter and Culture

The third quarter of the century was a momentous one in the history of the sciences and the penetration of the secrets of matter. Three of the most influential men reached their mental maturity during the 1850s and 1860s, and their findings had a profound influence on the future direction of society. They were Charles Darwin, Louis Pasteur, and Karl Marx. The first two differ radically from the third; what binds them is their belief that scientific methodology, not *Vernunft*, was the proper way to achieve a knowledge of reality, whether in the universe of matter or that of social structure and conditions. Some historians attribute to Comte the triumph of scientific outlook. They may be right. More accurately, however, research methodology arose as needed and according to the demands of each discipline. Comte provided methods more suitable for the several social sciences but not for pure science. Positivism was a convenient word taken up by many men and women of the natural sciences who had never read him.

Undoubtedly the great discovery of nineteenth century science was the evolution of species. The idea of evolution was, so to speak, in the air in the late 1700s, but it was not widely accepted in society. Christians believed that God created the universe including the Earth and all creatures inhabiting it, in six days and earned a well-deserved rest on the seventh: According to one Anglican divine, counting generations in the Old Testament, that remarkable act of creation had occurred in about 4004 B.C.

The matter was taken up by professional scientists who, at first, sought to reconcile recent discovered fossils and the biblical story. George Cuvier, a kind of official anatomist and naturalist under Napoleon I, recognized that new forms of life had appeared since the creation and others had disappeared. His explanation was sensible for the level of learning at the time: A series of catastrophes, of which the great flood was the latest, had destroyed some species and different ones had come from unflooded areas to replace them. This, the catastrophist theory, was challenged by Jean-Baptiste Lamarck, a paleontologist. He asserted in 1808 that certain species knowingly developed characteristics favorable to survival which they passed on to their offspring. There was no succession of catastrophes, merely the inheritance of acquired favorable characteristics.

Such a notion did not convince Charles Darwin who had sailed on the ship *Beagle* from 1831 to 1836 as a member of a scientific expedition to Latin America. He collected data on the fauna and flora, and the study of them raised questions in his mind. Why, for example, were there different forms of the same species of creatures on the various islands he visited? It became evident to him that each locale, with its special environment, sustained different forms. It was equally evident that species were not immutable. His reading of Malthus about the limits of sustenance and the competition carried on to obtain it gave him a working hypothesis. He devoted twenty-odd years gathering data to support it. Finally in 1859 he published *The Origin of Species*. In the same year Alfred Russel Wallace came out in print with a conclusion almost identical to Darwin's. Both posited that variations do exist in the same species, all of which produce more offspring than survive; there is struggle for limited resources needed to live and reproduce; some variations have greater chances of survival than others. Darwin concluded that species evolved over eons of time because of favorable variations in a particular milieu. Moreover, variation was not willed by any specie; it was a favorable or unfavorable outcome. He found no grand design in the lengthy process; in fact, he put aside his early religious beliefs, especially when all religious denominations condemned his theory as false and blasphemous. For Darwin the mutation of species was not up to God but to nature—hence, his term "natural selection." By this he meant that certain mutations were favorable and others not, and those species survived whose offspring inherited the favorable mutation. For example, whiteness in rabbits offers a high survival rate in snow; when snow melts, however, whiteness betrays them to their predators. Far more favored are rabbits that mutate in such a way to change color as seasons change and pass this mutation (which is not acquired) to their young. Natural selection did not mean that nature consciously selected certain species; the whole process was random. In 1871 Darwin applied his theory to humans when he published *The Descent of Man*.

Darwin's two major publications undoubtedly changed the way educated people interpreted material life. The notions that God created the universe in six days became increasingly difficult to accept at face value, and the widely held view that human society originated in a social contract was absolutely laid in its grave. *The Origin of the Species* sold out immediately when it appeared in book shops, and Darwinism became at once a subject of discussion and debate, sometimes very bitter debate as during the exchanges in 1860 between Bishop Samuel (Soapy Sam) Wilberforce defending the book of Genesis, and Thomas Huxley, Darwin's "bulldog," defending *The Origin*. This was the first major salvo in the war between religion and science, a war that continues today. During their debate Wilberforce facetiously asked his audience whether they descended from the apes on the side of their grandmothers as well as their grandfathers. Huxley, with his biting acrimony, replied that he would prefer to descend from an honest ape than from a man who, though endowed with brains, refused to make use of them.

The war was not waged exclusively between the spokesmen of religion and those of science. Most French naturalists rejected natural selection out of hand as an Anglo-Saxon plot. In Darwin's homeland, distinguished scientists believed that the struggle for survival debased humanity to the level of animals. Many asked if any human values could survive in a Darwinian world. The notion of nature as a place of brutal struggle was unacceptable to them as a mindless existence without any moral purpose. Where was the divine and guiding hand in all of life?

In time many churchmen and laymen began to accept evolution as part of God's purpose. God had first created life and then guided its evolution from primeval slime to intelligent humanity endowed, unlike animals, with a soul and therefore a purpose. What also emerged was a concept of nature different from that of the Enlightenment. To the *philosophes*, nature was beneficial if properly understood and organized. After Darwin, nature was "red in tooth and claw," a dark, hostile place where "ignorant armies clash by night," as Matthew Arnold dolefully wrote. Darwinism penetrated the arts as it penetrated every niche in society: "The rise of science as the prevailing mode of thought, predicted by Comte, owed more to Darwin than to any other figure," according to Roland N. Stromberg.

Inevitably Darwin's ideas influenced economic, social, and political philosophy. What became known as social Darwinism owed much to the writings of Herbert Spencer, perhaps the most celebrated of mid-Victorian thinkers. He had accepted the principle of evolution long before Darwin's first book appeared; he was, in fact, a Lamarckian and affirmed that he had discovered the laws governing the evolution of human society. In his *Social Statics* (1851) he already identified the poor with the unfit, therefore undeserving of aid merely to prolong their useless lives. As he put it, "to prevent present misery would entail a greater misery on future generations." To Darwin the "fit" were not necessarily the best; but Spencer took up the term "survival of the fittest" to mean the superior, those who won out in the struggle that had lifted human society to its present exalted state. The evolution of societies was progressive, evolving from primitive closed or corporative groups to modern open ones allowing individuals full freedom to compete. From this competition arose new societies better than the old. Another of his laws of social evolution posited the shift from communal to private property as a mark of progress. Spencer exercised an enormous influence on the new disciplines of sociology and anthropology. He also gave new life to Ricardian economics. Not only was competition among individuals necessary to improvement, so was competition among institutions, even between states, and for Spencer, war put nations to the test. This does not mean that he was an advocate of war; like authentic liberals he vehemently opposed the imperialism that Britain was undertaking in his old age. Unfortunately, war strengthened the state, and in *Man versus the State* he posited another law; evolution involved the expansion of personal freedom and the diminution of state power.

Not all Darwinians followed Spencer. Even Huxley came to argue that natural selection, the bitter struggle to survive, must not become the rule in today's human society. The fittest in society may not be the most ethically desirable. On the whole, the science of society that emerged from Darwin's theory was best adapted to middle class interests and most of his advocates came from this class. But, as with romanticism, we must not push this view to extremes. For one thing there never was a single bourgeois class; rather several strata existed under that general and at times vague designation. Once more we are dealing with tendencies, and many social reformers, or simply kind-hearted men like Huxley, opposed social Darwinism in its crudest form as that taken up by the American William Graham Sumner and his comment that "root, hog, or die" is the law of life.

In fact, Darwinism had its appeal to out-and-out socialists. Both Karl Marx and Friedrich Engels admired its creator. After all, Marxism was based on the idea of class struggle as the law of life, at least until socialism would bring conflict to an end.

Medical Science

In the eighteenth century a medical doctor John Lettsom, resorted to humorous doggerel to reveal the view of practitioners toward their patients:

> When any sick to me apply
> I physics, bleeds and sweats'em;
> If, after that, they choose to die,
> Why, verily, I Lettsom.

His verse also revealed the most common methods used on the sick: purging and bleeding.

By the early nineteenth century conditions had hardly improved. Traditional pathology, the means of treating diseases, held firmly to the notion that four humors determined a person's health. It was acceptable to doctors whose training was severely limited, and also to churchmen because it affirmed the mysterious and spiritual powers over which they claimed much control. But as such, it was a serious impediment to medical progress, and become increasingly incompatible with the expansion of scientific knowledge, including that of the human body, and the more materialistic concept of nature. The first major step in a new direction was taken by Rudolf Virchow, professor of pathology at Würzburg when he published *Cellular Pathology* in 1858. His system discarded the humors by making the cell the center of all medical study, and he revealed how white blood cells protected the body from foreign infectious cells. He laid down a pathology that began a medical revolution of sorts. Medicine was now ready to take its place as a major science and make its contribution to the cultural level of society. Although the important findings that were to come out of laboratories did not immediately improve the state of health of most people, they would in time. As parts of an increasingly materialistic culture, they had eventually a profound and progressive effect on public health. This role was hastened where society was educated enough to accept change, and rich enough to pay for it. The part played by states also expanded as the classes in power both provided wider educational opportunities, passed laws to improve public health, and subsidized better medical schools, laboratories, and institutes to encourage experimentation. In fact, even such a laissez faire government as that of Britain passed the Anatomy Act of 1832 which made bodies available to medical students for dissection. For centuries churchmen had forbidden the dissection of human cadavers. Before the century of our study, medical men were terribly ignorant of the human body. It is highly probable that artists knew more about muscles and bones than the average doctor.

Progress came about in several ways, at times by accidental discoveries, but more often by organized, methodical research in laboratories. We can more or less exclude hospitals until the later decades; their staffs were adamantly resistant to innovation and in their ignorance preserved them as places where the sick were more likely to die than benefit from a cure.

One of the major discoveries that came about in the 1700s but was hardly applied until after 1800 was inoculation against disease, particularly against smallpox. The wife of the English ambassador to Constantinople observed that the natives used a crude form of inoculation to protect themselves against the pox; they cut the skin and inserted some pox pustule in the wound. When she urged her friends in England to do the same, she was roundly condemned. However, there were already practitioners of it in England. Among them was Dr. Edward Jenner who learned that milkmaids who contracted cowpox never suffered from smallpox, a far more deadly infection. He waited twenty years, until 1796, to inoculate a boy with cowpox and later with matter from a smallpox pustule. The boy became immune to the latter, so Jenner made a second trial, equally successful. His experiments won professional approval and became part of medical practice. Unlike the hostility shown the ambassador's wife,

Parliament voted him a gift of £10,000 and a knighthood. Inoculation was adopted by Napoleon I, and all new recruits in his army were routinely vaccinated. For unknown reasons the Bourbon rulers abandoned this procedure. The Prussian army, however, had adopted it and made it part of the military's regular medical program. It is ironic that the victorious armies of France under the first Bonaparte were succeeded by incompetents and in the 1870–71 war lost some 20,000 men to smallpox; the Prussians remained immune. In the general population of advanced countries, where the upper classes rather rapidly had themselves inoculated, the number of smallpox cases steadily declined. Although inoculation was slow to be applied to the lower levels of society, it eventually became the means to offer immunity against diphtheria, whose bacillus was discovered in 1883, and then tetanus, and typhoid, the main killer of British soldiers in the Boer War. In the 1890s serums were developed for use on a mass scale.

Inoculation implied a knowledge of blood circulation, known of course since William Harvey discovered it in 1616. Yet the composition of blood remained a mystery. Doctors, like soldiers, were aware that the loss of this precious liquid led to death; but they were totally ignorant of the different types of blood. Early experiments at transfusions had often involved taking blood from an animal to put it into a human, with fatal results. In 1818 a Dr. Blundell of London temporarily revived a man by using syringes for exchange of blood, and in 1829 he saved a human life. Unknown to him, the blood types matched. Transfusion was subsequently tried, even though success was dubious, because patients sometimes bled to death during surgery. Only in 1901 were blood types discovered and identified, a step that was to save thousands of lives in World War I.

Surgical operations were more the work of barbers than of trained practitioners until the nineteenth century, and without an effective anesthesia, the process seemed closer to a form of torture than salvation. This was equally true of tooth pulling. And when Sir Humphry Davy discovered the anesthetic properties of nitrous oxide (called laughing gas), it was an American dentist who first tried it, and successfully. In 1847 an Edinburgh gynecologist tried Chloroform on his patients to ease childbirth. He too, was successful. But he received a foretaste of the conflict between religion and science when the strict Presbyterians cried out against the application of a soporific in childbirth; according to the Bible, Eve was informed: "In sorrow thou shalt bring forth children." Chloroform was denounced from pulpits as a "decoy of Satan" that would rob God of the cries of women calling on him for mercy. Concern, if not vociferous opposition, came from England, at least until Queen Victoria accepted Chloroform for her next two deliveries. Ether was also used at this time. It was now possible to carry out deep surgery and men trained in medical schools replaced the barbers.

This shift made for more skilled operations, but as doctors learned more about human anatomy and could operate more successfully, death from postoperative procedures continued high as a result of gangrene and blood poisoning.

Physicians knew little if anything about microbiology and the threat of germs. Happily Louis Pasteur's work was known to Dr. Joseph Lister, named Regius Professor of Surgery at the University of Glasgow in 1860. He soon realized that hospital air was charged with microbes that attacked the open surgical incisions of patients. Therefore he set out to discover an antiseptic, and finding the effectiveness of carbolic acid, began covering the wounds of compound fractures with dressing soaked in it. He then urged his colleagues to disinfect their instruments and to wash their hands. Many doctors had doubts about the added effort, but the downward rate of infection gradually convinced them. Lister received a peerage for his innovations.

Meanwhile in Vienna Dr. Ignaz Semmelweiss brought about a marked decline of puerperal fever in his ward by the use of aseptic and antiseptic measures. An acutely observant man, he noted that mortality was far too high in his ward because students came in directly from the dissecting room, and since they did not wash their hands, transported germs into the ward. After he refused them entry, mortality fell dramatically, from 12 to 1.27 percent. This evidence was not convincing to his colleagues, perhaps because he was Hungarian and they Austrian. This situation took place before the *Ausgleich*. He returned to his native land where, in 1865, he ironically died of blood poisoning.

A far happier career was that of Louis Pasteur. Although without a medical degree (he was a biologist) he had an enormous influence on medicine when he proved the existence of microbes and revealed both the harm they caused and how to combat them. A parallel to the Darwin-Wallace case arose when a German, Dr. Robert Koch made the same discovery while studying the germ causing anthrax in cattle. Koch at this time was a country doctor carrying on research in his home-made laboratory. After his brilliant work on the anthrax life cycle he became district surgeon in Wollstein where he built a small laboratory. When working on anthrax he discovered the technique of making pure cultures of organisms in order to study their life cycle. In 1877 he published an important paper on the investigation, preservation, and photographing of bacteria. He won recognition as a first rank investigator and obtained a position in the German Health Office in Berlin. There he devised new methods to obtain a pure culture outside the body. In 1882 he discovered the bacillus of tuberculosis; in 1883 that of cholera after visits to Egypt and India. He also found that cholera was transmitted via drinking water, food, and clothing. These were monumental discoveries because cholera and tuberculosis were major killer diseases, reduced after 1870 because most cities had improved their water supply and built more effective sewers.

Cities that did not repair their sewers inflicted a terrible medical cost on their citizens. For instance Hamburg, a free self-governing port city, postponed costly modernization of its water supply. It drew water without treatment from the Elbe River. Next to it was Altona, a city within the boundaries of Prussia and that state installed a water filtration plant there. In 1892 cholera of epidemic proportions struck Hamburg but had no affect on Altona. The street dividing the two cities was also the dividing line between the area of plague and that of immunity. There could no longer be any doubt that contaminated water was a major cause of the dread disease. The "miasmatists," believers that a stench of miasma was the source, were put to rout. In the 1890s Koch investigated malaria, still a mystery until the British bacteriologist Ronald Ross proved that it was caused by a certain specie of mosquito. Koch won the Nobel prize in 1901 for his tuberculosis research.

Pasteur, along with Koch, opened the new field of microbiology and continued to discover new forms of pathogenic germs and identified illnesses due to infection from them. Remembering Jenner's work on smallpox, he definitively proved that an injection of micro-organisms of diminished virulence protected against the more virulent infection of the same organism. He proved that vaccination could become a general technique applicable to all forms of infectious diseases, rabies included. Pasteur was a practical scientist who believed that his craft must serve society. When silkworm growers in southern France were suffering from an attack that was killing their worms, he discovered the culprit, pebrine, and a cure against it. When wine growers found their product turning to vinegar he found the cause, a microbe, and a cure, heating the wine to a temperature just high enough to kill the villain. This was the procedure that became known as pasteurization, subsequently applied to milk to impede spoilage.

There was another force active in the remarkable progress of medicine: nurses. Before the later nineteenth century, nursing in hospitals was professionally in low repute, and dangerous because hospital air was deadly. According to The *Times* (London) in 1857 nurses were "lectured by committees, preached at by chaplains, scowled at by treasurers and stewards, scolded by matrons, sworn at by surgeons, bullied by [wound] dressers, grumbled at and abused by patients, insulted if old and ill-favored, talked flippantly to if middle-aged and good humored, tempted and seduced if young and well looking—they are what any woman might be expected to be under the circumstances." Practically all nurses were teenage girls and working class women because only they accepted the conditions of employment: responsibility for seventeen beds, hours from 6 A.M. to 7 P.M. and a ridiculous wage of five pounds per year, plus food and lodging.

Reform of the profession began in Germany where the first nursing school was established by a Protestant pastor, Theodor Fliedner and his wife. Their school became a model, and Florence Nightingale attended courses there. When she returned to England she visited nursing arrangements in hospitals. After the Crimean War broke out she went to the front as a nurse, an act unheard of for a woman of her high position. Yet when the army's medical services broke down and more men died of disease than enemy fire, she reorganized the nursing corps to some good effect. She was a very determined woman with powerful friends. On her return home she used the sums offered by them to endow a nursing school at Saint Thomas Hospital. Soon other hospitals did the same.

Both the medical and physical sciences had effects on the general course of thought. In particular they reinforced the tendency toward the belief that only matter existed, that which could be observed, measured, and demonstrated. The immaterial, the soul or spirit, was a fiction perpetrated on society by advocates of traditional beliefs stemming from ages of gross ignorance about the world. After scientists like Antoine Lavoisier and John Dalton had demonstrated the indestructibility of matter and energy, there could be no doubts on this count. In 1855 Ludwig Büchner published *Energy and Matter* to prove that the human brain is of purely physical composition. His book went to sixteen editions between 1855 and 1889, evidence of the general interest in the subject. The traditional belief that the brain was spiritual, even the seat of the soul, was challenged by a Dutch physiologist in 1850 when he published *Doctrine of Food*, and asserted that there could be no thought without phosphorus, that is, material nourishment for a physical organ. As the German philosopher Ludwig Feuerbach put it "man is what he eats." Feuerbach also thought out the idea of religious alienation. To the old precept that God made man in His own image, he replied that man made God in his own image, thereby alienating himself from his true physical nature.

For materialists, mind was the same as matter and governed by the same scientific laws. Claude Bernard, attached to the Collège de France, published his famous *Introduction to the Study of Experimental Medicine* in 1865. In it he, too, affirmed that the brain was simply another organ of the body. His book became a text for medical practitioners; it also became the bible for several fiction writers. They were convinced that the methodology of research in the physical sciences was equally valid for the social sciences as well as for a new style of literature.

Science and Literature

The nineteenth century was the first in which the expansion of scientific knowledge carried a greater weight than law, religion, art, and letters in determining the public's outlook on age-old values. It was also the era when the novel as a literary type came into its own, rivaling other forms of creative writing. In its growth it passed through several stages and moved from the picaresque tastes of the past to romantic gothic stories. Around midcentury a new generation of writers, certainly influenced by science, began to find their own time and place suitable as subjects for their plots, and sought to relate the lives of ordinary people whom one could meet on the street, field, railway station, department store, barroom, or dockside. Known as realists they showed little or no interest in the past or the workings of the soul or the eternal forces of good and evil. Like the positivist literary critic Hippolyte Taine, they affirmed that there was neither good nor evil, only life in its hard-hearted manifestations, and their world was often uncharitable.

The first among them was Honoré Balzac. As a precursor and most prolific in the 1830s and 1840s, he still had the sentimentality of romanticism running through his work. Capable of prodigious energy he set out to display his society in its vast number of aspects, from the poor to the rich, the good to the evil, the caring to the indifferent, and the holy to the nonbelievers, all appeared in the many volumes of his *Human Comedy*. There was too much idealism in his outlook to place him squarely in the predominately pessimistic French realist school: His priests were too good, his nobles too benign, and his bourgeois too ill formed as characters. It is odd how little attention any of the realists paid to business men. The only truly honest one in Balzac went bankrupt; the others were caricatures. Dickens distorted them, as noted already, into materialistic monsters. For Balzac, reality was to be found in the highly detailed descriptions of indoor and outdoor surroundings, apparel, and his characters in their daily actions. He was criticized for depicting a scene in which people ate food; to the romantic mind this was vulgar.

Gustave Flaubert was far less productive; yet he wrote one of the great novels of the century, *Madame Bovary*. Emma, the chief character, was an anti-heroine. A provincial lady she was bored by a dim-witted husband. Seeking romance and affection through adulterous affairs with a series of lovers, she found neither. She finally killed herself in a moment of despair. There was nothing romantic about her life, nor was it heroically tragic, only prosaic. Flaubert was prosecuted for violating an 1819 law prohibiting published works that were an "outrage to public and religious morality."

Emile Zola took realism a step beyond, into "naturalism." Influenced by Claude Bernard, he wrote a treatise called *The Experimental Novel*. By this he meant that writers must investigate and verify their facts, then depict social reality. He also, like Balzac, set out to produce a massive study of his times, believing that the novel, like any scientific work, must find the laws that determined people's behavior, especially the influence of heredity and the environment. His main characters, all of the Rougon-Macquart family, are in the grip of genetic forces beyond their control, hereditary degeneration resulting from alcoholism. With Edmond and Jules Goncourt, *Germinie Lacerteux* is the victim of social forces she never understood. A country girl come to the city as a servant she fell pray to all forms of exploitation, described in detail with the pathos of a psychoanalyst studying a patient.

In Italy the exponent of *verismo* was Giovanni Verga. In his later masterpieces *I Malavoglia* (translated as *House by the Medlar Tree*), and *Mastro dom Gesualdo* he saw man's struggle for material betterment, his major theme, as foredoomed. His strong feeling for locale gave rise to a school of regionalist literature.

It is odd that the realist school found no adherents of similar stature in Germany. Undoubtedly romanticism was too deeply rooted in central Europe, as was idealist philosophy. The most popular novelists, in the midst of rapid economic and urban growth, preferred to write about the towns and villages of their grandfathers. Berthold Auerbach combined the older humanistic tradition with poetic sympathy for the life of simple folk. Whatever realism there was they overlaid with an optimistic faith in human power to overcome pain and suffering. They sought to embody the "conscience of Germany." They seemed blind to reality and mired in the mystique of the *Volk*. They ignored the powerful strain of materialism expressed by some of their scientists. For them man is not what he eats, but what he dreams.

The full strength of realism in Germany was achieved in the theater rather than the novel, a characteristic of the Germanic world. The father of truly naturalistic theater was a Dane by birth, Henrik Ibsen. His plays dealt with the themes common to French novelists: the dominance of society over the individual and the pressure to conform. Because Ibsen lived many years in Germany where his theater was greatly appreciated by independent producers, his influence there was strongest. The work of Gerhart Haupmann owes much to the Dane, save that he showed a much greater concern for the living conditions of the lower classes. His most gripping and humane play was "The Weavers" (1892). It was based on the Silesian weavers revolt of 1844. After 1900 he moved away from pure realism toward neo-romanticism. This, parenthetically, was a turning among more than a few realists around 1900, probably part of the general shift toward the irrational and mystical at the end of the century.

Unlike the Teutons, the Russians were more skillful with the novel, and to such an extent that such a backward country produced at least two of the greatest novelists of the century. The transition from romanticism to realism can be found in the writing of Alexander Pushkin, scion of an impoverished aristocratic family. He was the author of *Ruslan and Liudmila* (1820), *The Gypsies* (1823–24) and the historic drama *Boris Godunov* (1825). Like Goethe he was a universal genius. Although there was much lyricism in his poetical works, he contributed to the decisive defeat of imported pseudoclassicism, exaggerated sentimentalism, and second-rate romanticism. His later works opened the way for the realism of the creative novelists of the second half of the century. Ivan Turgenev does not quite fit in the category of great, but he was the closest among them to Western realism. His early stories about peasants whom he met on hunting trips were accurate descriptions of their lives, the torments they suffered at the hands of their brutal masters. His peasants were more real than those of Balzac or of Zola who painted them as avaricious monsters. As a liberal he was arrested, jailed for eighteen months, and then confined to live on his mother's estate. His best work, *Fathers and Sons* (1862), revealed the conflict of generations. Bazarov, a kind of antihero, was a nihilist, denying all laws save those of the natural sciences.

Fyodor Dostoyevsky also ran into trouble with the police. His early novel, *Poor Folk*, whose condition he knew well, inaugurated his own school of Russian realism. During his imprisonment in Siberia, where he read the *New Testament*, the only book available, he came to believe in a Christ who could raise the sinner to a new existence, and his youthful radicalism gave way to repentance and respect for the established order, combined with a belief in the messianic mission of the common people. The chief character of *Crime and Punishment* (1866) is a nihilist in revolt against society. It is a social novel in which money is a basic problem, as is the materialistic thinking of radical youth, and the willingness to murder for gain. Raskolnikov, the murderer, comes to realize that happiness is not achieved by a rational plan of existence but must be earned by suffering. Of *The Idiot* he wrote, "They call me a psychologist. It is not true. I'm only a realist in the highest sense; that is, I portray all the depths of the human soul." Dostoyevsky was very much a Slavophile, believing that the Russian people were superior to European intellectuals who were standing on the brink of destruction, doomed by their revolutionary materialism and denial of Christ. This was the message of his last major novel, *The Brothers Karamazov*: The secret of universal harmony was not achieved by the mind but by the heart, feeling, and faith.

Leo Tolstoy's realism lay in his mastery of detail and the subtlety with which he analyzes the personalities of his created characters. His greatest achievement, *War and Peace*, provides ample evidence of this ability. In his later years he went through an internal crisis about the meaning of life. To the annoyance of his family he became a recluse and mystical anarchist, denying the church, immortality, and the validity of government.

Russian realism was quite distinct. Save for Turgenev, it described a real world but sought not the laws of social development *à la* Zola, but the arcane forces that would save mankind. It was realistic but irrational, and indeed paved the way for the attacks upon liberal and scientific reasoning that came later in the century.

British realism did not deny reason as its creed, nor display the pessimism of the French. Rather it was earnestly moralistic; it combined deep human sympathy with rigorous moral judgment. Both George Eliot (pseudonym of Mary Ann Evans) and Charles Dickens described in exacting detail the physical surrounding in which their characters lived out their lives, and both were skilled in probing the minds of them. Most optimistic was Dickens. He clearly sympathized with the lower classes, made great melodramas of their predicaments, and was oversentimental about women. His belief in the essential goodness of human nature led him to dress his wicked characters in cloaks which they could—and often did—put aside suddenly to emerge as converted benevolent souls. The human heart beat loud in his fiction. Evans was far more a country writer. She knew the middle and lower classes of the Midlands. *Adam Bede*, for example, is a country story full of the smell of cows, the pungent smell of new mown hay, and the faithful representation of everyday things.

Realism, then, was a response to a changing society. It sought to combine in true descriptions both human nature and the physical world that impinged upon it. But the narrations were so personal and varied that one wonders if there ever existed a realistic school. Perhaps one characteristic does provide some unity. Unlike romantics, the realists came predominantly from the middle class; they wrote, consciously or not, for a middle class audience, even when their hearts were sympathetic to peasants or workers. After all, this was natural: The middle class was in the ascendant everywhere, its values the norm. It was the literate component of society, and the publishing houses were largely in its hands.

14

The Information Revolution

The remarkable flowering and dissemination of scientific knowledge came about so rapidly because of the increase of wealth available for education, investigation, and publication. The equally great flowering of creative literature and art is not so easily related to wealth and technology. Genius that does not depend on laboratories and instruments more sophisticated than paper, pen, and ink can flourish in all kinds of societies, including the economically backward. What we are concerned with in this chapter is less the quality than the content and orientation of imaginative work, and its influence on people in the process of being educated. The major part of society in 1815 was ill informed because they were uneducated. What most persons knew they had acquired by word of mouth from their parents, church preachers, and traveling merchants who carried, along with the lightweight objects they offered for sale from village to village, the news of distant events picked up along their journey. There were also town criers who announced official acts, there were educated bourgeois or literate artisans who read aloud the newspapers received by local tavern owners. Outside of the economically advanced urban regions only a tiny minority were functionally literate, that is, were capable of reading with understanding, and who were able to write comprehensible prose or poetry. These latter belonged largely to the clergy, middle classes, and nobility. If one reached down to isolated parishes inhabited by simple villagers, the local clergyman's literacy was shaky, probably limited to reciting some lines from a sacred manual if Catholic or Eastern Orthodox, the Bible if Protestant. Shifting from west and center to east the rate of literacy fell precipitously: Russia was territorially a massive land inhabited by uneducated serfs tied to routines because they were utterly lacking in the means to learn of change. Neither their priests nor their masters ever dreamed of literate serfs. Indeed, a literate serf was a contradiction in terms. The upper classes in the rest of Europe were about as frightened of lower class literacy as the Russians.

Yet, the ability to write and read certainly expanded, albeit slowly, in the first half of the century. The rate of progress cannot be stated with certainty because evidence is either lacking or unreliable, as is census data. Because governments were barely able to count the scraggly, lice-ridden heads of their masses, they were certainly incapable of deciding who was literate. Numerous studies based on counting the number of men and women who could sign official documents such as birth and baptismal certificates, marriage contracts, or death certificates are inconclusive because many witnesses to such events could sign their names but were not functionally literate. At best, I can suggest that between 1839 (school attendance records) and other documents in 1850, that literacy was highest in the northern and north western sectors of the Continent (perhaps 60 percent). This was Protestant Europe where study of the Bible required the ability to read. There were pockets of Catholicism where reading was encouraged if only to compete with the Protestants. The zone stretching from France to Austria and north Italy was next in line (about 70 to 50 percent). The Mediterranean basin was seriously backward (25 to 15 percent). Finally the East and Southeast was a vast area of the untutored, where the literate were like strangers in a strange land (20 to 5 percent). School attendance more or less accorded with these levels of literacy, as did the number of schools available. By midcentury it is almost certain that lower class youngsters were far more capable of reading than their parents, and almost grammarians compared with their grandparents. Schools had by then begun to progress enough to create a generational difference.

Schooling: Germany

Prussians were certainly the most educated, thanks in part to Wilhelm von Humboldt, educational adviser to the king of Prussia after Napoleon's conquest. Moreover the state had since the 1700s a compulsory education law for youngsters over seven years of age, the first such measure in Europe. However it would be naïve to believe that the law was everywhere enforced. Humboldt benefited from it and shaped both primary and secondary schooling by carrying out a more enlightened curriculum. His was a thorough classical system, emphasizing reading and writing at first, then some Latin, and German, but taught with other subjects so as to provide students with information other than grammar, and intended also to provide them with a sense of value and ethical judgment. The basic element at the primary level was the *Volksschule*, set up for the broad population, but especially for the sons of the middle class and offering a broader curriculum than the more exclusively classical studies of gymnasia. Like other educators he faced a teacher shortage and earnestly set out to establish centers to train young recruits. For some time teachers were retired army noncommissioned officers whose classroom abilities were limited to keeping order, by corporal punishment if necessary. Since private schools had been practically eliminated, pedagogy was concentrated in schools controlled and financed by the state and local populations. No one as yet objected to the leading place that religious instruction held in the curriculum, although parish clerics objected to laymen teaching such a sacred subject.

Humboldt concentrated secondary schooling in the gymnasia which pupils entered when nine or tens years of age. Here only qualified persons held academic positions. This measure raised standards by curbing patronage and the arbitrary powers of urban educational officers, traditionalistic as they were. The pastors also found their influence reduced. The plan of studies complemented the primary level, with more Latin, Greek, German, and mathematics. For the ten-year period of study other subjects were accessory. Humboldt, intent on reforming the entire Prussian educational system, instilled in the faculties that their role was both to teach and seek for new knowledge. That indeed man's knowledge is never complete. And apart from research, teaching must endeavor to train the whole person, not merely instill a specialty.

Baron Karl von Altenstein, minister of education from 1807 to 1840, followed in the path laid down by his predecessor, and also like him sought to defend academic freedom during the reaction following the Carlsbad Decrees. An energetic man, he reorganized or established some 30,000 elementary schools and thirty-eight normal schools, the seed ground of competent teachers. By 1848 about 80 percent of school age children attended classes in the Rhineland and 93 percent in Prussian Saxony. Illiteracy was on the way out as other German states followed Prussia's example. The exception was the Hapsburg Empire.

After the crisis of 1848 the king of Prussia, as head of the Protestant church, insisted that religion become the core of primary studies. His 1850 constitution separated church and state which gladdened Catholics but worried Lutherans. In reality the king continued to exercise extensive control over both education and the churches as head of the Evangelical High Council that he created in July 1850 and gave religious instruction a narrowly Evangelical and Lutheran bent. The church's supervisory powers over education broadened but stopped short of the universities.

German universities, like those throughout Europe, had declined during several centuries; in the early 1800s most of them existed mainly for training future civil servants. They, too, underwent extensive reform as the century progressed. By the 1830s the process of renovation raised them to the first rank in Europe. The liberal arts faculties attracted the greatest minds of the time, such as Hegel and Leopold von Ranke. After midcentury the science faculties prepared students to enter the chemical and electrical fields where the Germans became superior. Much of this advance resulted from the large degree of academic autonomy they enjoyed.

Germans showed a marked tendency toward mass education. Their mentality combined a respect for the soldier and the scholar. Prussians in particular readily joined the militia, but all Germans took to learning. Nowhere else did the prestige of university professors rank so high; merchants and industrialists never attained such a towering degree of acceptance. There was a profusion of doctorates for a degree was taken as the sign of the *gebildeter Mensch*, the cultured person. This desire for culture encouraged book production. In 1750 the number of books published came to 1,279 for all German states. That total rose to 5,000 in 1827, 9,053 in 1850 and 19,000 in 1890. This was the largest number in Europe and matched the total of university students: one out of 1,300 inhabitants, if Austria is excluded. At the secondary level, the total was one pupil for 249 inhabitants, second only to Scotland in 1866.

Schooling: France

France ranked second with one university student per 1,400 inhabitants and one secondary pupil per 570 inhabitants. Yet in 1829 fully 52 percent of army draftees were wholly illiterate. In the population at large, including females, about five out of seven persons could neither read nor write. As in each country, rates of illiteracy varied according to economic conditions. In the impoverished Massif Central, they reached 81 percent; in the rich Jura region, they reached only 17 percent. Wealth alone, however, was not the main determinant of schooling; Germans were not richer than the French and far less so than the British.

Educational policies of the Restoration government were largely left unchanged from those of the first empire. Napoleon had created the *Lycée* at the secondary level to provide him with civil servants and army officers. Discipline was military, and courses preserved their strong classical content of Latin and Greek, but provided more math and history. The Bourbons simply substituted religion for army discipline, time became marked by bells rather than drums, and attendance at mass became obligatory. There was no minister of education; all primary and secondary schools, as well as higher institutions belonged to the *Université*, an administrative superstructure topped by a grand master. Bishop Denis Frayssinous, royalist and ardently clerical, pursued policies comparable with those of his counterparts throughout the Continent: He hunted out all the liberal teachers, including those in the Sorbonne, and Guizot was one of those expelled. The books of the *philosophes* were forbidden. All elementary education fell under the surveillance of the clergy, and Jesuits began operating their own elementary schools.

Primary school curriculum was above all religious in content; at the secondary level it was religious and classical. Apart from Latin, philosophy was supposed to be the crown of the body of learning, but it was limited to logic and ethics, a common practice everywhere. History and geography disappeared from classes, physics and natural sciences never appeared. Conversely, mathematics enjoyed approval because it was "sinless."

The July Monarchy inherited a school system that reached only a very limited number of children, a situation common to predominantly Catholic societies. There were state as well as private, chiefly clerical, schools. Guizot returned to public office, not as a history professor but as minister of education. In 1833 he proposed a school reform bill that marked the first hesitant step toward generalized public schooling at the primary level. In this year there were at least 7,000 communes without a schoolhouse or teacher. Since Guizot was a Calvinist he favored public instruction, but most of the private schools were in the hands of Catholic teaching orders; in fact, many teachers in state supported schools were either nuns or clergymen. He had no desire to disturb these sectarian schools so he gave legitimacy to them by proclaiming the liberty of teaching, guaranteed already by the Charter.

His education law required all communes without some kind of teaching facility to provide at least a room, and hire at least one teacher. Aware of the miserly stipends of pedagogues, he included a minimum stipend of 200 francs a year for those at the primary level and double that for higher grades. He knew that no teacher of any value would be attracted by such a low income, so it was to be increased by fees charged to all parents save those living in poverty. The law sought no changes in the curriculum or its doctrinal base. The first article read: "Primary... instruction comprehends necessarily moral and religious teaching." This provision included secondary education and required all communes of 6,000 or more people and departmental capitals to maintain a high school. In addition, each department must support a normal school for training teachers.

For its time the law was a step forward. However, many communes, even when several small ones were allowed to combine their resources, did not set up any kind of learning facility. And the monarchy did little to enforce its law to the strictest letter. Moreover the measure made no provision for girls in a state where separation by sex was customary in all grades save the lowest; nor did it make education compulsory. Even the so-called opposition in the chamber had no wish for that. Adolph Thiers, sometimes the wit, warned his colleagues that obligatory and general schooling was like building a fire under an empty pot.

Catholics were pleased with Guizot's work, but now their concern was secondary education. What they resisted was state control of schools at this level; its agents supervised all schools and required teachers lay and clerical, to pass tests for competency. What the Catholic clergy demanded was freedom of teaching; what they really aimed at was a monopoly of all teaching.

During the reaction following 1848 they very nearly won their goal. Louis-Napoleon, eager for church support, not only sent troops to support the pope in Rome, he put up no resistance to a law in 1850 that gave the church complete freedom to establish high schools and control them without state intervention. Clericalism won its long battle against the very moderate anticlericalism of Orleanist liberals.

Napoleon, part romantic, part Saint-Simonian, recognized how limited the classical system of studies had become. His education minister introduced a system called "bifurcation." This involved offering a wider choice of degree programs, one emphasizing literature, the other science, with some overlap. Napoleon recognized that the old program that had provided one science course on a purely voluntary basis , for one hour per week, had turned out too many young men ignorant of science and quite unprepared for any but the limited jobs teaching literature or churning out low-paid articles for fly-by-night newspapers. Unemployed and underemployed intellectuals easily became revolutionary malcontents. His scientific track, however, had little chance of success: There were too few teachers, the literary tradition was too deep rooted, even for many scientists who insisted that the humanities were needed to turn out men capable of discernment and moral judgment. When the medical schools continued to require a humanities degree for entrance, "to keep out the uncultured ignoramuses," scientific specialization at the secondary level died as a choice.

When, in the mid-1860s, the emperor brought in Victor Duruy as minister of education, he allowed him to create a "special secondary education" for the sons of farmers and businessmen. The courses were not intended to produce scientists or grammarians: They included history, modern languages, and morals without academic philosophy. Given their watered down content, they represented in a sense education geared to social status: Most of the students came from the petty bourgeois in trade, the professions, and artisan industry. Education was still not compulsory or free; parents still had to pay fees that remained rather steep and excluded most teenagers from high school. Under 2 percent of boys aged between 11 and 17 went to state secondary schools. Those who did enter came from rather affluent families and 68 percent of them opted for the classical track between 1865 and 1880. The more technical degree never acquired respectability. Ironic was it that a degree in letters led either to the jobless intellectual proletariat or to high places in the expanding civil service or teaching. As in all states, the class distinctions of society largely determined the options of secondary school pupils. That the vast majority of students were male goes without saying. As noted already, Duruy's plan to inaugurate public education for girls led to his dismissal. The close relation between culture, social hierarchy, and state were very evident. France was a wealthy country but stingy.

Higher education in France in no way resembled that in Germany. All the universities had been abolished by the revolutionaries in the 1790s and none were reestablished until 1896. What existed until the latter date were faculties, chiefly of law, theology, and medicine. For most of the century standards fell as did the number of students. Most teachers abandoned lecturing; not more than a handful of students bothered going to class. Rather professors gave exams and students paid a fee to take them. Members of the faculties had no connection with important scientific discoveries and were not disposed to teach them. Major towns had faculties, but not necessarily all the faculties. However, all had faculties of sciences and letters. These were rather extensions of *lycées* and their examinations provided students with the bachelor's degree they needed to continue toward a doctorate. Research was hardly a prominent feature of university life. Some professors gave lectures, such as Guizot, and his style was typical: high-level rhetoric, "elegant popularizations" for the general public who usually outnumbered students in the audience. Most lecturing, however, was carried out by *suppliants*, substitutes. Members of the law faculty were too concerned with their paying clients to teach, just as doctors of the medical faculty with their patients. The sums spent on books and scientific equipment were negligible.

Before his dismissal Duruy was appalled at these conditions and wanted to create real universities in the German sense. Resistance from the professors proved too much. Rather he created outside the universities a special research institute, the Ecole Pratique des Hautes Etudes, and he had serious difficulty funding it. A great future awaited it, but it was insignificant compared to the Ecole Polytechnique, where engineers and scientists received their training. From the 1840s more money had been spent on higher education, but nearly all of it to create additional faculties in provincial towns. Nonetheless, faculties and professors outside of Paris remained largely unchanged and underfunded. Half the state's budget went to Parisian institutions, and mainly in the capital was higher education fairly comparable to the more adequately financed German universities as regards teaching, seminars, and research. More specialized training, needed to teach young men in commerce and industry, was provided in locally endowed schools set up by businessmen in major cities. The same financial sources, industrialists and urban councils, created institutes for scientific and technical training.

Schooling: Great Britain

Education in Great Britain differed in many respects from that of Continental countries. First there was no ministry of education in the early 1800s, and the government showed little concern to create one. Cabinets left schools in the hands of the Anglican church and this established organization collected a tithe to maintain itself and to pursue its pedagogic mission. It appears that the clerical hierarchy was far more concerned with the former than the latter. Economically the church was rich and its clergy enjoyed many sinecures offering a comfortable life devoted partly to religious services, but also to eating, drinking, and hunting. Its own schools were not centers of bustling intellectual striving; its universities at Oxford and Cambridge, the only centers of higher learning in England and Wales, were as moribund as possible without being dead. As in France and Russia there were few students, and not much more book learning. When Robert Peel was studying mathematics and his parents removed him temporarily for a trip to Italy, the teacher simply dismissed the other students until his return because none of them were interested in the subject. The younger sons of peers and squires went to university to prepare for the clergy, which promised a good living, or for law or medicine, or simply to live like gentlemen, and that meant gambling, drinking, and womanizing.

Fortunately the British had come to tolerate dissident Protestant sects, even the Catholics. Educational progress resulted less from the vigor of internal reform in the Anglican establishment than from competition among the churches. Protestants everywhere were committed to the Bible and desired their flocks to read the "good book." Therefore they felt the need to found schools to provide some basic elements of learning: reading and writing, and also mathematical calculation because so many of the students would enter business. The Scots, predominantly Presbyterian, were active educators, and literacy there rivaled that of Prussia. The Irish were more in line with southern and eastern Europe where neither governments nor churches felt any impulse to educate the young until the later decades of the century.

In England, dissidents, especially Quakers, founded their own schools. Their academies for secondary and higher education became centers of scientific and intellectual pursuits, even attracting sons of nondissenting parents. To compete, the Anglicans had to become more active; they built more schools, eventually surpassing the Quakers in number if not in pedagogy. These schools emphasized biblical learning as well as the three R's. They had no desire to spend large sums on primary schools, which were private, so they resorted to the monitorial system—older students taught the younger—an innovation of Joseph Lancaster and widely imitated because it lowered costs. Unfortunately it also lowered standards. There were numerous private secondary schools, founded by reform-minded masters dissatisfied with traditional institutions. They attracted the sons of better-off farmers and shopkeepers because they provided close supervision and were readier to include modern subjects in their curriculum.

At the same level were privately endowed "public" schools, which were really private and far more exclusive because of heavy fees. Their course of studies was narrowly classical, with ancient languages and history at the base. Teaching emphasized rote memory, like most schools, and relied on outdated textbooks. It was not uncommon for students to riot out of sheer boredom. Their salvation came in the 1830s through the initiative of head masters like Thomas Arnold of Rugby. He devised more stimulating methods of instruction and free inquiry among students. He improved the prefectoral system, that is, leadership without teaching by a senior in charge of a small group of young boys. He curbed bullying and ragging of the small by the big, of the young by the older. Chapel became the center of moral improvement.

Arnold, the father of Matthew, has been credited with the introduction of sports as part of student life. The game of Rugby undoubtedly originated there but he had little to do with it other than using it to prevent boys from other kinds of action, some cruel. As one scholar put it, " he occasionally stood on the touch-line and looked pleased." Nonetheless, from Rugby, school-organized sports steadily spread to other institutions and were found to be a healthful means of releasing unused energy, thereby reducing class room restlessness.

Undoubtedly, educational standards improved as more schools were built, teachers trained, and rising wealth made it feasible for parents to send their offspring to classes. The British were undoubtedly the wealthiest people in the world; yet, in 1866, there was only one secondary pupil for 1,300 inhabitants, and in 1870, only about half of school-age youngsters were receiving an education, save perhaps in Sunday school. Large numbers of them were still laboring full-time in factories and shops. The situation would change after 1867 when most wage workers acquired the vote and used it to influence governmental policies. As one suffrage reformer put it, "we must now educate our masters." Gladstone's cabinet came forward in 1870 with a bill drawn up by W. E. Forster, an Anglican of Quaker origins. He did for Britain what Guizot had done for France. Leaving established schools undisturbed—he doubled the grants to Anglican schools to consolidate them—then introduced publicly supported non-denominational schools to fill the gaps in the educational map. These new schools were to be financed out of local taxes and managed by elected school boards. This was a progressive measure and augmented tax support for education, a step that the state had taken earlier but with hesitation and stinginess. For nonconformists, however, the issue was the tithe they still had to pay to the Anglican establishment whose schools they would not attend. Finally in 1880 another act made primary schooling both compulsory, and ten years later, fees were eliminated.

Improvements at the lower levels eventually caught up with the universities. The first step came in 1828 when the nonsectarian University of London was founded by private grants. Then, in 1854 and 1871 legislation freed matriculation at Oxford and Cambridge from all religious tests. This opened fellowship and teaching posts to men of all denominations. In the 1850s both institutions began the widening of the fields of study they could offer, especially in the sciences. After all, they had now to compete with newly established universities at Durham, Manchester, and Birmingham. Scotland already had four centuries of higher learning with young, enterprising faculty and rather eager students. Scots also had more students from poor families. In England, workers went to mechanics institutes for technical education, a field in which official schools were deficient. Engineers did not go to universities; they acquired their special knowledge on the job after beginning as apprentices. This system worked well enough in the early stages of economic growth but as science and technology become more complicated, England fell behind the Continent in newly opening fields. There was nothing like the Polytechnique of France or the German universities with their great laboratories for research in chemistry and electricity. The British held to the ideal of laissez faire even in education long after it was not in their interest to do so. The result in the mid-1860s was an inferior number of students per head of the population and a sense of culture that disdained the pursuit of material progress.

Schooling: Russia

Russia, given the size of its student-age population, hardly had an educational system. There is no really accurate data on academic populations at the primary level. The increase at the secondary level was modest: 5,600 in 1809 to 7,700 in 1825 and 17,800 in 1854. Matriculation at the university level rose from 450 in 1809 to 1,700 in 1825, to 3,600 in 1854. Even with these huge percentage increases, however, education remained the privilege of a minute minority. Nearly all institutions of learning were located in towns and cities. Peasants, even the few who were free, were illiterate, save the few chosen by the church for training to become parish priests.

Instruction was both geographically centered and class determined. In secondary schools students destined for a university were taught in the classics; terminal students received training in what were considered practical subjects, such as law, math and natural history. All received extensive instruction in Orthodox religion. This class division was common throughout Europe, but nowhere was it so fully implemented. In Russia, in 1853 there were 424 students in the University of Saint-Petersburg, and 125 belonged to nonprivileged, that is, neither noble nor upper bureaucratic.

The 1848 revolutionary tide did not sweep into Russia, but it frightened the government, inducing it to tighten its control over all schools, especially universities. These lost whatever autonomy they had enjoyed; henceforth rectors were appointed by the education minister, not elected by the faculty. Deans, too, were appointed and were required to censor faculty lectures. Philosophy and constitutional law courses disappeared; logic and psychology were now taught by professors of theology. The only light in the dimming environment were students returning from study in German and French institutions, although there too, the post-1848 crackdown left few faculty who sought to open rather than close minds. What was lacking in Russia were competent teachers. Retired soldiers taught at the primary level, as did many members of the church. The first normal school was opened only in 1871. Then there was a rapid increase in their number after serf emancipation, but the number of trained teachers always remained inadequate.

Teacher shortages particularly weakened education for girls. Under Nicholas, schools existed to train daughters of nobles and upper civil servants. As elsewhere, standards were very low and the curriculum limited to household management, singing and dancing. These girls were locked away from the world in boarding schools that were more like nunneries than centers of learning. Alexander's education ministers opened these schools to all classes save those paying the poll tax, the lowest rung of the social ladder. However fees remained high. This was also true of new day schools opened for girls of the middle class. These latter were secondary establishments offering a far more serious seven-year course of studies. Because women were denied entry into universities, several were set up through private initiative and funding. The first female medical school opened in 1872.

After serf emancipation came a series of reforms already described. For education the most notable was the creation of provincial entities, the Zemstvos. Although controlled by the noble class, their members included many bourgeois, even some literate peasants. They took the need for education reform seriously and began imposing taxes to finance their schools. Their expenditure for education rose from 700,000 rubles in 1868 to 6,800,000 in 1885. For the state with the largest population, these sums were hardly adequate seriously to affect the level of literacy. Nonetheless as Russia began the process of modernization its population between the ages of seven and fourteen found the means to acquire more knowledge and expand its horizon. In 1881 one boy out of six and one girl out of thirty-two attended some kind of school. As in the West, these figures say nothing about the quality of education and the level of literacy. As might be expected, children of the middle class benefited the most; youngsters of peasants and urban workers attended irregularly, dropped out early, and in most cases, soon forgot what they had learned when they joined their illiterate parents in field and shop. For knowledge to remain intact, children needed a society that reinforced what they had learned. Russian society was too backward to provide that. The proposals for universal, free, compulsory education did not come to fruition before 1914.

Education and Society

European society has always produced an intellectual elite that governed, provided values, and produced wealth of which it pocketed a very large part: Of this elite only the religious sought to inform the lower classes and did more than inform, it determined what kind of information might be distributed and how people—even the secular elite—should conduct themselves. In the course of the nineteenth century this mission continued, only state authorities won the upper hand and assumed the control of information flows downward without fully realizing that they were opening the floodgates of knowledge.

The nineteenth century was revolutionary in more ways than building barricades. Such revolts, even when they succeeded, changed little save one ruler for another. The permanent revolutions were not carried out in the streets but in classrooms and editorial offices. Larger numbers than ever before of the young were inculcated with the skills of absorbing information, and then were provided with its sources: periodicals and books. If we can judge the modernizing efforts of Third World countries today, it is evident that significant economic and social progress is impossible without stable government and an informed populace. Education in the early and midnineteenth centuries, because it was controlled by officialdom both lay and ecclesiastic, created generations of youngsters convinced that the regime under which they lived was, as Voltaire put it, the best of all possible worlds. The schools turned out young men who became malcontents; a few of them diffused ideas that would seriously challenge the status quo, but not before the end of our period of study and under conditions unforseen by the seed bearers. Educational systems were on the whole successful in forming a series of generations that proved capable, once other forces intervened, of accepting modernization as a desirable—even a destined—goal for Europeans. These other forces were the periodical press and books.

Periodicals

Newspapers of various sorts had existed before the nineteenth century, but their content was narrow because information was hard to come by and communication slow. Their readership was limited to the literate few who could afford their high prices. The model newspaper was *The Times* of London, founded in 1785 by John Walter: It continued into the next century (it is still a leading daily) and set standards for high quality reporting and mechanical innovation. In 1815 its circulation was 5,000, its price seven pence; in 1850 its readership rose to 50,000 and its price fell to five pence; in 1861 it sold 70,000 copies at three pence.

In 1815 the circulation of important dailies was between two and five thousand. They contained odd bits of information sent in by readers or lowly paid agents. News could not travel faster than the mounted courier who brought it to editors. It took four days for London readers to learn about the victory at Waterloo. More adventuresome editors resorted to homing pigeons until a telegraph cable was laid between Dover and Calais in 1851. It, combined with overland lines or the wireless, reduced the time lag to a negligible factor.

The decline of the price of *The Times* resulted from technological innovation. A newspaper like *The Times*, as its staff grew with the addition of special-ized editors and full-time reporters, expanded from a workshop to a factory churning out information and presumably enlightened commentaries on events. At first newspapers were printed on hand-operated, wooden flatbed presses. These were replaced by the rotary press activated by steam power in 1814. Mechanical typesetting replaced the human hand. From a few hundred copies, technology made it possible to roll out thousands of copies daily. Paper was made of rags and its manufacture gave a livelihood to thousands of old rag pick-ers. Their incomes, however, disappeared when editors turned to paper made of wooden pulp to reduce costs.

For small journals the expense of gathering news remained a problem until the appearance of agencies specializing in this undertaking. In 1835 Charles Havas set up his business (still functioning); he culled articles from many papers, rewrote them, then sold them to subscribers. In 1851 Paul Reuter fol-lowed his example and began an agency that surpassed his and others until they all formed a monopoly to divide the world among them, thereby eliminating competition. They were simply following the lead of big industrialists and the rush to organize cartels.

In the first half of the century most journalists would have reacted with hostility toward such blatant commercialism. These were the political journal-ists, a large number of them with liberal or democratic leanings. Among the moderates stood Adolph Thiers, connected with the *Constitutionnel* and the *Siècle*, who made a fortune publishing newspapers and books. More to the left was William Cobbett's *Political Register* which had a wide circulation before and after 1815. He even continued to direct it from prison where he spent some time for unfavorable comments on the British government during the reactionary period after 1815 when heavy stamp taxes sought to put opposition journalism out of business by raising costs, and by resorting to the Six Acts of 1819 when censorship was reimposed.

The political press was most vigorous in France where it was largely responsible for the revolutions of 1830 and 1848 which began in Paris where leading journalists were also politicians, and literacy rates were high. Periodicals like *Le Bon Sens* of Louis Blanc, the *Réformateur* of François Raspail, *Le National* of Armand Carrel were engines of war against the Bourbon and Orleanist regimes. For these men, *The Times* was far too sedate and commercial. As Louis Blanc put it, journalism was not merely a job, it was a sacred mission, a call to arms to do combat against the evils of monarchy and clericalism. A political journal was less concerned with objective reporting than with editorials expressing the views of its editors and financial backers. Its goal was to win readers to its cause. This was equally true of the legitimist press, such as the *Gazette de France*.

Such papers had relatively few readers, a few thousand at most. Their prices were high, eighty francs a year and sold mainly by subscription. They were dependent on financial support from sympathizers and sales to taverns and bars where they passed from hand to hand, and were often read aloud for the benefit of illiterate workers. So they had a far wider influence than their subscription lists suggest. They accepted advertisements to help their budgets, but refused to let them influence their goal and grouped them on the last page. Louis Blanc once insisted that a merchant prove the efficacy of his product before accepting an ad. Given this outlook, it was no surprise that they opposed the owner of *La Presse*, Emile de Girardan, when he set out to commercialize his paper by relying on ads to meet expenses. He also played down politics, relying more on a gossip column written by his wife, theater reviews, human affairs, and serial stories. Many famous novelists published their stories first in journals like the one of Girardin, which explains why so many of them were excessively wordy and ill organized: Writers were paid by the word! Eugene Sue chopped up his enormous *Mysteries of Paris*, a highly romanticized depiction of the lower classes of the capital, to insert it in several papers. The same fate awaited *The Wandering Jew*. Melodrama was the mainstay of the serial story. Criticism of Girardin was bitter and provoked a duel between him and Carrel, which ended in the latter's death. Girardin, whatever his faults, had found the way to cut the price of newspapers by 50 percent in his case, and to expand his sales, which reached 20,000 in 1836.

The opposition press, determined to awaken the minds of its readers, had a difficult time surviving. The Bourbons, Orleanists, and Bonapartes sought every means to crush it. High stamp duties was one device. The July Monarchy resorted to the September Laws of 1835 to censor it, to arrest journalists, to impede sales by arresting street hawkers. Some editors spent years in jail; fines bankrupted the weaker journals. Even when the prosecutor was not sure of a conviction, he prosecuted to force the journal's owners to pay legal fees and deplete their budgets. All records were beaten by the *Tribune*: it was brought to trial eighty-six times, lost seventeen times, its director spent a total of fourteen years in jail and paid 87,474 francs in fines by 1833.

Unlike the political press, the general interest newspapers that succeeded won a large following. In 1863 the *Petit Journal* sold a quarter million copies; Henri Rochefort's *La Lanterne* sold half a million. He was one of the wittiest of journalists and became famous for his observation: "France has 36 million subjects, not counting the subjects of discontent." The success of his journal proved that politics could pay off if violent and scurrilous enough; he attacked the Second Empire without mercy. More sedate papers like *The Standard*, sold 130,000, the *Daily Telegraph* 150,000 copies, and when its price fell to one penny its circulation rose to 250,000 in 1880. The sales of the *Berliner Morgenpost*, the most widely read periodical in the German Confederation, were far less. The papers in Germany and Austria were more provincial than those in England and France, and managed with about 35,000 readers each. However there were more of them and their total readership equaled, possibly surpassed, those of Britain and France where the major dailies tended to be concentrated in London and Paris.

Books and High Culture

Expanding literacy also spurred book production, and the technical innovations that expanded sales of periodicals by lowering costs helped publishing houses to put more books on the markets at prices readers could afford. The kinds of texts they printed indicates the changing public taste. Early in the century religious tracts were popular. By 1900 volumes dealing with the relatively new field of social science were the best sellers; close behind were those concentrating on literature, history, geography, and medicine. Religious works far surpassed those in the sciences, although medicine ran well ahead of sacred literature. Trailing were volumes about philosophy and fine arts.

The rate of increase of books more or less followed both the rate of literacy and of population. In Britain and Germany the numbers climbed steadily; in France they leveled off from the eighties onward. This indicated that the consumption of printed literature did not increase per capita, a limiting factor in the French industry. Consumption of coffee and sugar climbed per capita; books did not. Apparently even with the decline of prices, books were too expensive for most households. Workers read Sue's *Mysteries of Paris* in serial, if they read him at all, not in the seven-volume bound edition.

Some authors enjoyed decent incomes from their literary efforts, a few became rich, and many barely survived. Large cities attracted aspiring writers and painters, and they did not always make ends meet. They became the essential element of the so-called "Bohemian" populace: inspired but impoverished, the raw material washed of its criminal features by the composers of opera, such as "La Bohème" of Giacomo Puccini. Among the prima donnas tuberculosis was fashionable and they died of it in melodious ecstasy. This fictional melodramatizing of the down-at-the-heel had great appeal for the well-to-do bourgeoisie. Poverty lay hidden behind the screen of romance. In reality, these aspiring immigrants faced literal starvation, and spent most of their time in quest of a meal. Their life was difficult and dirty, and no fantasizing could wash it clean. But, then, much of culture, whether highbrow or lowbrow, was composed of myth—from the fake romantic imagery of starving artists to the Wagnerian revival of medieval folk tales.

There did emerge in the century an institution that could not enrich writers but could aid them: the public library. Before their appearance in towns and cities readers unable to buy books went to private reading rooms where books and periodicals were available for a fee. In Germany there were such establishments for the more affluent with comfortable reading rooms as well as rooms for cards and billiards. But most of them consisted of one or two chambers, and it was even possible to borrow volumes for a fixed period of time.

Public libraries were free, supported by local taxes and open to all inhabitants of a city. As cities grew wealthier they budgeted larger sums first to build libraries and then to stock their shelves with reading matter of every variety. Their advent created a relatively new profession, the librarian, which offered employment to women in particular, as did schools as they acquired libraries. Indeed, the enormous expansion of cultural institutions was a notable step in the rise of a female work force entirely different from that of the textile mill and the clothing sweat shop. The culture of the nineteenth century was largely a middle-class creation, combining the older nobiliary traditions with new creations. Rising industrial towns fell under the control of wealthy manufacturers and profession-als, men who were often very busy, but whose wives and daughters enjoyed the leisure to devote themselves to artistic and literary activities. We cannot write here of a feminization of culture, but women were certainly active in organizing cultural events and persuading their husbands and fathers to finance them. As places like Manchester exploded from village to great city, it built up a symphony orchestra, a university, first-rate libraries, a literary and philosophical society, a theater, and a museum of nineteenth-century art. High culture was generally reinforced by theaters, concert halls, and opera houses, many of which were included in the work of urban renewal in older cities like Paris.

Centers that dated from the medieval or renaissance periods usually had gothic or classical churches that were renovated by architects in government employ. "Respectable" society needed churches and the middle classes went to them faithfully, at least the women and children did. Clergymen were still judged according to their skill at preaching, and church going was still classed as a form of amusement. But one that was now being challenged by other activities, not usually cultural but sporting. The lower classes in both Protestant and Catholic countries sometimes went to hear "hot gospellers" where they learned more about the roaring flames of hell than about the pleasures of heaven. The businessman had his circle, the tilted noble had his more exclusive center, like the Jockey Club in Paris, the working man had the tavern or pub and their children the street.

Popular Culture

The culture of the common people was created as a means of living with the harshness of their nasty, brutish and short lives. It was oral until written down by anthropologists and folklorists, its substance, storytelling, passed down by word of mouth from one generation to the next, half Christian, half pagan. Indeed, its persistence leads one to ask whether the rural population had ever been fully Christianized or whether the church missionaries had compromised with ancient superstitions too deep to be uprooted. Before the spread of literacy and of science, the lower classes believed in magic, especially black magic. Until recent times in southern climes people remained fearful of the evil eye, and might seek relief as readily from a local sorcerer as from the local priest. As in the Middle Ages, they invoked saints to succor them in times of drought or flood, or to safeguard crops, animals, and loved ones. Work animals enjoyed a value equal to that of humans. In the lower-class mind, and in that of many educated people, the sorcerer possessed powers equal to those of priests and were more willingly sought out than the medical doctor to cure illness. Doctors were often powerless defenders of public health in times of widespread plague, as during the cholera invasions. Such beliefs, of course, were common to uneducated peasants. Among them shepherds, those solitary men living alone with their sheep or cows much of the year, were held in special awe. Blacksmiths, working near their smelting furnace, were considered powerful because they had special relations with the devil. Such beliefs were not limited to the lower class; Goethe's Faust had recourse to the devil to recover his youth and virility. Goethe was composing a moral story; to the uneducated it seemed a normal response. Salvation would come from above or below; when both failed the unwashed masses would turn to socialism. In the ample bosom of the socialist goddess everyone stank for lack of washing facilities.

Socialist ideas could not make much headway in rural areas where popular beliefs were basically Christian with some remnants of paganism. How were propagandists of reform to deal with peasant culture that understood natural phenomena such as storms at harvest time as acts of malevolent demons, witches and vampires? Holy water was used not to bless oneself but to ward off vampires or the spells of sorcerers. In the Balkans corpses that did not stiffen in the tomb were transfixed with wooden stakes and had their limbs cut off lest they return as vampires. There was a gruesome side to the culture of the people.

In contrast popular culture of the cities was more given to hilarity than tragedy. Everyday life was tragic enough. What workers and their girls and wives wanted was fun, and this is why rituals, formerly an integral part of holy worship, were held on to for their comic elements. The lower wage-earning class of artisans, factory hands, shop assistants, and petty clerks celebrated the carnival with masks, fife and drum parades, lively dancing, cock fighting, bear baiting (even after these cruel sports were made illegal), and bull fighting in Spain and southern France. The solemnity of the holy days of lent lost much of its appeal as the century progressed. At other times of the year storytelling was popular. In worker neighborhoods and peasant villages the teller of tales, whether native or traveling, was widely acclaimed. There were plays that could depict the nativity of Christmas, or satirize an unpopular member of the upper class. It was common in France, when an older widower married a young woman, for the young bachelors to express their discontent at her loss to them by performing a *charivari*—loud cries and banging of pots and pans. Villagers had their fairs and urban workers their inexpensive promenade concerts. In Vienna Johann Strauss led his orchestra, playing waltzes and mazurkas for dancing couples; in Paris young men and women went together to the open-air concerts in the Champs-Élysées; in London the same took place in Surrey Gardens. In all these events the better paid workers mingled freely with the petty bourgeois. Both these groups lived in a world distinct from that of "genteel" society that frowned on body-contact dancing between the sexes as immoral.

Middle-class culture was essentially individualistic, that of the lower classes collectivistic. The rich could get along on their own, the less well off could not. Their cultures reflected their economic opportunities and their social strata. The expansion of capitalist systems of production and trade changed traditional ways of thinking and acting, generated the wealth that offered access to the world of literature and art that only the churches had offered in the past. With the material improvement of life high culture became more secularistic, low culture less mystical. With the spread of educational opportunities, the two even acquired some resemblance: Both the upper class and the lower class could waltz with their ladies, but not in the same place.

15

Modernization of Domesticity

The Family: From Full to Empty Nest

The history of the family became increasingly complex over the nineteenth century because the domestic group we call the family evolved from an economic unit into an affective household. Before the appearance of factory production, most families were created and held together by the necessity of survival. Each was a working unit with all members able to walk participating in the labor routines required to provide the necessities of life and obtained chiefly from farming the soil in the countryside and from artisan labor in towns. The domicile, or "nest", was full because the household was rather large; there were blood relations, and there were, in many cases, servants who were considered part of the family since they lived in and were ruled over by the father as head. Even in the upper class family each member had some task that contributed to its position in society.

With the introduction of the domestic system in the late 1600s rural families did not change their economic basis, only the tasks that each member performed as spinning and weaving were added to cultivation of land. The family economy remained intact. Of course the persistence of serfdom in central and eastern Europe deprived domestic groups of the freedom enjoyed by those living west of the Rhine River. The difference was more than a purely legal one; servility deprived the family of options about how it would function as an economic unit, and also bound it to the village in ways that had disappeared in the west long before the 1789 revolution in France.

The breakdown of this rural household began in Britain with the industrial revolution and enclosures. By 1830 farming areas there were undergoing considerable depopulation as more people moved into manufacturing towns, abandoning their rustic tasks, including domestic manufacturing, for disciplined work and, usually, life in small apartments, tenements, or row housing. This same displacement came later and more slowly to the Continent. The ruination of many artisans by factories forced them to change jobs as well as residence.

This process had a marked effect on the family but not in ways previously believed. Formerly historians and other social scientists theorized that economic modernization destroyed the large multigeneration, or stem, family and put in its place the smaller nuclear family of parents and children. Recent scholarship has contended that no such change occurred because the nuclear group had always existed. Indeed even its size had resisted economic changes in western Europe, falling only from 4.77 members in 1740–1821 to 4.3 in 1911, with moderate fluctuations in between. This observation is valid only for certain geographical areas, especially where there was already economic progress as a result of expanding trade and an active domestic production of cotton yarn and cloth. The two-generational family certainly predominated in the northwestern area. However in the life cycle of many families there appeared a three-generational structure when a son or daughter married, lived with the parents and produced children. But before long either the older parents died or retired to another dwelling or the younger ones moved to a farm of their own, terminating the stem setup. This phenomenon was widespread over Europe. But there were sizable areas where large multigenerational families were the norm, as in central and southern France, as well as in eastern Europe. Regardless of structure domestic units everywhere tended to be large. Especially upper class families were sizable because two or more generations remained under one roof. In those of the entrepreneurial manufacturing class, sons were given an elementary education and then taken into the business. Since they delayed marriage they lived at home until their late twenties or early thirties.

Age at marriage was one factor determining family size. It was common in western and central Europe for offspring to remain at home until they acquired sufficient wealth to support an independent existence—the son well established in a job or with land, and the daughter with a dowry created from savings over several years. Since their parents had also married late the father would be close to or past his sixtieth year and, given the limited longevity of life before 1900, either deceased or ready to retire. The son could then inherit most of the land, marry and begin his own family. This practice was equally common among urban artisans because the son had to become a master before he could marry. There were, it must be noted, a fairly large number of children who never married. What is called the European demographic pattern was characterized by late marriage, with permanent celibates making up about 20 percent of the population. Family size was equally determined by the woman's age at marriage.

The term *size* can be misleading because it has two meanings. I have used it when referring to generations inhabiting the same domicile. But even a nuclear family could be large because it produced many children. Numerous studies by demographers have hit on the average of four to six persons in nuclear households. In the second half of the nineteenth century, however, that number fell to two or three in France where family limitation led to demographic stagnation. The average for Britain was 4.68 in 1831 and 4.36 in 1911, a figure fairly constant in nonindustrial as well as industrial cities, and in economically-active small places. These figures are also valid for much of central Europe. This rather limited size was also part of the European pattern. The preceding two numbers, although they do not seem significantly different for each family, indicate a decline in birthrates nationwide.

Russia and much of the East had a decidedly different pattern. Before and after emancipation the stem family dominated. After all, the end of serfdom changed the peasants' legal status without changing the conditions of life that encouraged multigenerational households and large numbers of children. These were biological households; the size of land allotments was decided by the size of membership based on blood relatives. Numbers of these peasant groups ran from six to as high as twelve when two married sons and their brood cohabited with their parents. Large families of this type were longer lived than those in the west because children married much earlier: seventeen for grooms, fifteen for brides. These ages rose by about two to three years after the 1860s, but never enough to modify family size generationally or numerically. The father was considerably younger when his children married and was still in his prime when his grandchildren came into the world, and, alas, out of it because so many died in infancy. He was a true patriarch who ruled with a firm hand.

If the Russian family was large, that of the Balkan peninsula was larger. The *zadruga* was a biological household that could reach eighty in number but rarely did. Recent studies have revised the size down to an average of nine to fifteen in all, not much more sizable than its Russian counterpart. Only occasionally did it include nephews and uncles, or the female equivalents.

Clearly the nest was not emptied in the East. In the West, industrialization eventually took its toll, but not so much in the urban laboring family where children began working at twelve, contributed their wages to their parents, and remained at home because they could not afford to live alone on their meager earnings. In rural villages, however, teenagers departed because opportunities were limited, younger sons did not inherit the land, and daughters migrated at an early age to cities where they found employment either in textile mills or as servants in middle-class homes. By the 1890s, however, as girls received some education, they went off in search of jobs as teachers, sales personnel, railway office clerks, and secretaries. This trend continued to the point where male farmers began to complain that they could not find women to marry.

Conjugal Relations

Women could expect little affection in the family either as daughters or as wives, or even as sisters and cousins. The family as an affective group was a product of the social conditions in which it existed. The romantic experience with its exaltation of passion and commitment seems not to have penetrated domestic life. The families of some romantics were certainly influenced. The Byrons, Shelleys, and Hugos followed their own dictates which called for passionate love, at first with the spouse, later with someone else, preferably a muse in flesh and blood. But they were exceptional. The upper class like the lower class were far more traditionalistic. Property arrangements determined marital alliances at the highest strata in town and country where property married property and bank accounts married bank accounts. Love was and remained into the early twentieth century a minor matter.

Property was not a bargaining issue at the lower levels of society, save for the dowry that servant girls gathered to enhance their attraction even if they were comely. Bodily beauty, which was as short-lived as the rose under harsh conditions of life, had less appeal for rural men than physical strength. Peasant men looked for an extra pair of arms, essentially strong, capable of the arduousness of field work and harvesting. For the common peasant, a woman was simply another piece of farm equipment, and an acre or two of dowry. In Russia, physical beauty counted for even less as compared with submissiveness and the "endurance of a horse." There, in the extended family, the young wife had to anticipate the curt treatment of her mother-in-law and the sexual advances of her father-in-law. Given the youth of Russian brides they were possibly troubled by these attacks upon their vulnerability. On the other hand, they were probably not treated kindly in their own families before marriage and expected nothing better after it.

Throughout Europe, family relations lacked affection. As one male commentator put it, "Marriage is a way of learning how to hate women." This statement revealed the deep-rooted misogyny of men who expected passive obedience in women, not equality. The fear and hatred of women was deep-seated in the Christian clergy over centuries and was inculcated in nineteenth century men. Affectionate gestures between spouses or between them and their children were rare.

Of course there were numerous exceptions to these crass generalizations. To be sure, most proverbs of the time reveal a deep distrust of women, but these do not necessarily represent accurately the internal conditions of matrimony. Besides, we must not read the past in the light of our own values. There were husbands who beat their wives; given the physical stamina of farm women, there must have been some who were not only capable of defending themselves but of taking the offensive against their bullying mates. Parents beat children and pounded on each other. Mores allowed a good deal of violence in social as well as in private life. And this kind of savage state persisted into the late nineteenth century. Only education and economic improvement would soften the brutality of existence. Given our knowledge of human nature, admittedly a "soft" sector of knowledge, there surely were loving couples who gave more caresses than cuffs to their children, as well as to themselves. Brutality in the family, both urban and rural, resulted from excessive alcohol consumption, as well as from the exiguous living space available to married couples. As for the former I shall go out on a limb and propose that violence resulting from alcohol was more common in northern Europe where people consumed beverages high in alcohol. This was also beer-drinking territory. Beer is a drink with alcohol generated by fermentation. Far more deadly were the beverages produced by distillation. Fermentation produced a wine of 10° and a beer of 5°–6°, distillation a drink of 40° or more. In the cold winter of northern climates people consumed both beer and brandy accordingly. In their ill-heated and damp habitations, they imagined that alcohol would warm their blood. Alcohol, unfortunately, produces the opposite effect, cooling the skin's surface and weakening the body's defense mechanisms against cold and contagion. Wine-producing areas, chiefly the northern Mediterranean basin, were less afflicted by strong drink. Wine there was low in alcoholic content and served more as a source of merriment than of deadening the senses. In northern industrial towns, alcoholism was a serious problem, not merely a personal one, but a social one. It destroyed families and sent unhappy children into foundling homes. When violence occurred frequently in the family it was very likely the result of a lack of affection between husband and wife who were brought together more for convenience than commitment.

Happily there were ways of controlling wife beating in farming communities. The village impinged constantly on each household, and there was no private life nor family secrets among neighbors, just as there was no personal privacy within the confined living space of each family. When neighbors heard the husband's imprecations and the wife's screams, the young among them did not interfere at once, but soon after grabbed the villain, put him forcefully into a wheel barrow, and paraded him around the village while reenacting the beating as they imagined it. If the wife beat her husband, he was put backward on a donkey, and trotted around the village. Or the young set up a *charivari*, that is, shouted out loudly while beating on pots and pans outside the house of the offender. In England this was known as "rough music," and as *Katzenmusik* in Germany. So the custom was widespread. In these ways the village avenged the upsetting of established customs. Of course, as society modernized, village life changed and the state, with its organized police force, took over the defense of tranquillity. Not until the last decades of the century, however, was this transition notable in the countryside near urban centers; life in more remote areas remained largely unaltered until World War I.

Urban families were usually more complex than their rural counterparts. At the lower levels there was no property to bring a man and a woman together, so choice of mate was often a result of affection. Moreover there was a greater number of young people without family, and therefore parents had nothing to do with the decision to marry. In one respect many rural and urban couples had one practice in common: their living together without going through a marriage ceremony. These consensual unions resulted in the countryside from the refusal of landlords to permit their tenants or workers to marry. Refusal was widespread in Austria with the result that illegitimacy rates were the highest in Europe, up to 28 percent of births in Styria during 1870. At this date the rate in England was 5 percent. On the whole, peasants did not regard their offspring as bastards; only the church and the law declared them so. In cities, ill-paid workers simply could not afford the fees required for registration and ceremony so they simply moved in together and produced children. Such unions were as stable as legalized ones. Better-paid skilled workers usually could afford the costs of marriage and were often less tolerant of illegitimacy than landowners who hired rural workers without inquiring about their origins. Factory owners were also indifferent, their major concern focusing on the work habits of their employees.

The employer, like the landlord, was most likely to choose a wife from his own class and to be married by a clergyman, and a noble, in particular, lost standing if he married beneath his social standing; his family would make every effort to dissuade him and to locate a suitable bride for him. As with peasants, so with nobles: Love was not the prime motive for marriage. It was certainly less important than property, and a rich heiress, regardless of her looks, was surrounded by eligible suitors, often younger sons without an inheritance sufficient to live "nobly." The nobility had its own moral code, one adapted to the frequency of loveless unions. Wives were duty bound to produce children and avoid dangerous liaisons; husbands, on the contrary, were expected to support a mistress, and no small number of them enjoyed the benefits of a second family without causing great scandal, providing they were circumspect. A wife had little recourse against such conduct until the law allowed divorce, but noble women rarely took advantage of it. Her parents would certainly move heaven and earth to dissuade her. There were, of course, women of the aristocracy who took lovers. Queen Isabella of Spain enjoyed more lovers than her education permitted her to count. One could slyly suggest that Spain was a Catholic country and priests were tolerant if the church suffered no harm. It is true that the upper clergy of official churches lifted their eyes heavenward to avoid seeing the sexual peccadilloes of their noble supporters. Isabella was overthrown in 1868 because of her politics, not her morals. She was, nonetheless, an exception to the rule of wifely fidelity. Tradition was stronger than personal feelings. Indeed, family formation and life-style at the highest and lowest levels of society were traditionalistic, but in both of them tradition allowed a good deal of extramarital sexual venture.

Modernization of the family came from changed values and practices within the middle class, that is, within the most educated class in Europe, and domestic modernization had its beginnings in areas where it was most numerous, the west and center. Modernization involved the introduction of love and affection as the basis for a happy marriage, the rejection of infidelity precisely because the progressive minded wife came to expect as much pleasure in marital coitus as the husband, the recognition of the two as equally important in their relations, the more gentle and loving treatment of children as well as the willingness to provide for their education over many years, and the transformation of the domicile into an intimate haven or nest closed to outsiders.

Numerous forces worked in this direction. The romantic criticism of marriage for property's sake and the glorification of the passionate and spiritual in life gradually influenced conjugal mores. Evangelical and dissident religious movements insisted on moral purity which discouraged infidelity, and also on gentleness which introduced a humanitarian note into the often harsh symphony of home life. They preached against sin but did not want to brutalize the sinners. Rather they called for more humane treatment of all God's creatures: They decried cock fighting and bear baiting as cruel and contrary to divine will. The wife, along with dogs and other animals, must be gently ministered to and her physical frailty recognized. A kind of cult of motherhood emerged from all this, accompanied by a greater reverence for the birthing process and care of young children. The sermons of a well-known, very activist evangelical, Hannah More, has caused serious scholars to condemn her as an advocate of child whipping. Her advocates, however, retort that she looked upon beating as a last resort. She insisted that the sinful nature of the young be curbed by prayer and the inculcation of self-discipline. And, indeed, the modern family sought to instill a series of rules in the young mind that would guide it along the path of virtue during its adult years.

Of course, no single family lived up to all these recommendations. But they did serve as a guide in the civilizing process, and were elucidated in the numerous magazines and books written explicitly for educated bourgeois readers. Moreover it is important to bear in mind that the term *modern* refers to changed relationships of the nineteenth and early twentieth centuries. By today's standards they seem stuffy and confining, especially for women.

Women: Bondage and Liberation

The middle-class ideal family centered on the mother, and while it enhanced respect and affection, it was also restricting. As wife and mother the married woman was assigned to the home and her freedom was limited. Her world was, as the Germans put it, *Kirche, Kinder, Küche* (church, children, kitchen), the three elements that made up a wife's world. To her was assigned this private space while men functioned in the public sphere of business. In the early nineteenth-century bourgeois male mentality, there was a deep-rooted desire to dominate, both in the work place and in the home where his mastery extended over wife, children and servants. Until later in the century when new laws granted women control over their dowries, inheritances, and wages, the husband immediately on marriage assumed control over such property and used it at will, as George Sand discovered after she was married off by her parents. Moreover, the female, whether married or not, did not enjoy many legal rights, so that her signature on a contract had to be countersigned by a male relative or guardian. At least political progress came to their aid from the 1870s on when specific laws were promulgated not only protecting their property but giving them access to divorce from a philandering or brutal husband, and in Britain in 1907 enabling them to sit in local elected councils, or even to serve as mayors. But they still did not have the vote save in Norway.

The suffragette movement gained fairly large numbers of middle class women, and in Britain, resorted to very moderate acts of violence or outrage, such as shouting down political speakers. They sometimes resorted to hunger strikes when jailed, resulting in force-feeding by less than kindly prison personnel. This suffrage movement, unlike earlier ones that gave men the vote, had wider aims than the ballot as it merged into feminist agitation which sought complete equality between the sexes as well as special laws to protect women as wage earners from exploitation by men. Feminists were justifiably enraged by the denial of access to certain university classes and faculty posts, by the denial of equal pay for the same work, and by the barriers men guarded to close them off from supervisory and managerial positions. Feminism was particularly attractive to unmarried daughters of bourgeois families who had to earn a living. Less educated than their brothers they found a scarcity of genteel jobs. Many of them served as shop assistants in the family store, for small retail stores were the economic basis for multitudes of lower middle class families. Wives also served in these shops without having to abandon their domestic duties because living quarters were usually located behind or above the place of business.

The opening of professions brought into existence by economic expansion and new inventions were outlets for unmarried women from both the middle and lower classes. Enlarged enterprises needed myriad clerks to file and classify documents, and secretaries capable of typing and taking dictation in shorthand. As cities grew they opened libraries and museums with office and cataloging positions open to women who worked for smaller wages than men. The typewriter and shorthand certainly feminized the office as workplace, just as the invention of spinning and weaving machines had feminized the factory floor earlier in the century. They also took jobs in railroad companies where thousands of clerks were needed to control the movement of trains and to sell tickets. Compulsory elementary education was a boon. Earlier, teachers in primary schools included both sexes; in the new schools women who were trained either on the job as in Britain or in normal schools on the Continent occupied nearly all the class rooms, so the chance of employment was enhanced. Unmarried daughters of working class families entered these posts in large numbers; they found the ladder of upward mobility, even if they climbed only one rung. For men effectively kept them out of secondary and higher education. In the war of the sexes the battle lines were drawn in schools and in business offices.

More than ever the middle-class home became a haven where the weary husband came for comfort and affection. In earlier decades businessmen saw little of home because they put in days as long as their employees. The generation coming after midcentury steadily reduced their hours as factories and professional offices closed earlier. They saw more of their children; indeed, the literature pouring forth on family matters, along with the clerical pulpit, urged fathers to act kindly toward the young but not to spoil them. This message was intended for aristocratic fathers as well, but because they sent their offspring away to boarding school at the tender age of five or six they never saw them save on holidays. And girls were raised by nannies and tutors so the mother rarely enjoyed confidential relations with them either, her social life being a busy one. This pattern of life was also characteristic of the upper bourgeois whose wealth and pretensions rivaled those of the nobility. With time the class barrier came down between those with titles and those without, as long as their bank accounts were impressive. Prussian *Junkers* tried to maintain their lofty disdain of parvenu burghers, but Alfred Krupp, the steel and cannon maker, whose father had a few dozen workers in the 1840s, was invited to an imperial wedding because his employees in the 1880s numbered in the thousands. At this level of society wives were expected to produce a large brood to preserve the family. Although as medical science improved survival chances later in the century, noble families began to limit their births less family property become excessively fractured by inheritance laws based on the French code requiring equal division among all children including girls. English and Prussian lords were spared this by their use of primogeniture and entail; however, in Austria-Hungary, France and Italy, where Napoleon's Civil Code outlived him, land division posed a serious problem for nobles and bourgeois that was best solved by family planning.

It was the middling bourgeois housewife who benefited most from birth control. She did not at all take Queen Victoria as a model: the queen, who had a certain dislike of young children and who used chloroform to ease her deliveries, produced nearly a round dozen of children. Little did she need to bother raising them, and their futures were assured by their marriages to every reigning or near-reigning dynasty in Europe east of the Rhine River.

On the contrary, the middling bourgeois wife did not try to enter the labor force but rather to go into labor. Her work place was the home and her energies were not directed toward making money but toward the satisfaction of her husband and the upbringing of her children. By midcentury she was the product of a society far more health conscious than that of the earlier decades: inoculation became a routine at this social level and did not need the French law of 1902 requiring it. She was far more educated than her mother and grandmother, and therefore more eager to seek medical advice about her own health and that of her family. This simple fact was almost a revolution because she rejected the absurd nostrums of earlier generations of women full of grotesque notions about healing. Belief in the therapeutic power of prayer and quack remedies had not aided mothers to curb the high mortality of their young. The modern mother was more discerning, much better informed about health. In this respect the city-bred woman was far in advance of her rural sisters, and by the term "sister" I do not mean peasant woman: such a comparison would be distorted. The wives of the gentry, the rural middle class, were hardly more advanced than the peasant women hired to milk cows and look after the flocks. Gentlemen farmers did not marry women for their brains but for their breeding ability and their dowries. They distrusted intellectual women as much as they distrusted breed animals without a pedigree.

The middle-class wife after about the 1870s was a remarkably enlightened person. She cast off the fatalism of earlier generations who accepted infant mortality as the will of God. Rather she read the simplified articles of enlightened pediatricians—a new branch of medicine—who informed her that high mortality had nothing to do with God; it was the result of ignorance and neglect, and therefore could be reversed, as indeed it was. As a mother she sought the advice of professional health care workers; as a wife she came to accept the notion that sexual relations were not exclusively to procreate but were part of the pleasures of married life. She learned that coitus need not ineluctably lead to pregnancy. Many women came to hate the sexual act because it was the cause of great pain at birth and put their life in jeopardy. So the informed modern woman deliberately began to take measures to limit her pregnancies, and to free herself from the dangers of delivery and the burdens of rearing child after child.

Her husband's income was limited and when western Europe finally emerged from the long depression in the mid-1890s the rate of inflation rose steadily, putting many bourgeois families in difficulties. They required space, and it grew expensive; they required servants but fewer young rural women opted for domestic service, finding other occupations more attractive and lucrative. Under-the-attic rooms, once reserved for live-in servants, were converted by landlords into attractive apartments for young working class couples. The bourgeois wife, therefore, had to rely on more elderly women who worked by the day and left early to look after their own families. So the wife had to learn how to cook and do some housework herself. She readily became a consumer of recent inventions, such as the sewing machine which she used to clothe her children, and the vacuum sweeper which relieved her from the arduous task of cleaning carpets. These and the neighborhood laundry enabled her to manage with one maid-of-all-work, or even without a maid. In this way she acquired a certain freedom from having to supervise servants and also from children who now went off to the recently established state supported schools. This free time she used to educate herself.

To traditionalist men an educated woman was a dangerous creature. Women, to the Christian fathers of the early church, were sex driven and full of wiles to lure the unwary man. Their sexual hunger had to be controlled and that demanded the most repressive measures. Men held to this view for two thousand years, but it was consciously rejected by the women of the later decades of the nineteenth century. What prudish, woman-hating men had preached and that timid wives has accepted as gospel, was false. One of women's rights, although not written into constitutions, was precisely the right to orgasm—and to birth control. It has certainly been one of the fashionable myths among historians to believe that all Victorian women were Victorian. Fashion had it that decent people did not refer to legs as legs but as limbs: Even pianos had limbs. Virginity until the wedding night was inculcated into every young woman's mind, and self-discipline formed part of every young man's training to become a gentleman. Such notions mothers accepted but not too seriously. Admonishing their daughters to resist fondling by males, they nonetheless dressed them in evening gowns with low-cut necklines and corsets that pushed up their young breasts like plums ready for plucking.

Fashion had its codes. Men's attire had evolved from the colorful clothes of the last century into the black suit that made them all look like undertakers. Moral probity had won out. Women's attire evolved with each generation from the fairly simple gowns of the Restoration to the dresses of the 1850s with hoop skirts that spread outward over several feet, making it risky to sit down or impossible to pass through doorways that had not been widened. At the upper levels of society clothes were designed by men to confirm the useless role of women in society. These tentlike gowns symbolized also the glitter of prosperity from the 1848 revolution to the fall of the Second Empire. A more sober attire came with the long depression that lasted into the mid-1890s in the West.

It was during this time when many middle-level housewives were faced with limited budgets that made it difficult to maintain traditional standards. Faced with this dilemma wives began practicing the advice of books and articles on family planning. Children were much loved at this social level but given high rents, and increasing tuition in the private schools to which boys were sent, and, with higher levels of education demanded for entry into the lucrative professions, it was necessary to support youngsters longer before they would begin earning. So a large number of couples began to limit births. Most likely some wives began using sponges, douches, and diaphragms on their own if their husbands objected. Of course all churches condemned these tendencies, but not to much avail.

Population grew, especially that of the middle class, but growth resulted more from declining infant mortality than the birthrate: Families produced fewer children but kept them alive. This result made for a more cheerful home life. As middle class families, including wives, became more concerned with happiness in this world, there was less incentive to attend church services as regularly as ancestors had done. Women's literature became less and less religious as new subjects such as health and housekeeping demanded attention. A modern orientation opened the way to greater freedom for the housewife. Less burdened by family care, she adopted less restricting attire, took to tennis, long bicycle rides, other genteel sports like croquet and even foreign travel. This "new" woman was not yet the "flapper" of the 1920s, but she was evolving.

There were no signs of a similar trend in eastern Europe. The Russian middle class after midcentury was still in its early stages, lacked any real power save that which it could exercise in the Zemstvo. It was progressive in a backward society. Middle-class women could hardly emancipate themselves from prevailing mores; they attained the status that their Western counterparts had experienced before midcentury. Firmly under the control of their fathers before marriage and their husbands after they were confined to the narrow walls of their domiciles where they produced numerous progeny most of whom died early. A minute number of young women became politically active in the Populist movement, but they were atypical.

Throughout the Continent farm women still outnumbered those living in cities, although the earlier imbalance was steadily leveling as young women migrated toward the easier, attractive jobs in industry, services, and teaching. Girls of farm families were gradually acquiring enough rudimentary education and knowledge about life outside the village to be attracted to city lights. By the 1880s they departed, but unlike their predecessors, they were less likely to go into domestic service. Many went into textile mills where hours were now shorter and conditions improved as a result of enforced laws. Many of those who were married found work in the clothing trade where they used sewing machines, or they picked up cut cloth to stitch together at home, a situation convenient for women with children too small to pack off to school. This was a practice widespread among lower-middle-class wives whose husbands were clerks or salesmen, jobs that paid less than needed to live a middle-class lifestyle. Often this woman bought on time a sewing machine to increase her productivity. Unmarried girls also resorted to machines but their wages were so minuscule that without a husband's income to pay rent and food, they rarely could earn enough to support themselves. Before long they lost the machine and had to go into a clothing shop and accept the harsh conditions of sweated labor. Farm girls fallen into this plight must often have wished that they were back tending flocks and feeding chickens. They tried to maintain contact with their families, even to send a few coins home, but such generosity was often abandoned, and eventually contact ended as the girl grew into womanhood as a city dweller, cut off from the land.

When conditions became intolerable, especially during the crisis years, she turned to prostitution. In the eyes of bourgeois moralists she fell from grace; for her she simply turned to another option when in need. Unless she was gifted with physical charm that made it likely that she would enter the warm comfort of a brothel, she walked the streets as a common harlot. There she encountered conditions that were hardly more attractive than the sweatshop: cold and rain, male brutishness and a stingy hand, a pimp who exploited her, and the police who ran her into jail if she was not registered. Worst of all was the chance of venereal disease that was rampant in large cities, and, finally, tuberculosis, a malady that was especially deadly for females in textiles, clothing, and harlotry.

Only women employed in established industrial firms could benefit from new protective legislation. As politicians came to fear that declining birth rates would leave the military undermanned, they began to enact laws that were written to protect working women as mothers. In Britain the Factory and Workshop Acts of 1874 and 1878 limited women to a fifty-four-hour week. A series of laws between 1890 and 1910 aimed at particularly dangerous work such as match making where the nearly exclusively female work force was subject to phosphorous poisoning. An effort was made to set minimum wages in trades with sweatshop conditions and to provide some health insurance for women not normally covered. Night work was prohibited, a double edged statute that cut women from printing jobs on morning newspapers. In 1891 Germany also prohibited night, Sunday, and underground work, mandated paid maternity leaves of four weeks after birth, and limited the workday to eleven hours. France followed the same path without, however, including paid maternity leave.

Russian peasant women, whose numbers would probably come close to the combined female farm population of western Europe, remained continuously subject to harsh conditions. Those who became pregnant could hardly look forward to a happy event. Not only did infants die in massive numbers, so did mothers. They were the victims of unbalanced diets, overcrowded housing, which was also common to the West, their clothing was inadequate for the bitter winters of the northern parts, and, because even elementary hygiene was deficient, disease flourished. Worse, medical care was lacking, and poor in quality where it did exist. In consequence, numerous, maybe most, young women gave birth alone, in the village sauna, or the animal shed. When her family called in someone to aid, it was the *povitukha*, an old women steeped more in superstition than medical training, indeed, little better than a witch doctor. They were adequately prepared by experience for normal births, but useless and sometimes harmful if there were complications. Yet expectant mothers felt more at home with them, because birth was an act surrounded by ancient custom and prejudice. When trained midwives became available later in the century peasants did not summon them; they believed that a stranger would give the "evil eye" and harm the baby! Only the backward societies of southern Europe revealed a similar level of medical ignorance. Peasants everywhere put cost above life, and since a midwife, like a medical doctor, was too expensive they did without. The Russian Ministry of Health was sufficiently enlightened to recognize the problem, but expected local authorities to pay a salary to midwives educated in state supported training centers. This was a Catch-22 situation: The tsarist regime was distrustful of the Zemstvos and limited their budgets, yet called on them to provide local health care as well as education. Under this situation not much, if anything, could be done.

The peasant communities were no more helpful, insisting that health care was a private, family matter. Health care in imperial Russia, inadequate during normal time, completely broke down when famine struck in 1891–92. Unable to cope the ministry called upon the Zemstvos and other nonbureaucratic bodies to take up relief work. The problem of feeding a helpless population was compounded by a cholera epidemic that spared no one, least of all the women, in an already weakened condition. Further crop failure occurred in 1897, 1898, and 1901. The old regime proved to be utterly incompetent.

Children: Poverty and Progress

Only an extremely prolific female population can explain the considerable increase of Russians during the century because this vast country had the highest rate of child mortality in Europe. In 1884 about one-third of all newborns died before their first year. Beyond that life remained precarious. The conditions of birth described above lead one to believe that a not very subtle form of infanticide was practiced lest families become overburdened. Throughout Europe most doctors believed that swaddling was detrimental to an infant's health, and by midcentury swaddling had disappeared everywhere save the east where the very young were kept wrapped for six to twelve months. Peasant mothers breast-fed their infants while noble ladies resorted to wet nurses, so a low born child had one advantage, but too many disadvantages. They were given cow's milk when the mother worked in the fields and were even expected to digest a rough gruel when only a few days old, and solid food after six months! Relatively few survived this diet. Babies were subjected to extremes of temperature to "harden" them. Mothers, like busy ones everywhere, neglected their young, a habit as common in the upper as in the lower classes. Fathers had almost no contact with children; the parish priest persistently warned them against showing tenderness toward their young. On the contrary, he quoted from his superiors, "Do not spare your child any beating, for the stick will not kill him, but will do him good." Scholars have estimated that one out of eighty infants was murdered. After all, two tsars, Ivan the Dread and Peter the Great, had murdered their sons in fits of anger. Intellectuals who wrote their memoirs recall their youth as a time of physical and mental suffering, of the alienation that separated fathers and sons as described by the novelist Ivan Turgenev.

In western and central Europe infant mortality rates, although not as high as in the East, persisted almost unchanged before 1900. A striking decline, however, occurred in the five- to fourteen-year-old category. Governments acted to preserve their future manpower. New legislation in the 1870s and after sought to protect small creatures from brutal treatment by regulating wet nurses who often neglected their charges, and required the registration and inspection of lying-in houses, nurses and child-watchers. In Britain the Factory Act of 1895 forbade mothers to resume work before several weeks after birth and doctors urged them to breast-feed their newborn. In 1902 the French state compelled parents to have their children vaccinated.

Such impulses by politicians were undoubtedly inspired by the persistent influence of Jean-Jacques Rousseau. In the previous century his writings convinced many of his readers that childhood was worth the attention of knowledgeable adults, that the process of growing up was interesting and instructive about human nature. In a time when well-to-do mothers customarily sent their babies to peasant women for care and feeding, Rousseau urged them to offer their own breasts for nourishment.

Families were more likely to provide necessary care to a male rather than a female child. Fathers in Mediterranean areas were fanatical about this distinction: In Naples parents placed a small black flag in the front window if a girl was born, a custom that lasted until the 1860s. Where infanticide was practiced, girls were more frequently the victims.

Western parents, whether urban or rural, were not quite as brutal as Russians, but neither were they kindly disposed toward their offspring. The rich turned them over to the harsh regimen of governesses. The lesser classes were not cruel by nature but, taking the admonitions of the clergy seriously, feared spoiling the young by kindness. Only after midcentury when the surge of religious fervor had died down did medical doctors, psychologists and child specialists begin to publish advice that urged middle class parents to fondle their infants. Apparently their books sold well. Gustave Droz's *Monsieur, Madame, Bébé* reached its 131st edition in 1886.

British mothers were about the only group who did not resort widely to wet nursing. German and French women did so on a large scale, especially wives who busily worked in their husbands' shops. Some of them continued to swaddle their babies until late in the century, if only to keep them out of the way, but this practice was dying out. Working mothers were also disinclined to bathe their infants. Which is part of the answer as to why the rate of infant mortality fell so slowly.

Until the 1880s and compulsory education laws, adulthood came early to offspring of the working class and peasants. From the age of five or six farm children were expected to herd flocks of sheep, goats, and cows. Working mothers took their youngsters to cotton mills where they labored at light but sometimes dangerous jobs. From the 1830s and 1840s laws excluded children under nine from factory labor, but inspection and enforcement left much to be desired. Child labor in small workshops and farms went unregulated, with the result that apprentice lads were often brutally exploited by master craftsmen and by their own parents. The condition of life for everyone could become oppressive, so adults saw no reason to be soft on the young. Teenage girls were mercilessly exploited by their mistresses in garment sweatshops, an economic sector that remained unregulated until after 1900.

The gloom of childhood began to disappear about midcentury, chiefly as a result of changing outlooks of middle class parents. Rousseau's voice was kept audible by educational reformers who displayed a more optimistic concept of childhood. They no longer believed that children were naturally sinful or lustful. They recognized that youthful energies must not be suppressed but channeled in a desirable direction as a preparation for eventual adulthood. But they also believed that adolescence was a stage in the life cycle that had its own characteristics. Sports were useful for character training and were introduced into school curriculums. In the early 1900s General Robert Baden-Powell founded the Boy Scouts and the Girl Guides. These organizations attracted teenagers from the bourgeois who were inculcated with Christian ideas including love of God and country. The French never went in much for these groupings. But the Germans did wholeheartedly. Karl Fischer founded the *Wandervogel*, a young group comparable with the Scouts, but with less adult direction and greater freedom for boys. By 1911 it was becoming more conservative, and resembled the *Jungdeutschland Bund*, a nationalistic and clerical rival. German middle-class youth was also more patriotic. It was ironic that these youth movements, recruited at the moment of their founding, adolescents who just reached the age of military service in 1914. It is tragic that Scouts and *Wandervogelen* lined up in opposite trenches where they slaughtered one another for the "holy cause."

It is now possible to appreciate the close relation between cultural norms and the social conditions of women and children. For them, circumstances would not improve until economic progress raised living standards for society as a whole, and until governments, responsive to outside pressures, took legislative action on their behalf, both to educate them and protect them against the exploitation that was part of their past, and also until the high level of medical science, a cultural factor made available because of increased wealth, could save them from the unseen enemy, the microbe.

16

End-of-Century Politics: Persistent Autocracy

The German Empire

The years 1870–71 marked a turning point in the political condition of Europe. What brought about the turn was the consolidation of new states in the central region. Italian nationalists achieved unity, and imagined that their creation was now a great power. The truth, however, was that the centralized state was still too weak and peripheral to become the hub in the Continental wheel of fortune. That position was taken over by the Second German Empire. With the signing of the Peace of Paris in the Hall of Mirrors in the palace of Versailles during 1871, and the subsequent proclamation of the German *Reich*, the balance of power shifted from the west to the center. Germany became the arbiter of European state relations, just as Austria had been prior to 1848. The new situation, however, was not merely a repetition of the old. The Treaty of Vienna was as dead as Metternich, and the new Germany proved to be a far stronger hub than the old Austrian polity. Germany's move to the role of arbiter resulted from solid economic prowess, vigorous leadership, and a highly motivated society.

      Between 1870 and 1890 Bismarck continued to direct the internal and external affairs of his country with a firm hand, a hand that had become a fist to fight for unity. But once unity was achieved it opened as though to greet a future as yet uncertain. "Blood and iron" had achieved their goal; other tactics were now essential to mold the new state. Bismarck needed peace to consolidate the new regime, and the first step of unification already presaged the future. The chancellor refused to allow the North German Reichstag to take any part in the state-making process. The empire was to be the product of the ruling class. Not liberal-minded politicians but the king of Bavaria invited William to take the imperial crown. So did the head of the National Liberal Party in Prussia, a gesture that induced William to remark ironically, "Why, then, I am indeed indebted to Mr. Lasker for an Imperial Crown!" As Bismarck intended, the empire was given birth by the princes, not the parliament.

In a similar manner the new constitution was drawn up by nobiliary circles, not by a popularly elected constituent assembly. Either to please or to befuddle everyone it was a mass of contradictions. It set up a constitutional monarchy, but did not abolish divine right in Prussia. It created a federal form of government, but did not equalize power among the constituent states. Prussia retained the dominant authority that it had acquired in the Seven Weeks War against Austria. Finally it proclaimed universal suffrage for all men twenty-five years or older, but negated their votes by depriving the federal Reichstag of all power save that of obstruction. The real evidence of Prussia's towering position lay in the upper house, the Bundestag. The lower house represented the voters, the upper the constituent states, twenty-five in number. There Prussian delegates, chosen by William, occupied seventeen seats out of fifty-eight, a sufficient number to block any undesirable proposals.

As imperial chancellor, Bismarck enjoyed the dominance that came with success. The aristocracy, especially the Junkers with their unshaken hold east of the Elbe River, were fully behind him. The middle classes hailed him as a hero because he unified Germany, satisfied their national aspirations, and opened the way toward economic freedom and growth. The peasants accepted him, at least those who gave thought to the matter, because they assumed that unity would hasten their accession to land. On the surface it appeared that the Empire was a nice compromise between federalism and nationalism, between divine right monarchy and popular government. The federal states controlled education, law courts, direct taxation, public health, police, and land policy. However, they did not have any hold on the federal army, which was really the Prussian army, nor the foreign office. These two key institutions were in the hands of the emperor and his chancellor, and in the 1870s and 1880s that meant in the hands of Bismarck who, as chancellor, was responsible only to the emperor.

There was only one institution, apart from the imperial crown, that could weaken but not break his grip, the Reichstag. There were five political groups that occupied most of its seats. The German Conservative party defended the aristocracy. The Free Conservative party combined big landlords and big industrialists, the "alliance of rye and iron" on which Bismarck could always depend. The Center party was Catholic, with its mass confessional following in the Rhineland and the south. It was monarchist, favorable to a social platform reflecting the cooperative ideals of Bishop von Ketteler. The National Liberals and the Progressives were defenders of a typical liberal program, save that the National Liberals tended to let their nationalism weaken their commitment to individual freedom and responsible government. The Progressive party, a left-wing liberal grouping, was never strong, probably because it was antimilitarist and republican in a society with a bourgeoisie firmly devoted to the army and a strong state. The Social Democratic party was, by the later 1870s, committed to Marxism, and proclaimed itself a revolutionary movement. It won over the working class that was either indifferent to religion or not Catholic enough to vote for the Center party.

Bismarck's domestic policy was intended to make Germany a replica of Prussia. That called for strengthening the crown, limiting the power of the Reichstag, expanding that of the army, winning over the industrial middle class, preserving Protestantism as a means of social control, and wooing the rising urban proletariat. He did not achieve all of these goals. He was, however, successful enough to seriously weaken the "spirit of '48," that is, the spirit of individual freedom and its expression in the form of institutions responsible to the people. His task was facilitated by the ambiguity of the 1848 inheritance. The revolution, after all, had failed. Worse, the behavior of the Frankfurt Assembly had combined the ideals of liberal freedom with a nationalism that was hostile to claims of ethnic minorities such as the Czechs and Poles living inside the German Confederation. By the 1870s there was not an unequivocable tradition of individual rights and limited government. The party that most openly stood for these principles, the Progressive, was the weakest in the political spectrum.

Apart from tradition, the constitution was an instrument that the chancellor could use to his advantage. The fundamental law of the empire was basically a replica of the Prussian constitution of 1850. It did not include the three class voting system, which prevailed in Prussia, but it still allowed fiscal independence for the crown. As in the 1860s military budgets became a matter of constitutional interpretation. However, no crisis resulted because the National Liberals did not raise the issue of fiscal responsibility. At best, they sought to limit the time during which a law would be in effect. Sums voted for the army, or for any other purpose, would have a limit on their duration. This strategy was employed successfully by the English Parliament to bridle the monarchy. But in Germany, the law stated that fiscal legislation would remain in effect until new laws were approved. So if the Bundestag vetoed a bill to limit previously approved resources for the army, the existing laws remained in force; taxes could be collected legally until a new law forbade them. Moreover there was no legal way to control the Ministry; it was the creature of the crown, that is, of Bismarck. No wonder that the Reichstag was referred to as the "fig-leaf of absolutism." On several occasions the Ministry failed to receive a majority vote. In Britain and France, a Ministry would have resigned under these conditions. Not so in Germany. An adverse vote did not bring down ministers, it simply made clear that ministers were responsible to the emperor, not to parliament. Germany was indeed an enlarged Prussia.

Under these conditions, Bismarck could act at will, and he did. When opposition to army bills came up, he orchestrated a demagogic press campaign. The official newspapers that provided a minimum of news screamed against any effort to establish civilian control of the military. This was a subsidized press—nearly all papers were financed by some special interest group—and capable of arousing popular sentiment. It is too simple to isolate this phenomenon as distinctly German; it was as common in Britain and France. The British were simply indifferent to their army, but the French, a republican people, were as committed to the sanctity of the army as the Germans, a fact the Dreyfus trial revealed. Mass democracy proved to be a two-faced effort to balance individual freedom with *raison d'état*.

Bismarck stood for state power. He could not repeat the statement of Louis XIV in the late 1600s, "I am the state." But he made this claim for the emperor. To advance his goal of strong government, he felt the need to find an enemy that he could use to arouse the voters in his favor. This was not difficult. There were authentic enemies and those scared up by him.

He first attacked the Catholics, an odd target in as much as they were not opposed to the Empire. I suppose that every powerful politician has a moment of weakness, the unguarded moment. This was Bismarck's. The Catholic Center party was by no means hostile to his policies. He was a kind of "reborn" Protestant, but his motives were political, not religious. As a result, his policy was influenced by several factors. He was still reliant in the 1870s on liberal support. Liberals and the advanced middle class were secularist. Their secularism was abetted by Pope Pius IX when in 1864 he had issued the encyclical *Mirori Vos*, an attack on individualism and industrial society. Finally in 1870 he promulgated the doctrine of papal infallibility. It was concerned with matters of faith and morals, but it was not easy to distinguish between faith and constitutional government. To the Protestant people of the north, this was a call to arms, and the chancellor did not squander the occasion. To him, the hierarchy of the church was subversive, actively encouraging a Catholic league against Prussian authority. He therefore pushed through the Prussian Parliament, still elected under the three class voting system, a series of laws that deprived bishops of their disciplinary powers, extended state control over clerical education, made civil marriage mandatory, and dissolved religious orders, such as the Jesuits. This occurred in 1873, and his anticlerical program became known as the *Kulturkampf*, the struggle for civilization.

It rapidly turned into a fiasco. German Catholics rallied to the church and Bismarck soon realized that he had miscalculated their determination. His strategy to preserve royal control was to have an enemy he could use as a bogeyman to frighten voters, not one that could seriously detract from imperial power.

France served this purpose, and the efforts there to restore a Catholic monarchy fitted in with his illusion that the French were part of the pope's subversion. His policy, however, had not considered the emergence of a second enemy; in fact, even two. After the Center party increased its representation in the 1877 election, the National Liberals began to demand greater participation in formulating governmental policy. This the chancellor refused; his unspoken agreement with them was simple: He protected their economic interests provided they accepted conservative domination in the Ministry, and voted for the military budget. He never fully trusted liberals of any color.

He had no trust whatever in the Social Democrats; they were *the* enemy. It was the increasing strength of their party, and his estrangement from the National Liberals that led him finally to rescind the laws against the Catholic hierarchy, with the exception of civil marriage, state inspection of seminaries, and expulsion of Jesuits. The Center party accepted his half extended hand because it too, was fearful of atheistic socialism. In addition, the death of Pius IX and the accession of Leo XIII, more accommodating in many ways, eased the tension that had caused the conflict between church and state.

Relying now on the conservatives and Center, he pushed through the Reichstag in 1878 a series of measures outlawing socialist organizations and censoring their press. Leaders of the extreme left now went underground or into exile, and although their political network survived as an organization, it could hardly function as a party. Its members were not allowed to hold meetings, or rally voters except during electoral campaigns. Party congresses had to take place outside the Empire. And yet, workers as well as some petty bourgeois learned the names of candidates and voted for them in growing numbers. Continued economic expansion, favored by Bismarck, also increased the working class that voted socialist.

Bismarck hoped to overcome this proclivity by wooing labor to the Empire. To this end he promulgated legislation beginning in 1883 that created a pioneering social insurance system. It included insurance against sickness, financed by contributions from workers and employers with the former paying double the amount turned over by the latter. Next came accident insurance. Finally the capstone was put in place in 1889 with old age and disability pensions financed by payments from workers, employers, and the state. The politically conservative state now passed to the forefront of social reform, well ahead of liberal regimes west of her. Indeed Britain imitated the German model two decades later; the French hesitated until 1932.

Workers benefited but were not won over. They continued to vote for socialists whose strength in the Reichstag increased with every election save those of 1887 and 1881. From twelve seats in 1881 they advanced to thirty-five in 1890, when the new emperor dismissed Bismarck.

His removal opened a new chapter in German history. William II was determined to participate more actively in policy making, almost to be his own chancellor, an office he filled with men lacking the skill and iron mindedness of Bismarck. It was unfortunate that the old chancellor had built up a state and army that could become a menace to peace. For all of his demagoguery he no longer looked on war as desirable. He had recognized that the new Empire needed a long period of stability for its parts to become solidly forged into a national and nationalist state. He had of course expanded the army, but that was a defensive measure, as were the alliances he had arranged with Austria and Italy. He had even resisted until the late 1880s the urge to acquire colonies.

William lacked the skill to deal effectively with Bismarck's legacy. The grandiose *Reich* had perhaps become a world power too quickly, and had never successfully thrown off the weight of Prussia. The German army remained under the Prussian officer corps, just as the imperial civil service remained subservient to Prussian bureaucrats. Throughout the realm Germans had a world outlook consisting essentially of three values: militarism, nationalism mixed with racism, and authoritarianism. Even the workers who voted for socialists were more than lightly imbued with this outlook, a factor that helps to explain why the Second Workingman's International failed to overcome nationalist rivalries on the eve of World War I. This outlook also makes clear why authentic liberalism could not penetrate deeply the German populace. Bismarck successfully duped the liberals into supporting the army by voting his budgets, and split their party asunder when it took sides on his antisocialist laws.

William inherited a powerful army and bureaucracy, a burgeoning economy, an industrious people creative in the arts and fairly docile in politics, and an absolutist state with a veneer of parliamentary rule. This was Wilhelmine Germany. As ruler, he sought, like Bismarck, to win over the workers by rescinding the antisocialist laws. The workers responded by voting in ever greater numbers for Social Democrats whose representatives went from forty-four in 1893 to 110 in 1912.

Such ingratitude deepened his dislike of parliamentary institutions which he viewed as inimical to the military. The word military indicates a new element in Germany, the navy. The Kaiser despised the English and was determined to build a fleet capable of challenging their mastery of the seas. Supporting him was a Navy League with considerable influence in the Reichstag, and other pressure groups defending the army, colonialism, tariff protection, big business and *Junker* agriculture. He was infuriated by parliamentary control of budgets, even though he had little opposition there. He boasted that he had never read the constitution, and affirmed, "The soldiers, the army, and not the decisions of parliaments, forged the German Reich." He had even thought of carrying out a coup d'état against the Parliament, in imitation of Louis Napoleon in 1851, but remembrance of the fate of that ruler was perhaps the reason he never tried it. Lack of decision was not his weakness; rather it was the unpredictable decisions that he made without consulting his chancellors that caused trouble and created enemies. He broke a longtime understanding with

Russia; he alienated an otherwise friendly Britain by his naval policies and the dubious claim that he had formulated the military strategy used in the Boer War. If his claim is true he should have hidden it; British strategy in that war was far from brilliant. Finally he aroused the French by his clumsy intervention in Morocco. Far more dangerous in the end was the expanding role of army and navy officers in foreign affairs. From the lowly military attachés who sent home erroneous or false information to Field Marshal Helmuth von Moltke, the younger, who on his own initiative in 1909 assured the Austrian government that Germany would fight if Russia declared war on Austria, even if Austria provoked an attack. This reversed Bismarck's intention of a defensive, not an offensive, alliance; Austrian provocations toward Balkan powers blurred the distinction between the two. He repeated this assertion in the summer of 1914, again without consulting the foreign minister. In 1871 the elder Molkte had insisted that in war time the army must rule. By 1912 a large number of voters was becoming disenchanted with the dominant role played by the military—and even with the regime itself. In 1912 the Social Democrats, Catholic Center, and Progressives won 7,744,285 votes out of 12,207,529 total. This was practically a vote of no confidence, which the government chose to ignore. Subsequently, it had only six years left before its overthrow.

Austria-Hungary

The old Hapsburg state had a similar fate in store for it. Francis Joseph, emperor since 1848, had grown older without growing wiser. Unable to offer effective leadership himself, he was incapable of choosing the men who could. Since the 1867 agreement that put Austria and Hungary on an equal footing, creating the Dual Monarchy, only one constitutional change occurred, the establishment of a lower house of Parliament in 1873. The upper house represented the seventeen provinces; the lower was supposed to represent the people, like the Reichstag in Germany, but the indirect process of elections gave preference to the owners of property and to men with higher education degrees.

Although representation was narrow, the men in control of the dominant Liberal party were enlightened Germans and Czechs. They had a progressive outlook and set out to drag Austria toward a higher stage in the modernizing process. They reformed the court system, gave greater freedom to publishers, abolished restrictions on Jews, improved military administration and discipline, put through laws to encourage economic growth, and removed schools from clerical control while at the same time making religious education purely voluntary. Education had been made free and obligatory in 1869, but provincial diets more or less ignored this measure for the next decade. And yet, the 1870s formed a kind of gilded age; when the emperor dismissed the Liberal ministry in 1879 because it was bent upon inaugurating an authentic parliamentary regime, he brought that age to an end.

Neither he nor his new chief minister, Edward Taaffe, were able to solve the major problem confronting them: the nationalities and their wish to become either fully autonomous, as Hungary was, or completely free of Hapsburg rule. Taaffe made concessions to the Czechs, such as giving official standing to their language. However this did not satisfy the Bohemians who truly hated their German overlords; and it aroused other Slavs to demand equal treatment. It equally enraged the German-speaking population of Bohemia whose anger forced Taaffe to resign.

Government was not made easier after the fall of Liberals. As their attraction for voters waned, two new parties entered the lower house. The Christian Socialists were led by Karl Lueger, longtime mayor of Vienna. It was an odd assortment of intelligence and fanaticism. It called for legalizing trade unions and a social security program like Germany's. Apart from this it responded to its electorate of disgruntled artisans and small businessmen suffering from the competition of large-scale industry and commerce. Because they blamed their troubles on Jewish financiers, the party became anti-Semitic. When the suffrage was broadened in 1907, Christian Socialists showed their true colors, merged with the conservatives, and found their strength in rural constituencies.

That left Vienna open to the Social Democratic party. Founded by Victor Adler, it was Marxist but revisionist, which meant that it ceased to be revolutionary—if it ever had been—and sought to win power by means of the vote. Like all Marxist parties it proclaimed that all workers were brothers, but it had no solution to the nationalities problem. But then neither did the Christian Socialists. Maybe there was no solution that could save the territorial integrity of the empire.

Hungary was a major obstacle in this respect. Under the governance of a House of Magnates and a House of Deputies elected by well-to-do Magyars, the Hungarian speaking population firmly opposed any extension of political rights to Slavs. Composing less than half the population of the state, Magyars were determined to impose their language on everyone by requiring its use in courts, schools, the civil service, even on railroads signs. Francis Joseph, as king of Hungary, raised no objections until the Hungarian deputies called for the use of Magyar in Hungarian units serving in the imperial army. He then threatened to grant the suffrage to Slavs, which effectively silenced the Hungarians. But he offered no viable solution to a situation threatening the very existence of his regime. For the ethnic problem was not merely an internal one; it included the extreme nationalism growing explosively in neighboring Slavic states, in particular Serbia where a new dynasty incited an extreme hatred of both Germans and Hungarians as oppressors of Slavs.

Nationalism in the Balkans

The Balkan peninsula in southeastern Europe has often been referred to as a powder keg with a long fuse. For the historian it is more like a stretch of quicksand in which the scholar can sink, never to rise. I shall not narrate events there in detail and, I hope, avoid the danger. We noted earlier (see chapter 10) that the Treaty of Berlin of 1878 had guaranteed the independence of most new states. Local councils of landowners had customarily invited German princes to ascend their thrones, and sometimes this arrangement brought order for awhile and the first steps toward modernization. But these thrones were shaky at best, and there were several palace revolutions that changed monarchs, but rarely improved living conditions. The peninsula was still economically backward, overrun by bandits, and overtaxed by rulers to build armies.

The 1880s constituted a decade of turbulence resulting from the continued control of Macedonia by Turks. This territory in the center of the peninsula was bordered by Greece, Bulgaria, Montenegro, and Serbia. Its population consisted of natives of the bordering states, each of which laid a claim to some part of it. In 1885 Alexander of Battenburg, king of Bulgaria, engineered a coup that recovered East Rumelia, a territory taken away in the 1878 Berlin settlement. This angered the Serbian ruler who went to war against the Bulgars, but his defeat set the stage for his downfall. Serbia was saved when Austria forced a peace treaty on Bulgaria. Alexander fared no better; the Russians provoked a coup that brought him down, to be replaced by another German, Ferdinand of Saxe-Coburg-Gotha. He was no more than a figurehead; the whip hand was that of Stephen Stambulov, son of an innkeeper, who ruled with more than a whip. To achieve his goal of economic reform in a poor land, he thought it necessary to do away with opponents. He accomplished much before he was overthrown in 1894 and assassinated the next year.

Ominous changes occurred after 1900. The throne of Serbia, long the seat of the Obrenovitch dynasty friendly to Austria, was seized by the Karageorgevitch dynasty, after the murder of the incumbent. Peter I was violently hostile to the Hapsburgs because they had taken over Bosnia and Herzegovina in 1878. Because numerous Serb-speaking people lived there, Peter burned to annex these protectorates to his kingdom. Under his encouragement Serbia became a center of fanatical nationalism, and he very likely fostered secret societies, like the Black Hand, whose members were sworn to assassinate Hapsburgs.

More threatening to Balkan nationalism was the seizure of power in 1908 by young Turks whose aim was to modernize the weakened Ottoman Empire. The so-called sick man could perhaps recover. As it turned out, the new regime in Constantinople was as brutal as those of the past. Conditions in the Balkans worsened until, finally, in 1913, a Balkan League spontaneously appeared, and declared war on Turkey. Serbia seized much of Macedonia, but to check her ambition, Austria championed Albania, now free of Turkish overlordship, in order to block Serbia's drive to the Adriatic Sea. Albania's new status as a free state won recognition in peace settlements. Tranquility, however, was short-lived. Bulgaria sent an army against Serbia and Greece, starting the Second Balkan War. When Romania invaded Bulgaria the war was brought to a close.

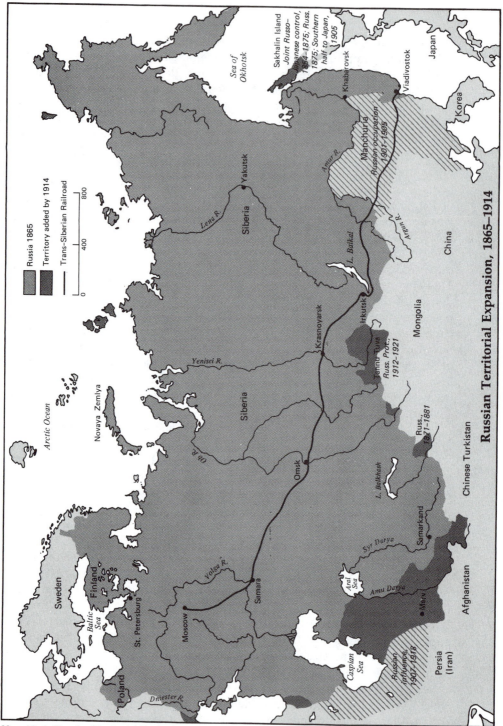

Map 16–1 Russian Territorial Expansion, 1865–1914

Greece received what she had occupied, southern Macedonia, and Serbia the northern section. Rumania kept south Dobruja. The Bulgars were left with their resentment and sense of injury. No one believed that peace would last, and it did not. The Balkan wars were merely the prelude to the main play.

Russia: The End of Reform

The impulse toward reform lost headway before the murder of Alexander II. His minister of education, Count Dimitry Tolstoy, rapidly crushed academic freedom in Russian universities out of fear that the faculties and students were spreading ideas subversive of autocracy and orthodoxy. Only the natural sciences were left intact, but teachers watched. In secondary schools, the hours devoted to science as a discipline were reduced to a minimum and partially replaced by expanded courses allowing more controlled indoctrination of students: literature, history, geography, and languages—all with a strong dosage of religion.

The emphasis on orthodox religion was inspired by a zealot named Constantine Pobedonostsev, procurator of the Holy Synod, essentially a lay minister of religion and subordinate to the tsar who was supreme head of the church as well as of the state, a set up known as caesaropapism. The new tsar, Alexander III, was a thorough-going reactionary. Upon his accession in 1881, he issued a Law of Exceptional Measures. It invested provincial governors and police officials with extra powers to crush enemies of autocracy and orthodoxy. In Russia enemies included revolutionaries, of course, but also outspoken critics of the regime. The marriage of church and state went far beyond that of western Europe earlier in the century. After all, Queen Victoria was official head of the Anglican church, but England's Parliament had passed laws that denied her the privilege of using the church to crush other religions. There was a marriage of altar and throne in France under Charles X, but the pope, not the king, was head of the church. Russia's political situation had no equal elsewhere save in the Moslem Ottoman state; it had been ideally arranged, purposely by Peter the Great in 1725 to enhance the tsar's power. Under Pobedonostsev's control, the worst kind of obscurantism penetrated and overwhelmed the regime; this became manifest when Nicholas II ascended the throne in 1894. But his predecessor opened the way to the kind of hysterical autocracy that became typical of the last Romanovs.

It is ironic that while the political regime restricted many of the benefits of modern culture, a kind of industrial revolutionette was making headway fueled by extensive loans from the west, France in particular. There seems to have been a schizophrenic condition between the government and the economy, with the former acting as though the latter was not occurring. As the economy became more heavily dependent on science and technology, the police were closing out suspect faculty and students from universities, as well as severely censoring books and the periodical press. When students went on strike in the 1880s and 1890s, mounted Cossacks were sent against them, roughly swinging long whips to lash them. Thousands of students were recruited into the army as punishment, or simply expelled. To obviate such protests a ministerial circular instructed secondary school principals to exclude students from the lower classes. Teachers were even required to sign certificates of political loyalty if they wished to keep their jobs.

There was not an unbridgeable chasm between the government and the social results of economic development. Even conservative ministers recognized the need for some protection of factory workers, and laws were passed to protect the health of women and adolescents by ending night work and limiting excessively long hours. A factory inspectorate was created to enforce these laws. It was, however, not large enough to become truly effective, a condition that prevailed in other Continental countries.

The reaction in Russia under Nicholas was curious in its unique character. Under Vyacheslav Plehve, minister of interior (1902–1904), it assumed sinister dimensions with the condoning, by inaction, of anti-Semitism on a scale not experienced in recent times. Pogroms broke out, the worst occurring in Bessarabia on Easter Day 1903. Enraged, drunken mobs looted and killed during two days, led by paid agitators. Waves of pogroms followed elsewhere. Rioting peasants were no more spared than Jews. In the villages masters were again allowed to flog disobedient peasants.

Autocracy, however, employed more sophisticated methods than brute repression to control the urban lower classes. Plehve accepted, reluctantly, proposals by Sergei Zubatov, who had been head of the Okhrana in Moscow since 1896. Zubatov had played an active role suppressing the terrorists of the 1880s. He continued this work in the Okhrana, which was a counterrevolutionary arm of the Department of Police. He trained his agents to recruit young revolutionaries because he believed that they and most workers could be won over to the regime by a form of benevolent paternalism. He intended to use the Okhrana to prevent the diffusion of socialist ideas among the proletariat. During 1902–1904 this approach was fairly successful. Workers were drawn into its cooperatives and mutual aid societies by Zubatov's agents who were both young laborers and policemen posing as workers. They encouraged bargaining with management and even took part in strikes.

This was an odd situation and unique to Russia. All states used police spies and *agents provocateurs*, but only in Russia did the police actually subsidize trade unions that were illegal before 1906. These activities infuriated managers as well as Witte, who was minister of finance. But Plehve was influential enough to have him removed. As strikes continued and assumed massive scale in 1903, his muted distrust led him to dismiss Zubatov. In Saint Petersburg his place was unofficially taken by Father Georgii Gapon. His Assembly of Russian Factory and Mill workers attracted a sizable number of skilled and educated workers who made the assembly a crypto trade union seeking to control the shop floor by bargaining. They were not revolutionaries and believed that the tsar would intervene to rectify the injustices of the factory system. The events of 1905 shattered that old belief.

These events resulted largely from military failures. War had broken out in February 1904 when Japan, antagonized by Russia's refusal to recognize her spheres of influence in the Far East, attacked Port Arthur without a declaration of war, and nearly destroyed the Russian fleet there. When the Baltic fleet came to the rescue, the Japanese navy sank most of it. The Japanese were equally successful on land, driving Russian divisions into Manchuria. By early 1905 the tsar was ready to make peace. He was confronted by a revolution at home and Plehve had been assassinated by a new terrorist movement.

Undoubtedly the assassination was planned, the revolt was not. No resort to barricades had occurred in Russia since the Decembrist movement in 1825. Rather, the insurrectionary strain in history was made up of rioting and the political murder of leading figures. In the 1870s there arose a movement known as populism; thousands of well-meaning young men and women became convinced that peasants were innocent and good, so all that was needed to bring about reform was to enlighten the rural folk whose vast numbers would compel the tsar to relieve their plight. When the populists went out to the villages, however, they encountered the usual hostility—or at least distrust—that peasants felt toward city dwellers. Fearing a trick, the villagers notified local authorities who promptly arrested the naïve young people.

The youths who remained politically active had learned a bitter lesson. They now turned to anarchistic terrorism, and over the next three decades a not insignificant number of high officials, including a tsar, were either shot or blown apart. This phenomenon, incidentally, was widespread, although concentrated in countries that were only beginning to modernize, like Russia. Many terrorists eventually went over to the Social Revolutionary party: Its main goal was the division of large estates among the peasants and cooperative enterprise.

There was by the 1890s a Social Democratic Party, Marxist in inspiration, but it soon split into two sections: the Mensheviks, more or less revisionist, for political action, orthodox in their belief that Russia must pass through a long period of capitalism before the workers would be ready for a socialist uprising. The Bolsheviks fell under the control of Lenin. As a professional revolutionary he impatiently hammered on the theme that in Russia the capitalist phase would be very short, and that the socialists needed a small, strong party composed of an elite of revolutionaries trained and ready to seize power at the right moment. This is reminiscent of Blanqui, but different in that Lenin was more concerned with party organization and planning, and a keener observer of the conditions that signaled the right moment. Naturally all these organizations functioned underground, and their leaders had to live in exile. Their newspapers were printed usually in Switzerland and smuggled into Russia. They were frequently caught and many of them were languishing in jails or in Siberia when troubles began in 1905.

Several events contributed to both the expectation of reform and to the following violent uprising. Delegates from the Zemstovs were meeting in the capital during November 1904. These local bodies, distrusted by tsars and their bureaucrats, were complaining that the government was overly centralized and inefficient. The three serious famines that had occurred in the past twelve years had shown the incapacity of the central administration to succor starving peasants. Yet the Ministry willfully restricted the budgets of both Zemstovs and municipal councils (*dumas*) out of fear of losing power. Undoubtedly, one of the fatal flaws of the imperial regime was its deliberate limitation of action by local men eager to advance conditions of life in their localities, Frustrated, their delegates were meeting to petition the tsar to accept constitutional reforms. Nicholas's hesitations aroused the anger of liberal bourgeois who began rallying to nascent political groupings. More decisive was a spontaneous strike of some workers in the capital. A father Gapon had been organizing them in an "official" union. On January 20, 1905 some quarter million workers joined the strike and Gapon gathered them to present a petition to the tsar. Nicholas was nowhere to be found when a huge demonstration gathered two days later. On order troops responded with fusillades: More than thirty demonstrators were killed, three hundred wounded. Like the massacre in the Boulevard des Capucines in Paris in February 1848, this event turned a demonstration into a revolt.

The insurgency was like a great circle without a center and with a circumference continuously moving outward like artillery fire. Its dynamic came from the masses, stimulated by peasant riots, worker strikes, and a mutiny of sailors on the warship Potemkin. Even the modest middle class demanded reforms. Overtaken by events and powerless, Nicholas offered in August to create a consultative assembly, a gesture that placated only moderate liberals. In defiance workers began a general strike in October, bringing the economy to a halt. At last came the real revolutionaries bent on overthrowing the regime. Thoroughly frightened the tsar issued an October Manifesto: it provided for constitutional government through the creation of a national Duma and democratic elections.

At once liberals accepted this proposal, but they split into two groups: moderates, calling themselves Octobrists, and radicals, calling themselves Cadets. Revolutionaries, now out in the open, called for a true change, but the people's furor was fading, and the army remained loyal and ready to act. As in 1848, the loyalty of the army was the key to salvation.

We need not dwell on this, the last revolution before the great slaughter of war engulfed the Empire. The laws that created the Duma resembled those of Prussia and Austria: a bicameral body, partly appointed by conservative provincial bodies, partly elected with balloting weighted in favor of nobles and wealthy bourgeois. The Ministry was responsible only to the tsar who enjoyed an absolute veto, and the power to issue decree laws. The first Duma was dissolved by Nicholas, as was the second, after which the suffrage was narrowed to exclude the opposition. The only positive achievement was carried out by P. A. Stolypin when he was interior minister. He ended the dependency of peasant farmers on the *mir* by offering them freedom to leave, buy land, consolidate scattered strips, and market their crops. Between 1906 and the outbreak of war, Russian agriculture progressed as never before, and there emerged a strengthening of a class of independent farmers, the real *kulaks*. He also gained a reputation as the enemy of rebels when he set up in 1906 a network of courts-martial to try those who were caught. The courts condemned about 500 people to death. The noose, "Stolypin's necktie," was used to hang them. He was also instrumental in encouraging the tsar to ignore the Dumas. For his pains, he was assassinated in 1911. Now power of a purely personal kind fell into the hands of Gregorii Rasputin, a mystical sectarian, drunkard, and debaucher. As a faith healer he acquired strange powers over the tsarina because he seemed to save her son, a hemophiliac, from bleeding to death. Russia was now practically in the hands of a reckless ner'do'well, and, with a tsar too weak-minded to rule effectively, under the spell of his wife, a hysteric.

Political Culture: Center and East

The difference between the German Empire, on the one hand, and the Dual Monarchy and Russia, on the other, is striking. The Germans worked out a system of government combining elements of autocracy and those of parliamentary practice, and placed enough trust in this combination to absorb it into the cluster of values that formed part of their culture. The term *limited autocracy* seems like a contradiction, and in a sense it is. Although it worked well enough for over a generation, the ill-matched forces became less well articulated once its creator, Bismarck, was no longer present to hold them in some kind of accord. But even he, toward the late 1880s, was becoming doubtful about the desirability of such a system. He began to consider seriously the proposal to remake the Constitution and enhance the powers of the crown. So was William II, but he never acted on this impulse. There was no need to. The relation between the executive and legislature was sufficiently flexible to give him all the power he needed to build a navy and the mightiest army in Europe. And the German nobility and bourgeoisie, imbued as they were with national patriotism, always approved the policies of the chancellor and the emperor. The form of government seemed perfectly compatible with the powerful capitalist economy that emerged, and the social hierarchy that provided a dominant place for them.

That dynamic economy had, of course, also brought forth an enormous working class. If we can judge by their votes, this industrial proletariat was less than committed to the imperial regime. At least a large part of it cast their ballots for socialists. However they did not always, or even most of the time, vote for revolutionary socialists. From the 1890s proletarian culture blended into that of the mainstream, and so did the electoral stance of most social democratic deputies. The party leadership persisted to define itself as revolutionary, but everyone knew that it was no longer a "revolution making" party. And that precisely because it was dominated by the powerful trade unions who preferred strikes to revolts. The party seemed like an imposing lion, but one could observe that when it roared it had no teeth. This was because socialist culture had become overlaid with nationalist pronouncements that were only slightly less deafening than the clamorous drum beating of middle-class patriots. Racism too, formed part of German political culture, but it did not necessarily take the form of violent anti-Semitism. The latter as a political force was confined to the hard-core conservatives, whose political influence declined. Racism was a state of mind that excluded the "nonpure" from gentile parlors and the clubs of rich men, as well as the workers' sporting circle. This kind of ethnic exclusivity was also widespread in the West, but other cultural factors prevented it from becoming fanatical anti-Semitism after 1918, as it did in Germany.

The Dual-Monarchy and Russia were more openly autocratic, their belatedly created parliaments, elected by a narrow suffrage, had almost no control over the crowned heads. Their political culture was the culture of aristocracies, only slightly affected by liberal ideas about citizenship and individual freedom. Economies just emerging from feudal conditions and narrowly limited to favorable geographic sites did not yet call forth a sophisticated bourgeoisie or an organized proletariat. Both countries were predominantly agrarian with only a few industrialized cities. The farming populations, now legally freed from serfdom, were not yet fully free in their mentalities. The imperial regimes were making efforts to modernize and borrowing heavily from the West to implement grandiose schemes. Their economies could not self-start themselves. Modernization had made a first step, but the ruling political forces were still functioning in accord with old regime ideals. The policies of government aid to the economic growth was in the tradition of mercantilist ideals, and mercantilism called for a firm autocratic state. Indeed, the last of the Hapsburgs and of the Romanovs believed themselves the anointed of God, their right to rule of divine origins. The last of the Hohenzollerns would not have disagreed, even when he was telling risqué jokes to his intimates. The political outlook of the ruling classes was essentially out of joint with the vast means of destruction created by modern economies. When these rulers went to war in 1914, they acted as though they were going to a jousting match when in reality they were charging toward a bottomless chasm.

17

End-of-Century Politics: Liberalism Triumphant

France: The Republican Solution

Given the accumulation of various governments in France, they have been numbered like monarchs and popes. After the defeat of the Commune, royalists were looking toward a second restoration, so convinced were they that their hour had come. They would not only provide a head of state, they would put a crown on him. Like sorcerers' apprentices they had all the elements, but when they put them all together what did they get? Voilà, a republic. As it turned out they had one element too many; instead of one pretender to the crown they had two. Worse, the Bourbons and the Orleanists did not see eye to eye. The Count of Paris, heir of Louis-Philippe, was committed to a liberal regime and the tricolor flag. Henri, the count of Chambord, heir of Charles X, was a true legitimist emotionally devoted to the white lily banner of his prerevolutionary ancestors. Worse still, he claimed precedence over his cousin as the older and more entitled. An agreement accepted his claim; he was childless and his crown would pass to the count. Henri's insistence on the white flag, however, prevented a restoration because even most aristocrats, to say nothing of the bourgeoisie, would not abandon the red, white, and blue. But to Henri, without the white banner, he would be like the king without clothes. To the men of the National

Assembly, however, the white flag was the equivalent of the red flag that Parisian workers had tried to impose on the Second Republic: a provocation to revolt.

Hoping that Henri would either change his mind or drop dead the monarchist majority in the National Assembly chose the king maker of 1830, Thiers, as temporary head of state, and went about drafting a constitution. This document, written in anticipation of a restoration, provided for a president of a republic (a word included while royalists held their noses), a bicameral legislature composed of a senate elected by indirect suffrage for seven years and a chamber of deputies elected by direct suffrage for four years. All adult males enjoyed the ballot. As usual, no one thought of giving the vote to women.

During the four year interval between the election to the National Assembly and the promulgation of the Constitution of 1875, republicans did not sit idly by. On the contrary, they rejected the claims of the monarchist majority to draft a constitution, and armed themselves with an active press, defiant oratory and much personal courage. In these turbulent times Leon Gambetta made his career as he became the most influential leader of the so-called radical republicans. Their cause was aided by the deaths and resignations of aging royalists in the assembly. These vacancies required by-elections in which republicans ran and their steady success indicated that the electorate had indeed voted on war or peace in 1871, and was now turning away from monarchism as a permanent form of government. Theirs was not an easy task: the police censored and often closed down their newspapers, which they reestablished under different titles, prohibited or broke up their political meetings, sometimes brutally, and intimidated opposition candidates. Even Thiers was won over when he told royalists complaining about republican victories, "the republic divides us least." If he had hopes of being elected president, they were squashed when he was forced out of office by a disgruntled majority that chose the aging General Maurice MacMahon to keep the executive seat warm for the rump of one of the pretenders.

Conservatives, bent on holding power in the legislature, passed an electoral law in 1875 that maintained the single-member constituency. Within its narrow confines the clergy and local magnates could weigh heavily on peasants and rural artisans who often depended on them for loans and information. The law provided that each *arrondissement* was entitled to one deputy. Since a large number of these districts were predominantly agrarian and had a limited population, rural France was greatly over represented. The northern, more populous part of France, was entitled to 220 deputies for 19 million inhabitants; the less industrialized southern and western parts had 280 deputies for 16 million inhabitants. Most states of Europe had imbalances of this sort, and only the British made a serious effort to correct them. But then, Britain had far more larger cities than Continental states where agriculture still employed more than half the population. Despite this setback republicans won the elections of 1876 with nearly 56 percent of the ballots. They occupied 300 seats in the new Chamber of Deputies, a somewhat fragile majority. Of these Gambetta and his followers held 180, the extreme left led by Louis Blanc and Georges Clemenceau won 80. Ligitimist followers of Henri came back a mere twenty strong, whereas Orleanists occupied forty-five.

What counted in this election was the near disappearance of center groups, the possible nucleus of a party committed to a moderate policy including further reform. The left center of conservative republicans and the right center of constitutional monarchists won about eighty places, but they were not a unified group, the issue of the clergy dividing them. The church hierarchy, from parish priest to cardinal, used the pulpit and probably the confessional, to rail against republicans. It would seem, then, that the electorate was either red republican or black reactionary. This assertion has some validity in the kind of political games that politicians liked to play. In reality, the question by 1876 was not whether France would become monarchist or republican, but what kind of republic would emerge from the play of forces influencing voters. This became evident in the so-called Sixteenth of May crisis. MacMahon had called upon a moderate republican, Jules Simon, to form a Ministry, and then dismissed him and used his constitutional right to dissolve the Chamber of Deputies, with the necessary assent of the Senate. During the elections that followed in 1877 his administration made every effort to stymie republican candidates. By this time Gambetta had organized most of them into a Republican Union, the possible nucleus of a large party, but it did not survive the 1870s. Once the threat of a restoration was removed, the political left split into several groups. Possibly single-member constituencies encouraged fractionalization: within their relatively small districts republican politicians operated pretty much on their own, forming their clienteles, looking after local interests, creating their little fiefdoms, shifting from group to group, and enjoying an independence of decision found mainly in the Latin countries of the Mediterranean basin. It is not a gross exaggeration to suggest that they carried their headquarters and files in every pocket of their working suit save the back one, which they kept for party loyalty. This system, or rather nonsystem, worked well enough: republicans received only 54.4 percent of the vote, yet they won 318 seats out of 526. The system worked in their favor, even though enormous pressure had been exerted by the executive. By the time MacMahon resigned in disgust during January 1879, the republican Ministry that had so annoyed him had restored all the civil servants, judges, and prefects who had been dismissed as uncertain before the election.

The crisis had been provoked by the president when he, in accord with the Senate, had dissolved the chamber. Dissolution was constitutionally legal, but the way MacMahon carried it out turned republicans against it and it was never resorted to again prior to 1914. This result only added to the independence of deputies who now enjoyed four years safe from having to face their electors unexpectedly. This kind of free-wheeling, combined with a miserly salary that barely covered expenses, probably was a cause of the corruption that pervaded both chambers. The British went from reform to reform, the French from scandal to scandal. That the republican form survived the peccadillos of deputies and their shifting alliances indicated that the French had learned to live dangerously.

One factor that counted heavily in the 1877 campaign was the connection between royalism and the papacy. In 1871 the right had accused the left of wanting to continue a disastrous war, an accusation that won them most of the voters who wanted peace. In 1877 (as in 1875) the republicans accused Catholic monarchists of wanting to drag France into a war against Italy and Germany in order to restore the Papal States. At this time there were virulent conflicts between church and state in both Italy and Germany where Bismarck implemented the *Kulturkampf*. Peasants were warned that if Henri was restored he would bring back the feudal regime and restore their land to clergy and aristocracy. This message must have penetrated rural France because the 1881 elections were especially favorable to republicans.

Equally significant was their victory in the 1879 senatorial elections; they captured the bastion of the conservatives. It was this event that precipitated the resignation of MacMahon. He was the second head of state to be forced out of office, the first being Thiers in 1873. MacMahon's successor, Jules Grévy, began the process that steadily emasculated the office to the point where the president retained little more power than Queen Victoria of Britain. Neither was entirely without influence: Grévy, a petulant, small-minded man, kept Gambetta from the premiership until it was too late to build a strong republican center. Henceforth France was governed by her two representative bodies; even the office of prime minister lost some of its power as a result of the lack of party discipline. Instead of two major parties as in Britain, French politicians split into numerous groupings. Fortunately there was a common denominator holding them together, Freemasonry. In its numerous lodges republicans of every color gathered in a common brotherhood devoted to the Republic and to anticlericalism. Even socialists were later brought in because during the two decades prior to 1900, numerous republicans recognized the need for unity and lived by the belief that there were "no enemies to the left." The danger was on the right.

The belief in a common cause, however, did not encourage unity of a practical sort in the Chamber of Deputies. This made it difficult for premiers to form solid, harmonious ministries. A ministry had to represent as many parties or groups as possible in order to win approval in the Chamber. This meant that a splinter party whose few members might hold the votes needed for survival could exert pressure on the executive far beyond what its membership warranted. In Britain, Disraeli and Gladstone usually held the premiership long enough to devise consistent programs and carry them out with party support over three to five years; in Germany Bismarck was chancellor for nineteen years. In France a ministry was considered solid if it lasted nineteen months; a fair number endured only nineteen or so weeks. Gambetta's "great" ministry endured less than three months. The chambers were obstreperous, at times outright obstructionist.

Obstruction of social reform was the specialty of the Senate. Created by the Constitution of 1875 to bear as much resemblance as possible to the upper chambers of the Bourbon and Orleanist monarchies, where peers of the realm had sat and often fell asleep, it survived the virulent attacks upon it by republicans until they won a majority of its seats in 1879. The extreme left, known then as Radicals, continued to demand its abolition. But the more moderate of the left, who became known as Opportunists, controlled it and retained it. They modified it: Life senators disappeared in 1884, and the electoral systems was slightly changed so that provincial small towns became important in the electoral process, without seriously reducing the rural bias of most successful candidates. For Roger Magraw, "the senate faithfully fulfilled the reactionary role for which it had been conceived, its collection of geriatric politicians and bureaucrats carried from its benches to their graves after passing their declining years obstructing progressive legislation." It is important to bear in mind that conservatives, usually consisting of landed magnates and big industrialists, retained most of their power in an age of democratic revolution by controlling upper houses.

The German *Bundesrat* consisted of noble delegates chosen by rulers of the member states; the Austrian Consultative Assembly was merely that, an advisory body without power. Great Britain's House of Lords consisted chiefly of landed peers who inherited their seats, and, as we shall see, was as obstructionist as the French Senate. That the Lords had their powers clipped by commons in 1911 resulted from the rise of urban populations and the pressure of labor for social reform. The French electorate counted in its ranks far more independent small farmers, equally independent artisans, and socially conservative bourgeois. In the 1870s most of them rallied to the Republic, but they wanted freedom for themselves, equality of rights, and the fraternity of patriots. Clustered in small- to medium-sized towns and minuscule villages, they knew little of big industry and the factory proletariat, and resisted any effort to raise taxes to pay for social reforms that would benefit urban workers. They lacked civic-mindedness, (*incivisme* as the French call it) and were individualistic almost to the point of anarchy. The thrust to social reform was also weakened by the large number of workers who defied unionization as a means of influencing politicians. Their leaders, won over either to Marxism or anarchism, called for the overthrow of the Republic, not the reform of it. In the end they neither overthrew it nor obtained much reform. There was an obvious relation between the nature of government and how it fit a society. A nearly inactive regime clearly suited most of the voting population. Only a handful of extremists on the right and left of the political spectrum displayed a visceral dislike of the Republic and threw poisoned darts at the picture of Marianne, the Phrygian-hatted, big-bosomed woman who visually symbolized the Third Republic as the continuator of the first and second.

Most French were delighted when, in 1882, the government proclaimed July 14, the date on which the Bastille was taken in 1789, as a national holiday.

Henceforth main streets in every village and town were bedecked with tricolor flags, and the *Marseillaise*, the national anthem, was belted out by school children as they learned their ABCs. On July 14 of every year good citizens danced in the streets, and in 1914 they died by the thousands for the Republic. By all counts this was a happy marriage uniting government and people, albeit often boring between national celebrations.

The Republic of the Opportunists was politically progressive and socially conservative. As one of them put it, "my heart is on the left, my pocket book on the right." Another Jules, surname Ferry, was their outstanding politician. His major legislation was intended to wean children away from the church's teaching and to win them to republican ideals. As minister of education he put through the legislation that inaugurated free, secular and compulsory education at the elementary level. Like all good republicans of the early 1880s he was a hardened anti-clerical. As premier he ended the prayers said at the opening of each meeting of the Chambers, and abolished all religious congregations that had not received authorization, especially the Jesuits, and set about closing their schools. He was not able to implement his sweeping changes at once for lack of competent lay teachers to replace the nuns and Christian brothers who taught in both church and state-supported establishments. A complementary purging cleared away several hundred judges named years earlier when monarchists ruled the judicial roost. He naturally replaced them with solid republicans. He also rescinded the regime under which prefects appointed mayors; a new law called for the election of mayors by municipal councils, themselves chosen by local voters.

Ferry was finally overthrown by a combination of the right, out for revenge, and the Jacobin Radicals who denounced him for his support of colonial expansion in Indo-China. The extreme left, still intent upon recovering the sacred soil of Alsace, accused him of wasting resources that should be husbanded for a war against Germany. And it was the Radicals, led now by Georges Clemenceau, who imposed upon his successor the appointment of General Georges Boulanger as war minister. Radicals supported him because he was the only general in the army, not yet purified as judges had been, who professed his republicanism. He courted favor with common soldiers by improving their conditions, with striking workers by having his men share rations with them, with republicans by depriving Orleanists pretenders of their army rank, nationalists by his bellicose rhetoric against the Germans, and the Parisian crowds by elaborate parades. His ambitions for political advance led him to being dismissed as minister and dropped from the army because of frequent absences for political campaigning. When Clemenceau cut him off, he won support, both financial and political, from royalists hoping to use him to restore the throne. In 1889 he was elected to a seat from Paris, as well as other districts. Nationalist and royalist mobs thronged the capital's streets, calling for an invasion of the Chamber of Deputies. Disgust for the regime was deepened by a recent scandal involving

President Jules Grévy's son-in-law, and his retirement under pressure. The handsome, dashing soldier then disappointed his backers: When threatened with arrest he fled to Belgium where he shot himself beside the grave of his mistress. The whole affair collapsed like the proverbial house of cards. During the crisis the Opportunists failed to call out the army to defend the Chamber; they were not sure which side the soldiers would take. Their fears were probably unfounded. Although it is probable that officers from field grade up harbored monarchist and clerical sympathies, they were not prepared to imitate their forebears of 1851–52 and serve as the shock troops of a coup d'état. After all, the colonial policies of the Opportunists had called on the army for penetration of "backward" areas. The unfortunate defeat in Tonkin was avenged and Indo-China made safe for French settlers, never more than a handful.

The politicians who ruled in the 1890s were known as the *Progressistes*; they were really Orleanists without the title. Like a cancer cell, Orleanism had penetrated the Second Empire, it also entered the bloodstream of the Third Republic. This was accomplished by means of the *ralliement*, a shift of Catholics from the right center to the left center. Pope Leo XIII, reversing the intransigent hatred of Pius IX for liberalism, called on his flocks to rally to the Republic in order to Catholisize it, to remove its anticlerical legislation.

Reconciliation of this sort was anathema to Radicals. Their favorite joke was: "What is worse than a bad priest? A good priest." Leo XIII was a good priest; in fact, he was stealing their thunder. His bull, *Rerum Novarum*, published in 1891, called for the protection of wage earners, collective negotiation of working conditions, even the legality of trade unions. In France they had acquired legal status in 1884, precisely during the time when Bismarck had outlawed Social Democrats and was hounding union organizers. The *Progressistes* were happy to welcome the Catholics who made no political issue of their religion. Most *Progressistes* were nominally Catholic, even when they were anticlerical as indeed they were, and most of their wives were church going and baptized their children. This, incidentally, was a common problem for politicians on the left. Their attacks on the clergy made home life rather difficult because their wives were devout, as wives were supposed to be. To find wives who did not attend mass, one had to go to the Protestant and Jewish communities. Even on the far left, wifely religiosity was a bitter embarrassment. Given this condition, one can understand why anticlerical politicians vehemently and categorically refused to give women the right to vote. To give them the vote would have amounted to political castration. This was not a matter of morality. In politics there were no morals, or perhaps more accurately, politics has its own morality, and that of France was not of the highest.

In 1892 the Panama Canal Company, after it went bankrupt, was exposed for its financial manipulation of deputies. A multitude of small investors lost heavily. Key officials of the company were Jewish, a situation seized upon by the extreme anti-Semite Edward Drumont. In his newspaper *La*

Libre Parole he ran a series of denunciatory articles that led to an investigation by a parliamentary committee. Only one of the bribed deputies confessed and he went to jail; the others were exonerated at the end of hearings punctuated by the shouts of enraged crowds held back by police lines.

Distrust of incumbent politicians ran deep in voters' minds, leading them to believe that voting for the left would purify the chambers. In consequence the Radicals profited in the 1893 elections, and in late 1895 Leon Bourgeois put together a government committed to social reform. His philosophy, known as *solidarité*, called for a system of social security to moderate the insecurity that troubled the daily life of wage earners. In contrast to the extreme individualism of *Progressistes* his notion of solidarity held that all people are bound by a quasi-contract to help and defend one another. To finance the cost of social insurance he proposed a moderately progressive income tax. His bill won only a slight majority of deputies but only a third of senators. His loss there raised a constitutional issue: Was a ministry responsible to the Senate as well as to the Chamber? The deputies had brought down many premiers, but not yet the upper house. Radicals urged Bourgeois to ignore the conservatives; however, he was at heart a moderate man, a pacifist even, and resigned rather than fight. The event was of great moment; the Senate, graveyard of social reform, had successfully defeated the first attempt to initiate the same kind of legislation that Bismarck had provided for the German lower classes. France was just emerging from a long depression when unemployment had racked wage earners. Their plight did not move most senators, and the emergence of several socialist parties merely frightened them. They dug in their heels against further measures beneficial to wage earners. Big capital and inherited wealth flourished in this environment. The costs of imperialism and armaments would be paid by regressive sales taxes, which made up roughly one-half of state revenues, by taxes on real property that drew heavily upon small farmers, and by tariffs that raised the prices of the daily necessities urban workers had to buy.

The years following Leon Bourgeois' fall were filled with the din of the Dreyfus Case. Alfred Dreyfus was a Jew and the only Jew to be found in any army General Staff in Europe. France was unique. Most officers were Catholic and, if not monarchist, were sympathetic to authoritarian regimes. The French clergy was riddled with anti-Semitism, and the Order of Assumptionists were merely the most fanatical among them. But hatred of Jews does not fully explain why Dreyfus was charged with treason, tried by fellow officers who relied on a forged document, illegally concealed other papers from his defense lawyer and, after finding him guilty, condemned him to "Devil's Island," the "dry guillotine" that sliced away a man's life day by day. During and after the trial France was divided between Dreyfusards and anti-Dreyfusards. The latter consisted of all kinds of people, many solidly republican, many attempting to use the affair to overturn the republic. There now emerged right wing groups whose ferocity matched that of the army that shot communards without blinking an eye. They

Stiff-backed, Dreyfus stands in the dock at his first trial. The evidence against him consisted mainly of confusing reports from handwriting analysts.

Captain Alfred Dreyfus was first tried and found guilty of treason in 1894 by a military tribunal. Because he was a Jew, his trial aroused populist anti-Semitism, even after his defenders proved that the decision was based on a forged document.

contributed to an emerging irrationalist current of thought challenging the deep-rooted rationalist tradition for which the French were both famous and, to romantic nationalists, infamous. This cultural about face was hastened by *"L'Affaire,"* shorthand for the Dreyfus case. The incredible dishonesty of the military court was made known, first by Senator Auguste Scheurer-Kestner who risked his career when demanding a retrial, Émile Zola who openly challenged the high command with an exposé of the trial, which he titled "J'accuse" and published in Clemenceau's paper *L'Aurore*. Behind them were numerous republicans who organized a defense rally, a block, to save the regime. They were Radicals and socialists from the teaching profession, workers from factories and petty bourgeois anticlericals. They provided the progovernment majorities that enabled the two succeeding ministries to free Dreyfus, and later to rehabilitate him.

For extreme nationalists Dreyfus was "morally" guilty of treason simply because he was a Jew, and the army could do no wrong. Such was the position taken by Charles Maurras, founder of the pre-Fascist Action Française, who fused a reactionary monarchist tradition with extreme chauvinist and populist nationalism. Supporting them were the Camelots du Roi, gangs of activist youths, most from well-to-do families, and notorious for street brawling on Saturday and going to mass on Sunday. Their alliance with the church was really a sham. Nationalism was their religion.

This extremism provoked the final solution to church-state relations. Between 1901 and 1905 moderates and Radicals dissolved most Catholic teaching orders, closed their schools and separated church and state. In the long run the church benefited from this surgery, and began its recovery as a Christian institution, aware that militant nationalism was at odds with a religion devoted to the equality of all peoples. It was a remarkable act when the pope excommunicated Maurras in the 1920s.

By 1902 Radicals were in command of France and of themselves, having organized a modern political party in this same year. Many observers believed that France had moved leftward. That was a false impression; rather most Radicals had moved closer toward the political center out of fear of socialists. As a group they had helped found the Republic, defended it heroically against its enemies and, to a certain extent, made it a more just government. With that mission accomplished, they should have taken up their reform program: social security, a progressive income tax, state ownership of the Bank of France, railroads, mines and utilities, and abolition of the Senate. But Radicals now controlled the upper house, and felt more comfortable curbing the church than expanding the state. When Clemenceau became premier in 1906 he was no longer a Radical, yet he put forward a major program of reform. Much to the relief of the party's rank and file the Senate voted it down. Clemenceau himself found it difficult to address the demands of teachers and postal workers. When they went on strike he had them fired and set the police on them, proclaiming that he was the first cop (*flick*) of France. As for the Radicals, an unfriendly critic commented, "they are like radishes, red on the outside, white within."

The United Kingdom: Unrelenting Reform

The British, a term I am using to include the English, Welsh, Scots, and Irish, were fairly detached from the events that transformed central Europe and France in 1870–71, just as they had been in 1848–49. The government, since the days of Castlereagh and Canning, had prided itself on its policy of "splendid isolation." Of course, this policy did not hinder the protection of British interests in the Near and Far East, or more recently, in Egypt. The country was on the threshold of expanding into Africa and Asia, and eventually these activities would influence the political situation at home. In this chapter I shall concentrate on domestic affairs, reserving colonial expansion for later.

By the 1870s, the destiny of the British lay in the policies of two parties, the Conservative and the Liberal. Disraeli had put together a powerful coalition that was attached to tradition, but was also willing to initiate reforms precisely to stave off revolutionary threats to established institutions: the monarchy, the Anglican church, the aristocracy, and private property. In this endeavor he was successful; however, he could not isolate the country from an economic depression that swept over western Europe. His liberal opponent, Gladstone, made use of a general election to blame him for hard times; he also castigated him for supporting Turkey whose Moslem troops had occasionally massacred Christians in the Balkans.

Gladstone's attacks paid off and he returned as prime minister backed by a sizable Liberal contingent. This situation gave them the chance to get even with the Conservatives, who had granted the suffrage to urban workers in 1867, by granting it now to agricultural laborers, most of whom worked on the estates of Tory landlords. Of course there were large estate owners who had joined the Liberal party without abandoning their less-than-liberal Whig leanings. At the first excuse they would bolt the party and join the right, but for the moment they accepted their fate. So the third reform act of 1884 gave the vote to rustic field laborers who could also organize trade unions. In addition it enfranchised the industrial workers and miners not included in the 1867 act, usually because they were living outside a parliamentary borough. This reform made necessary a complete alteration of the agrarian basis of electoral districts. Since the Middle Ages, representation was based on a landed area, a borough, or a county. As its critics pointed out representation was founded on "sticks and stones," not on men. The Redistribution of Seats Act of 1885 brought a drastic change by dropping the land factor and taking population as the determinant of electoral districts. Seventy-nine boroughs with fewer than 15,000 inhabitants ceased to be seats, and thirty-six with under 50,000 lost one of their two members. Only the universities and boroughs between 50,000 and 165,000 remained two-member constituencies. The counties were split up into single-member districts. Clusters of people now became the voting unit, and approximate numerical equality the principle. These same conditions were extended to Ireland, with the result that a native movement opposed to rule from London, and led by Charles Stewart Parnell, carried all the seats and became an important minority in Commons, siding with the major party that advanced its cause. At first the Irish members supported Gladstone, but that support was a kiss of death.

The new system markedly reduced the disproportionate rural representation common in Continental countries, but it tended to give excess representation to simple majorities and to fortify both central and local party organization. Conversely, politics was brought closer to the large masses of urban centers and the electorate grew enormously, a phenomenon that had been underway much earlier. Before long the very nature of electioneering was transformed. In 1868 Liberals by means of active campaigning had won a large majority. In contrast Disraeli had merely sent a written address to his electors in Buckinghamshire. His successors were no longer permitted such off-hand tactics. On the contrary, constituencies now had even to be nursed between elections. This required a high degree of party organization, and, as it turned out, greater concentration of decision making at party headquarters in London. It was there that strategy was planned and the human machinery activated to implement it. Within the House of Commons party discipline became more rigorous by the use of party whips. There was, contrary to politicking in France, a loss of freedom, but a gain in efficiency. This gain was mandated by the press of more business in Parliament as it responded to a more modern society that expected a higher volume of services from government than ever before. The relation between society and government attained an unprecedented intensity. As regards social needs the authorities responded fairly rapidly—there was not even a need for pressure groups like the Chartists. As regards economic needs, British politicians remained more bound to laissez faire traditions than Continentals who saw in government the lever to lift their industrial output and to protect it from outside competition. But more on this matter will come later.

Not all these changes occurred at once; they would appear as the need for them grew. Before 1900 parties were as yet fairly fluid in their membership, and maverick members could upset their balance of interests. In the Liberal party, Joseph Chamberlain, mayor of Birmingham, was leader of its radical wing. His program had several points in common with the French left, such as a progressive income tax, and separation of church and state, that is, the state financed Anglican church. He also called for free primary education. The education act of 1870 had included compulsory education, but fees were dropped only in 1890. He also called for payment of a salary for members of Commons. It had always been assumed that the men who ran for a seat were financially independent, part of the ruling élite, or supported by a rich patron, a practice that precluded any independence in the House: Clients voted as their patrons commanded. This meant that a person not elected by the voters could influence parliamentary behavior. Wealthy patrons not only financed elections, they often hired thugs to break up the crowds gathered to hear the rival candidate. A Corrupt Practices Act, passed in 1883, sought to put an end to such rowdiness, and the act did curb it, save for particularly heated campaigns.

While violence associated with politics was on the decline in England, Wales and Scotland, it spread and intensified in Ireland. The economic crisis of the late 1870s hit the Irish peasants with particular severity. Barely able to make ends meet before the fall of farm prices, they were now faced with hunger and eviction from their tenancies. A proposal to aid them was flatly rejected by the House of Lords; many peers were absentee owners of vast Irish estates that were divided into large holdings rented to natives who then further divided their tenancies into much smaller plots that they rented to dirt farmers. This disastrous system was responsible for the backwardness of Irish farming, and for the mass migration of families to foreign lands. Ireland was the only country with a declining population. It must also have had the highest level of rural violence, surpassing Russia. By the autumn of 1880, it was "Captain Midnight" who ruled the countryside as desperate men burned the hay stacks and barns of Protestant Anglo-Saxons, and maimed their cattle. Prominent persons awoke to find graves dug before their doors; others were dragged from their beds and assaulted by masked bands. As more peasants were evicted for nonpayment of rents, violent acts rose in number. From just over 2,000 evictions in 1877, the number swelled to well over 10,000 in 1880; and violent acts proportionally rose from 263 to 2,590.

Few English politicians took a keen and understanding interest in Ireland. Gladstone was the exception, and during his grand ministry of 1880–85, he sponsored several bills that could have improved conditions in the Emerald Isle. In 1881 he put up for debate a measure that would provide the "three F's": fixity of tenure, fair rents, and free sale. Parnell rejected this measure as insufficient, but it passed and became law. Chamberlain brought the Irish leader and the premier together: they agreed that about 100,000 tenants with rent payments in arrears and liable to eviction, would receive government aid to pay their rents. In return Parnell would use his influence to curb violence. His influence, unfortunately, was too limited to prevent the Phoenix Park murders which snuffed the lives of two high English administrators. The culprits were members of the Invincibles, a murder syndicate. In a desperate effort to forestall popular support for such violence the Arrears Act provided financial aid to distressed farmers, but the budget it proposed was inadequate. The Irish problem had simply gotten out of hand, a condition denied by English administrators, although generally admitted to be true by a competent observer. The Arrears Act entered the code of written law; it proved of little use, however, because of the unwritten law that firmly defended owners' rights.

The next logical step of course, was home rule, two words spelled in capital letters by Irish children learning their *ABCs*. In a disappointing phase of his long career Gladstone proposed home rule in 1886. The measure was defeated in June by a sizable majority of 343 to 313. Ninety-three of the Liberal party condemned it with their vote. The radical Chamberlain, who imagined that unenforceable reforms could prevent separation, vehemently denounced it and quit the party in order to set up a rival group, the Liberal Unionists. The parent party never recovered from this defeat, and that of the next election which returned a Conservative majority, and Lord Salisbury, their premier, held office for thirteen of the next seventeen years.

The Conservatives recognized that they had an issue that stirred English voters who were never friendly toward the Gaelic race; even English workers looked upon Irish immigrants as scabs. They all denigrated Parnell, who indeed was vulnerable because of an adulterous liaison. To strike from another front,

The Times published a letter purported to have been written by him and approving the Phoenix Park murders. Hard on this exposé, Lord Salisbury put through a new Crimes Act, which enhanced the use of police action in Ireland. The letter was later shown to be a forgery, but it did its pernicious work while Parnell was alive.

The Tory's policy became one alternating between blows and caresses. They brutally dealt with the more violent natives, then provided funds enabling tenants to purchase land. By 1909 about half the arable land belonged to former tenants. This, however, did not satisfy the Irish demand for home rule. In England home rule became a nasty phrase, not used in polite society. Gladstone and his ilk were ostracized by the queen and the London upper strata. The Liberal party came to rely on the Scots and the Welsh to fill out their ranks and garner votes. They also came to rely on the labor vote verging to a new political left, first the Independent Labor party and in 1906 the much larger Labor Party. Since its members generally stood by Liberal ministries, they were called Lib-Labs.

Both Liberals and Labor confronted a serious obstacle to their programs in the House of Lords, the ultimate stronghold of obstreperous conservatism of a highly partisan sort. Salisbury and, after him, Arthur Balfour were in the tradition of Disraeli in that they favored the factory acts that controlled hours of labor in large factories and the removal of children from the work force. In 1897 Conservatives enacted legislation that codified all factory laws since 1833, and added provisions that limited the workweek of women and teenagers to between fifty-five and sixty hours, eliminated night work for them, and required adequate time for meals. Sanitation in the workplace was improved and machinery enclosed to cut down on accidents. These regulations were extended to clerks in shops, miners, railway workers, even newsboys. Because these measures emanated from a Conservative majority, they sailed through the House of Lords. In contrast, Liberal measures such as an employers responsibility bill that would have compelled factory owners to compensate workers for injuries resulting from production processes, was rejected, as was home rule and several other reforms. A sizable majority of peers were clearly determined to frustrate Liberals. Like Salisbury and Balfour, they were a largely closed aristocracy representing a small privileged class, and convinced that the greatness of England was due to patrician rule. They watched with deep concern the entry into Commons of men from the petty bourgeoisie and working class. The house of 1906 had fifty-three Laborites, all reared in working class homes, and new style Liberals such as the Welshman David Lloyd-George, the son of an elementary school teacher and raised by an uncle who was a shoemaker. How, peers asked themselves, could such men with their crude local accents, effectively govern the country? The answer was obvious, and acting on it, the Tory lords consciously set out to block Liberal proposals for reform. Such blatant partisanship steadily undermined the moral and constitutional basis of their position. In fact, their intransigence encouraged the formation of the Labor party.

So did the judicial hierarchy who shared the head-in-the-ground posi-

David Lloyd George was a member of Parliament and a leader in the move to lay the fiscal foundations for a welfare state. His budget of 1908 raised taxes on the rich to provide the poor with old-age pensions.

tion of the upper House. An example was their decision after a strike in 1901 against the Taff Vale railroad. When strikers destroyed some property, management sued the union and obtained a decision holding that the union was responsible for all material losses resulting from pickets set up by its members. This early decision set a precedent that would have bankrupted unions and overturned the provisions of the 1871 Trade Union Act that had afforded protection to union treasuries. On appeal the case went before the Lords serving as the highest court of the realm. The decision went against the union that was forced to pay £32,000. Union membership leapt up, and leaders now realized the need to enter politics, to back the new Labor party with manpower and money. In fact, workers could not have run in elections nor met their personal budgets without union contributions. The union movement became the patron of workers in Commons.

The Liberal party, with the support of Irish, Welsh and Labor members returned to power in December 1905 with Henry Campbell-Bannerman as prime minister and Lloyd George at the Exchequer (Treasury). When H. H. Asquith succeeded him in 1908 the budget contained provisions for an old age pension. The conditions were modestly generous: Every British subject seventy years old and older, with an income under ten shillings a week and with no criminal record, became entitled to an annual pension. The sum to be received varied, but the maximum stood at £31 10s. Because there was no fund built up by contributions the cost had to be met by general taxes. This bill abolished the old Poor Law and ended the humiliation attached to public charity. Everyone who qualified was to receive a pension by right.

The bill providing for compulsory insurance of wage workers covered sickness and disablement. Workers would contribute four pence per week, employers three pence, and the government two. Free medical treatment was added, as well as money payments to replace lost wages. Unemployment insurance, unknown on the Continent, was included as an experiment and limited to industries where loss of jobs was common. Compensation would continue over fifteen weeks.

This bill, which passed Commons, was both pioneering in the field of social security and extremely expensive, creating a deficit of £16 million. This deficit was to be met by a greatly increased income tax, progressively scaled to absorb more from the rich than the poor. It placed a heavy burden on large landed estates, the kind owned by most peers. One of them fulminated, "This is not a budget, it is a revolution!" Naturally they rejected it out of hand, despite the warning by no less a person than Edward VII.

The Lords were, in the vernacular of the street, on a roll, and too purblind to recognize that they were heading for a fall. Asquith dissolved the Commons and called for new elections. The budget aroused everyone from apathy, turn out was heavy, and the Conservatives and Liberals returned with nearly an even number of seats. However, Irish and Labor members rallied to Asquith, allowing him to form a new Cabinet. The budget passed once more, only this time (1909) it contained an addition depriving the Lords of the power to defeat financial bills. When they again killed the budget they provoked a constitutional as well as a budgetary crisis a little reminiscent of that in Prussia during the 1860s. There the National Liberals were ignored and later rallied to Bismarck. In Britain the Liberals and their allies rose to the fight. In 1911 a bill to deprive Lords of budgetary control passed the lower House, and if the upper House amended or destroyed it, George V promised Asquith to create as many new peers as needed to get a favorable vote. This was the same threat used by the crown in 1832 to move the first Reform Bill through an equally hostile upper House. Rather than become inundated by new members, Conservatives abstained and Liberal peers passed the measure. The new act prohibited the Lords from delaying for over a month any bill classed as financial by the speaker of Commons, and also left them with only a suspensive veto of two years duration over all other measures.

In this same session an act provided members of Commons with a salary of £400 per annum. This resulted from another court case in 1909 denying the legality of union payments to Labor members.

The British succeeded where the French and other Europeans failed: the privileged class, the aristocracy, was removed as an obstacle to social modernization, this term meaning the lessening of the insecurity that characterized laissez faire society.

The German state certainly provided nearly as much social security as the British and more than the French. The kind of government, it is evident, was not a factor determining how states protected their citizens; the level of economic growth needed to finance social security was of major importance, as was social structure. The more agrarian a society, the less inclined it was to intervene to improve the lives of its subjects. France and Russia, although vastly different in many respects, shared this disinclination together; so did the poorer states of the south.

The Mediterranean: Italy and *Trasformismo*

In Italy, unification was completed in 1870 when Rome was taken away from the pope; the eternal city became the capital city. The form of government did not change; Italy was a unified state functioning under a limited monarchy, a Senate chosen by the king, but like him, unwilling to interfere actively in government affairs. These were carried on by the Chamber of Deputies elected at first by only 2 percent of the population, then 7 percent when the franchise was broadened in 1882. The highly centralized administration was borrowed directly from France, but the French state, as noted earlier, enjoyed far more power than its Italian equivalent.

In 1870–71 the occupation of Rome did little to improve the problems carried over from centuries of division, foreign rule in the North, and incompetent rule in the South. The drawn out Risorgimento had been an era of selfless heroism, high-minded idealism and worthy dreams. What remained were the age old problems that now faced the new regime.

Most disheartening was the lack of a modern infrastructure, a paucity of capital for investment because the high costs of unification had exhausted both public and private reserves, technical skills at the levels of management and labor, and natural resources, there being neither iron nor coal with which to build a capital goods basis for industrial take-off. Worse, the men who held power, undaunted warriors in the struggle for unity, were not well trained in the strategy needed to resolve pressing problems.

At the lower levels of society the masses were highly illiterate, up to 90 percent in the *Mezzogiorno*, a result of deliberate policies of former rulers. Theirs was the psychology of agrarian folk, their lives entirely devoted to land cultivation in ways that went back to the ancient Romans. Even the urban wealthy were dominated, more so than in France where land was also highly prized, by the desire to invest in the soil. This proclivity tied up large amounts of capital in a not highly profitable but socially prestigious enterprise. There was little of it left over to be mobilized for industry or for research and development.

The Risorgimento unified the peninsula but did not overcome sectionalism. It had been carried out by the noble and middle class, while most of the farming population had stood by. There were as yet few Italians, but rather Piedmontese, Lombards, Venetians, Romans, Neapolitans, Sicilians, and so forth, all speaking their own dialects. Administratively, Italy was Piedmontized to a greater extent than Germany was Prussianized; but culturally Prussia weighed heavily in the Empire while Piedmont was a featherweight to the south. Localism of speech and habits would give ground only after the spread of elementary education, but the national government was both too poor and the Catholic church too entrenched in schools for pedagogy to become, as in France, the major force creating a national consciousness. Mobilization in 1914 would continue the process of forming a sense of Italianness that the school system had only begun to inculcate in the south.

The North and South were not only two different sections, they were two different worlds. Political unity had the unexpected effect of deepening the chasm between them: The end of internal tariffs opened the traditional industries below Rome to the lower prices of more advanced enterprises above the Po River. Railroads, symbol of modernization, hastened the destruction, leaving the *Mezzogiorno* with little but unimproved agriculture.

A schism just as deep but of moral dimensions existed between Catholics who were obedient to Pius IX's command to oppose the government that usurped his territories and capital, and those who defied his excommunications. The Roman question, the pope's anathemas against the secular state, threw many into the torment of divided allegiances. It was far easier for anticlericals to win converts in France where vast stretches of population were dechristianized by 1914, than in Italy where propapal feelings were thoroughly ingrained. This situation merely deepened the Italians' longtime and intense distrust of politicians regardless of their electoral pronouncements. Excluded from the suffrage, the masses looked on government with its fiscal exactions as a necessary evil that had to be appeased but resisted. In the deep south this cynicism led to banditry, the Neapolitan Camorra and the Sicilian Maffia, terrorist organs necessary to keep in their place agents of the national state as well as those of local polities.

Governing such a state would have taxed the ingenuity of Cavour. His disciples formed the *Destra* or conservative element in the Chamber of Deputies. They received all the fulminations of Pius and had to expel thirty bishops who refused to accept royal authority. The narrow franchise cut them off from the country and, left with huge deficits, they taxed everything, including flour in their orthodox belief that budgets must be balanced; they forgot that Cavour rarely had balanced budgets. The tax on flour, in a nation of pasta eaters, was too much. In 1876 the *Sinistra* (left) won power and more or less held it until 1914. What distinguished the right and left was less a matter of principle than of political strategy. Agostino Depretis of Piedmont and after him in the 1890s Francisco Crispi of Sicily, brought the south into the political arena. Along with the southern tricks of the trade. After expanding the suffrage slightly in 1882, and raising the tariff to protect Italian industry, premiers resorted to a practice called *trasformismo*, that is, they abandoned trying to rule with a divided left for a policy seeking a majority culled from all groups of the Chamber and gathered around a man rather than a party program. Depretis as premier in the 1880s held power by making deals with all factions to piece together a ministry. This did not always require monetary payment; deputies loved honors, and after a majority supported a particular measure, the next day's official journal would announce that about fifty to sixty deputies had been named *cavaliere*, a prestigious title, similar to the designation "knight" in Britain. Unfortunately, more energy went into this practice than into carrying out major reforms. It did not solve the cleavage between north and south. On the contrary, the economic crisis of the 1890s bore heavily on a fragile economy like Italy's. There was a steady stream of emigration to France, and North and South America. Desperate Sicilian peasants initiated riots of almost revolutionary proportions in 1893, and Crispi, a Sicilian, crushed them unmercifully. Hoping to divert Italians from their troubles he sent the army into Ethiopia where it suffered a disastrous defeat in 1896, which brought him down.

General conditions improved throughout Europe after 1900. Giovanni Giolitti, a Piemontese, assumed the premiership and strove to form a broad liberal party of the left. The newly formed Socialist party, at least its right wing, was tempted. Giolitti's liberalism led him to pass factory legislation, to nationalize large insurance companies and the railways, and to encourage collective bargaining between legalized trade unions and employers. Now that workers were free to strike, they resorted massively to it, especially since the Italian economy entered its revolutionary phase. He too, caught the imperialist bug and seized Libya from Turkey in 1911, the same year that he introduced universal male suffrage even though only half the population was literate. At least he no longer had the church against his government; Leo XIII had urged Catholics to take part in politics to capture the seat of power, and halt the spread of revolutionary socialism, the same policy he urged upon the faithful in France. Impatient with him were the revolutionary wing of the socialists, and a rising nationalist movement that cast its eyes on the northeast, the Trentino, Fiume and the Dalmatian coast where Italian-speaking peoples had remained under Austrian rule after 1866. These lands were *Italia irredènta*, unredeemed Italy. Inspired by the high-sounding poetry of Gabriel D'Annunzio, who urged them to "man the prow" and sail out into the world, Giolitti had to hold them in check because Italy had joined Austria and Germany in 1882 to form the Triple Alliance.

The Mediterranean: Spain as a Lost Cause

The governments of Spain joined no foreign alliance; none could even effectively rule the country. Between the overthrow of Isabella in 1868 and 1875 the state shifted from monarchy to republic with ill effects until the army put Isabella's son, Alfonso, on the throne. The premier, Don Antonio del Castillo, headed a conservative party and drew up the constitution of 1876. Modeled deliberately on that of Britain it provided for two houses with, as in Italy, a very narrow electorate consisting of large property owners. Because the so-called liberals hardly differed from conservatives, debates in the Chamber were high-flown oratory but meaningless. Both groups vied for power and little else. At the least they provided stability, but maintained it by letting politicians, clergy and army officers enrich themselves at the expense of the common people. The death of Alfonso in 1885 changed nothing since his wife acted as regent until 1902 when her son took the crown.

Near the end of the interregnum, Spain lost Cuba and the Philippines. Worse, the state coffers were empty and the army devastated by the loss of about 200,000 troops who perished from wounds and disease in 1898. Among the lower classes poverty and illiteracy led to increased frustration and anger that sought outlets in socialism and the militant trade union movement known as anarchosyndicalism. The unity of the country became threatened by separatist urges among the Basques in the north central region and among Catalonians in the northeast. These movements were not peaceful; on the contrary, terror and assassinations marked an increase of violence that reached a peak in 1909 when the army tried to draft young men in Barcelona to fight in Morocco. There followed five days of the most aggressive anarchy: Twenty-two churches and thirty-four convents were attacked and put to the torch. Hastily assembled troops shot nearly two hundred workers in street fighting.

These events were the prewar culmination of changes in people's attitudes and values. In the past, when Spanish peasants had fought against French invaders, they had taken arms to defend crown and church. To be Spanish meant to be Catholic. But Spain was not entirely isolated by the Pyrenees from liberal currents in the north. A century of crass exploitation by the church and its close alliance with reactionary political forces had aroused anticlericalism among the lower classes in town and country where anarchist ideas spread as rapidly as skepticism among the urbanized middle classes. Church attendance declined, civil marriage increased, and fewer infants were baptized in the largest cities. Spain and southern Italy were the proletariat of Europe.

Peripheral States: The Small Fry

These states were small in size, yet their economies were more modern than those of Mediterranean polities. Switzerland enjoyed the benefits of a mountain fortress, developing unperturbed by her larger neighbors. The federal cantons had enjoyed considerable self-rule after 1848. The central ones were Catholic but drove out bishops trying to enforce the pope's infallibility. About two-fifths of Swiss were Catholic, the remainder Calvinist. A new constitution in 1874 made civil marriage obligatory; it also allowed more extensive federal control over religious institutions, and over the cantons themselves.

Belgium was predominantly Catholic, which did not at all hinder industrial development. Middle-class parties controlled the legislature where Catholics and liberals fought over schools. Since the former predominated and ruled, even after manhood suffrage was approved in 1893, elementary education provided religious instruction, which, however, was not compulsory. Belgium was not conspicuous for social reform and workers there were less well off than those in Britain. There were several issues to turn attention in other directions. Apart from that of religious instruction, that involving language was divisive. Walloons, most of whom were upper class and Francophone, made certain that French was the official language. Flemish-speaking Belgians, however, threatened separation, and applied enough pressure to win official status for their language in the northern provinces in 1898.

This tiny state was the center of two contrasting phenomena: It was one of the most highly industrialized on a per capita basis in Europe; and its king, Leopold II, owned one of the largest colonial territories relative to his country's size. The Belgian Congo provided him with an enormous personal fortune. The Belgian Parliament took it over only when news leaked out revealing that the king allowed his agents and tenants complete authority over the natives and that they inflicted the most brutal conditions on their workers, using chains, the lash and torture to keep them in line. The scandal was even greater than the one in Britain when the opposition learned that Balfour, when Conservative prime minister, had allowed the introduction of coolie indentured laborers into South Africa to work the diamond mines. Liberals and Labor raised a howl but he did not change his decision.

The Netherlands were slower to industrialize than Belgium, relying more on trade and agriculture. With the vote limited to only 14 percent of the population, the forces concerned with social conditions were slow to appear. With a population two-thirds Calvinist and one-third Catholic, religion was as important an issue as in Belgium. Both religious groups allied against the liberal demand for secular education, and provided state subsidies for nondenominational public schools and denominational private schools. The latter drew more students than the former at both the elementary and secondary levels. Apparently the British rather than the French model guided them.

Scandinavian countries were all solidly Lutheran so there was no struggle over religious education. There was not much social conflict either. Rule by middle class parties was more benign than in Belgium and the Netherlands. There was ready acceptance of trade unions and humanitarian reforms by the parties in power. Norway separated from Sweden in 1905, a formal step that simply expanded the intensive autonomy Norwegians had enjoyed for decades. Norway was unique in that women won the right to vote and stand in elections in 1913.

Conclusions

Western Europe became the center of modernization in its fullest sense: political democracy, economic growth, legal equality, and social mobility. It was here that the privileged aristocracy, absolute monarchy and ecclesiastic control of culture were most decisively overcome. It is clear that the theory as an indicator of general tendencies has to be limited to Britain, France, Italy, Belgium, Norway, and Denmark. And even in these countries, there were limits to some aspect of the theory. Britain oppressed the Irish, France the native Algerians, Italy the Libyans, and Belgium the Congolese. Both Norway and Denmark failed to come through with sizable industrial growth, the Danes relying for their wealth on highly advanced agriculture, the Norwegians on fishing and forestry. Even in the more liberal and industrially advanced nations, there were sizable pockets of economic retardation: the highlands of Scotland, southwestern England, central and southwestern France, and southern Italy. The island of Sardinia was one of the most impoverished areas of Europe, rife with banditry and semifeudal oppression. And yet, the political institutions everywhere, reflecting economic growth and contributing to it, were radically different from those of 1815. Russia had most successfully resisted the general trend of history by 1914, but Clio was to punish such intransigence three years later and set in motion an entirely new trend running contrary to modernization theory.

18

Second Coming
of Socialism

Karl Marx: The Red Specter

When Marx fled Germany after the 1848 fiasco he settled in London where he spent the next thirty-five years of his life. In the *Communist Manifesto* he had warned that a red specter was haunting Europe; if such was the case it was not the Marxist specter; he was hardly known save to the police. Yet, when he died in 1883 his ideas formed the basis of a major socialist movement already in existence. He became one of the seminal thinkers of our period, ranking with Darwin, Pasteur, Dostoyevsky, Balzac, Byron, Saint-Simon, Ranke, J. S. Mill, and Freud. During most of his exile he lived in terrible poverty, relieved only when his longtime friend and collaborator, Friedrich Engels, scion of a wealthy family, provided him with an income. He imposed great sacrifices on his family, wept at the death of newborns who died of malnutrition and resulting disease. To his intimates he was loving and kindly; to his critics, even to his followers, he was biting and disdainful. Even when wrong his errors were grandiose, and received as gospel by thousands of disciples.

I cannot devote adequate space to analyze all of his phiosophy, and must restrict this section to his main ideas. First of all his approach was historical and much of his lucubration went into finding the laws of social and economic development over time. The cornerstone of his system was what he called the "mode of production." Society advanced as modes of production changed; thus men moved from an ancient or slave mode, to a medieval mode, to a capitalist, and eventually would enter into a communist mode. Unfortunately he never fully clarified the precise meaning of mode of production. It was primarily economic, and changes in technology, engineering skills, raw materials and labor organization were essential components. These were the "forces of production." But equally essential were the "relations of production," that is, the legal ownership or lack of it, of the forces. These two components formed the basis of society upon which rested a "superstructure" of ideologies, political formations, religion and culture in general, all of which were conditioned by the basis or substructure.

As a student of Hegel he picked up the dialectical method to explain change: first there appeared the thesis, which in time generated its opposite, the antithesis. These two sort of fought it out and from their struggle emerged a new condition, displaying aspects of both but different, a synthesis. Put simply: The medieval or serf mode of production was challenged by the capitalist mode and from their conflict there would emerge a new synthesis, communism combining the collective facet of medieval society and the high productive capacity of capitalist society. Unlike earlier socialists Marx did not try to describe the future life under communism, save on one occasion when he mentioned that it would offer each individual a range of choices that equaled Fourier's imagination.

Marx spent long hours in the library of the British Museum gathering data to explain why capitalism, after its triumph over feudalism, was itself doomed. His cornerstone in this endeavor was the labor theory of value, devised by Ricardo early in the century. Marx's interpretation posited that human labor and only human labor created value. Of course the market value of a commodity did not result from the efforts of one or two workers, but from the "socially necessary" or average labor time of all employees in a plant who were hired to produce value. Marx divided value into two parts: that which was required to enable the worker to live at a subsistence level. The creation of this value, say, required four hours. But the worker continued for another ten hours and produced "surplus value," which the employer, a mean, greedy monster according to Marx, appropriated for his own use. He was really a robber of the value generated by the exploited worker who was denied the full value of his efforts. Marx spared no invectives when denouncing the exploiter and his system; he did not view the capitalist as an owner managing his own mill, working long hours and reinvesting to expand. He saw him rather as a rentier, idle all the day and living in luxury at the workers' expense.

But Marx also pictured him as caught in a round of keen competition, having to mechanize and innovate desperately to stay in business, a contradictory portrait of the idle capitalist. Regardless, the man was caught on the horns of a dilemma: To survive he had to introduce machines to produce; however, in doing so, he reduced necessary human labor time, the source of his surplus value. The result was that with an increase of the mass of value, its rate declined, and this declining rate was driving lesser capitalists into bankruptcy; they were being pushed down by a few large monopolists into the proletariat. The direction of society, in consequence, was a diminishing number of rich bourgeois, and a growing number of impoverished proletarians. Unable to rise above subsistence, and pushed below it as recession worsened, the wretched masses would spontaneously rise up in revolt, overthrow the few remaining capitalists and then follow the lead of the communists toward a new life. Such a schematic course of events sounds more like a fairy tale than an analysis of capitalist development. As things turned out it was, but it was one of the most appealing facets of a mix of ideas that became known as Marxism. For Marx there was no magic, no fairy godmother, just the undeniable laws of history working themselves out through conflict.

Another popular aspect was Marx's proclamation, probably derived from Guizot, that all the past is the history of class conflict: slave against master, serf against lord, worker against capitalist—unending until the final inevitable upheaval. And this final revolution would make itself. Marx and Engels wrote that they were simply the midwives of the new order whose birth would occur as a natural ordained process. They insisted that no revolution could be successful before its time, which explains why Marx was angrily critical of Blanqui and anarchists. All societies must pass through the necessary phases before they were ready for the final reckoning; all the resources of capitalism must be exhausted before it would reach its highest stage and become ripe for overthrow. By this reckoning, Great Britain was to become the battleground and Marx along with Engels sought to penetrate the British working class. Marx's contacts led to his invitation to address the inaugural congress of the first Workingman's International in 1864. But neither capitalists nor workers thought of him as a pioneering theorist; they hardly knew of his existence.

Organization of Labor: Great Britain

This title, the organization of labor, had become the battle cry of artisans in the spring of 1848. It was taken from the cover of Louis Blanc's little book, and he, as head of a special commission, had assembled representatives of most trades, to find a solution to their problems: low wages, long hours, and joblessness. At this time most workers were craftsmen employed in shops of various sizes. The true proletarians, people of limited skills tending machines in large establishments, consisted largely of women and adolescents in textiles, and more skilled male laborers in the iron and machine works making locomotives and rails for the rapidly expanding railway networks.

Very few thinkers and activists gave much attention to organizing female workers because most theorists still believed that women should stay in and maintain the home and raise children. For men, there were two ways to organize their labor: trade unions and political parties. The two were not one and the same, nor necessarily connected. Early socialists gave little, if any, attention to unions, the exception being Robert Owen who set up the Grand National Consolidated Trades Union in 1834. It came the closest to combining unionism and socialism, but soon died for lack of support. In Britain labor organizations were legalized in 1825. But what was declared legal by Parliament was not necessarily recognized as such by the courts. Royal judges looked upon worker groups as entities in restrain of trade and therefore not legal, so that union members remained in a kind of limbo between recognition by Parliament and non-recognition by tribunals. Justices were particularly ready to deal with strikers, peaceful or not, and many an unhappy union leader found himself packed off to jail, or worse, sent off to the Australian penal colony.

This problem did not exist on the Continent where labor or even nonlabor organizations were outside the law. Guilds were recognized east of the Elbe, but they were entities of master craftsmen who employed journeymen as wage workers. These latter often belonged to tolerated, but not legalized groups called *compagnonnages* in France. Officially, all trade groups in France were outlawed by the Le Chapelier law of 1791. But while this statute was rigorously enforced against unions, called *syndicats ouvriers* in France and *Gewerkverein* in Germany, it was not against associations of employers. With the rapid growth of industry and transport, a new laboring class came into being, a true factory proletariat. It did not entirely displace the traditional craftsmen, some of whom succumbed to competition from mechanized production, but many of whom survived by concentration on the making of goods, usually luxuries, that enjoyed an expanding market as wealth increased.

During the years of plenty after 1850, workers and their leaders put aside revolutionary yearnings to concentrate on more effective union organization. The early forms of socialism were dead, and newer ones were still in gestation in the minds of thinkers. The British flirtation with Chartism was long over; in fact, unionists had not actively supported the Chartists. Most of them were highly skilled and now concentrated on limited aims: to resist the worst forms of legal and industrial oppression by setting up trade unions with membership limited to the skilled. This was the New Model unionism, charging high dues, filling treasuries, hiring professional personnel, even lawyers to defend them against hostile judges. These were national organizations with branches in the major industrial and mining centers, with headquarters in London. Their general secretaries began to meet and plan together. They all agreed that their aim was to improve working conditions and win a larger portion of national wealth for their members. And this was to be done by bargaining rather than picketing, certainly not by revolt. The very idea of a general strike had no appeal. Their strength lay in stone masons, iron molders, steam engine makers, and so forth. A prime example was the Amalgamated Society of Engineers headed by Will

Newton. The members were not graduate engineers, but mechanics, skilled men who had passed through a long apprenticeship. Societies of this sort had considerable bargaining power and were generally successful. Their power was enhanced in 1868 when their leaders, called either the "Junta" or the "Clique," organized the first Trades Union Congress. Henceforth during each annual meeting, elected delegates put together a program of action for the coming year. It was now, when a parliamentary committee was set up, that unionism took on political significance as a pressure group.

Working with the Liberal party, they induced Gladstone to pass the Trade Union Act of 1871 which gave unions adequate legal status: No union could be regarded as criminal because it was in restraint of trade. Then the Criminal Law Amendment Act allowed unions to sue in courts for recovery of funds stolen by an employee. Nothing was done to protect unionists when on strike however. Judges sent picketers to jail merely for informing workers that a strike was underway. In 1874, therefore, union leaders struck a bargain with Conservatives. The result was new legislation that permitted peaceful strikes, but "peaceful persuasion" of nonstrikers was not won until 1906.

The complacency that took hold of organized labor was considerably dissipated by the long depression of the 1870s. Strikes to resist wage reductions were not successful, and both skilled and unskilled workers suffered setbacks in the 1880s. However, a new era began as the so-called "new unionism" made headway. It meant simply the organization in one union of men belonging to different trades. The industrial union took its place beside the narrower craft union. Its first success was a huge strike of dock workers who managed to win some improvement of their abominable working conditions. There followed a great increase in union membership and of work stoppages. The worst year, 1893, saw 30.4 million work days lost due to strikes. When miners were locked out, workers began to call for a general strike, a notion that the craft unions had earlier rejected. There even took place the beginnings of unionization among women when their matchmakers organization went on strike for safety measures against sulfur poisoning, and won their strike. There were also women in some of the textile laborers unions. Their number, however, never grew significantly. They held back because their wages were too low to enable them to pay dues based on men's income. Women often held more than one job, or worked irregular hours to take care of their children and perform household duties, which left them with either no time or not enough concern to take part in union activities. Finally their husbands discouraged them from joining. For men, the aim was to earn enough to support their families and keep their wives at home. While most women were employed in textiles, many worked in shops where conditions were as dangerous as matchmaking: Those in mirror manufacturing were exposed to noxious chemicals; in cigarette and cigar rolling they inhaled tobacco dust. More women than men suffered from tuberculosis. Small wonder that unionists wanted to keep their wives and daughters at home. The skilled could do so; the growing army of semiskilled and unskilled could not. The government passed laws protective of women and adolescents, but did nothing to improve wages.

Trade union leaders by the 1890s finally decided the time had come to organize their own party. On the whole, the Liberals were sympathetic to wage earners, and among its ranks were the "Lib-Labs," labor members who were Liberal and voted for bills favorable to labor. Keir Hardie had founded the Independent Labor party, but in 1895 all twenty-eight candidates lost; workers simply voted for Liberals. Only when the courts struck at the very existence of their unions did laborers decide to go it alone. In 1901 the Taff Vale Railroad sued the striking union, not individual members, for damage to its property. The judges upheld the company, a precedent that could drain union treasuries and destroy them. The House of Lords upheld the decision. The result was a massive labor turnout in the 1906 elections and a stunning defeat for Conservatives. The Liberals benefited enormously. The newly organized Labor party sent some thirty members into the House of Commons, a small victory but promising for the future. This Labor party was the creation of the trade unions and created precisely to defend them against the courts, not on the picket lines, but in the seat of legislative power. New laws protected union treasuries. As the creature of unions the Labor party was not a truly socialist organization. Its program did not call for an end to private property; it did not even allow individuals to join. Its membership consisted chiefly of trade unions, and organizations such as the Fabian Society, formed in the 1880s by Sidney and Beatrice Webb. It was really a brain trust of intellectuals like George Bernard Shaw. Its watchword was "gradualism," that is, the peaceful takeover of private business by public corporations, beginning at the municipal level with the acquisition of public utilities. Because many large cities already owned water, gas, lighting, and transport, the Fabians believed that public ownership was on the march. There was no need for a revolution.

Fragmented Socialism: France

Revolution was the watchword of the Continental left, and the French, with a long tradition of social upheaval, took it seriously. With the same skill and energy they used to erect street barricades they elaborated theories of social and economic reorganization, all anticapitalist.

The contagion was such that worker syndicates could not resist. The survivors of the Commune of 1871 recovered quickly enough, albeit there were fewer of them. As early as 1876 a labor congress assembled but little was accomplished until 1879 when the economy was in the throes of a serious recession. Delegates to a congress in Marseilles voted overwhelmingly to set up a socialist organization. The problem was, what kind of socialism? Here they could not agree, and the 1880s witnessed a germination of theories that sprouted like weeds almost overnight. It would be too tedious to cover them all. The moat important were the *Possibilistes* led by Paul Brousse, a medical doctor and a moderate who called for all the social reforms that seemed possible of rapid enactment, beginning, like the Fabians, with municipal ownership. His more radical critics referred to his scheme as "gas and water" socialism. As a political party it did not count for much and eventually split. More successful with voters were the Independent socialists, founded by Benoît Malon who was more or less a latter day disciple of Louis Blanc. In the 1890s leadership was assumed by Jean Jaurès, an ex-philosophy professor turned politician. He began his career as a moderate republican and ended it on the extreme left well before he was brutally assassinated by a fanatical nationalist in 1914. He moved leftward because he became convinced that social justice was impossible under capitalism. A large-hearted Southerner, he was an inspiring orator and an effective leader. The Independents called for the national ownership of transport, large industry, finance and communications.

Marxism penetrated France in the 1880s largely through the efforts of Jules Guesde and Paul Lafargue, Marx's son-in-law. They set up the Labor party as a highly centralized organization, with Guesde as absolute head after the suicide of Lafargue. Its politics were based on class struggle and an eventual revolutionary seizure of power in accord with the teaching of Karl Marx. Unlike the other parties which depended heavily on the "red belt" around Paris the Guesdists' electoral base lay in heavily industrialized northern districts. Finally there were the followers of Blanqui, naturally committed to revolutionary action without much thought to strategy or goals, convinced that the people would rise up spontaneously when called to build barricades. They usually sided with Marxists when doctrinal conflicts arose.

From the 1893 election to 1914, socialist parties steadily improved their organization. In fact, it was only the political groups of the socialist left that formed true party formations with dues, departmental sections and annual congresses to debate and vote on programs. And to subsidize official newspapers. The *Revue Socialiste*, founded by Malon, was open to all theorists and became a highly respected organ. The 1893 elections returned thirty-seven socialists, most of whom eventually rallied to a new party founded in 1905.

Unity had, after much hesitation, been almost forced on the factions by the Second Workingman's International. Founded in 1889 it had grown exponentially as socialist parties arose in nearly all countries. Since they all believed in the brotherhood of workers they looked to the International as a league of socialist parties, the means of reconciling their differences and uniting their forces. Times and the law had changed; socialists were no longer outlaws, save in Bismarck's Germany until 1890, and danger came less from classic conservatives than from extreme nationalists, the type of fanatic who murdered Jaurès.

The International brought unity, more or less; it also imposed certain policies on member parties. In 1899 Alexandre Millerand, a prominent independent socialist, joined the ministry set up to save the Republic from nationalists and clericals. This ministry contained the general who had crushed the Commune of 1871. Acting on his own, Millerand did not consult his party, a serious breach of discipline. That and entering a bourgeois government raised the issue of "ministerialism." Should socialists collaborate with nonsocialist and even antisocialist politicians? Jaurès defended Millerand; Guesde attacked him and brought the issue before the next congress of the International. There the Germans condemned any collaboration as a betrayal of class conflict. Millerand was condemned and ejected from the party, ministerialism was equally condemned. The Germans had spoken and the French obeyed in the interest of unity.

The French gave to their new party the clumsy name, Parti Socialiste, Section Française de l'Internationale Ouvrière, but everyone called it simply the SFIO or Socialist party. Unity in this case was more apparent then real. Its program was largely Marxist, emphasizing class struggle and revolution. Jaurès reluctantly bowed to these imperatives, accepted the red flag of the Marxists and sang the International. But he and most socialists were solid patriots, and those running in rural districts resoundingly reminded their peasant crowds that a socialist regime would not take over their small farms, only large estates and divide these among them. In France no one could resist the peasant hunger for land, which explains why the so-called move to the left was really a form of directionless marching in place. I described already what happened to the Radical party.

Many artisan workers distrusted socialist politicians. Artisans were a curious lot: Eager to preserve their crafts, a goal they identified as social consciousness, and individualistic to the point of anarchism. Given the huge number of them concentrated in the Parisian basin, they inevitably carried major weight in the reorganization of craft unions following the Commune. These unions or *syndicats*, much put off by squabbling socialists and their numerous factions, steered clear of politics and were searching for a way to attain working class goals of reform without resort to the "games" of politicians. In the early 1890s there emerged precisely the man to guide them around the governmental mire. Fernand Pelloutier, a sickly but energetic organizer and thinker. He and his disciples took over the *Bourses du travail*, municipal employment agencies, and transformed them into labor centers with rooms for union offices, libraries for propaganda and information, space for converting workers to the revolutionary doctrine of social upheaval by means of a general strike. This drastic step, many believed, need not become a violent act, but regardless of its form, it was the nonpolitical means of abolishing government and transferring power to workers unions. In other words trade unions would drastically change their character as defenders of labor interests, take the offensive, destroy capitalism by refusing to serve its labor needs, and finally give birth to a new anarchist society based on artisan labor. In 1894 he created the Federation of Trade Syndicates.

The following year trade unions, legalized in 1884, organized the Confédération Générale du Travail. Influenced by the *bourses* this General Confederation of Labor declared itself a revolutionary formation and would have nothing to do with political parties, least of all the Marxists. Its membership included only industrial unions to avoid the narrow interests of purely craft affiliations. Its anarchist tendencies were reinforced when it fused with Pelloutier's federation in 1902, after his death. In its congress at Amiens in 1906 it called for direct action by workers to attain a nearly stateless society based on the local *syndicats* as units of social organization and production.

It would be an error to believe that the CGT's program represented the aims of all workers or their unions. The very large trade associations of the north, with thousands of members, had no more votes in annual congresses than the small craft unions of the Parisian basin. The small units, fully devoted to anarchism, outnumbered and outvoted the big units whose leaders were typical unionists, that is, generally republican and concerned with bread-and-butter issues. After Léon Jouhaux was elected general-secretary of the CGT in 1909 the anarchosyndicalist elements in its program were submerged into the fairly typical union demands just mentioned. For the more traditionalistic union leader the idea of a general strike was "general bunk." During the decades since 1890 many workers ignored the siren calls of anarchists and voted for socialist candidates, yet, some of the old program remained indelible, raising the level of abstention and weakening the impact of socialist deputies in the Chamber. This tendency was unfortunate. The SFIO was not able to exercise power commensurate with its potential electorate. Given that it was devoted to international peace it may have been able to prevent the outbreak of war in 1914. The failure here, however, lay in German hands.

The Model Marxists: Germany and Russia

The style of socialist politics and labor organization varied from state to state, depending in part on the level of economic development, the degree of political freedom, the size and nature of the working class, and cultural tradition. In Britain the large, stable trade unions dominated the working class and created a political party to defend its interests. This procedure was in keeping with Britain's cultural tradition of pragmatism, large labor groupings and an advanced economy. In France the division between the CGT and the SFIO resulted from the age-old doctrinal splits among socialist thinkers, the divisive power of Gallic rationalization, and the persistence of numerous artisan workers and their leaning toward anarchic solutions.

In contrast, Germans combined the cultural idealist tradition and found in Marxist philosophical categories an "idealism turned on its head," with the rigorous discipline of work and home life so prevalent in Prussia. The party that emerged the strongest owed its survival to dedicated leadership, tight organization, intellectual rigor, and an unrelentingly rigid corps of theorists that prided itself as the guardian of true or orthodox Marxism, and it enjoyed the blessing of Friedrich Engels who lived into the 1890s. Unlike Britain where union leaders created their party, the German Social Democrats set up the major trade unions to win over the votes of laboring men.

The first successful attempt to organize workers was not a Marxist convert, but a talented, flamboyant ambitious Jew named Ferdinand Lassalle. He undoubtedly picked up his socialist notions from Louis Blanc, but partially drained them of their democratic content and looked to the state of Prussia to inaugurate socialist cooperatives. He was secretly negotiating with Bismarck since he too, was antiliberal. In 1863 he organized the General Association of German Workers, a combined political party and labor union.

In contrast, two Marxists from Bavaria, Wilhelm Liebknech and August Bebel, formed a social labor party in 1869 at Eisenach. The two organs were at odds until Lassalle's death in a duel, then they merged on a program that included the deceased notion of the state. Before long, however, the Marxists gained complete control and kept it during the twelve years that the party was outlawed by Bismarck. It survived, assumed the name German Social Democratic party (SPD), and steadily increased its representatives in the Reichstag. When the Kaiser abolished Bismarck's antisocialist laws the party became the largest Marxist organization in Europe. Karl Kautsky, founder and editor of *Die Neue Zeit*, became the keeper of Marxist purity, and to his critics, its chief theoretician-theologian. He fought off those who wanted to add an agrarian element to protect peasants, as Jaurès did in France, and as the revisionists proposed in Germany.

The revisionists, led by Edward Bernstein, wanted to transform the party from a self-proclaimed revolutionary movement into an organization seeking reform by legal, legislative means. He was certainly influenced by the British Fabians during his exile in England. His concept of socialism was ethical; a collective society would come about because it was morally justifiable, not because it was predetermined by economic laws. Although continuing to believe he was a Marxist he revised, really rejected, most of Marx's basic premises: The poorer were not becoming poorer; monopoly capital was not destroying the lesser bourgeois because new careers were increasing their numbers; the workers were not suffering more but less as laws curtailed hours and labor unions pushed wages upward. Even economic and financial crises were less severe than in the past.

Revisionism, seen as a right-wing deviation, was severely condemned in party congresses after 1900. But this was willful blindness to trends both in the world economy and within the labor-socialist movement. The majority delegates to party meetings were proclaiming their orthodox goals: class struggle, a coming revolution, the triumph of pure Marxism. The truth was quite different as the new century opened. Power in the party lay not in the hands or heads of thinkers, but in those of party and trade union bureaucrats whose main concern was sound administration, discipline, and well-filled treasuries to pay their salaries. They were no longer the labor militants of the years of struggle; the youngest among them had never suffered imprisonment and exile. They were white collar types, hardly different from government or corporate executives and clerks. A strange reversal had occurred: The revolutionary party that had created unions to win labor voters had been taken over by the huge trade unions whose chiefs had effectively pulled the Marxist teeth of the party. The final tooth came out when party leaders agreed that the party could not deviate from accepted practices without the consent of the trade union executives. In angry opposition a left revolutionary wing emerged, inspired by Rosa Luxemburg. But, like the revisionists, its policies were condemned. Social democratic parties arose in most European countries, modeled more or less on that of Germany, the largest and most efficiently organized.

The least typical was that of Russia. Soon after its creation in the 1890s it split into two hostile factions: the Mensheviks who were more or less moderate Marxists, and the Bolsheviks who fell under the dictatorial leadership of Lenin. From Switzerland where he lived in exile, he laid down the party line regarding organization and strategy. The Bolsheviks were a revolutionary cluster, limited in membership to persons ready to devote their lives and their time to the party, who were fully committed to its mission and convinced that it could do no wrong. The party, not the individual member, was of prime importance. The program was uncompromising in its emphasis on revolution—before 1905 opposition groups had no legal institution to express their concerns, and the Duma created in that year had no place for vigorous resistance to the tsarist regime. In Russia, Marxists had to be revolutionary if they were to remain faithful to their traditions. Mensheviks believed that Russia had to pass through a capitalist phase; Lenin, however, revised Marx to the extent that he argued that the capitalist phase had already run its course, and that men of true faith could seize power by sheer will, a concept known as voluntarism and condemned by the orthodox as heresy. Yet it was the addition that Lenin made to Marxism and left as his heritage, along with the dictatorship of the proletariat, to wit, of the party, after victory.

Socialism of various types had made notable progress since 1870. The Marxist variety had come to dominate but nowhere did it become a ruling party legally or otherwise. It is odd that it scarcely penetrated the British Isles. Henry Hyndman had organized a Social Democratic Federation, claiming it was in accord with Marx's teaching. Marx thought otherwise and made no secret of his contempt for Hyndman whose influence was negligible. So was Marx's. When he was buried in Highgate cemetery, British labor hardly shed a tear.

19

Apex of Capitalism

Industrial Balance: Great Britain

We have already observed that the military balance of power shifted to central Europe in 1871. The new German Empire henceforth could deploy the strongest army in Europe, and it rapidly acquired the economic foundation to maintain such a formidable force. Britain, of course, remained the prime naval and maritime power, but as the century ended her economy revealed the first signs of weakness and it became a serious strain to maintain a navy second to none. Worse, Kaiser William II deliberately set out to challenge both her economic and maritime supremacy.

Now the British economy did not suffer absolute decline. It was adversely affected by the crisis of 1873, a result of excessive railway construction in the United States, which struck her financial institutions. Germany was harder hit by this down turn because the French indemnity payments had flooded stock exchanges and there was wild speculation in railroad shares that lost most of their value when the bubble burst. Both British industry and trade were more seriously hurt by the steady fall of prices from the late 1870s to the mid-1890s. France shared that suffering but sheltered home markets with steadily rising tariffs. There was in Britain a rising clamor for protective tariffs and imperial preference, led by Joseph Chamberlain. He had started his political career as a left-wing Liberal, but he bolted to the Conservatives as he became the champion of colonialism and urged the formation of a free trade zone enclosing Britain and all her territorial holdings. It is doubtful that such a sham could improve the home economy; the colonies could not absorb all of the vast array of goods coming out of factories, nor could the domestic market. As always, the stimulus of British industry was foreign markets, and these included Europe, North and South America, India, and finally other colonies. Unfortunately, many of these foreign markets were being either curtailed or closed by the return of tariff protection as national industrial groups pressured their governments to save them from outside competition.

British industrialists were not very skilled at finding ways to overcome such obstacles. At the highest levels there were brilliant engineers, but there were not enough of them. And there was a paucity of men with sufficient up-to-date technical training to employ new scientific methods. It is ironic that Englishmen and Scots had carried the know-how of mechanics to the Continent in the early 1800s, but in the late decades they had to import German engineers to retool for new types of production and transport. Overemphasis on classical education had delayed the spread of technical schooling, and the British were now at a disadvantage. Factory owners were slow to accept a higher degree of mechanization in the manufacture of products other than textiles and iron. Unfortunately exports of textiles steadily declined, and this weakening sector was historically an important stimulus of machine production. In this latter category there were increased sales of machines—spinning and weaving devices—to foreign countries that were building their own cotton, silk, and woolen factories, with the intention of competing with the Lancashire mills; Britain was equipping her rivals in the textile markets. Even in metals they failed to realize the advantages of steel over malleable iron for railway tracks, locomotives and precision tools. Articles such as typewriters, bicycles, automobiles, dynamos, clocks, harvesters, printing presses, cash registers, engines, and so forth, required more efficient processes, such as assembly lines that were too upsetting both for labor and management. Clever workers, frustrated by a lack of promotion and recognition, left for the United States where they could advance to managerial positions in a fluid industrial structure.

Management was also less dynamic. Many family firms were in the third and even fourth generation. Consequently there was nepotism, with important positions held by less-than-competent persons who were more given to the pursuit of golf balls than new inventions and production technologies. Inventors, like Graham Bell, followed the workers to the United States, and foreign inventors rarely came to Britain to exploit their discoveries. The English advanced prodigiously after 1850 in coal production (see Table 19–1).

By 1914, however, her miners' output had fallen behind that of the United States, and the diggers and haulers began to feel the hot breath of the

Table 19–1 Coal Production of Great Powers, 1850–1914 (million tons)

	1850	1880	1900	1914
Britain	57	149	228	292
France	5	19	33	40
Germany	6	59	149	277
United States	—	65	244	455
Dual Monarchy	1	15	39	47
Russia	—	3	16	36

Germans. The British export of coal fueled the machines of Continental competitors, hardly a blessing. Worse, British mines were old by modern standards, and less productive, because coal seams were narrow and hard to work. This factor, combined with the greater depth of shafts, raised the cost of extraction. Normally, prices would compensate for costs, but competition discouraged price rises, therefore the rate of profit fell.

The increased reliance on steel posed difficulties for the British. Its production required types of iron ore whose deposits were less extensive in Britain than in Germany and the United States. Table 19–2 reveals why the English, once the biggest exporter of iron products, had both to import steel, and lost out in markets demanding steel objects.

Britain's disadvantage was more than paucity of ore, it was having begun early and invested heavily in the technology to make malleable iron. Germany and the United States started out with the new technology that, once more ironically, had originated in England with the Gilchrist-Thomas furnace! British mill owners were not mentally willing to scrap their old foundries to invest in the new, especially as the new required much larger plants to operate efficiently. Now it is important to observe again that Britain's decline was only relative, not absolute.

Table 19–2 Steel Production of Great Powers, 1880–1914 (million tons)

	1880	1890	1900	1914
Germany	0.7	2.3	6.7	14.0
Britain	1.3	3.6	5.0	6.5
France	0.4	0.7	1.6	3.5
Russia	—	0.4	1.5	4.1
Dual Monarchy	—	0.5	1.2	2.7
United States	1.3	4.3	10.0	32.0

The Small Producers' Paradise: France

The same was true of France. If production per capita is used as a measure, the French ran about neck and neck with her neighbors. However, it was not per capita but total production that counted in the hierarchy of industrial nations and French manufacturers tended to have a protectionist rather than an entrepreneurial mentality. They had complained bitterly about Napoleon III's free-trade policy, and they rallied to the Third Republic because its rural and small town politicians led the way toward high tariffs during the depressed years of the 1880s and early 1890s. There developed a fairly close relation between government and the economy—a widespread phenomenon in Europe as the old ideal of laissez faire was proclaimed from factory tops but ignored within. Official subsidies along with protection from foreign competition became regular practices.

The French economy suffered a minor setback resulting from the huge indemnity imposed by the Germans, and a major one from the loss of textile mills in Alsace. Yet the French were a rich people. They exported capital as though they had an inexhaustible supply. In the 1890s the *Progressistes* ministries encouraged such exports, especially to Russia, the ally they were seeking in order to end the nation's diplomatic isolation. More than 25 percent of foreign investments went to Russia, and after 1905 French loans enabled the tsar to ignore the Duma because he was financially independent. No wonder Nicholas II was willing to salute the revolutionary tunes of the *Marseillaise.* Apart from the imperial coffers, Russian industry, transport and oil drilling benefited from foreign, especially French, investments, and paid high interest rates.

It is doubtful that the French economy suffered from a shortage of capital. Changing technology in metals had the same effect in France as in Britain. During the crisis years inefficient foundries closed, but there was ample capital for the larger steel firms of the de Wendel and Schneider families that adopted new technologies. Smaller plants simply did not seek more investment capital, resorting as far as possible to self-financing out of profits, a very old practice. They would have been hard put to find lenders anyway, because another old practice was for banks to prefer to invest in government bonds. They earned less, but ran fewer risks.

It was not capital but domestic customers that became another economic retardant. From the 1870s the population just about stopped growing, increasing not above 10 percent. Of course people had more money to spend. Even peasants, in order to update equipment, began to pull their gold francs out of old socks they had stuffed in a mattress. And before 1900 more than 40 percent of the active population was engaged in farming. Unfortunately more than half the cultivated holdings were too small to provide a comfortable living, and among these were the plots of numerous farm workers whose land merely supplemented low wages. The result was a large population with too little income to buy expensive industrial products. Moreover, agriculture was beset by the blight that struck the vineyards from the 1870s to the mid-1890s. Then came a surplus of wine, with cascading prices and severe privation. Because roughly 7 to 8 percent of the total population was involved with grape and wine production, as well as with wine sales, buying power for industrial products was limited. And as before, retail outlets remained small, family units, with low turnover and high prices, which further dampened purchasing. When war broke out in 1914, France was not prepared either financially or demographically to stand up to Germany.

The New Colossus: Germany

The new German Empire was born with its economy already in adolescence. The advanced age was due to the industrial headway in Prussia during the preceding two decades. The beginning did not seem auspicious because the French indemnity rapidly entered the money market, the bloodstream of any economy, provoked inflation and wild speculation in railroads and joint-stock companies venturing into mining, metals, any activity that promised quick profits. The Germans refer to this feverish search for a fast mark and the rapid expansion of plants to unprecedented size as the age of the *Kolossal*. It resembles the railroad mania of Britain in the 1840s. As then, unscrupulous German promoters corrupted ministerial officials to win favors, such as an end to a law requiring government approval of new companies. Journalists were bribed to write articles favoring their schemes. This was a forerunner of the Panama Scandal in France some twenty years later. But in 1873 the results were catastrophic. The speculation mania had widened to include Vienna and it was there that the stock market crashed on May 8. There were 300 bankruptcies in a few days, accompanied by an epidemic of suicides. The crisis then spread to Germany with identical results. Thousands of small investors lost all their savings. Everywhere sales fell, along with prices, wages, and employment. This was one of the worst recessions of the century. Recovery required three years.

After it the German economy took off on wings of coal, steel, chemicals and electricity. These were the new dynamos of economic progress, and the Germans excelled in them all. Textiles, so important in the initial Industrial Revolution, languished. Entrepreneurs took full advantage of the empire's natural resources: coal in the Ruhr, iron ore in Lorraine, potassium in wide areas. The French excelled in the new field of automobiles, whereas the Germans excelled in ship building using steel, and steam turbines, plus the most up-to-date tools and machines in the building process. Thanks to a modern merchant marine, exporters set out to conquer overseas markets. Thanks also to the best system of engineering, science and technical education, employers could hire a most knowledgeable work force. Because many firms emphasized research and development, they built advanced scientific laboratories as an integral part of the factory and staffed them with university trained researchers. A good part of the personnel in these plants were white-collar professionals. There was no "great depression" in central Europe during the 1880s and early 1890s; that was largely confined to the areas west of the Rhineland.

One reason for this was the active role played by national as well as local authorities who actively promoted economic growth: industry, agriculture, forestry, and trade were provided with excellent communications, transport by roads, rail, canals, and deepened rivers. Public undertakings included railroads, mines, ironworks, shipyards and various factories. These enterprises came to one-tenth of the national total in 1907. In the early years of the new century between 20 and 25 percent of investments in Germany were made by public authorities and nationalized concerns. Nowhere else was the public sector so large, and it contributed to general economic advances. Clearly the hands-off policy of Britain and, to a lesser extent France, was not widely applied in the lands of the Kaiser. Moreover investment banks were far more aggressively involved in management and planning than elsewhere. And banking executives snapped their ringed fingers at free trade, for it was they who occupied numerous board seats of companies they backed financially. In fact, they sat on boards in numerous concerns, forming interlocking directorates as a step toward forming cartels. It was through such practices that entrepreneurs obtained the financing they needed to build vast industrial empires. Werner Siemens, Emile Rathenau, August Thyssen, Albert Ballin were the most dynamic. Bismarck and his advisors urged the formation of cartels to cut down competition, maintain prices and avoid crises like that of 1873. He wanted no mass unemployment, no collapse of stock markets or financial scandals. He sought to win over businessmen with such favors just as he sought to win over laborers with social security. He was far more successful with the former than the latter. As it turned out, workers rallied to the big trade unions in search of protection and some sense of identity. Only unions of massive size could stand up to such colossal businesses.

The Peripheral States: Slow and Not Always Sure

The economic gap between the central core of industrialized areas in northwestern and now we must add north central Europe, on one hand, and the periphery states on the other, widened around the turn of the century. There were several exceptions which resulted mainly from the discovery of new sources of power. For example, oil in Romania. This product had been used for lamps since the Middle Ages. Landowners, being chiefly concerned with growing wheat, showed no interest in creating an industry to produce oil for lighting interiors, or even for outdoor oil lamps when cities began to illuminate their streets. Not until the invention of gasoline powered motors and automobiles made their appearance did foreign know-how and capital take over the fields for large-scale development in the 1890s. The same occurred in the Caucasus fields near Baku in southern Russia and in Austrian Galicia. Because the other regions of Europe had no significant oil filled strata, they readily imported their needs from these areas and the United States. The local populations of oil-producing states found some menial employment, but most of the profits went to foreign investors.

The discovery of hydroelectric power had a more beneficial effect for areas with swift, permanent rivers and streams. Electricity as a source of energy could not be sent off to foreign lands; it had to be used within a given radius. Benefiting from the streams of the Alps and Apennines, Italy began seriously to industrialize in the 1890s. Its efforts, however were largely confined to cotton and silk textiles in Lombardy and Piedmont. The other two props of the Industrial Revolution, iron and coal, did not make much headway before 1914. The government subsidized a few small foundries that profited from turning out only the finest steel, such as that used for medical instruments and scientific equipment. Railroads were laid even before political unity, but did not stimulate a true industrial take off. They did not even bridge the cultural gaps between north and south. Below the Po Valley, and especially south of the Tiber was a land of noble-owned estates, scarcely productive, and a mass of grossly impoverished peasants who had to save ferociously merely to buy the shirts for their backs or the black dresses that barefoot women wore day in, day out. The only escape was emigration and millions took that route. Fewer people left the north where an industrial take off was occurring in automobiles, engineering, metallurgy, and chemicals.

As for Spain, save for the northeast, it was a land full of religious faith combined with despair and hopelessness. By 1900 there were no longer any colonies to exploit. Here too there was an impoverished south.

The land of the Dual Monarchy was highly diversified, the German and Czech areas considerably wealthier than those that dipped toward the Balkan Peninsula and Poland. Railroads and the Danube River offered some stimulus to industrial growth. This consisted largely of consumer goods industries like textiles and food processing where the labor force was mainly female. After 1890 the northeast section of Austria produced an industrial boom stimulated by metals and engineering firms. The boom was not really a take-off because a market with a high level of buying power did not exist save in the city and region around Vienna. Hungary had no industry save some flour milling. A major drawback were the national rivalries. The Empire built roads and railroads to hold its disparate parts together; unfortunately its outlays were the result of ethnic pressures rather than that of a rational plan to link industrial centers to raw materials and markets.

In Russia, industrialization was largely dependent on the influx of foreign capital, led by the French franc. The groundwork was laid by Count S. Witte, finance minister from 1891 to 1903 when he was forced out of office by conservatives distrustful of modernization. During these twelve years he used state funds and borrowed money to build railroads, then raised tariffs to stimulate a machine building industry. An additional inducement was tax remission, which he preferred to outright subsidies, guaranteed profits and government orders paid for at above-market prices. Foreign loans were made available through state banks whose number, a mere 871 in 1890, rose to 4,781 in 1900.

To raise part of the money he needed, he resorted to higher direct taxes and required peasants to pay them in the autumn; this forced them to market their crops when supply was plentiful and prices low. He also placed burdensome imposts on salt, tobacco, matches, lamp oil, vodka, and sugar. He mercilessly forced peasants to pay their redemption dues. "The budget and the balance of payments came to depend on the peasant not eating his fill." His policies were harsh, but no worse than those of English enclosing landlords or Anglican landowners in Ireland. And he got results, as the above tables make clear.

Save for Belgium, the other outlying areas of Europe were predominantly rural. The Netherlands was active in trade but slow to industrialize. Balkan states were not even as modernized as Spain, and Scandinavia prospered largely on forest products, save Sweden where high grade steel and electrical machinery were symbols of economic modernization.

Russia benefited from her economic backwardness after midcentury by borrowing technology and management know-how from already-industrialized nations. Despite the ambivalence toward modernization of many high officials, and shared by the tsars, the imperial treasury financed native and foreign entrepreneurs who hired armies of workers and built factories and foundries far larger than those in central and western Europe. With exploitation of coal, iron, and oil in the southwest and south, they benefited from nearby raw materials and the lower costs of manufacturing in spacious plants housing the latest inventions. Industrial production for the period 1860–1913 has been estimated at 5 percent a year. By 1913 Russia held fourth rank among advanced economies. There was, however, a very wide gap between her and the third rank in total output and an even wider gap in output per capita.

Agriculture: A Loaf of Bread, a Jug of Wine

In late nineteenth-century Europe it was not easy to make a living, not to mention a good living, from land cultivation. There were several reasons for this. Improvements in rail and oceanic transport exposed once protected local markets to the pressures of world producers. Farmers of all sizes concentrated on cereals, wheat in the west, rye in the east, and herds of beef cattle. Prices were normally determined by local production and demand. But when wheat from the great plains of the United States and Canada, as well as beef from Argentina, were cheaply brought to Europe, agricultural prices collapsed in the 1870s and

1880s. British farmers, whether large or small, were the hardest hit because they had little influence in Parliament. Even the largest landlords suffered from falling rents, and were forced to dismiss laborers and to reduce the arable. By 1900 planted acreage was only one-half its 1872 level, and the number of farm laborers declined by a third while the general population rose by 43 percent. There was some recovery after 1900 when world prices moved upward. But British agriculture turned to other more lucrative produce: milk, meat, butter, fruit, eggs, vegetables, and pedigree stock for export.

French farmers, most of them cultivating rather small plots, and unable to lower costs, were particularly threatened by foreign imports. They were, however, very numerous up to 1914 and enjoyed the vote, which made deputies and senators listen and obey. Tariffs climbed steadily up to and beyond 1900. The champion of protectionism was Jules Méline, a conservative republican who believed that the authorities must act to keep peasants on the land. As a leading proponent of "agrarianism," he was convinced that a strong peasantry was needed to protect France against her foreign enemies as well as against her internal enemies, the socialists. Protection was only partially successful; rural laborers continued to migrate toward the nearest cities, but at a more modest rate than in other countries; urban industries could not absorb many of them.

Large industrialists were not particularly favorable to tariffs, but like large estate owners, accepted them as part of the tacit bargain between themselves and big rural interests. The growers who held onto their little plots were aided by governmental programs that subsidized cheaper transport to markets, gave tax advantages and subsidies to rural cooperatives that provided credit, storage facilities and at-cost equipment and chemicals for their members. Protected by the highest tariffs in the west, there was less incentive to modernize agricultural techniques. But farmers, better educated than in the past, did resort to chemical fertilizers that raised yields to unprecedented heights. The result was a country capable of feeding itself by 1914.

It could also drink its fill. Data on French agriculture from the 1870s looks so bleak because vineyards were invaded by an aphid, the Phylloxera, that wiped out all major vineyards until the 1890s. The resulting drop in wine production was a catastrophe never before experienced. After all, ordinary table wine was consumed throughout the land once railroads began shipping cheap southern wine into northern cities, and finer wines from Burgundy, Champagne and Bordeaux were leading exports. But they too were victims of the aphid. Replanting French vines on selected American rootstock overcame the Phylloxera, and after 1900 wine production recovered—so much so that an excess caused prices to plunge, which provoked serious agitation among southern grape growers. The only solution at the time was to distill wine into a cheap brandy that was fit only for industrial usages.

The German wine industry was hardly important enough to seriously affect agricultural data. Rather, the potato was to Germany what wine was to

France. Her farmers grew half the potatoes produced in Europe. Discounting wine, agriculture in the Empire was a net contributor to the general economy. Although agricultural productivity in France, even in nonviticultural sectors, lagged well behind industry, productivity in the Rhineland and eastward ranged from 60 to 90 percent of norms, fairly favorable rates compared with 123 percent for industry and mining. Animal weight doubled and milk production trebled. Since nearly 4.2 million acres of land were taken out of cultivation, it is evident that small farmers in particular were abandoning cereals for dairying. But *Junkers* in the northeast enhanced their output of rye and barley, chiefly for export as cheap fodder to Denmark.

As in France the move to tariff protection was led by the alliance of steel and rye. Arguments for tariffs were identical to those in France, with the same admixture of old-fashioned romantic agrarianism. In effect, in republican France and semi-parliamentary Germany the tariff issue was as enveloped in political as in economic and social policies. Small farmers in the Rhineland and landlord *Junkers* also saw eye to eye on protection even when their politics differed on other matters. Rhenish farmers in particular but those in Bavaria and Württemburg also benefited from governmental aid to cooperatives. Mutual societies stemming from the Schulze-Delitzsch tradition were devoted largely to rural credit, while the more numerous Raiffeisen cooperatives, managed by peasants in their villages, provided credit, collective buying at cost, warehousing and other services at the local level. The state, in the Prussian tradition, subsidized more agricultural education than other governments, only Denmark being on an equal footing.

Neither in France nor Germany did cooperative services alter the structure of land ownership. Big noncompetitive estates prevailed in eastern Germany thanks to tariffs; in the West and South small and medium farms held on. Only 4 percent of Rhineland farmers owned more than fifty acres of land. This was a serious hindrance to rural modernization and improved living standards. Little growers harvested potatoes for the same reason the Irish did, to eat them day after day.

Agriculture in eastern Europe was largely devoted to cereals grown on exceptionally large estates, with small farmers and their women providing much of the paid labor force. Hungary and the Ukraine became the bread baskets of industrializing countries. Germany and Britain were their principal markets, even though they had to compete against American wheat on the London exchange where prices were considerably below those held high behind tariff walls. Easterners could not benefit from protection because they had to export most of their surplus which far surpassed the needs of local populations. On the large estates owners introduced some of the most up-to-date equipment and scientific methods. Politically conservative, they were economically entrepreneurial, generally more so than protected *Junkers* or Russian gentry.

Outside the Ukraine and the southern black earth regions, the land mass of Russia was not richly endowed. The cold climate severely limited the growing season and as throughout southern Europe, rainfall was distressingly short during summer. When weather was adverse, as in 1892, catastrophe resulted, and on a massive scale. Given the almost medieval transport, help could not rapidly be carried from prosperous to suffering regions.

Undoubtedly peasant emancipation as carried out did not bring improvement, at least not until after 1900. Increasing peasant unrest did not result from Populist preaching but from increasing anger at their plight, and it poured forth in 1905. This was the problem facing Peter Stolypin, made prime minister after the revolt. In his view the legal emancipation now required emancipation from the *mir*. It had not impeded the riots of 1905, so its usefulness was nil. Better, he decided, to create a free, landed peasantry and trust in the more prosperous farmers. He began by abolishing redemption payments as well as the corporal punishment meted out to nonpayers. Each peasant won the right to claim his share of communal land, along with the use of meadows and woods. By a two-thirds vote of its male members communal restraints on land purchase could be abolished, a percent lowered to one-half in 1911. Stolypin also granted the Peasant Land Bank the power to facilitate the sale of plots or their exchange. By 1915 about 2 million households had become land owners. Clearly the reforms were beginning to attract the rural population, but Stolypin's assassination, bureaucratic clumsiness, and the outbreak of war slowed the process. Because the consolidation of strips was much slower than conversion to private holding, the conditions of farming hardly improved before 1914 for the majority of peasants still without land. Of course conditions varied: The Ukraine grew rich on exported grain, and everywhere *kulaks* enjoyed a "golden age" in the impoverished Russian context.

Peasants, when freed, were leaving the *mir* and not claiming parts of it, or they sold their shares. Some left for nearby cities, but by 1914 some 2 million migrated east into Siberia, where they settled in the only suitable land for farming in a narrow band between the frozen north and parched south. Russians pressed eastward as Americans westward, but in much smaller numbers, even after the building of the Trans-Siberian railway eased their passage to a new life.

International Trade: Return to Protection

The changed balance of economic power can be readily observed in data on international trade of manufactured goods (see Table 19–3).

Germany was the only major economic power to achieve a progressively higher rate of exports. She never won parity with Britain, but surpassed her in the most lucrative fields: steel, chemicals, machinery, and electrical equipment. Germany's advantage lay not so much in transoceanic markets; it was rather the developing economies of her eastern and southern neighbors that needed the kinds of high-technology commodities her manufacturers were eager to turn

Table 19–3 World Exports, Percentage by Country 1890–1913

	1880	1899	1913
Britain	41.4	33.2	30.2
Germany	19.3	22.4	26.6
France	22.2	14.4	12.1
Dual Monarchy	8.0	—	5.0
Belgium	5.0	5.5	5.0

out. This situation partly explains why the imperial merchant marine, despite its rapid expansion, came nowhere near that of Great Britain. In 1914 Britain's share of steam vessel tonnage was over 44 percent, that of Germany only 12 percent. Of course the English relied on European markets, but tariffs posed serious obstacles especially since her lack of high import duties gave her diplomats little leverage when bargaining for entry rights. So merchants relied more heavily on transoceanic buyers within and without the empire. Unfortunately as older colonies achieved dominion status, like the Union of South Africa, their own economic interests led them to protect their growing economies against a flood of cheaper British goods. The French for some time had been closing in on themselves behind protective walls like a fortress. They exported their capital but little of their other commodities, save luxuries. What is interesting to note is that no countries could rely on exports to colonies to balance their exports and imports. Both Britain and France bought more than they sold, ending with negative balances. What filled the gap were so-called "invisible" incomes: interests on loans, insurance fees, profits from shipping. So trade balances were maintained. Besides, rising populations increased domestic markets.

Demography: The S Curve

Modernization had a double effect on the population of Europe: it raised the head-count sharply for over a century, and then it nearly leveled the total. Before 1815 population growth was unpredictable. In a prosperous decade or even a quarter century, couples raised their birth rate and, if the death rate was not devastating, they increased the population. But, as we already observed, nature was not eternally generous; cold winters, wet springs, and too-dry summers destroyed crops. Then the birthrate tended to remain constant while the death rate leapt ahead, rubbing out previous gains. With the advent of industrial growth, however, an increase in real per capita incomes took place, birth rates rose and death rates declined. The economic cycle, then, was directly related to demographic trends. So was official policy concerning sanitation both personal and public. Urban renewal plus more humane treatment of foundlings aided the decline of infantile mortality, and here probably was the reason for population growth. Not declining death rates among the over-60 population at midcentury, but declining death rates at the infant and young child (5 to 12 years of age) categories were decisive. In modernized states, the predicament of high child mortality was relieved. This was not a problem solved entirely by government medical bureaucracy. Urban cleanup was undoubtedly decisive, but so was the rising level of education and the rising level of expectations.

Economic and medical progress led to two contradictory trends after midcentury: child mortality fell, but so did natality. Fewer children died, but fewer children were conceived. This condition brought about the leveling of the incredibly rapid growth of population, beginning around the 1890s. An absolute drop in population did not follow; on the contrary, the number of Europeans grew but at a slower rate as Table 19–4 shows.

Both moderation and leveling revealed that internal or family brakes were being applied. Germany excepted, the highest rates of growth were in relatively backward states where birth control was not widespread. In general governments had no policies to check population growth; on the contrary they encouraged it. Rather there were moderating forces at work in various areas of connubial life. First, a reduced birth rate made its appearance earliest among the upper classes where couples consciously decided to reduce family size. Earlier in the century the well-to-do, whether rural gentry or upper bourgeois, had insisted on producing large families; their wives were little better than milk cows taken on to bear huge broods, more than half of whom would die before their first year of life. Wives were as vulnerable, so widowers wore black, shed a few tears, and after several months took a new wife, not infrequently the younger sister of their dear departed. And so the process went on. There were big houses, ample revenues, lots of servants to take care of large families.

Table 19–4 Population Change by Country, 1881–1911(in millions)

	1881	**1911**	**Percent Increase**
Germany	45.2	64.9	43.6
England and Wales	35.9	36.0	0.3
Scotland	3.7	4.7	27.0
France	37.4	39.2	4.8
Dual Monarchy	37.9	49.5	30.6
Russia	97.7	160.7	64.9
Spain	16.2	19.9	22.8
Italy	28.5	34.7	21.7

By the 1870s, however, attitudes changed. The long economic downturn very likely was a damper, if not on a husband's ardor, then on his pocketbook. A big brood had become a heavy economic burden. Children were no longer dying so early, thanks to improved hygiene and new educational laws. Also the technological demands of business required that children remain much longer in school, and therefore a continuing financial burden on parental budgets. It behooved a couple, ambitious for the careers of their offspring, to curb their fertility to concentrate limited resources on one or two heirs, rather then dissipate an inheritance over many.

So limiting family size became a way of life for the middle class. All sorts of literature appeared informing women how to avoid pregnancies without having to abstain from intercourse as the Reverent Malthus had advised much earlier in the century. Once more technology came to the aid of amorous couples: The vulcanization of rubber produced the condom, far more effective then the entrails of animals. The diaphragm also appeared in the 1840s, and was improved by the 1870s when spermicide was added to its shield as an additional safety measure. Quite clearly social and cultural history met amicably when the condom and diaphragm provided a rather slippery bridge between them. Only after the decline of religious influence could the condom rise to the demands of modern society.

A declining birthrate became the hallmark of a society that was urban and well-to-do. Reduced birth rates were not the sign of a decadent society, but of one grown rich and self-satisfied. Children had to be limited in numbers so that each could receive a better education in an exclusive private school. The better-off worker, often financially superior to petty bureaucrats, corner grocers, barbers, tailors, and candlestick makers tended to imitate the better-off white-collar class. The proletariat, however, did not take either to abstinence or contraception and went on producing large families, a matter that worried conservative thinkers who warned that as the upper levels pursued a practice threatening their survival, the laboring class, seen as a fortune-grabbing mob, would despoil them of their wealth and bring civilization to an end.

Small wonder that conservative politicians put their trust in the farming families who, they believed, continued to ignore birth control. Table 19–4 bears out their belief. But this was clearly not the case in France where peasant couples spaced their births to complete the family size early, stopping with two or three offspring. Faced with a situation approaching demographic suicide, French politicians almost unanimously outlawed contraceptives. But all in vain. In fact, without an influx of immigrants from Spain, Italy, Poland and Belgium, France's population curve would have turned downward from about the 1870s on. England was also dependent of Irish immigrants to offset threatened stagnation. English conservatives were as upset as the French by declining birth rates, also forbidding dissemination of contraceptive information. Charles Bradlaugh, the atheist denied a seat in Parliament, and Annie Besant, a Fabian socialist, were arrested for passing out brochures on birth control. The Scots, in contrast, were as actively fecund as ever.

The situation was quite different east of the Rhineland. Rhenish, Bavarian, and Austrian Catholics, unlike the French, were quite prolific, as were the vast orthodox peasant families of Russia. Mediterranean Europe, strongly Catholic, also remained prolific, too much so for the economic conditions, and population control was carried out by emigration rather than by contraception.

The earliest mass emigration involved Irish fleeing from destitution, poverty and actual starvation resulting from the potato famine during the 1840s. From then on the number of exits diminished but remained high, draining the country of its young. The same was true of the German Federation, but the rise of industry put a stop to it, and by the 1870s the Empire steadily attracted impoverished peoples on its eastern and southern borders. England and France were also melting pots, accepting people of all nationalities and religions. Both states had huge territorial empires from which they drew many immigrants while only a few of their nationals left for the colonies. The French in particular were a people in bedroom slippers; nothing could induce them to leave the hexagon. South Africa and Australia drew the largest contingent from England, Algeria from France. From about the 1870s, movement by Europeans to non-European lands grew to unprecedented proportions.

As with the Irish, Italians and Spaniards fled indigence for the cities of North and South America. Many east Europeans traveled to central and west Europe in search of jobs, but probably as many left because of persecution; such were the Jews who finally settled wherever they were not subject to pogroms. Poles fled Russian rule, Slovaks that of Hungarians. The largest melting pot was certainly the United States whose major cities teemed with foreign accents.

Lack of jobs and harshness of life also led to what we call perpendicular migration, that is, people fleeing their mountain villages for what they hoped would become a more prosperous existence in the flat lands of the Continent. Over past centuries highlanders had cut timber, hunted, herded cattle, and, with back-breaking labor, dug into mountainsides to make flat terraces in which they planted and harvested meager crops. Their offspring found life too hard and lacking in opportunities. They fled the Alps, Apennines, Pyrenees, Carpathian, and Ural ranges, as well as the beautiful but inhospitable Massif Central.

The movement of peoples had been going on since homo sapiens first appeared on earth, and almost always in search of food. In the more recent past, population had become somewhat more stabilized; families and villagers had stayed put because they were ignorant of lands and peoples beyond their customary horizon; as serfs they were not permitted to leave; travel was daunting and very expensive before railroads and steamships. In addition, governments wanted subjects in place to collect taxes and recruits; the ruling classes' traditionalistic minds distrusted change. All these anchors were cut loose by modernization that rolled over Europe from west to east like a huge tidal wave, uprooting everything in its way. Probably some thirty million Europeans left for foreign shores between 1800 and 1914. Europe exported commodities, money, and people. The expression "the Europeanization of the world" is not an exaggeration; no land mass and its inhabitants were left untouched financially or culturally.

20

Europe's Fin de Siècle

Europe as a Cultural Unity

Fin de siècle is a term denoting intellectual and social conditions around 1900. At the turn of the century there was still not a unified Europe, at least not one that could be called a continental community. The quality of life among the vast regions differed too much, and advanced communications notwithstanding, the peoples of the several nations were unfamiliar with one another. For the Frenchman in the street or in the field, Russians could have been moon creatures for all they knew about them, and vice versa. Even the educated were remarkably ignorant of peoples living beyond national frontiers, and as yet not very well informed about fellow nationals living beyond regional boundaries with natural frontiers. Public education, while in the process of eradicating illiteracy, concentrated on making students in primary schools aware of their nationality. Courses and textbooks therefore informed young formative minds about national history, language, geography, and military prowess. Europe as a distinct unity existed only on two levels, the diplomatic, and the cultural. The migration of peoples was minor compared to the migration of ideas, of dominant currents of thought. Even the emergence of extreme nationalism, while it glorified one nationality over others, was nonetheless a European-wide intellectual phenomenon, and was part of a general cultural reaction against the prevailing exaltation of science and devotion to materialism.

Revolt against Positivism

By the turn of the century the positivist ideology associated with Auguste Comte had lost its original allure. It is true that in 1898 the Sorbonne celebrated his centenary, and four years later placed a stone sculpture of his bust in the square before its main gate. The faculty there was only now emerging from its old regime way of thinking. But throughout much of Europe and Latin America the Comptian type of positivism had become a secular religion substituting for dogmatic Catholicism. To many thinkers the term positivism signified a belief in the benefits of science, material and mental progress, the supremacy of reason. L. T. Hobhouse, granted the first chair in sociology at the University of London, firmly believed that the human mind had attained a higher stage of evolution and would continue to improve. Yet, among some older Comptian disciples, there were growing doubts about the present state of the human race, or, if not doubts, a degree of disillusion about the quality of the civilization that economic development had produced. Renan was one of them, and for him human nature began to appear less controlled by reason, knowledge more subjective and elusive, the past less understandable and the future less predictable.

The sciences of engineering and technology had produced wonders during the century, and particularly from midcentury on. The way peopled lived, worked, traveled, and played had all been changed drastically by material inventions. By 1900, many thinkers who were critical of science, who believed that Europeans were becoming decadent, had to own up to these wondrous accomplishments.

Precisely toward the later decades a host of theoretical scientists began to question the assumptions of the physicists, engineers and chemists whose work was based on or motivated by the "positivist" concept of the world: that nothing exists save matter because only it was apparent to the senses and to reason. But a new generation of thinkers began to ask, what is matter? Theoretical physicists and astronomers, Einstein among them, discovered that matter is energy, energy is matter, and that space and time are not separate but interdependent, reducible to common units. The only thing that is permanent is not matter but change. Their universe, therefore, seemed insubstantial, elusive, and did not fit the Newtonian physics that the practical sciences had assumed was indestructible. Within a generation midcentury certainties were swept away. The absence of synthesis made the physical world far less positive.

This philosophical attack on positivism was a revolt against the simplistic materialist, mechanistic views that were the content of scientism. The attack also cast its salvos against the rationalism of the utilitarian creed, more specifically aiming at the belief that individuals were consciously motivated by reason when choosing between pain and pleasure, and that the actions of individuals, each seeking his own advantage, would ultimately bring about a better life for everyone.

These critics were not irrationalists; rather they were social thinkers concerned with the irrational only to exorcise it. They probed it to tame it and direct it toward constructive human purposes. They sought to vindicate rational inquiry into the problem of consciousness and the role of unconscious forces determining human action. Henri Bergson's first book laid out the problem. He distinguished between a "superficial psychic life" to which the scientific logic of space and number could properly be applied, and a life in the "depths of consciousness" in which the deep-seated self "followed a logic of its own." Put another way, he limited science to expanding society's influence over matter. But to attain to a true knowledge of nature and life, it was not rational "intellect" but "intuition" that was needed. To him, intuition was "instinct become conscious of itself." In his most famous book, *Creative Evolution* (1907) he rejected Darwin's theory, arguing that evolution was the result of *élan vital* or vital impetus, the mysterious force that was continuously generating and developing new forms of life. Evolution was a creative, not a mechanistic, process. Science was useful for accomplishing tasks, but it could not uncover reality because it left out the concept of duration and the perpetual flux that is inexpressible, grasped only by intuition. Reality is "flux, a continuity of flowing, a becoming." Before and after World War I, Bergson enjoyed an enormous following. His philosophy of "becoming" made him a dynamic cult figure, led him steadily away from his Jewish heritage and toward the Catholic church; he would have converted before his death in the 1930s but Hitler's persecution of Jews decided him against it.

The time element, duration, was equally influential in the thinking of historians. The Neapolitan, Benedetto Croce, turned his attention to establishing the difference between written history and science. His contention was that history had been made by the action of men and their motives and actions were unpredictable, therefore, it was impossible to postulate any laws of historical development. The German, Wilhelm Dilthey, also posited that historians could not adopt the methods of natural science, for like all "human studies," history was concerned with man and the human mind rather than physical reality, with individuals rather than types, and with values which were not the stuff of science. A knowledge of the past did not depend on perception or abstract thought but on understanding (*Verstehen*), the capacity to relive and to empathize with the experiences of other men. We can readily discern here a resurgence of German idealist philosophy, especially that of Immanuel Kant. It is worthwhile noting that this concern for recovering the immediacy of past experience penetrated the content of novelists such as Marcel Proust and Thomas Mann.

Sociologists above all were bent upon exploring the forces governing day-to-day decisions of individuals and groups, and the impact of the subconscious on popularly held beliefs. Sociology like history had come to emphasize the importance of empirical methods of research. But turn-of-the-century scholars more or less rejected the nineteenth-century belief that the patient accumulation of data would reveal truth. Theoretically inclined scholars argued that this accumulation offered no means to penetrate beneath the surface of human experience. The goal for scholars of society was to penetrate the popular mind and discover the levers of popular action. In other words, to understand human motives and their results, it was no longer sufficient to study what humans did, but why they acted as they did and whether they acted out of rational choice.

Pursuing this goal, an entire school of sociology emerged, far removed from the determinist sociology of Comte. If there was an element of determinism, it was neither progressive nor staged according to levels of progress from a lower to a higher state, as predicated by Comte. Max Weber, a German sociologist, concluded that the major force behind the development of capitalism was the Calvinist ethic of hard work and frugal living, a combination that soon led to financial accumulation and therefore the investment capital needed to advance trade and industry in places where Calvinism was dominant: Scotland, England, and Geneva. In this study Weber put forward his notion of ideal types as a means of studying humans by groups, such as professions, and penetrating their motives.

Increasingly scholars saw the need to bring together the methodologies of specialized disciplines to study the actions of individuals and the groups they formed. The result was social psychology which combined sociology, psychology and physiology. The dethroning of man from the lofty and central position he formerly held in social thought was carried out by professional scholars. Gabriel Tarde and Gustave Le Bon studied collective groups: the former argued that human action did not result from reason but from imitation and habit; Le Bon that when individuals were swept up into a "mob" their rational faculties gave way to the bizarre urges of panic and passion. Graham Wallas's *Human Nature in Politics* (1908), when combined with the studies of Vilfredo Pareto and Gaetano Mosca pretty well destroyed any notions that human action, especially political action, resulted from logical thought. The subconscious, not the conscious, ruled conduct whether political or social. It is interesting to note that Wallas was a Fabian socialist, the Italians nationalist conservatives who attacked Giolitti for deceiving the people. Their investigations revealed to their satisfaction that people were motivated and controlled by myths, the creation of which politicians were masters. Georges Sorel, a retired engineer turned socialist, published *Reflections on Violence* (1908) to reveal how myths, such as the second coming, had nothing to do with reason yet held great and irrational powers over large masses. Interested in French syndicalism, he borrowed the idea of the general strike, and held it up as a belief that could inspire workers to take heroic action.

The way to liberation was to act, not to think, least of all to reason. The leaders of the CGT were not at all influenced by Sorel; its leader, when asked whether he was familiar with the book, replied that he read *The Three Musketeers*. At this point it is important to distinguish between the concept of myth and the utopian lucubrations of the earlier century. A myth was an imagined belief created to induce the masses to act in a certain way, and Sorel saw it not as a goal to attain, but as a stimulant to action for action's sake; there was no end, only continued striving. The purveyors of utopias, on the contrary, were within the rationalist line of thought; they appealed not to the passions but to what they felt were man's essential goodness and sense of justice. Moreover their utopias had no historical dimensions. Once attained, the goal of happiness was fixed, static; there was nothing more to become.

Sorel was in the line of thinkers going back to Friedrich Nietzsche whose works were becoming known only after his death in 1900. For Nietzsche "God is dead." Christian mythology and teaching were responsible for the decline of civilization by preaching subservience and humility, and by subordinating the sensual to the spiritual. Modern democracy was equally to blame for imposing equal rights on a weakening society. To restore man to his rightful place and vigor, there was need for heroes, "supermen" who had the will to exercise the power existent within themselves. The right morality was what their heroic vigor dictated, for society was in need of a new morality, of new values in which evil and good combined to give free reign to the will of superior beings. The will to power was the instinct to freedom. It was not identical with the idea of free will of middle class philosophers and Christian theologians. It was a more basic urge combining reason and passion to attain its ends. These goals were not fixed for all time. On the contrary, the heroic type could make and remake himself as well as society. Like Bergson, Nietzsche was a philosopher of the becoming.

Emile Durkheim, professor of sociology, was concerned about the condition of society, but differed radically from the devotees of myth as a factor influencing human action. His studies made clear to him the importance of common beliefs that bonded individuals into a society. These beliefs he labeled the "collective consciousness," that guided and controlled people. In the past the small, functioning, local group had served the most valuable purposes in society. But rapid change had caused such groups and their norms to fall apart, and men were now suffering from *anomie* or normlessness. It resulted from the extreme division of labor that separated people and made them critical of traditions. It was the product of "egotistic" as opposed to "altruistic" societies, in which individuals lost their self discipline and the meaning of life. Durkheim's solution was the industrial syndicate that united management, labor, and consumer in a new social unit. It was to act as an antidote to the destructiveness of class warfare.

Not all thinkers were concerned with humanity as sick and in need of a new source of inspiration. The theorists of the social unconscious usually hoped to use it for some public, really political, end. Psychology, without its adjective "social," concentrated rather on the individual and the particular derangement causing mental illness. The founder of psychoanalysis, Sigmund Freud, was concerned not with society's neuroses but that of his individual patients. His theory, not widely accepted before 1914, held that neurosis resulted from impulses or desires buried in the subconscious, and buried there because of sexual repression. At one moment he wrote that the unconscious was the true psychic reality!

The revolt against realism and the attempt to give social meaning to literature and art was carried on as a form of neo-Romanticism, best expressed as "art for art's sake." This was an attempt to liberate art from any moral, religious or political goal. It was also a search for beauty for beauty's sake. This trend was best expressed in poetry by the symbolists, and in art first by the impressionists whose blurred images became recognizable only from a distance, then by the expressionists who wanted to penetrate outer appearances as revealed to the eye and paint the soul experiences that underlay reality.

Integral Nationalism

Undoubtedly the most politically motivated attack on liberal rationalism came from advocates of an extreme form of nationalism, which underwent considerable change. The patriotic writers of the earlier century were essentially democrats: Jules Michelet, historian of the French PEOPLE, and Joseph Mazzini, who awakened a national consciousness among educated Italians. They and their fellow believers conceived of the human specie as divided among nationalities and argued that each nationality should enjoy freedom and a territorial state to develop in accord with its God-given characteristics. For, indeed, each national group had its distinct personality. But distinction did not mean superiority. The human species was likened to a great garden of world dimensions, and in it, each nationality formed a distinct flower bed, adding its own coloration to the beauty of the entire display. Free national groups would live in harmony, end war, and each make its contribution to raise the level of civilization.

The wars of national liberation that eventually united Italy and Germany and created a host of states in the Balkan Peninsula heightened the feeling of national identity. The Franco-German conflict of 1870–71 awakened French patriotism to a feverish pitch, just as the 1863 revolt in Poland aroused strong anti-Russian sentiments as a means of Polish identity, a situation similar to that in Ireland, another territory and its people ruled by a foreign power of different religious faith.

Henceforth the nationalist creed became a form of religion as it abandoned its liberal origins to identify itself with right-wing political forces. Particularly in the 1890s, stimulated by the Dreyfus affair, fanatics like Charles Maurras and Maurice Barrès put forward their doctrine of "integral nationalism." There were three basic ingredients composing it. First the belief that the soil of France—and they referred only to their homeland—was sacred. The French nationality has become rooted in it over centuries of time. The annexation of Alsace was therefore not merely a land grab, it was the tearing away of part of the soul of the nation. Second, the belief that Frenchmen formed a race, with distinctive traits inherited from previous generations. Nationality was in the blood of all patriots and bound their loyalty to the fatherland, the *patrie*. Foreign immigrants, therefore, could not become French. And this view brought out the third ingredient, anti-Semitism. No Jew could ever become truly French. They were racially different, inferior, a menace, not merely to the purity of blood by intermarriage, but to the necessary cultural bond, Catholicism, that provided the spiritual base for the organic unity of the nation.

Anti-Semitism was by no means a novelty. In the mid-1850s Arthur Gobineau had published his *Essay on the Inequality of the Human Races*. His tenet was that human races were unequal; at the pinnacle stood the Teutonic people. Distrust of Jews was also an ingredient in German nationalism. Richard Wagner and his son-in-law Houston Stewart Chamberlain preached it, and in 1879 the famous Prussian historian, Heinrich von Treitschke published *The Jews Are Our Misfortune*. Anti-Semitism was a cultural expression; it was also a fact of everyday life. As a state of mind, it existed everywhere; as a practice, as actual physical violence, it was most widespread in Russia and Poland where pogroms were on the rise; as a political issue it was widespread and permanent, even after Jews were granted civic rights in the Dual Monarchy and Germany. In France it flared up briefly during the Dreyfus affair. In reality the Jews contributed many of the greatest intellects of the century and, with non-Jews, provided the inventions, science and culture that improved the conditions of life.

The Condition of Europe

Life in Europe was far more urbanized than it had been since the ancient Roman Empire. In 1850 there had been forty-four cities with populations exceeding 100,000; in 1914 there were 180. Great Britain had the largest number, but Germany was now a close second, even though a third of her people lived in rural villages compared to about 5 percent for Britain. France was about equally balanced while the rest of Europe, save the Low Countries, was predominantly rural. In Russia the growth of cities in this category was phenomenal, but they were still mere clusters of closely housed people existing in a vast hinterland of scattered villages even more agrarian now as estate industry moved to urban centers or disappeared. Only 15 percent of Russians were classed as urban on the eve of World War I.

Since midcentury cities had undergone considerable change. Those above the half-million mark, and especially the great capitals of the major states, were far cleaner and healthier than they had been in earlier times. Municipal government had become more efficient. Power had been pretty well taken away from the corrupt placemen through electoral reform and put in the hands of men, mostly middle class, who better understood the need of urban renewal. The building of underground sewers, and the laying of pipes to provide clean water continued at a pace equal to that of the 1850s and 1860s.

Water remained a major problem none the less. As in the past, urbanites had to fetch water from a neighborhood well or fountain and carry it home in some kind of container. This was usually a job left to women, whether servants or housewives. In many cities private companies contracted with authorities to pipe clean water into apartments or buildings. The General Water Company, founded in France during 1852, obtained monopoly rights with very favorable contracts: city leaders taxed their citizens to provide land, lay pipe, and build pumping stations; the company managed the facilities and collected fees from those who subscribed. These latter were never more than a small minority of the well-to-do inhabiting first floor apartments. Small cities often had a water supply superior to their sewers. Both national and city administrations enacted laws intended to eliminate insalubrious housing and facilities, but only rarely did they effectively enforce the statutes. Lack of adequate underground sewage and clean drinking water caused typhoid plagues in 1886, 1893–94, and 1901–2 in France; general lack of cleanliness resulting from improperly functioning toilets, excess humidity, and the accumulation of fecal matter and dirt kept the rate of tuberculosis high, and helps explain why life expectancy in 1900 was not much higher than in 1800. Hosts of adults, even well-to-do, endured unpleasant chronic illnesses.

We must not paint too black a picture. The nineteenth-century cities were on the whole cleaner and safer than ever before. Certainly the capital cities as well as large provincial ones were marvels of modernization. All major streets were now paved with stones, were illuminated by electric lights kept aglow all night, had broad sidewalks for pedestrians, and electrified trams moving on tracks that provided cheap transport. They replaced the old horse-drawn trollies and, although noisy, did not cover the streets with manure. The numerous animals drawing delivery wagons and carriages did that. But after 1900 motor vehicles made their appearance and animal traction began its slow decline. With cheap transport the better-paid workers made their move into the better housing of suburbs.

Improvements in public hygiene and in private housing definitely benefited the health of urban dwellers. The city now was a more salubrious locale than the rural village, especially in rich nations. The British and Germans, the two wealthiest, surpassed the French and other nationalities in the number of flush-toilets and washing facilities. The so-called conquest of water and cleaner water for personal use, very likely encouraged better habits in personal hygiene.

Yet, Europeans still held ambivalent views about the use of water for cleaning the body. For centuries bathing the entire body in a tub of some sort was used as treatment for the ill. Very few dwellings had the luxury of bathrooms. Some rich people installed bath tubs and servants heated water to fill them. But most people, and especially the Victorians, obeyed the churchmen's warning about the moral dangers of complete nudity. So people who bathed wore linen gowns and soaped themselves through them lest they touch the intimate parts of the body and incite immoral thoughts, or worse, acts. Masturbation was loudly condemned by all the moralists, and there were many of them. The prudery for which Victorians are famous—or infamous—has undoubtedly been exaggerated. Yet there were norms that had prevailed, and that became less respected by the 1890s, the "gay nineties", and the human body acquired rights previously denied it, especially as cheap transport carried vacationers to the seaside and swimming or at least wading, became fashionable. Bathing suits covered the entire body, but revealed its contours all the same.

Bathing the entire body in the privacy of one's home was a major undertaking that very few people ventured into more than once a year, if ever. In earlier times the rich did not even wash, they simply changed clothes, or underwear if they wore any. Yet by the late nineteenth century medical doctors were calling for more cleanliness. Fearful of epidemics city fathers provided public baths for a low fee, or free of charge. This encouraged a weekly, monthly, or annual full-body washing. There were luxurious privately-owned bathing centers for the upper class. And yet the cleanest people in Europe were the Scandinavian villagers with their steam huts where whole families gathered to sweat out their dirt. The dirtiest were the peasants everywhere. Rural cultures looked on layers of dirt as a protective coating useful against a hostile nature filled with evil spirits that could invade the body. City folk of the lower classes were not much cleaner and since many had migrated from farms they clung to the belief that layered dirt was a protection, not against evil spirits, but against the cold and damp. Given the lack of heat and the high humidity of their dwellings perhaps they were right. After all, even the bourgeois of both sexes limited their ablutions to the face and hands, using a large bowl and water poured in from a pitcher. Because most men wore beards they did not even have much face surface to cleanse. Europeans were a smelly people, exuding odors both from their body and the eau de cologne and other perfumes they used to disguise them.

Apart from medical campaigners, the agency that most contributed toward encouraging personal hygiene was the elementary school in both town and village. Teachers, especially as more women entered the profession—many men considered washing effeminate—were instructed by medical inspectors to require clean faces, hands, and clothes. Many young pupils had their first acquaintance with running water and flush toilets in schools, perhaps also their first encounter with toilet paper. The rise of cheap newspapers undoubtedly contributed as much to cleaner behinds as to enriched minds.

Modernizing Education

A major step toward building a progressive society was the enormous expansion of formal learning in schools, and compulsory attendance at the elementary level. Obligatory attendance not only led to the decline of illiteracy, it removed children from the work place they had occupied since time immemorial. Equally important was the enforcement of instruction for both sexes. Schooling for boys had been growing for decades, but only from the 1870s were young girls drawn into classrooms in large numbers. In the more economically advanced states, literacy rose sharply for both sexes, without attaining equality, however, before war began in 1914. The ability to write as well as read was limited in the population at large to western, especially northwestern and north central Europe. In the Latin countries schools had only limited penetration in rural areas, and the line separating north from south within each state disappeared only in France. Germany was the model for all to follow; pedagogy there was strict but effective, and the kindergarten was a major innovation for the tiny creatures left there by parents going to work. Eastern Europe raised its literacy rates in cities and their surroundings, but illiteracy was the common condition in the countryside. And even in cities, female illiteracy persisted. The tsarist regime did not consider it worthwhile to educate girls, in fact, considered it dangerous. Girls had no need of reading, the local priest taught them all they should know. In such a society, women, especially working women, found that literacy was a dead end; all the institutions, including the family, stood against the advance of women.

Increase in numbers of students, especially of young people from the lower middle and working classes, forced changes in the courses offered. Older centers of learning retained their classical curriculum above the primary level. New schools, however, offered courses in science and modern languages. Middle class fathers were strongly committed to providing their sons with practical knowledge that would help them find jobs in industry or commerce. Secondary schools responded, but old universities did so meagerly and reluctantly. It was the newest institutions that offered the best training in science and engineering. In France, the *Grandes Écoles* were models widely imitated; but they were not universities in a true sense. In Britain, apprentices had learned on the job, but with the founding of higher learning centers in the industrial cities, engineering and science enjoyed eminent places in the curriculum. This was equally true in Germany where the sciences were integral parts of programs of study. Germany in 1901 spent the highest portion of its budget for education, 12 percent, England spent 10 percent, France 8 percent, Spain a mere 1.5 percent, Russia even less. The high level of Germany was to be further raised in 1906 when secondary education became obligatory.

In modern society education became more expensive, secular and essential. Moreover teachers attained a higher status than in "preindustrial" societies. Before universal primary instruction, teachers were a very "mixed bag." Some were well educated, others were not more than a page ahead of their students. Obligatory education required a huge output of pedagogues. The British used an apprenticeship system, in keeping with the Lancastrian system designed to hold down costs. On the Continent, ministries of public education feverishly set up teacher training colleges, and the French normal school program was the most rigorous. Unfortunately, the status of communal educators was not financially enhanced; in fact they were grossly underpaid. A highly trained elementary school teacher, who had invested time and money in training, earned about the same salary as a semiskilled laborer, just slightly more than laundresses and textile workers.

University professors, in contrast, were a recognizable academic elite and almost an economic one. They were well paid, provided assistants, enjoyed light teaching loads and extended vacations. Their status was far above the simple high school teachers who had to spend more heavily on suitable attire and set an example of cleanliness and probity. With families to support, they had to "moonlight", that is, they held the job of secretary to a communal council and to a mayor. On the whole they were, regardless of sex, more humane. They were less given to thrashing youngsters, to abusing them. In France, laws existed prohibiting the beating of the very young. But, then, the French were always making laws that no one could or would enforce. Besides, parental and social values did not disparage physical punishment. Many parents were brutal, physically, toward their offspring; they beat them; why then should not a person *in loco parentis* do the same?

It is almost certain that the life of children improved. By 1900 there were fewer of them per family; there were far more social workers, backed by extensive legislation, to protect them, to help parents understand them. There were also more official agencies to assist families, and that were solicitous of widows with young children. There were no welfare states as yet, but there was a concern for the health and well-being of children. Humane principles had penetrated the ruling classes. Protestant, Catholic, and Orthodox churches extended their social services, providing shelters for people in distress, including children who were orphaned or abandoned. Middle-class parents were even more solicitous of their children than in the past and since the middle class grew in number, their offspring came to occupy a large nitch in the world of the young.

Condition of Women

The expansion of schooling for girls offered opportunities by 1900 that no one had dreamed of at midcentury. The French education ministry recognized sexual differences, but was inspired by the revolutionary ideal of equality and had as its goal for girls the motto "different but equal" (*égalité dans la différence*). "Vive la différence" later proclaimed a deputy, and indeed, females and males were educated in separate school buildings; there was no mingling of sexes, a common policy in Europe. Girls secondary schools offered a much broader curriculum than the classical schools for male teenagers who, often, ended their classical studies with a degree that had no practical value unless they had family ties that opened careers in government service once they passed civil service tests. Far too many ended as unemployed intellectuals or low-grade clerks in private business.

Young women, on the other hand, could enter teaching, which they did in vast numbers, but only at the low-paying primary level. Their high school diplomas were not of much use professionally because the gate opening into professional careers was indeed strait. A few succeeded in their exams in law and medicine, after they were allowed to matriculate in universities in western Europe, and those with medical degrees could practice, but those with law degrees were not admitted to the bar until a few years before the war. The highly educated woman was not at an advantage vis à vis the lesser educated. She was lucky if she found a husband; the middle class woman without an inheritance or dowry, if not good looking, very likely never married. She worked in the family store or office, or became a governess, the rather unenviable position of many penniless women of good education and background.

The lives of upper-class married or financially independent women varied. There were more than a few who devoted part of their time to charitable causes: visiting or assisting some poor families or widows, or teaching Sunday school for working women still illiterate who could find free time to attend classes. These women did not at all conform to the belief that Victorian gentlewomen were closed off in their homes, took no part in public life, and lived a useless existence. But most middle- and upper-class women spent their time going from one social event to another, shopping, being fitted for dresses and shoes. They above all went in for sports like tennis, croquet, and bicycling, and changed clothing fashion to accommodate an active life. The bustle disappeared, skirts were made more simple to allow body movement, they even donned "bloomers" to preserve their modesty when mounted on a bicycle. They also wore ornate bathing costumes at the seaside. When they were bored a not inconspicuous number turned to drugs which were easily obtained from a friendly pharmacist. Many patent medicines were heavily loaded with narcotics. The more daring found them insufficiently exciting; they met together in the afternoon to inject one another with morphine. After all, the good doctor Freud was also a user of drugs to calm his nerves. Their daughters were the "flappers" of the 1920s.

Lower-class women had equally varied lives. Those married to skilled workmen quit their own jobs to become full time housewives and mothers. Those married to lesser skilled men often continued working until the first pregnancy. Because women at this level married early their rate of maternity was considerably higher than that of upper-class women. Yet, they had to work to make ends meet, which usually meant part time work sewing either at home or in a small clothing firm. Single women and especially widows had to earn a living and since employment in textile mills was stable or declining as a result of mechanization, they turned to sewing or lace making, usually in a small shop, working under "sweated" conditions: long hours, little rest, and low pay. For them, the "gay nineties" were not gay at all.

Life for peasant women seems to have changed somewhat for the better. The introduction of harvesting machinery on medium size farms lightened the heavy work of wives and daughters during late summer and early autumn. On farms too small to use machines, women and girls continued to aid men with cutting, and carrying, and picking grapes in viticultural areas, while performing housework when not in the fields. With improved prices and markets after the mid-1890s, they could afford to add a few comforts to their houses: an extra room, a cooking stove using coal in replacement of the hearth for preparing meals, a chair rather than the usual backless bench for table dining and resting, a new-fangled pump to draw water from the well, and a midwife at birthing rather than an old women with little knowledge and dirty hands.

Modern Social Structure: The Bourgeoisie

Society did not evolve in quite the same way midcentury visionaries had forecast. Those like Marx who foretold the rise of a factory proletariat were correct; however, their belief that the middle class would be pushed downward into the working class by monopolists and that their conditions would worsen were not. The condition of factory workers grew better during the 1890s when wages rose faster than inflation. Equally important was the enormous increase in the white collar class in western and central Europe. This was an element of the middle strata, but differed markedly from the older middle class, which had been largely a propertied group with much of its income derived from rents on real estate and the interest of government bonds. The white-collar group was, like wage workers, dependent largely on salaries. It included a variety of categories, from well-paid functionaries to simple office personnel. Their salaried incomes differed, as did their standing in the eyes of society. Yet, there were common bonds: their advanced education, sense of superiority, and hostility to socialism.

At the lower level, office personnel and lower bureaucrats earned about the same income as skilled workers, but usually had more job security. On the other hand their conditions of work were neither easy nor regulated by factory legislation. If they were simple clerks they could easily put in an eleven or twelve hour day, and spend most of it pouring over hand-written quantitative data sent in from other offices. There were lawyers waiting in vain for litigants, accountants in search of clients who did not trust them, doctors and dentists short of patients. The more advanced societies offered opportunities for upward mobility: Between 1900 and 1920, 35 percent of managers in British industry rose from the petty bourgeois, only 25 percent from the far more numerous working class. In France there was less mobility because the majority of managerial jobs in family firms were reserved for relatives. In these two states the bourgeoisie had become the ruling class: The nineteenth century was the time of their rise to power and prestige.

In central and eastern Europe, it was by no means a "bourgeois century." In Germany the average businessmen were not held in high esteem as a class. On the other hand famous university professors and big steel magnates were even courted by William II. The magnates held immense fortunes and readily imitated the noble ruling class. They saw themselves as feudal lords ruling over thousands of workers, usually in a paternalistic fashion. Below them were layers of white collar employees whose ideal was the civil servant who enjoyed the social prestige and job security they did not. From about 1898 to 1903 about 27 percent of them were jobless and lacked unemployment insurance. Engineers complained that the public looked upon them as "superior locksmiths." Their great fear was to fall into the ranks of the proletariat. To avoid this they formed their own craft unions and held aloof from those connected with the Social Democratic party they abhorred. But even organized they were politically impotent.

The entire middle class in Russia reflected an economy just beginning to modernize. Businessmen were held in low esteem; merchants were the most advanced among them but still drank tea out of a saucer rather than a cup, lived miserly in a few dirty rooms of the big wooden mansions they owned, and were politically subservient. The drive for economic change came from the government, that for mild social reform from the few professionals in the Zemstvos.

As Rudyard Kipling once wrote, "East is east and west is west and never the twain shall meet." The West was a market society where status and norms were established by competition in the market. Much of central Europe and the East was a status society where birth and family rank rather than enterprise distributed reward and influence. It is important to recognize this distinction; it is equally important to recognize its limitations. Germany was not identical to Russia, nor Austria to Hungary or Bohemia, or even Italy to Spain, or France to Britain. Societies modernized, but at different rates and in different ways. The French abolished noble titles after 1875; the British preserved the peerage, reduced its power, and put many of its members on corporate boards, if only for show.

Modern Social Structure: Laborers

Wage workers varied considerably between the skilled and unskilled and the difference was considerable. The highly trained boiler maker lived in a world apart from the navvy laying railroad track or the docker whose job depended on the strength of his back, and whose earnings fell as his back weakened. Worse, the unskilled were easily replaceable by a continuous stream of urban immigrants; they were all like replaceable parts of a vast machine. The presence of so many ill trained men and women relying on muscle rather than brain helps to explain why even in the 1890s a third of London's population was classed by Charles Booth as living at or below the poverty line. And yet, London was the world's wealthiest city, but exceptional only in that respect, not in the structure of its population. Most of the poor also included the elderly, especially old widows helped out by William Booth's Salvation Army, and people unable to work because they were sick and not covered by health insurance.

Conditions were in general quite better for the majority of wage earners. Their incomes rose faster than inflation, thereby increasing their buying power which, in turn, stimulated economic growth and political stability. In western and central Europe they benefited from government regulations limiting hours, imposing safety devices for machines, better aeration, rest periods, sickness insurance and old age pensions. An English historian once affirmed that social history is simply history with government left out. The truth is that one of the main trends of the century was the increasing penetration of government into society. The strengthening of trade unions was equally instrumental in the steady improvement of factory and shop conditions. A far greater number of workers now enjoyed what only a few had known in the past: a sense of security, a lessening of the hazards of life in the workplace. This was a new condition of major importance and largely explains why, at the turn of the century, there was a feeling that progress was a reality, a buoyant throbbing that put the mass of the population in a frame of mind highly distinct from that of the increasingly pessimistic intellectuals.

Workers of course had grievances. They expressed them by lowering productivity, which was a kind of strike against management whose profits were rising at a far sharper rate than wages. There were still wide gaps between the upper and lower classes, and confiscatory income taxes were still far in the future. Lloyd George's budget of 1909 was very moderate, downright timid, albeit a first step that was not imitated in any other country. Only the highest paid workers could afford to move to the suburbs; most continued to inhabit rundown apartment buildings lacking adequate plumbing and sanitation, with small often windowless rooms, and overcrowded given that workers' families were still large and rents were high. Men still fled their noisy children and complaining wives to gather in pubs, cafés, taverns, where they socialized with their male comrades and still drank a good deal. Given the cheap cost of watered wine and beer or schnapps or vodka, most of them did not spend excessively on alcohol. Besides, the married among them had only the few coins their wives allowed them for drink and tobacco. No wonder the French worker called his wife *la bourgeoise*; she kept the purse strings. The days of paying wages in barrooms were over, prohibited by law in order to save families from penury. When the wife was wise and skilled at home economy, the husband's wage and whatever she could earn by lace making, or any other domestic enterprise, could improve the family diet. The consumption of meat, sugar, tea, coffee, and milk went up at all levels of society. *Fin de siècle* Europe attained a level of wealth and comfort unknown before. Modernization, however varied its advance over the Continent, was also a mental construct rooted in the idea of progress, and a way of economic and social organization that had over the century raised the standard of living for the majority. The great tragedy was that it created nation-states, highly integrated and patriotically driven, but ruled by men whose minds had not yet evolved to a level that made them recognize war as a menace to the Europe they held dear.

21

The Diplomacy
of Imperialism

Trouble Spots

The year 1871 was memorable, not only because Germany and Italy emerged as unified states, but because of the shift in the locus of power. Germany now stood head and shoulders above any other single European state as a military colossus, and was fast acquiring the industrial strength to enhance her new standing. Her rivals were beset by troubles within their borders rendering them nearly impotent: Austria had still to work out a manageable balance with Hungary; Russia was mired in a reform effort that brought forth more problems than could be solved; France was torn between political factions struggling for dominance; Britain was enjoying her "splendid isolation." Bismarck, the instigator of war, was now a satisfied statesman. However, the Austrians, like the French, were not satisfied, both finding it difficult to accept their lowered status as has-been great powers. The French in particular were bitter and nearly all republicans were committed to *revanche*, the recovery of the territories lost to the new German Empire. But even the most bellicose Frenchmen understood that another war would be ruinous, possibly even destructive of the territorial state. Leon Gambetta's watchword was never to talk openly about recovery but never forget it. Alsace-Lorraine remained a trouble spot, however not a serious one for the foreseeable future.

Nonetheless, Bismarck set out a policy to safeguard Germany. It included further strengthening the army, isolating France and improving German defenses by negotiating pacts of friendship with Russia and Austria. This latter step resulted in the League of Three Emperors in 1872–73. It was not a true alliance, but an entente or understanding, aimed at preserving the status quo and suppressing revolutionary movements and socialism. Memories of the Paris Commune were still vivid, and police agents everywhere were tracking down members of the First Workingman's International, a Pan-European organization of socialist cells created in 1864, and which was on its last legs in the 1870s.

Bismarck used the League to isolate France; he hoped also that by bringing Hapsburgs and Romanovs together he could reconcile their differences in the Balkans. That peninsula was the geographic cradle of the Eastern Question. As we noted already, the Dual Monarchy, given the large number of Slavs living within its borders, had no desire to condone events and policies that stirred up the Ottoman sultan. Russia, on the contrary, had an ambitious policy aimed at controlling the Straits, thereby achieving free access to the Mediterranean Sea.

Elements that composed the Eastern Question were many: Balkan nationalism in the form of Pan-Slavism, as well as particular patriotisms such as those of Romanians, Serbs and Bulgars; the weakness of Turkish rulership combined with the efficiency and savage cruelty of the army; irreconcilable policies of Russia and Austria, and finally the determination of Britain to shore up the sultan. Balkan national groups undertook a full-scale rebellion in 1876. As usual the Turkish army massacred thousands of rebels, which, as usual, provoked a loud outcry in the west. But only Russia declared war on Turkey and military success led to the treaty of San Stefano in 1878. Its terms would have practically eliminated Turkish rule in the Balkans and created a big Bulgaria as a client state of Russia. No other state was prepared to accept this arrangement. Bismarck, hoping still to reconcile his two allies, hosted an assembly of all powers, the Congress of Berlin in 1878. The changes imposed by the diplomats reduced Bulgaria by removing Rumelia from her borders. They created Serbia and recognized tiny Montenegro as a sovereign state. For her victory, Russia was allowed to take a few Turkish towns on the Black Sea, and in recompense the sultan recovered much of the central area of the peninsula, Britain acquired Cyprus, Austria occupied Bosnia and Herzegovina, and France was given the green light to move into Tunisia, which she did in 1881. The aspirations of several Balkan peoples for freedom and territorial states were sacrificed to the avarice and rivalries of the great powers. But now Russia, like a dog deprived of its bone, nursed a grievance against Bismarck, who, in turn, was caught between the two states he relied on for security. To please one, he had to anger the other. Not only was tension among the major powers heightened, jealousies arose among the Balkan polities that had united against the Turks; as the Moslem menace declined, national rivalries surged.

Hoping to escape his dilemma, Bismarck negotiated an alliance with the

Dual Monarchy. This arrangement was intended to be defensive, and the final signatures were made on October 17, 1879. Russia was the focus. Should the tsar's armies attack either signatory, the other was pledged to come to its assistance with all strength. If another state initiated an attack (France, of course), the ally would observe a benevolent neutrality, unless the attack was made with the aid of Russia, then both signatory powers would fight together. The treaty that created the Dual Alliance was valid for five years and renewable; it was to be kept secret, but its general intent was soon common knowledge in diplomatic circles. By no means was Bismarck giving Francis Joseph a free hand: if he attacked he would receive no aid. Making the terms known was also a warning to the tsar. Bismarck's essentially pacifistic intentions were further strengthened by a renewal of the League of Three Emperors in 1881, a kind of sop to Russian frustrations after the Congress of Berlin. Luckily for the chancellor, Alexander remained friendly to Germany and chose his foreign ministers accordingly. Meanwhile Italy joined the Dual Alliance in 1882. In doing so the government had an eye on Tunisia; even a brief look at a map will reveal that whichever power controlled the peninsula, as well as Sicily and Tunisia, held an intermittent bridge spanning the central Mediterranean Basin, could indeed control a vast hinterland that might revive the glorious wealth and power of Renaissance Italy. In search of support in case France objected, the Crispi Ministry hoped to establish stronger ties with Germany, the conqueror of France. The Franco-German war had enabled Italian troops to occupy Rome. But more decisive than memories were hard facts. Italy was a new government feeling its way, and impressed by Bismarck's *Kulturkampf* that put the church in its place. But Bismarck's response to Italy's approach was: "The road to Berlin lies through Vienna." Simply put, if Rome wanted an alliance with Berlin, it must make peace with Vienna. Whether the Ministry held its nose or not is unclear, but it signed the agreement that created the Triple Alliance and consolidated central Europe as a block between East and West, effectively cutting France off from Russia. Bismarck could breathe easily in the belief that French *revanchistes* were completely isolated. To pound the nail in their coffin he signed a Reinsurance Treaty with Russia, the only possible strong ally of France.

It was unfortunate for Europe that Bismarck did not enjoy permanent status as chancellor. Whether his subtle diplomacy, often devious but also effective, could have continued balancing the ambitions of Austria and Russia remains a matter of conjecture. Perhaps not because it failed to take into account the conflicts arising from the colonialist impulse that surged forward from the 1870s on.

Imperialism: Second *Mal de Siècle*

The first malaise of the century, following the upheavals and restless need for war of Napoleon I, was a widespread feeling of unease, a deep fatigue resulting from a generation of conflict. Young men who had hurled themselves heedlessly into battle, who had overturned nearly all the old values, suddenly found themselves without the call of bugles, without the roll of drums, without orders and battle plans, without a cause until they were caught up in the enthusiasm of romanticism, liberalism, or socialism. Just the opposite was the malaise of the century's last quarter: Young men were deliberately stirred from the torpor of decades of peace by a call to arms to conquer the unknown stretches of Africa and the torrid lands of Southeast Asia. They threw off languor with a sense of patriotism forgotten since the 1790s, and felt a need, as D'Annunzio urged, to man the prow and sail out into the world.

This restless energy was certainly a cause of the revival of imperialism. A new generation took up with the same élan as the romantics the ideal of civilizing and Christianizing all the heathens of the world. Leading the way were young explorers who cast off the decades-old indifference to colonization. Colonies, early liberals had argued, cost more to maintain than they were worth. Britain did not have to take over Latin America to enjoy rich markets there, and gained an even greater source of profit in the United States, a lost colony. The adventurous of the early century went into business; those of the late century went into the bush of black Africa, the last continent to offer the lure of exploration into the unknown. Among the earliest was Dr. David Livingstone, a Scottish medical missionary. He learned about the extensive slave trade carried on by Arabs who preyed on the blacks for profit. The British journalist, Henry Stanley, sent to recover Livingstone who was never lost, sent home dispatches that awakened public interest. The slave trade became a basic factor in what Rudyard Kipling called the "white man's burden" to free and civilize not only blacks, but the unfortunates with brown skin in central Asia and those with yellow skin in the Far East. The French were more active than the British, and Catholic missions provided some forty thousand of all Catholics to carry out the process of conversion in every part of the "backward" world.

Sometimes preceding, sometimes following the clergy were explorers prompted by devotion to geographic discovery. Pierre de Brazza claimed lands for France in equatorial Africa while the German Karl Peters provided claims for Germany in the eastern part of the black continent. Others, like Cecil Rhodes, prompted more by love of money and power, laid out claims for Britain in South Africa. Missionaries and explorers opened the interior of Africa geographically and provided tabloid dailies with the tales of their conversions and adventures. At the same time they opened the minds of Europeans to the myriad possibilities of Africa, the wealth of mineral resources, of gold and diamonds, and of naked natives in need of Lancashire cottons to protect their morals and modesty.

Undoubtedly economic motives stirred European manufacturers, financiers and traders. The home economy was in recession and foreign markets had great appeal both to entrepreneurs and wage workers. Trade union leaders were just as eager to encourage business recovery. The British had already pene-

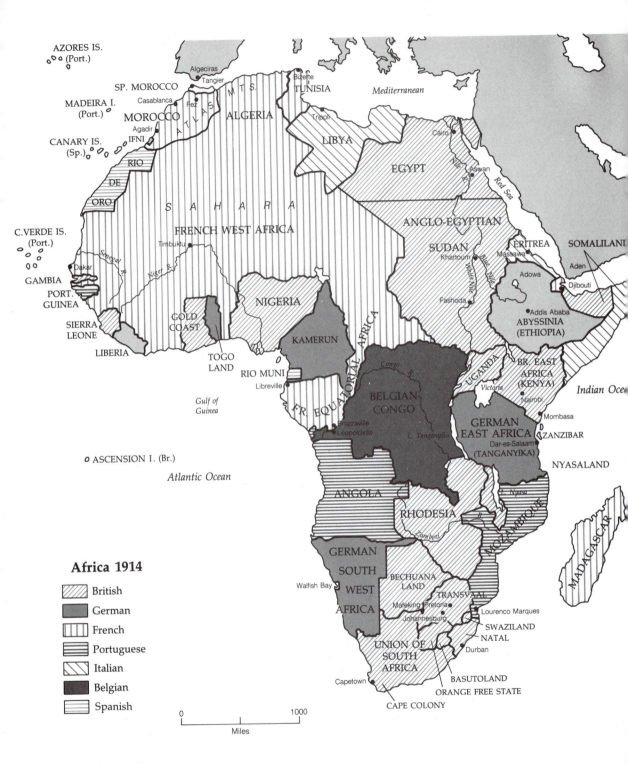

Africa 1914

British	
German	
French	
Portuguese	
Italian	
Belgian	
Spanish	

0   1000

Miles

Map 21–1 Africa, 1914

trated Egypt in the 1870s and Disraeli was a convinced expansionist. The *khedive* had defaulted on his debts and an international consortium had to be set up to manage his country's budget. The French soon pulled out but the British stayed, and when, in the mid-1880s, natives revolted in the Sudan, an army under General Charles Gordon went to quell it. When he and most of his men were overrun, the British, after much hesitation, sent in a fresh force under General Horatio Kitchener who taught the rebels the superiority of modern weapons. The Nile Valley was pacified and occupied by the 1890s. It would later become the northern bastion of an empire that stretched from its mouth southward to the Cape of Good Hope.

During these years the French were expanding their holdings from the southern Mediterranean shore to the Atlas Mountains, and from east to west across the vast stretch of Equatorial Africa, as well as into the island of Madagascar where they met strong native resistance. The British also met fierce opposition from the Afrikaners in the south, where rival claims led to the Boer War of 1899 which the British won by sheer force of numbers and weaponry rather than generalship; another war nearly broke out when British and French forces met face-to-face at Fashoda in the Sudan. When news of the impasse reached the capitals of Europe, the nationalist press worked up popular passions, exacerbated by British set backs in the Boer War and the Dreyfus case in France. It was a happy coincidence that Theophile Delcassé, the new French minister, was not an Anglophobe. He hoped, in fact, to achieve a rapprochement with his Channel neighbor, and bring her naval power into the understanding that France had signed with Russia in 1892. Worse, a war against Britain would play into the hands of Germany, so the French forces were ordered to retreat. Finally the watershed of the Nile and the Congo separated British and French spheres of influence.

This compromise was merely the final phase of a process that had been going on for two decades. And almost miraculously without a serious military engagement among the powers that were carving Africa into colonies. In the mid-1880s, when the vast basin of the Congo was being contested, Bismarck and Jules Ferry agreed to summon a meeting in Berlin of all interested parties. At issue was the International African Association founded in 1876 by Leopold II, king of Belgium, to manage his personal domain. Britain and Portugal became apprehensive about free navigation on the longest river in the continent, as well as other rivers. The Berlin Conference resulted in a treaty in 1885 which recognized that any power that effectively took possession of African territory and notified other powers could lawfully claim it to be within its "sphere of influence," a term first used during the meeting. The treaty really opened Africa to partition, and by 1911 that process was nearly complete with the Italian grab of Libya. Only Liberia and then Ethiopia remained free of foreign control after its native warriors beat back the Italians in the mid-1890s. The same procedures were used to partition south east Asia and China. Here, however, the takeover led to war between Russia and Japan and the latter's success put a halt to the tsar's ambition in the Pacific. That was a small loss; territorially, the Russian empire was rivaled only by China, but the Chinese emperor was no longer a free agent, his territory having been divided into spheres of influence under foreign control.

Looking at a world map of 1914 one is amazed that such a tiny cluster of European states could have appropriated so much territory without a major war. Of course a vast and devastating conflict broke out in this same year, but by this time the acquisition phase of imperialism was long over; the Italian grab of Libya was merely the last bite of a huge meal. And imperialist grabs of land, having most of the time been diplomatically settled, was only a remote cause of World War I.

It has been argued that nonbelligerent settlement of conflicting claims did arouse lingering animosities that determined the line up of sides when war finally broke out in 1914. This view has some validity, but if it were fully acceptable then France and Britain should have fought each other because France's retreat at Fashoda provoked much Anglophobia in Paris and screaming headlines in the nationalist press. Likewise the British and Russians had overlapping claims in Afghanistan and Persia. Despite several agreements by Russia to share out Persian territory as well as Persian wealth as repayments of British loans, stressed relations continued until 1914 when oil was discovered in the British sphere. But their dispute did not dissolve the entente arranged between them in 1907. For Britain the German naval menace was of far greater weight than Germany's holdings in East and West Africa that intruded upon the dream of a string of colonies from north to south. There was, none the less, one area where conflicting claims did deepen already strained relations: Morocco.

Germany entered the race for colonies late, found most of the territorial meal already devoured and digested, and therefore saw in Morocco a chance to enlarge her holdings, limited to east and southwest Africa. Of course the intrepid French were already there with knife and fork, ready to put a good Gallic sauce on her Algerian neighbor. Since German businessmen had free access to markets there, the Kaiser was determined to keep the French from closing it to outsiders. The French had a special interest there because Morocco's southern frontier with Algeria was not laid out, and some oases were essential to communication between Algeria and French Equatorial Africa. This frontier was a matter of dispute with the Moroccan sultan. William II, willfully determined, landed at Tangier in 1905 to make known his recognition of the sultan's independence. If he had the intention of detaching Britain from her recent understanding with France, he failed absolutely. As in the past, the dispute was to be settled by an international conference. In Algeciras in January 1906, Germany found no support save that of Austria. The conferees recognized Moroccan independence, but put her police under joint Spanish and French control, and her finances under a state bank to be directed by a Swiss. Tension arose again in 1908 and once more

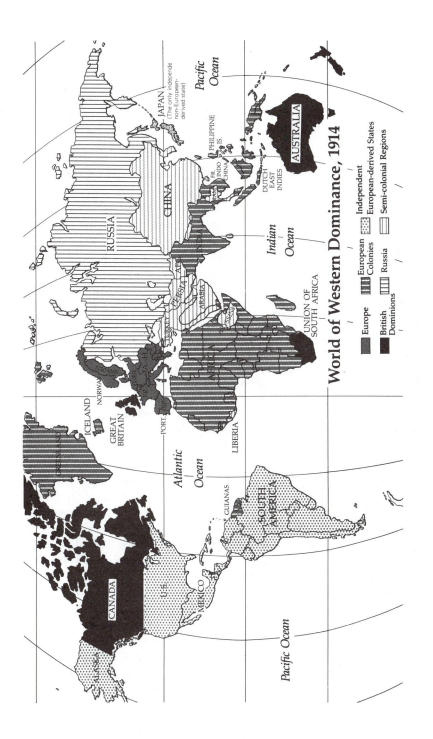

Map 21–2 World of Western Dominance, 1914

in 1911 when the Kaiser sent a gunboat to Agadir. The British fleet prepared for action. Finally he grudgingly recognized the French protectorate over Morocco in return for two strips of land in the French Congo. The Germans received a mere token for their efforts, which had aroused hostile public opinion in all countries; even Lloyd George, a pacifist and opponent of the Boer War, spoke in favor of war rather than surrender to German bullying. France and Britain drew closer together. Their understanding dated from 1904 and preceded the Moroccan crises. The Kaiser's acts prompted the two signatories to begin joint discussions between their general staffs, which simply sealed it. The crises, however annoying, did not cause a general war to break out; they were settled as other crises had been, by conference and peacefully, even if not always gracefully.

This does not mean that colonial expansion was entirely peaceful. European countries did not fight one another during its process, but the natives generally resisted violently and uncounted thousands of them died, as did the dervishes at Khartoum, the Zulus and Afrikaners in South Africa and the Chinese in the Boxer Rebellion of 1899. Put simply, Europeans possessed superior organization and training, vastly overpowering weapons and firepower, the wealth to supply their soldiers, and the determination to conquer.

Such determination signaled a turn about of public opinion in Europe. What occurred was only possible when huge masses of people became concentrated in cities, literate but not well educated, and militantly gullible. The mess press that built its readership with the aid of sensational headlines, that was increasingly nationalistic and xenophobic, convinced it readers that the nation's well-being and future depended on acquisition of colonies. This was one of the most potent myths employed to arouse public support. Scholars who argued that colonies were a drain on the national wealth and provided employment for the useless sons of upper class families were drowned out by the cacophony of colonial advocates arguing that imperialism pays. All serious studies agree that it paid for a small group of capitalists and promoters who reaped sizable sums from concessions granted to their monopoly companies set up to exploit nature and natives. In the diamond mines of South Africa where Rhodes made his fortune, blacks provided a form of slave labor and when their number was not sufficient or they died too quickly, the Balfour Ministry permitted the importation of Chinese indentured labor. The Michelin tire company earned huge profits from its rubber plantations in Indochina. Numerous companies founded to transform raw materials imported from colonial holdings undoubtedly created jobs at home and enhanced the bank accounts of their stockholders.

But before profits trickled homeward, tax payers had to bear the costs of conquest and then of creating an infrastructure of railroads, highways, electrical communications, bureaucracies, police forces, military occupation to preserve security and health services for natives. Public benefits in the form of increased employment and taxes on colonial investments did not even approach the costs. Nor did other acclaimed benefits materialize: few of the redundant Europeans moved to colonies; they went to North and South America to find work in cities and industry. Trade with colonies never rose to meet expectations; the bulk of British exports went to Germany and elsewhere in Europe, and the Germans found a better market in Britain than in their foreign holdings. The French exported huge sums, but most of it to Russia and east Europe. Few asked the simple question: how were black, brown, and yellow peoples going to buy high-priced European goods when they rarely knew where their next meal was coming from? They were not down-at-the-heel, they had no heels save those nature provided in their mother's womb. Missionaries clothed some naked tribes they converted, but decades passed before most natives abandoned their tribal attire for the cloth of Lancaster or Roubaix.

I am asserting that colonial conquest was a great hoax perpetrated by a grasping minority at the expense of the majority. Imperialism was as much a psychological as an economic and a military force. The Europeans who set out to rule had a long tradition of conquest to reinforce their claim to rule. The ancient Romans, who conquered most of the then known world, were convinced of their superiority. The crusaders of the Middle Ages went off to slaughter and be slaughtered because "God wills it." The Spaniards who conquered Latin America were as mixed a lot of sinners and saints as the Europeans of the late 1800s. The most devastating conquest, that was almost coterminous with the imperialism of Europe, was the American conquest of the West. No other people to my knowledge set out deliberately to annihilate the natives; but, then, no Europeans left their homelands in numbers sufficiently large to carry out authentic genocide. Most European settlers exploited natives; they did not unnecessarily kill them.

The Triple Entente: A Diplomatic Revolution

In 1890 no diplomat would have believed that opposites could come together to form a viable association. France was a republic, and the politicians in charge were men of deeply conservative social views. As we observed already, they were even prepared to cooperate with Catholics in order to preserve private property from the threat of socialism. Yet, France was and remained the center of revolutionary movements, and socialists were winning more votes from the rising urban masses. Moreover, it was in 1890 that anarchosyndicalists began the celebration of May First as a labor festival and demanded an eight hour work-day. How was it possible, then, for a republic to form an entente with the bastion of reaction, imperial Russia. The answer is not difficult: Politicians have nearly always displayed the ability to hold their noses in order to shake hands with the contemptible in order to safeguard what they consider national interests. In the year 1890 the Kaiser also dropped Bismarck whose involuted policies had kept France isolated for two decades. The new Kaiser, his chancellor, and his advisors on foreign policy, wanting to wash their hands entirely of Bismarck, abandoned the Reinsurance Treaty that had bound the German and Russian empires in a vague sort of friendship. The break shocked the tsar, and even though he remained on good terms with the Kaiser—they addressed each other as Willy and Nickey in their correspondence—their severance proved to be permanent. France and Russia were now like two unhinged polities, each with a grievance against the Teutons: France over Alsace, Russia over the intrusion of Germany into the Near East as made clear in plans to build a railroad from Berlin to Baghdad, and German incursions into lands around the Persian Gulf. In 1891 France and Russia began an exchange of intentions that, after the embarrassing Panama scandal, ended in the Dual Entente in 1894, with each signatory promising to aid the other militarily if attacked by a power of the Triple Alliance. This agreement, like those of the Alliance, was defensive. The tsar had no intention of aiding the French to recover Alsace, nor had the French any intention of contributing to Russian imperialism in the Near and Far East. When, during a visit to Marseilles the tsar saluted while a naval band blared out the sanguinary notes of the *Marseillaise*, everyone present realized that what had taken place was not merely an understanding, it was a miracle, and only the first.

In the mid-1890s neither country displayed a friendly face to Great Britain. The French still planned to play a role in the Sudan, and Russia in the primitive territories northwest of India, both areas where the English had vital interests. The British had been at odds if not at daggers drawn with the tsarist regime since the years immediately after the Congress of Vienna. Russia's ambitions in the Near East were most vigorously opposed by the Foreign Office, and the Crimean War had not eliminated the source of their differences. That military defeat had embarrassed the tsar and induced him to end serfdom. However, it did not deter him or his successors from pursuing policies intended to dismember Ottoman power in the Balkans, the ins and outs of which we have already observed.

Toward the turn of the century the British Foreign Office looked more kindly toward Germany. The Kaiser was Queen Victoria's grandson and most of her children were married to German consorts. The Conservative party under Robert Marquis of Salisbury leaned so far toward Germany that he even offered to begin negotiations aimed at some kind of mutual understanding. The Kaiser and his advisors never said no, but neither did they say yes, or even maybe. In fact, their actions took the appearance of being especially designed to annoy the British, as well as the Russians. The uncalled-for interference in South African affairs, and sympathizing with the Afrikaners during the Boer War seemed specifically intended to outrage the British. Two other strategies had the same effect: the effort to penetrate the Near East by constructing the Berlin-Baghdad railroad, assuming the role of protector of the sultan, and the decision to build a navy approaching the strength of the British fleet. This was the brainchild of Admiral Alfred von Tirpitz, backed by the Navy League, and enthusiastically approved by William. Given the size of Germany's foreign trade, second to Britain's, a fleet capable of safeguarding merchant ships was not unreasonable. But all foreign offices in Europe concluded that Germany, with the largest army and a powerful navy, and ruled by an erratic sovereign, was a menace. In short order a race to build naval ships began, much to the delight of metal producers, ship builders and cannon makers. Not only more ships but bigger ships began to slide down the ways, the apex of tonnage reached with the first dreadnoughts, the creations of Sir John Fisher, First Sea Lord. The costs of such "floating gun-carriages" were enormous and raised heated debates in the Reichstag and the House of Commons, both sensitive to public fears and exaggerated patriotism stirred up by the mass press. The question was: How many ships to build? Sane responses were not always at hand. Winston Churchill once explained how conflicting demands were settled: "The admiralty had demanded six [dreadnoughts]: the economists offered four: and we finally compromised on eight." This was in 1909. By then British foreign policy had made a complete about-face.

For centuries the English had followed a policy of isolation from Continental entanglements of long duration. By 1900 the Foreign Office began to question this tradition. The British were separated from the mainland by the Channel, but imperial commitments were worldwide and on each occasion when they brought British forces into near collision with a major power, they stood alone, without allies. As her relations with Germany deteriorated it became evident that, apart from a pact with Japan, she stood alone because her one ally would not come to her aid against such a mighty empire.

The increasingly dangerous situation that Germany helped to create was appreciated by Delcassé, foreign minister in Paris. He acted first to settle differences with Italy, ended the tariff war and offered the bait of extensive loans so necessary to Giolitti's near empty treasury and a green light to Italian ambitions regarding Libya. So successful was he that the Germans began to doubt the reliability of Italy as a member of the Triple Alliance.

He next sounded out the government in London, and was welcomed with open arms. The new king, Edward VII, visited Paris in 1903. The crowds there jeered him on his arrival and, fickle as always, cheered him on his departure. Police subsidies and threats could inspire very sudden about-faces among leading journalists, and therefore with the masses. With the ground prepared, diplomats settled the remaining disputes and signed documents that created an entente. As we noted this agreement stood the test of the Moroccan crises. In fact, it was the second step that led to the formation of the Triple Entente when Britain and Russia settled their disputes. Russia agreed eagerly because of her humiliating defeat by Japan.

The major powers were now divided into two competing alliances. This situation did not make war between them inevitable, but more probable. Figuratively, there now existed a powder keg. It remained to be seen who or what would add a fuse and light the match.

The End of an Epoch

The outbreak of war in late July and August of 1914 brought to an end a century of international peace. War broke out for a number of reasons. The enormous buildup of arms and armies put at the disposal of nervous politicians and ambitious generals the means of warfare on a scale never known before. War budgets doubled and tripled in the quarter century between 1890 and 1914. In Germany and France that increase had begun immediately after their mutual conflict in 1870–71. Armies grew in size, and the vast economic wealth that had been created over the century was put at their disposal.

Public opinion was also mobilized. The growth of urban crowds, and the steady spread of nationalist feelings created the willing cannon-fodder that threw the full weight of the populace into the scale of decision making. The immediate cause of belligerency was a combination of the extreme nationalism of the populace, particularly in the Balkans, and its manipulation by politicians in pursuit of irreconcilable goals. The Russians were determined to further weaken Turkey and the revolution that brought reformers known as the Young Turks to power in 1908 made the tsar and his foreign minister Alexander Izvolsky more eager to act before the "sick man" recovered. They intended to use Bulgaria and Serbia as tools against the new Turkish regime. Just as determined were the Austrian emperor and his foreign minister, Alois Aehrenthal, to thwart Serbian expansionist ambitions. The Serbs looked on Bosnia and Herzegovina as Serbia *irredenta*, that is, a land historically Serbian. To frustrate that idea Austria ended her legal occupation of them by illegally annexing them in 1908. Serbia, backed by Russia, denounced this step and nearly provoked a war the next year. In this affair Austria and Russia acted irresponsibly, and demanded the support of their respective allies. From this time on the German General Staff began actively to intervene in political matters when its head informed his Austrian counter part that Germany would stand by her commitments. He did not think it necessary to act through the foreign minister. In reality this was a side show because the German ministry and the Kaiser supported Austrian policy in the Balkans.

Encouraged by Russian ambassadors, the Balkan states formed a league for mutual protection. In 1912 its member states attacked Turkish forces, driving them to the Straits. Soon after they fell out, however, when they attempted to divide the land they had conquered. Serbia wanted access to the Adriatic Sea. Because Austria objected vigorously an international conference created the state of Albania, blocking the Serbs and granting them some land in the interior. Serbia was furious and instrumental in leading an attack on Bulgaria by the other Balkan states, starting the second Balkan War.

The final act occurred in June 1914. A Serbian fanatic killed the Austrian heir to the throne at Sarajevo in Bosnia. The assassination was planned by a nationalist group called the Black Hand, headed by the Serbian chief of military intelligence. Austria, assured by her German ally of support, sent Serbia an ultimatum that could only lead to war. And Austria declared war on July 28. In support of Serbia, Russia began to mobilize. So did Austria and Germany—and hostilities began. The long peace—however relative—was over. Europe entered the age of global war.

Suggested Readings

Historical Geography

E. W. Fox, *Atlas of European History* (1964); N. J. Pounds, *An Historical Geography of Europe* (1979); H. D. Clout, *Themes in the Historical Geography of France* (1977); W. H. Parker, *An Historical Geography of Russia* (1968); G. East, *The Geography Behind History* (1965).

Agriculture

W. Abel, *Agricultural Fluctuations in Europe* (1980); G. Grantham and C. Leonard, eds., *Agrarian Organization in the Century of Industrialization: Europe, Russia, and North America* (1989); J. Blum, *The End of the Old Order in Rural Europe* (1978); R. Price, *The Modernization of Rural France* (1983); G. T. Robinson, *Rural Russia Under the Old Regime* (1969); F. W. Wcislo, *Reforming Rural Russia* (1990); R. J. Evans and W. R. Lee, eds., *The German Peasantry: Conflict and Community in Rural Society* (1986); H. Clout, *Agriculture in France on the Eve of the Railway Age* (1980); M. Tracy, *Government and Agriculture in Western Europe* (1989); E. Kingston-Mann and T. Mixter, eds., *Peasant Economy, Culture, and Politics of European Russia, 1800–1921* (1990); P. Lowe and M. Bodiguel, eds., *Rural Studies in France and Britain* (1990); D. Goodman and M. Redclift, *From Peasant to Proletarian: Capitalist Development and Agrarian Transition* (1981); F. Dovring, *Land and Labor in Europe, 1900–50*

(1950); F. Coppa, *Planning, Protectionism, and Politics in Liberal Italy: Economics and Politics in the Giolitian Age (1971)*; R. Moeller, ed., *Peasants and Lords in Modern Germany* (1986); L. Loubère, *The Red and the White: A History of Wine in France and Italy in the Nineteenth Century* (1978).

Economic Development

The Cambridge Economic History of Europe (1941–); *The Fontana Economic History of Europe* (1971–); A. S. Milward and S. B. Saul, *The Economic Development of Continental Europe, 1780–1870* (1973) and *The Development of the Economies of Continental Europe, 1850–1914* (1977); P. Mathias and J. Davis, eds., *The First Industrial Revolution* (1990); D. Landes, *The Rise of Capitalism* (1966); J. Baechler, et al, *Europe and the Rise of Capitalism* (1988); W. O. Henderson, *The Rise of German Industrial Power, 1834–1914* (1975); P. Bairoch and M. Lévy-Leboyer, eds., *Disparities in Economic Development since the Industrial Revolution* (1981); A. Kahan, *Russian Economic History: The 19th Century* (1989); J. P. McKay, *Pioneers for Profit: Foreign Entrepreneurship and Russian Industrialization, 1885–1913* (1970); R. Cameron, *France and the Economic Development of Europe, 1800–1914* (2d ed., 1966); J. Mokyr, *The Lever of Riches: Technological Creativity and Economic Progress* (1990); J. E. Vance, *Capturing the Horizon: The Historical Geography of Transportation since the 16th Century* (1990); C. E. Freedman, *Joint-stock Enterprise in France, 1807–1914* (1979).

Urban History

P. Hohenberg and L. H. Lees, *The Making of Urban Europe, 1000–1950* (1985); H. J. Dyos, ed., *The Study of Urban History* (1968); D. Pinkney, *Napoleon III and the Rebuilding of Paris* (1958); A. Briggs, *Victorian Cities* (1965); D. Fraser and A. Sutcliffe, eds., *The Pursuit of Urban History* (1983); J. P. McKay, *Tramways and Trollies: The Role of Urban Mass Transport in Europe* (1976); J. Johnson and C. Pooley, eds., *The Structures of 19th-Century Cities* (1982); J. A. Yelling, *Slums and Slum Clearance in Victorian London* (1986); G. Stedman Jones, *Outcast London: A Study in the Relationship between Classes in Victorian Society* (1971); J. Merryman, *The Margins of City Life: Explorations of the French Urban Frontier, 1815–51* (1991); N. Evenson, *Paris: A Century of Change* (1979); D. Crew, *Town in the Ruhr: A Social History of Bochum, 1860–1914* (1979); D. R. Brower, *The Russian City between Tradition and Modernity, 1850–1900* (1990).

Population

W. R. Lee, ed., *European Demography and Economic Growth* (1979); R. Lawton and W. R. Lee, eds., *Urban Population Development in Western Europe* (1989); A. Brändström and L. Tedebrant, eds., *Society, Health and Population Growth during the Demographic Transition* (1988); A. Coale and S. Cotts Watkins, eds., *The Decline of Fertility in Europe* (1986); E. van de Wald, *The Female Population of France in the 19th Century* (1974); D. E. Eversley and D. Glass, *Population in History: Essays in Historical Demography* (1965).

Government

E. N. and P. R. Anderson, *Political Institutions and Social Change in Continental Europe in the 19th Century* (1967); R. Kann, *The Problem of Restoration: a Study in Comparative Political History* (1967); C. Morazé, *The Triumph of the Middle Classes* (1966); R. J. Goldstein, *Political Repression in 19th-Century Europe* (1983); G. Iggers, ed., *The Social History of Politics* (1985); N. McCord, *British History, 1815–1906* (1991); A. Briggs, *The Age of Improvement* (1959); D. Read, *England, 1868–1914* (1979); H. Schulze, ed., *Nation-Building in Central Europe* (1987); T. S. Hamerow, *Restoration, Revolution, Reaction: Economics and Politics in Germany, 1815–71* (1966) and *The Social Foundations of German Unification, 1858–71* (1969); O. Pflanze, *Bismarck and the Development of Germany*, 3 vols. (1990); H. Böhme, *The Foundation of the German Empire* (1971); G. Ritter, *The Sword and the Scepter: The Problem of Militarism in Germany*, 4 vols. (1969); R. Kann, *The Multinational Empire: Nationalism and National Reform in the Habsburg Monarchy* (1950); R. Magraw, *France, 1815–1986* (1986); S. Elwitt, *The Third Republic Defended: Bourgeois Reform in France, 1880–1914* (1986); D. Pinkney, *Decisive Years in France, 1840–47* (1986); T. Zelden, *France, 1848–1945*, 2 vols. (1980); H. Lebovics, *The Alliance of Iron and Wheat in the Third French Republic* (1988); N. V. Riasanovsky, *A Parting of the Ways: Government and the Educated Public in Russia, 1801–55* (1976); A. Verner, *The Crisis of the Russian Autocracy: Nicholas II and the 1905 Revolution* (1990); T. Shanin, *The Roots of Otherness: Russia's Turn of Century*, 2 vols. (1986); A. Carrié, *Italy, from Napoleon to Mussolini* (1962); S. J. Woolf, *A History of Italy, 1700–1860: The Social Constraints of Political Change* (1979); S. M. Saladino, *Italy from Unification to 1919: Growth and Decay of a Liberal Regime* (1970); J. A. David and P. Ginsborg, eds., *Society and Politics in the Age of the Risorgimento* (1991); D. Mack Smith, *Cavour and Garibaldi, 1860* (1954); R. Carr, *Spain, 1808–1975 (1966);* B. Jelavich, *History of the Balkans* (1983); P. J. Pulzer, *The Rise of Antisemitism in Germany and Austria* (1963); P. Birnbaum, *Anti-Semitism in France: A History from 1789 to the Present* (1992).

Collective Action

L. Charles and Richard Tilly, *The Rebellious Century, 1830–1930* (1975); W. Mommsen and G. Hirschfelf, eds., *Social Protest, Violence, and Terrorism in 19th- and 20th-Century Europe* (1982); G. Rudé, *The Crowd in History: A Study of Popular Disturbances, 1730–1848* (1964); D. Pinkney, *The French Revolution of 1830* (1972); P. Stearns, *1848: The Revolutionary Tide in Europe* (1974); P. Amann, *Revolution and Mass Democracy: The Paris Club Movement in 1848* (1975); T. Margadant, *French Peasants in Revolt: The Insurrection of 1851* (1979); R. Stadelmann, *Social and Political History of the German 1848 Revolution* (1975); J. Sperber, *Rhineland Radicals: The Democratic Movement and the Revolution of 1848–49* (1991); P. Noyes, *Organization and Revolution: Working Class Associations in the German Revolution of 1848–49* (1966); J. Rath, *The Viennese Revolution of 1848* (1957); S. Edwards, *The Paris Commune, 1871* (1971); F. Ridley, *Revolutionary Syndicalism in France* (1971); S. Harcave, *First Blood: The Russian Revolution of 1905* (1964); G. Surh, *1905 in St. Petersburg: Labor, Society and Revolution* (1989); D. Geary, *European Labor Protest, 1848–1939* (1981).

International Relations

The American Historical Review (Forum on the balance of power) 97, 3 (June 1992); G. Ferrero, *The Reconstruction of Europe: Talleyrand and the Congress of Vienna, 1814–15* (1963); N. Rich,

Great Power Diplomacy, 1814–1914 (1992); M. S. Anderson, *The Eastern Question, 1774–1923* (1966); A. J. P. Taylor, *The Struggle for the Mastery of Europe, 1848–1918* (1954); F. R. Bridge, *The Hapsburg Monarch among the Great Powers, 1815–1918* (1990); G. Kennen, *The Fatal Alliance: France, Russia, and the Coming of the First World War* (1984); J. Joll, *The Origins of the First World War* (l984); F. Fischer, *War of Illusions: German Policies from 1911 to 1914* (1975); K. Hildebrand, *German Foreign Policy from Bismarck to Adenauer: The Limits of Statecraft* (1989); A. P. Thornton, *Doctrines of Imperialism* (1965); D. Fieldhouse, *Colonialism, 1870–1945* (1981); W. Baumgart, *Imperialism: The Idea and Reality of British and French Colonial Expansion, 1880–1914* (1982); D. Headrick, *The Tools of Empire: Technology and European Imperialism in the 19th Century* (1981); J. Halstead, *The Second British Empire* (1983).

Social Conditions, Structures, Theories

P. N. Stearns, *European Society in Upheaval: Social History since 1750* (1975); R. Bezucha, ed., *Modern European Social History* (1972); J. M. Merriman, ed., *Consciousness and Social Class Experience in 19th-Century Europe* (1979); E. Sagarra, *A Social History of Germany, 1648–1914* (1977); G. Dupeux, *French Society, 1789–1970* (1976); R. Price, *The French Second Republic: A Social History* (1972); H. Perkin, *The Origins of Modern English Society, 1780–1880* (1968); C. Black, ed., *The Transformation of Russian Society: Aspects of Social Change since 1861* (1967); M. Daunton, ed., *Housing of Workers: A Comparative History, 1850–1914* (1990); E. P. Thompson, *The Making of the English Working Class* (1963); E. P. Hunt, *British Working Class History, 1815–1914* (1981); E. Hobsbawn, *Workers: Worlds of Labor* (1984); J. Benson, *The Working Class in Britain, 1850–1914* (1989); J. Schmiechen, *Sweated Industries and Sweated Labor: The London Clothing Trade* (1984); R. Magraw, *History of the French Working Class*, 2 vols. (1992); L. R. Berlanstein, *The Working People of Paris, 1871–1914* (1984); M. Perrot, *Workers on Strike, 1871–1890* (1987); M. Neufeld, *The Skilled Metalworkers of Nuremberg: Craft and Class in the Industrial Revolution* (1989); V. E. Bonnell, ed., *The Russian Worker: Life and Labor under the Tsarist Regime* (1983); R. Zelnik, *Labor and Society in Tsarist Russia: The Factory Workers of St. Petersburg* (1971); W. R. Lee and E. Rosenhaft, eds., *The State and Social Change in Germany, 1880–1960* (1989); E. Hennock, *British Social Reform and German Precedents: The Case of Social Insurance, 1880–1914* (1988); J. F. Stone, *The Search for Social Peace: Reform Legislation in France, 1890–1914* (1985); L. S. Weissbach, *Child Labor Reforms in 19th-Century France* (1989); D. Higgs, *Nobles in 19th-Century France: The Practice of Inegalitarianism* (1987); A. J. Mayer, *The Persistence of the Old Regime* (1981); D. Cannadine, *The Decline and Fall of the British Aristocracy* (1990); S. Becker, *Nobility and Privilege in Late Imperial Russia* (1985); F. Dawes, *Not in Front of the Servants: A True Portrait of English Upstairs/Downstairs Life* (1974); T. and M. Beck, *French Notables: Reflections of Industrialization and Regionalism* (1987); F. M. L. Thompson, *The Rise of Respectable Society: A Social History of Victorian Britain, 1830–1900* (1988); G. L. Geison, *Professions and the French State, 1700–1900* (1984); P. Pilbeam, *The Middle Classes in Europe, 1789–1914* (1990); R. Macleod, ed., *Government and Expertise: Specialists, Administrators and Professionals, 1860–1919* (1988); K. Gispen, *New Professions, Old Order: Engineers and German Society, 1815–1914* (1989); G. Anderson, *Victorian Clerks* (1976); P. McPhee, *A Social History of France, 1780–1880* (1992); D. Lockwood, *The Blackcoated Worker: A Study in Class Consciousness* (1958); J. Wishnia, *The Proletarianization of the Fonctionnaire: Civil Service Workers and the Labor Movement under the Third Republic* (1991); R. Gallately, *The Politics of Economic Despair: Shopkeepers and German Politics, 1890–1914* (1974); A. Moulin, *Peasantry and Society in France since 1789* (1991); F. Wunderlich, *Farm Labor in Germany, 1810–1945* (1961); F. W. Wcislo, *Reforming Rural Russia: State, Local Society, and National Politics, 1855–1914* (1990); C. Worobec, *Peasant Russia: Family and Community in the Post-*

Emancipation Period (1991); M. Perrot, vol. ed., *A History of Private Life,* vol 4 (1990); M. Chase, *The "People's Farm." English Radical Agrarianism, 1775–1840* (1988); J. Gillis, *Youth and History: Tradition and Change in European Age Revolutions, 1750 to Present* (1974); E. G. Spencer, *Management and Labor in Imperial Germany: Ruhr Industrialists as Employers, 1896–1914* (1984); A. S. Lindemann, *History of European Socialism* (1983); J. Braunthal, *History of the Internationals,* 2 vols. (1967); G. Lichtheim, *Marxism, An Historical and Critical Study* (1961); L. Loubère, *Louis Blanc* (1961); Derry, *The Radical Tradition: Tom Paine to Lloyd George* (1967); J. Joll, *The Anarchists* (1964); G. de Ruggiero, *The History of European Liberalism* (1927).

Women and Feminism

R. Bridenthal and C. Koonz, eds., *Becoming Visible: Women in European History* (1982); B. G. Smith, *Changing Lives: Women in European History since 1700* (1989); P. S. Robinson, *An Experience of Women: Pattern and Change in 19th-Century Europe* (1982); S. K. Kent, *Sex and Suffrage in Britain, 1860–1914* (1987); C. G. Moses, *French Feminism in the 19th Century* (1984); S. House, *Women's Suffrage and Social Politics in Third Republic France* (1981); R. J. Evans, *The Feminist Movement in Germany, 1894–1933* (1976); J. Quataert, *Reluctant Feminists in German Social Democracy, 1885–1917* (1979); A. T. Taylor, *Feminism and Motherhood in Germany, 1800–1914 (1991);* L. Edmonson, *Feminism in Russia, 1900–17* (1984); M. Baxter and J. Quataert, *Socialist Women: Socialist Feminism in the 19th and 20th Centuries* (1978); J. Slaughter and R. Kern, eds., *European Women on the Left* (1981); R. Stites, *The Women's Liberation Movement in Russia: Feminism, Nihilism, and Bolshevism, 1860–1930* (1991); M. J. Peterson, *Family, Love, and Work in the Lives of Victorian Gentlewomen* (1991); B. G. Smith, *Ladies of the Leisure Class: The Bourgeoises of Northern France in the 19th Century* (1981); P. Branca, *Silent Sisterhood: Middle Class Women in the Victorian Home* (1975); L. Tilly and J. W. Scott, *Women, Work, and Family* (1978); I. Pinchbeck, *Women Workers and the Industrial Revolution, 1750–1850* (1930); L. Coons, *Women Home Workers in the Parisian Garment Industry, 1860–1915* (1987); A. John, *By the Sweat of Their Brow: Women Workers at Victorian Coal Mines* (1980); R. L. Glickman, *Russian Factory Women: Workplace and Society, 1880–1914* (1984); T. McBride, *The Domestic Revolution: The Modernization of Household Services in England and France, 1820–1920* (1976); M. L. Stewart, *Women, Work, and the French State: Labor Protection and Social Patriarchy, 1879–1919* (1989); B. Farnsworth and L. Viola, eds., *Russian Peasant Women* (1992); C. Dyhouse, *Girls Growing Up in Late Victorian and Edwardian England* (1981); J. F. McMillan, *Housewife or Harlot: The Place of Women in French Society, 1870–1940* (1981); J. Walkowitz, *Prostitution and Victorian Society: Women, Class, and State* (1985).

Family

P. Laslett and R. Wall, eds., *Household and Family in History* (1972); C. E. Rosenberg, ed., *The Family in History* (1975); J. Goody, *The Development of the Family and Marriage in Europe* (1983); E. Shorter, *The Making of the Modern Family* (1976); M. Mitterauer and R. Sieder, *The European Family: Patriarchy to Partnership* (1982); J. Cuisenier, ed., *The Family Life Cycle in European Societies* (1977); D. Levine, *Family Formation in an Age of Nascent Capitalism* (1977); R. Evans and W. R. Lee, eds., *The German Family* (1981); D. Ransel, ed., *The Family in Imperial Russia* (1978); L. Tilly and J. Scott, *Women, Work and Family* (1978); L. Tilly, *Women and Family Strategies in French Proletarian Families* (1978); M. Segalen, *Love and Power in the Peasant Family: Rural France in the 19th Century* (1983); R. Fuchs, *Abandoned Children:*

Foundlings and Child Welfare in 19th-Century France (1984); C. Worobec, *Peasant Russia: Family and Community in the Post-Emancipation Period* (1991); D. Ransel, *Mothers of Misery: Child Abandonment in Russia* (1988); J. Woycke, *Birth Control in Germany, 1871–1933* (1988); H. R. Gillis, *For Better, For Worse: British Marriages, 1600 to the Present* (1985); L. Davidoff and C. Hall, *Family Fortunes: Men and Women of the English Middle Class, 1780–1850* (1987); D. I. Kertzer, *Family Life in Central Italy, 1880–1910* (1984).

Culture and Intellectual Life

F. L. Baumer, *Modern European Thought: Continuity and Change in Ideas, 1600–1950* (1977); R. N. Stromberg, *European Intellectual History since 1789* (1986); G. L. Mosse, *The Culture of Western Europe: 19th and 20th Centuries* (1961); R. Williams, *Culture and Society, 1780–1950* (1959); H. S. Hughes, *Consciousness and Society: The Reconstruction of European Social Thought, 1890–1930* (1961); E. Weber, *Movements, Currents, Trends: Aspects of European Thought in the 19th and 20th Centuries* (1992); W. M. Simon, *Positivism in the 19th Century* (1963); F. Manuel, *The Prophets of Paris* (1962); W. Dampier, *A History of Science and Its Relations with Philosophy and Religion* (1949); O. Chadwick, *The Secularization of the European Mind in the 19th Century* (1975); R. Carlisle, *The Proffered Crown: Saint-Simonianism and the Doctrine of Hope* (1987); G. Iggers, *The German Conception of History* (1968); M. Mendelbaum, *History, Man and Reason: A Study of 19th-Century Thought* (1971); J. Halsted, ed., *Romanticism* (1965); D. Bratchell, *The Impact of Darwinism* (1981); A. B. Spitzer, *The French Generation of 1820* (1987); R. Wohl, *The Generation of 1914* (1980); P. Gay, *The Bourgeois Experience from Victoria to Freud*, 2 vols. (1984–86); H. W. Paul, *From Knowledge to Power: The Rise of the Science Empire in France* (1985); G. Weisz, *The Emergence of Modern Universities in France, 1863–1914* (1983); J. S. Allen, *In the Public Eye: A History of Reading in Modern France* (1991); L. Clark, *Schooling the Daughters of Marianne: Textbooks and the Socialization of Girls in Modern French Schools* (1984); S. Barrows, *Distorting Mirrors: A Vision of the Crowd in Late 19th-Century France* (1981); W. Logue, *From Philosophy to Sociology: The Evolution of Liberalism, 1870–1914* (1983); E. Weber, *Peasants into Frenchmen: The Modernization of Rural France* (1976); J. Devlin, *The Superstitious Mind: French Peasants and the Supernatural in the 19th Century* (1987); R. McKibbin, *The Ideologies of Class: Social Relations in Britain, 1880–1950* (1990); M. Wiener, *English Culture and the Decline of the Industrial Spirit, 1850–1980* (1981); V. Lidtke, *The Alternative Culture: Socialist Labor in Imperial Germany* (1985); M. Lambert, *State, Society, and the Elementary School in Imperial Germany* (1989); J. Albisetti, *Schooling German Girls and Women: Secondary and Higher Education in the 19th Century* (1988); S. Kassow, *Students, Professors and the State in Tsarist Russia* (1989); R. Altick, *The English Common Reader: A Social History of the Mass Reading Public, 1800–1900* (1951); W. D. Smith, *Politics and the Sciences of Culture in Germany, 1840–1920* (1991); N. J. Smelser, *Social Paralysis and Social Change. British Working-Class Education in the 19th Century* (1991).

Nationalism

B. Shafer, *Nationalism, Myth and Reality* (1955); L. Snyder, *The Meaning of Nationalism* (1954); M. Sutton, *Nationalism, Positivism, and Catholicism: The Politics of Charles Maurras and French Catholics, 1890–1914* (1982); E. Weber, *Action Française* (1962); M. Hughes, *Nationalism and Society: Germany, 1800–1945* (1988); L. Snyder, *Roots of German Nationalism*

(1978); G. Ely, *Reshaping the German Right: Radical Nationalism and Political Change after Bismarck* (1980); H. Schulze, *The Course of German Nationalism, 1763–1867* (1991); G. Mosse, *The Nationalization of the Masses: Political Symbolism and Mass Movements in Germany from the Napoleonic Wars through the Third Reich* (1975); E. C. Thaden, *Conservative Nationalism in 19th-Century Russia* (1964); M. Petrovich, *The Emergence of Russian Panslavism, 1856–1870* (1985); H. Kohn, *Prophets and Peoples: Studies in 19th-Century Nationalism* (1961); A. D. Smith, *Theories of Nationalism* (1971).

Religion

H. McLeod, *Religion and the People of Western Europe* (1981) and *Class and Religion in the Late Victorian City* (1974); J. Groh, *Nineteenth-Century German Protestantism: The Churches as Social Models* (1982); A. Vidler, *The [Catholic] Church in an Age of Revolution* (1961) and *A Century of Social Catholicism, 1820–1920* (1964); B. M. G. Reardon, *Religious Thought in the Victorian Age* (1980); M. Crowther, *Church Embattled: Religious Controversy in Mid-Victorian England* (1970); J. McManners, *Church and State in France, 1870–1914* (1972); H. Paul, *The Edge of Contingency: French Catholic Reaction to Scientific Change from Darwin to Duhem* (1979); A. Jemolo, *Church and State in Italy, 1880—1950* (1960); G. X. Freeze, *The Parish Clergy in 19th-Century Russia: Crisis, Reform, Counter Reform* (1983); J. M. Phayer, *Sexual Liberation and Religion in 19th-Century Europe* (1977).

Medicine and Health

G. Vigarello, *Concepts of Cleanliness: Changing Attitudes in France since the Middle Ages* (1988); F. B. Smith, *The People's Health, 1830–1910* (1979); F. Cartwright, *A Social History of Medicine* (1977); K. Haeger, *The Illustrated History of Surgery* (1988); L. Granshaw and R. Porter, eds., *Hospitals in History* (1989); K. Walker, *The Story of Medicine* (1954); B. Latour, *The Pasteurization of France* (1988); E. B. Ackerman, *Health Care in the Parisian Countryside, 1800–1914* (1990); R. Evans, *Death in Hamburg: Society and Politics in the Cholera Years, 1830–1910* (1987); N. Frieden, *Russian Physicians in an Era of Reform and Revolution, 1856–1905* *(1981)*; M. Hildreth, *Doctors, Bureaucrats, and Public Health in France, 1888–1902* (1987).

Leisure and Sports

M. Marrus, ed., *The Emergence of Leisure* (1974); R. Malcoleson, *Popular Recreation in English Society, 1700–1850* (1973); J. Lowerson and J. Myerscough, *Time to Spare in Victorian England* (1977); P. Bailey, *Leisure and Class in Victorian England: Rational Recreation and the Contest for Control, 1830–85* (1978); C. Rearick, *Pleasures of the Belle Epoque* (1985); E. Weber, *France Fin de Siècle* (1986); T. Mitchell, *Blood Sport: A Social History of Spanish Bullfighting* (1991); D. W. Gutzke, *Protecting the Pub: Brewers and Publicans against Temperance* (1989); P. Goodhart and C. Chataway, *War without Weapons* (1968); Johan Huizinga, *Homo Ludens: A Study of the Play Element in Culture* (1970); P. C. McIntosh, *Sport in Society* (1963).

Index